Ziegfeld

Also by Ethan Mordden

Make Believe: The Broadway Musical in the 1920s

Sing for Your Supper: The Broadway Musical in the 1930s

Beautiful Mornin': The Broadway Musical in the 1940s

Coming Up Roses: The Broadway Musical in the 1950s

Open a New Window: The Broadway Musical in the 1960s

One More Kiss: The Broadway Musical in the 1970s

The Happiest Corpse I've Ever Seen: The Last 25 Years of the Broadway Musical

All That Glittered: The Golden Age of Drama on Broadway, 1919–1959

Ziegfeld

THE MAN WHO INVENTED SHOW BUSINESS

Ethan Mordden

St. Martin's Press

New York

ZIEGFELD. Copyright © 2008 by Ethan Mordden. All rights
reserved. Printed in the United States of America. For information
address St. Martin's Press, 175 Fifth Avenue, New York, N.Y. 10010.

www.stmartins.com

Library of Congress Cataloging-in-Publication Data

Mordden, Ethan.
    Ziegfeld : the man who invented show business / Ethan Mordden.—
1st ed.
        p. cm.
    Includes bibliographical references and index.
    ISBN 13: 978-0-312-37543-0
    ISBN 10: 0-312-37543-3
    1. Ziegfeld, Flo, 1869–1932.   2. Theatrical producers and directors—
United States—Biography.   I. Title.
    PN2287.Z5M67   2008
    792.02'32092—dc22
    [B]

2008028746

First Edition: November 2008

10 9 8 7 6 5 4 3 2 1

To Clint Bocock

Contents

Acknowledgments

To my good friend and agent, Joe Spieler; to the staff at Lincoln Center Library for the Performing Arts; to Dave Prado; to Jon Cronwell; to Erick Neher; to Vicki Lame; to my copy editor, Elizabeth Kugler; to Kevin Sweeney; and to my Golden Age editor, Michael Flamini.

Ziegfeld

Introduction

They were called "managers." The forerunner of the modern "producer," the manager in fact did more than simply commission a piece, raise the capital, assemble the creative team, hire the performers, and book a theatre. That is the activity sheet of the Golden Age producer—a Michael Todd, David Merrick, or Hal Prince. But the manager as such rose to utmost power in a different time, in the 1890s. This was before Irving Berlin and Jerome Kern, before Ethel Merman and Bert Lahr or George Abbott and Jerome Robbins. George M. Cohan hadn't played Broadway yet. Richard Rodgers wasn't even born.

The manager owned the entertainment industry in the 1890s. Stars made it go—the matinée idol, the charm diva, the Shakespearean. Or Sarah Bernhardt, as ever looking forward to her next farewell tour. But the manager owned the works. Every so often, a performer would claim that the public was in charge. "The customers are boss," said Jimmy Durante, a Golden Age clown. "You have to please them, no matter how it hurts." Yet it was at the manager's pleasure that theatre cultivated its public. The manager decreed when, where, in what genre, and to what end. And no two managers were exactly alike.

For instance, there was the writer-director-designer manager known for a certain type of play, even a type of staging. David Belasco favored what we might call the Melodrama of Realism, nineteenth-century thrillers or tearjerkers staged in twentieth-century *verismo*, here imaginatively pictorial but there so authentically ordinary as to seem a kind of revelation of the humdrum. Many managers were "characters," and Belasco was the most characterful. He dressed like a cleric, took first-night bows with the solemn humility of the true egotist, and ran knockdown, drag-out coaching sessions with his women stars. The Belasco kind of manager was as famous as any star player and more magnetic than many; theatregoers might attend "the new Belasco" without knowing anything about it.

Or there was the manager known for a style—Charles Frohman, most notably, with his love of English whimsy, of literate drawing-room settings, and of women of finesse. David Belasco had his own theatres under his own name, first a placeholder that he took over till he could build his dream house, with a stage carved deep for spectacle and his personal living quarters behind the second balcony. And of course the lordly Frohman had *his* theatre. But Frohman was less interested in putting his name forward than in advertising his ambition. The Frohman theatre was called the Empire, and Frohman ran one, as we shall presently see. But more: if Belasco was a controversial manager—an innovator in realism to some and a hokum hustler to others—Frohman was a classy manager. The classiest playwright was Sir James M. Barrie and the classiest of the actors was Ethel Barrymore, the princess of an American theatre dynasty, the Drews. Both Barrie and Barrymore were Frohman attractions.

Most managers attained power after startlingly lowly apprenticeships. Belasco, in his early twenties, served as Frohman's stage manager down at the Herald Square Theatre, and Frohman himself scrabbled about till his first important job made him advance man for Haverly's Mastodon Minstrels.[1] But Frohman was unique among managers for his honesty. He signed no contracts: just gave his word. And kept it.

---

[1] A key operative in the days of The Road, the advance man traveled ahead of a company to its next date to see to the state of the theatre, the placing of the posters, the overtures to the press, and so on. Jack Haverly was the foremost manager in the genre of the minstrel show; his Mastodons were an assemblage of minstrel troupes in a gigantic ensemble boasting an unprecedented forty "stars." Haverly's motto, "40—Count 'Em—40," is the first known usage of this cliché of advertising.

There were, as well, managers of genre. Weber and Fields were performer-managers but also archons of a form of musical known as burlesque. In decline in the 1890s, burlesque spoofed myth, literature, or drama with anything-goes fun centering on a star comic (or, as here, a comical duo) and pretty girls. Joe Weber (short and dumpy, at least in his getup) and Lew Fields (tall and lean) practiced "Dutch" comedy[1] and made a point of co-starring with beauty stars of the day, especially Fay Templeton or Lillian Russell. Half of each Weber and Fields bill was an original one-act, and the second half was a parody; the biblical play *Quo Vadis?* got the Dutch treatment as *Quo Vass Is?*. Weber and Fields were genuinely beloved, and their public thought of them primarily as performers. Still, the bulk of their work was *managing*: choosing the material, running the company, mapping the annual tour.

And here, too, management had its own theatre, Weber and Fields' Broadway Music Hall. But Oscar Hammerstein—the first one, grandfather of Richard Rodgers' later partner—built and lost several playhouses, including a few that were sized for opera. Oscar I was the manager of an attitude, one that saw all musical theatre, from vaudeville to Mary Garden, as being commercially interrelated. To Hammerstein, there was only one audience; he was the crossover manager before the notion existed. When the Metropolitan Opera bought Hammerstein's Manhattan Opera out of business because the competition was impoverishing them, Oscar simply plunked his opera troupe into Victor Herbert's *Naughty Marietta*.

Ziegfeld will do business with all these men. But the manager he was most closely allied with was a fifth kind—neither an artist like Belasco, a producer with a stable of writers and stars like Frohman, a performing entity like Weber and Fields, nor a music lover like Hammerstein. This other manager was a realtor, an owner of theatres—so many that he

---

[1]From *Deutsch,* or "German." Dutch comics had nothing to do with the Netherlands: they used exaggerated German or Jewish accents.

came to control the American stage by controlling what appeared on it. The powerful are seldom loved, but Abraham Lincoln Erlanger was hated by virtually everyone in the business, and he basked in it: for there lies the truest power. Yet in his greed Erlanger contributed to the amazing expansion of theatregoing in the 1890s and in the three decades after: by building more theatres to control. And the more theatres there are, the more plays one must produce to realize the original investment. A stingy business never discovers anything; a greedy business grows because its public does.

Indeed, the very makeup of the audience was undergoing refinement, from sporting males and music-hall rowdies to married couples, families, and matinée matrons. At the same time, the nation was undergoing a terrific cultural evolution, the population becoming concentrated in cities when European immigration was at its height. Thus, the urban spectator in New York and Chicago—the first to decide if a show was worth the ticket—responded to ethnic stereotype humor like that of Weber and Fields and sent it triumphantly off on a road tour that would advance the cause of what is now called multiculturalism.

The saga of Florenz Ziegfeld Jr. occurs precisely during this era of expansion and assimilation. It couldn't, in fact, have occurred at any other time. A generation earlier, there was too little theatre and not enough variety of ethnicity in the performers for the art of Ziegfeld; later, the theatre would presumably have matured in different directions. Another manager might have shared Ziegfeld's instincts for the use of PR in promoting a star or a genre. But would anyone but Ziegfeld, the son of a music pedagogue, have had a classical background and an early rebellious fascination with popular entertainment? This led Ziegfeld to the realization that classical is basically ennobling and pop is basically stimulating. On one hand: Goethe. On the other hand: sex.

Some managers were artists and some businessmen; Ziegfeld was a visionary, though he himself would never have articulated it thus. And what Ziegfeld envisioned was a theatre as rich as Hammerstein's, featuring Belasco's pictorial grandeur, exploiting Frohman's class, and unveiling Weber and Fields' "beauty chorus." When, in 1893, Ziegfeld arrived in New York looking for his first project, theatre was still operating exclusively in old forms. Ziegfeld, too, loved old forms. But he also modernized and innovated.

Did he do it all himself? At times, he seemed to be hiring the creators, not creating himself. At other times, he seemed to be urging his team to fulfill his conception, an auteur by other means. A generation into his career, Ziegfeld became The Great Ziegfeld, his shows unlike other men's shows because he pursued a concept of the stage as a place of surprise and delight. He mixed the familiar with the fresh so deftly that his public lost its place in history: the fresh reassured them and the familiar was shocking. The customers were not boss: Ziegfeld was.

We see him early to rise and making production notes while still in bed. We see him pelting one and all with verbose telegrams, orders of the day. He can't pass a telephone without making twenty calls—but each conversation brings the next show closer to what Ziegfeld has in mind. We see him brusque with men and captivating with women, his gallantry so casual that when he bestows diamonds he simply pulls the piece out of his pocket neat, no box. The *Follies* is like that: something extraordinary suddenly appears.

Ziegfeld lived in the news media, as the entertainment business learned to; and he crowded everyone who worked for him for more surprise, more delight; and he left the classical to others while trading heavily in Goethe's Eternal Woman. She "draws us upward," the poet observes, because one can get enough poetry but one cannot get enough sex. When Ziegfeld began, it was as if all theatre was in code, the looks and flirty double meanings locked up where they could do no harm. Ziegfeld freed them. And show biz now begins.

CHAPTER ONE

Ziegfeld's Chicago

We start with a photograph of Flo and his three siblings at a tender age. It is perhaps their only picture to survive, for it is the one we always see. Flo, the oldest at twelve or so, is standing, dressed in what appears to be a school uniform, complete with a military cap, and showing just the hint of a smirk. The others are seated in front of him: Carl, ten, dressed like Flo and looking up from writing something in a book; baby Louise, four, dolled up and leaning on Carl's shoulder; and William, six, the cutest of the group in his little boy's first suit, topped off with a pocket watch and chain. He looks a little uncertain.

They were middle-class kids, all born in Chicago, where their immigrant parents had settled. Flo's father, Florenz Ziegfeld Sr., had a vocation to educate the young in music, and with so many music schools already established in his native Germany, he decided to play the missionary in America. After earning his certificate at the Leipzig Conservatory of Music, in 1863, when he was twenty-two years old, Ziegfeld returned home to what was then the duchy of Oldenburg, on the North Sea between Hamburg and the Netherlands, made his farewells, and set off. By 1865, still a bachelor, he had put down professional roots in Chicago, and not by chance. New York, where he briefly dallied, enjoyed some musical infrastructure. But Chicago had next to none—and, to boot, counted a huge German population, the largest ethnic group in the city. Milwaukee, Wisconsin, only thirty miles straight up the shores of Lake Michigan, to the north of Chicago, was a German colony in all but name. However, Chicago was extremely fast-growing and had just reached the stage when the first families of business seek to become first families of culture. Chicago was thus an ideal starting place for a European musician with ambition.

And Florenz Ziegfeld was ambitious, organizing his tutorials around a partnership with piano manufacturer W. W. Kimball and music publisher George Root. It was a natural alliance for anyone with expansive plans, for in a time when one had to go somewhere to hear music or make it oneself, every middle-class home had a piano and a pile of song sheets and light-classical piano solos or violin-piano duets. "My Old Kentucky Home." "Favorite Airs From the Operas." "The Banjo, Grotesque Fantasie, American Sketch." Mastering the piano, buying one, and updating the repertory of the home musicale created one of America's biggest businesses. Entering into an alliance with all three branches addressed a wide public.

In the event, Ziegfeld's first enterprise failed. Meanwhile, he had met and married a fellow immigrant, the Belgian Rosalie de Hez, in 1865. Back home in Germany, the Ziegfelds were burghers of some repute, but Rosalie claimed a most distinguished grand-uncle, the count Étienne-Maurice Gérard, one of Napoleon's generals at Austerlitz, Jena, Wagram, and in the Russian campaign; war minister under Louis-Philippe, the citizen-king; and a marshal of France. Because Rosalie was Roman Catholic and Ziegfeld Lutheran, they hit upon an odd religious arrangement for their progeny. Florenz Edward Ziegfeld Jr., born March 21, 1867,[1] was baptized a Catholic, but Carl and William were entered into the Lutheran confession and Louise was christened a Methodist.

With a spread of eight years framing the four births, one might expect some close bonding among the children, but what little we can glean from the archives suggests that young Flo was intimate only in a

---

[1] A stubborn factoid, born of a typo in Ziegfeld's *New York Times* obituary, gives the year as 1869. All secure sources give 1867.

generalized way. Certainly, he didn't see anything the way his family did. For all the Beethoven and Schubert that filled his ears in youth, he developed no interest in classical music. He could play the piano, of course; piano lessons were automatic in the household of Herr Doktor Florenz Ziegfeld Sr.[1] Then, too, Flo Jr. attended student recitals and joined the Herr Doktor's staff as soon as age allowed. But none of this resonated in the older, independent Flo. Beethoven and Schubert were, to his taste, noble, transcendent, and idealistic. In short: hard work. If Flo is not actually smirking in that photograph of the Ziegfeld little ones, he is at least at some remove from whatever lies in store for the rest of his generation, and he seems to know it.

So never did Flo embrace the family business the way his two brothers eventually did. He remained on conventionally loving terms with his people, even joining his touring shows when they reached Chicago for Ziegfeld family reunions. Nevertheless, Papa, Mama, Carl, William, and Louise were what Flo was bound to leave behind him when he reached young manhood and pursued his destiny. What he took with him was Chicago.

Surely the most mythologized of American cities—more so even than New York or Los Angeles—Chicago grew like a mushroom, from trading post to metropolis in a single generation. It was tycoon heaven, where the business of the place is business, almost passionately founded on its main industries of stock butchery, grain, and lumber. All the nation's railroad lines led to Chicago, and as countless trains steamed into the center of town, two human beings a day were killed or maimed where tracks crossed streets. In Japan, they would say, "That's karma." In Chicago, they said, "That's business."

Built on prairie that turned to mud half the year, Chicago had a sanitation problem, a weather problem, a potable water problem. One

---

[1]Some writers have poked fun at the older Ziegfeld, questioning his right to "Doktor." In fact, the use of this term was, in the Germany that he came from, as much a mark of respect for a learned man as a factual representation of his educational pedigree.

bathed with minnows. The very concept of Chicago was the reordering of nature, yet civic pride plumed itself as much on the hazards of growing too fast as on the profits. Congested, plundering, insatiable—Chicago wasn't a model town: it was an American town, *the* American town, the city as capitalist text. Did any other major municipality so wed its government to its industries? "City of the big shoulders," Carl Sandburg called it, because it was tough and violent and filled with hustlers and stank to high heaven, and no one wanted to leave it.

There was excitement in Chicago life, born of the unmonitored swelling of an urban giant on a site both inviting and treacherous. Lake Michigan offered connection to the lumber fields of the north and the other Great Lakes, and, once the Illinois and Michigan Canal was dug, young Chicago enjoyed nearly limitless commercial expansion. The place really was young. Little more than cabins and a fort on Indian lands when Chicago incorporated, in 1833, it opened the canal only fifteen years later, simultaneously taking on telegraph communication and the construction of its first railroad.

That was in 1848, nineteen years before Florenz Ziegfeld Jr. was born. So the Chicago he grew up in was a frontier town and a cultural capital at once. It was a setting, a layout for startling events unlikely in other towns. It was where a woman star of early musical comedy, the English Lydia Thompson, could respond to vituperative newspaper editorials by horse-whipping the responsible editor in public, suffering arrest, paying a fine, and continuing her run at Crosby's Opera House after losing only a single performance to legal technicalities. Chicago sided with Thompson, not with the editor; this city liked its personalities on the rich side.

Who was *the* Chicagoan of Flo's day? Perhaps Philip Armour, the farmboy from New York who became the nation's leading meatpacker, up at work before the sun was, to hold a day-long levee at his rolltop desk with messengers, employees, colleagues in trade, and callers of various kinds: the dedicated industrialist.

Or Gurdon Saltonstall Hubbard, an Old Settler (as they were called) who took part in every Chicago adventure from fur trading through the ethnic antagonisms of the 1860s to the Great Fire: the local Character.

Or Jane Addams, the social reformer and Quaker saint. Or Theodore Thomas, the first conductor of the Chicago Orchestra (the forerunner of today's Chicago Symphony), the Chicagoan as artist, a friend of the senior Ziegfeld and a fellow German émigré.

Or Florenz Ziegfeld Jr. For though Flo made nothing of himself till he moved to New York, there is more than a little of the Chicago can-do hustler in Ziegfeld's style. He's the guy with an angle who bluffs his way into his first million, loses it on a gamble, and starts bluffing all over again. There's a helter-skelter in Ziegfeld the man, too, a hunger for chaos. It is as if he can do his best work only with everything going off at once: just like Chicago, where the nightclub stood right next to the art museum with railroad yards behind them, and where the Women's Christian Temperance Union made its headquarters in a drinking culture so thirsty that some saloons stayed open all night.

Florenz Ziegfeld Sr. could do nothing to instill in his first born a love of great music, but he did finally make a go of teaching music to Chicago. Senior's Chicago Musical Academy, founded in the year of Junior's birth, 1867, struggled for about five years, took the more "arrived" name of the Chicago Musical College, and at length caught on as a fixture of the city's cultural life. Thriving in its quiet way, it remained the Senior Ziegfeld's legacy till it was absorbed, in 1954, by the School of Music of Roosevelt University.

Herr Doktor's approach at his college was petit-bourgeois, catering to the offspring of Chicago's neverending supply of upwardly mobile families while maintaining respectful relations with Society and the city's musical establishment. Well-brought-up young ladies took piano, though the Chicago Musical College offered courses as well in the reed and brass instruments and in harmony and composition. Above all, Ziegfeld's close ties to the imposing conductor of the Chicago Orchestra must have contributed greatly to the school's prestige, especially among the socially elect.

Letters have survived that testify to Ziegfeld's very European manner of requesting permission of the Chicago great and near-great to arrange for the personal dedication of a musical composition—for instance, to Mrs. Potter Palmer, society's undisputed doyenne, on behalf of Fritz Scheel. "Herr Scheel is one of the greatest conductors in Germany," Ziegfeld writes, "and a composer well worthy of your kind consideration." In America as in the Old World, the patronage of the powerful was a necessary support in the business of making music. Theodore Thomas was a celebrity and Mrs. Palmer a grandee: and Florenz Ziegfeld Sr. was simply a family man always renewing cordial relations with what the French call *le gratin,* "the crust."

Ziegfeld's school moved from one address to another in its first years; at times it was housed in rented offices while the faculty pursued tutorials in individual students' homes. During one lean period, Ziegfeld had to operate entirely out of the family residence. Aside from the usual reasons—fluctuations in enrollment and such—was the Unique Chicago Reason that affected everyone in the town from aristo to bum: the Great Fire of the night of October 8, 1871.

Young Flo was four years, six months, and one week old when Catherine O'Leary's cow legendarily kicked a kerosene lamp into the hay of her barn and destroyed a city of 340,000 people. And a legend it is. Though the press hounded Mrs. O'Leary till her death, a reporter revealed that he and two other journalists had invented the story, based on the finding of an overturned oil lamp in the O'Leary barn. While no one knows what exactly sparked the Great Fire, what built it so big so quickly was a concentration of makeshift wooden structures, a poorly equipped fire department . . . and "the wind."

This last item was the effect of the cold night air being drawn into a vortex created by rapidly rising hot air, creating hurricane-like winds. These tore chunks of lumber off burning buildings, hurling them into the distance to ignite new fires. Thus, Chicago burned not in one steadily advancing military formation of flame but in little sorties of fire that leaped over untouched areas, thereby generating chasms in which fleeing humanity could find itself trapped.

Everyone living in Chicago in 1871 could tell you, ever after, exactly where he was when he realized that the city was burning. He could tell you what he saw and what he heard—a shower of flame, an orange wall, a seething mountain; a war of a thousand cannon, the screams of the damned. Most folks had simply been pulled out of bed by the noise or roused by neighbors. Still, with every Chicagoan intent on presenting the narration of His Fire, one would expect a Ziegfeld family version to have come down through time. Yet there appears to be no such story. One writer tells us that Ziegfeld Sr. spent the first hours of the fire trying to save some of the school pianos. Surely not. The Ziegfelds lived in the central business district known as the Loop, whither the fire headed after bursting out to the south in an immigrant shantytown so baked by a hot, dry summer that it was all but dying to crisp. Indeed, a serious but ultimately containable fire had raged there just one night before.

So Ziegfeld Sr. could have wasted no time wrestling with pianos. He would immediately have taken his family to the place where everyone else instinctively went: the lake. Besides parents Florenz and Rosalie, there was just young Flo and Carl, barely toddling. All four made it through the holocaust—as, ironically, did the mainstays of Chicago, the millionaire's city: the lumberyards, the grain elevators, and the stockyards. There is yet more capitalist instruction in the miraculously speedy rebuilding of the town. It was as if the nation couldn't afford not to reimplement this essential piece of the prosperity machine. Some Chicagoans claimed that the Great Fire did them all the favor of excavating the foundation for a new and improved metropolis.

This was the level of energy and self-belief in which young Flo grew up, and the family found a new residence, at 1448 West Adams Street, a thoroughfare that ran for miles from the Art Institute in the east on into the Illinois countryside in the west. This house, at last, was not temporary quarters; Senior and Rosalie remained there from then on.

Shouldn't the Herr Doktor have sought a more suburban location for his school and family, perhaps on the north side, where the money lived? Or did the Senior Ziegfeld enjoy being in the very center of a boom town as much as his son did? Enlisted as a junior officer in the running of the Chicago Musical College, young Flo couldn't wait to get out of the place and into the world of People Who Do Things, into the

Chicagoness of life. As the school's assistant treasurer, then treasurer, and so on up to general manager under his father's presidency, Junior was dutiful but distracted, all the more so after attending the great theatrical event of his adolescence.

The touring spectacle entitled *Buffalo Bill's Wild West* and billed as "America's National Entertainment" was a show without a theatre: a great outdoor representation of the facts and legends of the world of cowboy and Indian, settler and scout. Formed in 1883, *Buffalo Bill's Wild West* featured shooting acts, horseback-riding stunts, historical and generical reconstructions ("Battle of the Little Big Horn," "Attacks on the Settler's Cabin"), and a genuine hero, Bill Cody himself. In 1885, Annie Oakley swelled the drawing power of the posters, for Oakley, too, was famous. If Bill Cody was admired for his abundance of manly qualities, Oakley was as well: she not only shot like a man, but did so with the confidence of the surest hand that ever drew.

A woman without nerves! And what was Bill Cody? Nothing less than the man who avenged all of America for the slaughter of Custer's cavalry. His show depicted the terrible battle and left it at that—but every spectator knew the tale of Buffalo Bill's real-life "duel" with Yellow Hair,[1] a Cheyenne brave who symbolized the other side in the We Versus They of America's push westward. As Bill himself told it, a month after Custer and his men bit the dust, army scout Cody and his trackers met up with a Cheyenne war party led by Yellow Hair.

"I know you, Pa-he-haska," Yellow Hair called out to Cody. "If you want to fight, come ahead and fight me."

Instantly, Cody spurred his horse, and the two rode at each other like two terrors. At thirty yards, Cody fired his shotgun, wounding Yellow Hair. Cody's horse tripped and Cody went down, but he and Yellow Hair kept firing till Cody got close enough to stab the brave in the heart. Then, in Cody's own words, "jerking Yellow Hair's war bonnet off . . . I scientifically scalped him in about five seconds."

---

[1] He is sometimes called Yellow *Hand,* a mistake perpetrated by Wild Bill himself. More correct even than Yellow Hair is his name in Cheyenne, Wey-o-hei.

Is this Manifest Destiny or the theatrical version of it? Real life and theatre had not yet begun to blur into one in the 1880s, but *Buffalo Bill's Wild West* might have been a signal act in the history of wagging the dog, of staging real life. The show began with the "Grand Entry of the Rough Riders of the World," and had the public in a thrill till the last moment. It was not only exciting: it was authentic, with two absolutely guaranteed heroes in Cody and Oakley. Mark Twain claimed that the show "brought back to me the breezy, wild life of the Rocky Mountains and stirred in me like a war song. Down to its smallest detail the show is genuine—cowboys, vaqueros, Indians, stagecoach, costumes and all."

Cody's show compelled because it was "real." But it was something else: big. Yet it was designed for utmost flexibility, to be pulled up and set down again in over a hundred playing venues in a single year. And we note with interest that the man who put it on was no cowboy but a member of the New York theatre world, Nate Salsbury. Previously the capocomico of Salsbury's Troubadours, this now forgotten manager was the kind who conceives, writes, directs, and produces without performing himself. Among his work was *The Brook* (1879), a historian's prototype of musical comedy in its farce plot allowing for specialty numbers. *The Brook* was small and the *Wild West* vast, but we sense Florenz Ziegfeld Jr. seeing in Salsbury's art generally an alternative to the Chicago Musical College, a source of surprise and delight.

Cody himself was something special, like the outstanding personalities coloring the Chicago scene; you'd buy tickets to them. Cody knew how to dress, too, in finely decorated buckskins, boots rising almost to the hip. He knew how to hold himself, how to move, where to stand in a group photograph. Heck, he knew exactly when in history to present himself, with his good side showing.

Flo would doubtless have seen a lot of content in *Buffalo Bill's Wild West*. And in one of those apocryphal bits without which no important American life would be complete, we are told that Flo came out of the audience to match shooting skills with the pros, even that he ran off as a member of the *Wild West* company till his father went hurtling after to drag the boy back to music.

Well, maybe. We expect something of the like from Flo at this time, for Dutiful is not one of his styles, and his father had clearly stamped Flo's future, signed and then sealed it in the venerable European tradition of the father who is at once patriarch, despot, and bureaucrat. The stamp read: DUTY TO THE CLASSICS.

But Flo never argued with men who barred his way; he simply went around them. And it is true that he had had some informal lessons in gun handling from his father; it was not uncommon in a rough place like Chicago. However, for reasons that Flo seems never to have shared with anyone, after *Buffalo Bill's Wild West* left Chicago, Flo did not continue in any direction, instead settling down at the Chicago Musical College for ten dead years.

Till the Chicago World's Fair came along—more exactly, the Columbian Exposition of 1893, the biggest event in Chicago life since the Great Fire. Paris and London were famous for their fairs, and Philadelphia put on America's Centennial Fair, in 1876. But this new fair would be the biggest of all: in honor of the four hundredth anniversary of the discovery of America. It might have been held in any number of cities. Washington, D.C., obviously, had a political claim. New York had a cultural one, and St. Louis, the so-called Gateway To the West, a thematic one.

Chicago was on the short list, too, and as Chicago would hear no arguments from rivals, New York started one. A furious newspaper war sprang up between the two, New York calling Chicago a country bumpkin of a city, coarse and without Tone. "Chicago slaughters and packs its hogs," the *Chicago Tribune* replied. "New York puts them on committees."

However, Chicago was, again, the most American of towns. Didn't the nation as a whole lack Tone? Democracies don't have Tone: they have energy. Chicago's all but overnight rebuilding after the fire seemed a singularly national act, made of two things Americans really valued: money and efficiency. In order for Chicago to plan and execute a fair worthy of the history it represented—for it did indeed win the competition—the authorities gave the city an extra year, as if 1493 were the first date everybody learns in school.

All agreed that it was worth the postponement, for the fair turned out to be a tremendous success. Folks called it the White City, because of the mixture of plaster and hemp painted white that was used in its construction. It was set up south of the metropolis, in Jackson Park, and at the fairgrounds' center was a canal bedecked with gondolas and surrounding a little fantasy island. Elegant monsters of architecture guarded the scene—the Fine Arts Building, the Transportation Building with its fabulously ornate façade and Golden Doorway, the Electricity Building. In lonely glory stood the Statue of the Republic. It could all be thought of as a gigantic stage set, not least because virtually none of it was intended to last. The foreign exhibits included replicas of Samoan, Bavarian, and Algerian villages—and in the Dahomey Village one could enjoy the "natives" in a lavish war dance.

This is more theatre, isn't it? And Flo must have taken note of it, because we'll be hearing more about the Dahomey Village, the war dance, and the question of how indigenous these Dahomeyans were in a Ziegfeld show thirty-four years later. Amid all the travelogue, those who wanted to savor the American style could visit *Buffalo Bill's Wild West*, parked just outside the fairgrounds, or a huge log cabin known as the Idaho Building. There was a Wild East at the fair, too—a Bedouin village and a mock-up of Cairo, complete with the Temple of Luxor.

Still, many fairgoers preferred to these educational exhibits the fair's Midway Plaisance, the first of its kind. Is this where sideshow barkers introduced their "Hurry, hurry, hurry!"? The Chicago Columbian Exposition in fact originated a great many items now taken for granted, such as the picture postcard, the American volume of Baedeker's travel guides, and the Ferris wheel, after George Washington Gale Ferris Jr., who designed it to rival the outstanding ornament of the previous world's fair, in Paris, in 1889, the Eiffel Tower.

Still another "first" will bear on our narrative decades hence—the midway "kooch dance." A legend as insistent as that of the O'Leary cow tells us that a certain Little Egypt performed the hoochy-koochy on the midway—the *danse du ventre*, or "belly dance." Well, there *was* a Little Egypt at some point in the evolution of the kooch dance, but despite what one reads in almost all sources, she wasn't at the Chicago fair. Furthermore, the women who were elaborating upon the art of kooch at the fair's sideshows were not remotely the "strippers in all but name" that tradition places at the launching of kooch. Neverthless, false legends have a way of giving birth to facts, and as early as the following year, *The National Police Gazette* magazine of March 31, 1894, flourished on its cover a black-and-white drawing of the "Danse du Ventre in Brooklyn, N.Y.," wherein a crowd of men avidly watch "Fatima give a fascinating exhibition." In a sleeveless, diaphanous top, her back arched to thrust her tummy forward and her facial features in something like ecstasy, Fatima does indeed appear to be making the most of that minor-key melody always used to evoke the sensuality of the East. You know: the one that kids sing lubricious lyrics to. (One version begins, "Oh, they don't wear pants on the sunny side of France . . .")

The hoochy-koochy bears on our tale as the first-known irruption into American entertainment of what in due course became the basis of the striptease—that is, a sexy dance to dirty music. Nothing like this existed anywhere onstage in America at this time. But the notoriety of kooch made it irresistible to the managers then presiding over the devolution of burlesque.

This once great form of Lydia Thompson and many others suddenly seemed horribly dated, with its pun-filled dialogue and sing-'em-muck scores. Burlesque did have one exploitable element: the girls. What if the "tights" that the girls of burlesque were famous for changed from very loose fitting bathing attire covering them from neck to toe to . . . well, *tights*? Would the girls be willing to kooch—or, at least, to appear in drag as a bon vivant at bedtime after a party, slowly taking off the many parts of his dress suit? What if some writer was to rid burlesque of its puns and corn and start talking about sex?

All this took decades to accomplish in the dark alleys of a progressively degraded burlesque, while Florenz Ziegfeld Jr. was effecting his revolution in the presentation of the erotic right at the heart of Broadway. However, in 1893 at the Columbian Exposition, young Flo was busy assisting his father in events connected to the fair. Theodore

Thomas was of course the fair's music director, beckoning to choral groups around the country to come to Chicago to perform between ambitious orchestra concerts of European masters. Herr Doktor Ziegfeld's position as a Thomas colleague gave him access to the proceedings in some advisory capacity. But the senior Ziegfeld saw a splendid opportunity in mounting his own musical variety show, well off the fairgrounds in the Loop. A completely unsuitable building was commandeered, the First Regiment Armory, at Michigan Avenue and Sixteenth Street. Blithely rising above its castlelike appearance—it had everything but a moat—Senior dubbed it his "International Temple of Music," renamed it the Trocadero, and sent Junior to Europe to assemble and bring back a troupe of music-hall artists.

While Flo was abroad, the armory suffered a fire. So his father found another spot, this one an adaptable single-story building with a peaked roof. (This is the nightclub that was next to the Art Institute, also on Michigan Avenue, but at East Monroe Drive.) Another legend: Junior returns not with the stuffy class acts his father expects but with rowdy kitsch—bell-ringers, yodelers, and other Tyrolean whatnot; and the Trocadero fails.

On the contrary, both Ziegfelds had agreed that the Trocadero would present a bill of mixed light-classical and popular fare. One of the Trocadero's achievements, for instance, was the signing of the Hamburg Bülow Orchestra, a perfectly respectable group. Some writers have confused the Bülow name with the famous Wagnerian conductor Hans von Bülow. No: the Hamburg Bülows were led by the Fritz Scheel who hoped to dedicate a piece to Mrs. Potter Palmer a few pages ago.

The Trocadero enterprise did at first go badly, but this had nothing to do with the quality of the performers. What hurt the Ziegfelds was the quality of the fair. Who was going to spend an exhausting day rambling around the White City, stuffing himself with sights and snacks, then top it off with a jaunt into town for cabaret?

Then young Flo had an idea. There was no way to outdraw a world's fair. But one might draw alongside it, so to say. All one needed was a headliner—and not an established star like Buffalo Bill. Someone to

CHAPTER TWO

The Big Blond Boy

Eugen Sandow was a bodybuilder and a sex object at a time when there were very few bodybuilders and no sex objects at all, at least not in public and never of the male gender. Technically, Sandow was a vaudeville performer with a strongman act, but he ultimately became a summoning term for an ideal of power and beauty fused in one entity. Though he died in 1925 and had given up touring his act in 1906 to market his workout program and gear, the word "Sandow" lasted for generations as a marker of the herculean attributes. Each new contestant to the title would be called "as strong as Sandow," and everyone knew what was meant. In short, Sandow was the top of his line in a line that Sandow virtually invented. Continental European in origin and English by adopted citizenship, this first of the modern-day Beautiful Males attained the uniquely American status of the pop celebrity who survives the first fifteen minutes to become more or less permanently famous.

Sandow was born in Königsberg (today Kaliningrad), the cultural capital of East Prussia and a major port city on the Baltic; his birthdate of April 2, 1867 made him a mere two weeks younger than Ziegfeld. Sandow's family name was the most ordinary available in Germany, Müller, and his given names were Friedrich Wilhelm, presumably in honor of the line of Prussian kings.

Why did the young man take the name of Sandow? Of course, many who went on the stage in those days adopted a marquee billing, especially those working a strongman act. But they tended to give themselves definitive names—Goliath, Hercules McCann, Charles A. Sampson, Cyclops. Sandow's biographer David L. Chapman provides the simplest of explanations: "Sandow" is an alternative spelling of Friedrich Müller's mother's maiden name, Sandov. Besides, isn't it silly to be called Goliath or Cyclops? Like them, Sandow presented feats of strength and took on challenges from the audience to beat him at weightlifting. As one of Sandow's favorite stunts was "the human barbell"—packed with a grown man at each end of the bar—no one could.

And unlike his rivals, Sandow wasn't just strong: Sandow was lovely. Handsome, with curly blond hair and an upturned blond moustache, with a tiny waist veeing up through intensely articulated muscle separations to classically wide shoulders, with incredibly white skin, hairless but for a few wisps at the place of sin. So Sandow was heavy but exquisite, a thing of beauty. The other professional strongmen were so many Zampanos—the boorish lunk in Federico Fellini's film *La Strada*—next to this above all youthful pretender to the title of World's Most Perfect Man. When Ziegfeld crossed paths with Sandow, they were both just twenty-six years old.

They met at the Casino Theatre, one of Broadway's most popular houses and the first one specifically designed for musicals. Built in 1882 at the southeast corner of Broadway and Thirty-ninth Street, the Casino stood sentry at the northern limits of "Broadway," though Abbey's Theatre (later the Knickerbocker, now demolished) was just south of it, literally next door. (The Metropolitan Opera House, not part of Broadway but a theatre nonetheless, stood a tiny bit to their north, at the northwest corner of the intersection.) Historians always mention the Casino's Moorish look, its elaborate interior suggesting a Moroccan harem and its western façade that of a Venetian palazzo, with a domed tower at the corner. It was a house of choice for big shows: *Florodora* (1900) played there, and, still popular in the 1920s, the Casino offered such hits as *Wildflower*; the first Marx Brothers musical, *I'll Say She Is*; and two operetta classics, *The Vagabond King* and *The Desert Song*. The Casino was torn down in 1930, but by then "Broadway" had moved into its present-day address, spreading north from Forty-Second Street, with its infrastructure of luxury hotels with gala reception rooms and the fabled "lobster palaces" where the great met the ambitious for dinner and, in private rooms, more.

That will be the Broadway that we of today associate with Florenz Ziegfeld Jr.: a dressy and publicized Vanity Fair filled with glamor, wit, and first-nighting. For now, however, we find Flo alone and demoralized in the Casino Theatre on a sweltering evening in July 1893. He is attending a performance of that tired old burlesque *Adonis* (1884).

At least, that may be how Flo saw it. He was in New York to find that exploitable unknown who would turn his father's cabaret into the talk of Chicago—the next big thing. And here was Flo at *Adonis,* the *last* big thing—arch, prissy, and dull. To Flo, *Adonis* was your father's musical, your grandfather's musical, Abe Lincoln's musical.

To give *Adonis* its historical due, it was the outstanding hit of its day, roughly halfway between *The Black Crook* (1866) and *The Merry Widow* (1907). With a libretto by William F. Gill and music by Edward E. Rice (and many others), *Adonis* ran 603 performances in its first New York engagement, a record to that time. It was broken by *A Trip To Chinatown* (1891), seven years later. Still, *Adonis* had something that none of these other hits did: an enduring star. Henry E. Dixey enjoyed such réclame in *Adonis'* title role that to stage it without him would have been unthinkable.

"To stage it, period, is unthinkable," says Flo. I'm guessing. Because *Adonis* is made of the hammy coquetry that Flo was to encourage the theatre to outgrow. Flo liked his erotica neat and fulfilled, not coy and gibbering, and *Adonis* foofoos around almost as soon as its opening chorus of invisible spirits has ended. The ancient Greek sculptress Talamea calls forth her mentor goddess, Artea, who pops up through a trap door:

TALAMEA: Great Goddess, I am miserable.
ARTEA: You, the great sculptress, miserable? Wherefore?
TALAMEA: I love!

ARTEA: Your art? Yes!

TALAMEA: Of course, I do. But it is not that.

ARTEA: What, then? A man?

TALAMEA: No, alas.

ARTEA: A *lass*? You love a *lass*?

Actually, that sounds kind of modern, after all. However, it is a statue that Talamea loves, her own figure of Adonis. In a Transformation Scene, Artea brings the marble to life: Henry E. Dixey, all white from wig to toes, in a sleeveless long-tailed coat over tight shorts and skin-close leggings. No woman could have been so revealed onstage at this time; even for a man the look was daring, and no small reason why Dixey collected so many admirers. Though he fluted about throughout the evening in various disguises, including drag, Dixey was thought to be a model of comely manhood, and his physical appeal explains why *Adonis* was so successful.

At length, the hero finds the adoration of many women so exhausting that he turns back into a statue, posing for the final curtain as he was first seen, leaning against a pillar, one arm resting on the stone and the other artfully draped in one coattail, pointing off to some otherland. The curtain fell.

Now comes the history. Because the curtain immediately rose again—not for the *Adonis* company's calls, but for all five feet eight and a half inches and 220 pounds of Eugen Sandow, leaning on Adonis' column in his own costume, showing as much skin as might be legally risked. The Casino audience gasped. And Florenz Ziegfeld Jr. came to.

Why the theatre was following a full-length musical with a strongman act is easily explained: the Casino's manager, Rudolph Aronson, had taken the house over to vaudeville after failing to make "comic opera"—the house specialty—pay. But Aronson's variety bills didn't go over, either, and he was in a "try anything" mood when Sandow suddenly turned up. *Adonis* had already opened, and perhaps Aronson thought an epilogue of Sandow might illuminate the theme.

Henry E. Dixey was trim and small-waisted, with legs fit for tights—but as soon as Sandow quit his pose at the marble pillar, stepped forward, and went into his posing routine, the Casino public learned what an Adonis looks like. Dixey's looks favored the standards of the day; Sandow was to set new standards, starting that night. To Dixey's slim and supple, Sandow countered with big and cut, and as audiences of that time were more vocal in their reactions than those of today, Flo can't have failed to take note of the cries and murmurs of the ladies in the house. No one in the *Adonis* company had struck Flo as useful to the Trocadero. But Sandow was something else.

"The face was that of little more than a boy," *The New York Herald* reported. "Smooth, with rosy cheeks and a little blond moustache." But "the neck was massive, and the shoulders seemed a yard apart." This was no play Adonis, but something out of mythology. A god, yes—but, better, a new one, requiring a fresh cult. Flo loved new things, and he snapped Sandow up on the spot, brought him to Chicago, and started the beating of mighty drums to focus the town's interest, create a sellout opening with plenty of press coverage, and then let the quality of the attraction make its appeal. "Stardust," Flo called it years later in an interview, defining it as the "extraordinary power to draw humanity in streams to the playhouse."

This must be said of our protagonist: he let experience teach him how the knots were tied. One rule he had absorbed this early on was Don't Hustle the Midway. The manager of cheap acts never gets out of the neighborhood. To reach Broadway, one hustles class. Indeed, Flo had got his start hustling the midway. First came the Dancing Ducks of Denmark, an animal-abuse act. (Gas jets heated the metal grid on which the ducks were placed, making them squawk and hop around.) Then came the Invisible Brazilian Fish, a bowl of empty water, and so beyond audacity that one wonders if this is more apocrypha.

Flo would never set foot on the midway again. He was about to go pricey with Sandow and the "Trocadero Vaudevilles," as Flo billed them. As Sandow's opening night approached, Ziegfeld teased the town with posters and heralds and bragging. "It is but fitting and just," ran one of Ziegfeld's declarations, "to crown our most sanguine expectations with exhibitions by this powerful giant, whose hobby it seems is to toy with a thousand pound ball and lift a double-team of draft horses."

All this ballyhoo occurred in no more than two weeks, for Sandow met Chicago's public on August 1, 1893. Interestingly, not only the usual blend of gossips, the curious, and the "I was there"s greeted him: members of Social Chicago were present as well. After the acrobats, clowns, and song-and-dance people heated up the stage, Sandow introduced himself in his usual way—the heavy lifting, his marvelous standing backflip, and of course the flexing display. However, something new was added—and here we see a first manifestation of Ziegfeldian showmanship: the grandes dames of Chicago were invited backstage to feel Sandow's muscles.

In one version, Ziegfeld wraps the stunt in philanthropic righteousness by requiring of each applicant a three-hundred-dollar charitable donation. That may have happened. We do know that women regularly trooped backstage to examine Sandow because *The Police Gazette* covered it. As with its piece on the *danse du ventre,* the *Gazette* gave the tale national circulation with a cover story on January 27, 1894, during the Trocadero Vaudevilles' post-Chicago tour. THE LADIES IDOL-IZE SANDOW ran the headline, and while one of them is sitting in a chair as if overcome, another has laid a gloved hand on Sandow's right biceps as he stands topless in leggings, high stockings, and lace-up boots. Anna Held, Ziegfeld's next star and first great love, set down in her memoirs a notion of what these women were thinking: "How handsome you are! Your muscles ripple under your skin like the thrills of a Viennese waltz!"

For a woman of any class to get so close to that much male skin in public was unheard of in 1894. It tells us how edgy Ziegfeld's approach was going to be, how certain he must have been that liberating the sexual content of the popular stage would address a ready public and hasten the end of Victorian cautions. And note that Ziegfeld was an equal-opportunity panderer. The man who became notorious for—this is the phrase he devised for the 1922 edition of his *Follies*—"glorifying the American girl" knew which boy to glorify, too.

After Chicago, Ziegfeld left brothers Carl and William to assist their father at the Chicago Musical College and launched a tour. The Trocadero Vaudevilles now picked their way west in one date after another, reaching California in April 1894, in time for San Francisco's own Midwinter Fair, set up in Golden Gate Park. In the creativity of his PR, Ziegfeld always did his best when working in major cities to a competitive press, and he had all of San Francisco as keyed up for its first look at Sandow as Chicago had been.

We know relatively little about the Trocadero Vaudevilles as a package—a real gap in the biography, because the Sandow tour was in effect Ziegfeld's first produced evening of theatrical entertainment. The window cards herald the usual agglomeration of performers, with an emphasis on circus acts—trained dogs, a white-faced clown in a ruff, another clown with an accordion, an acrobat, and, more typical of the Great American Variety Show that was vaudeville, a duo of Old French Gentleman and Coquette With Fan. There was a Russian dance troupe in the mix, and the aforementioned Bülow Band. After Chicago, Ziegfeld signed up a trapeze act billed as the Jordan Family: Lewis and Mamie Jordan and a number of children, some Jordans and some not. This must have been quite some act, as Mamie was the first woman in history to execute a double somersault, and the Jordans got co-star billing right after Sandow. One of the Trocadero Vaudevilles posters gives its illustration entirely to the four members of "The Marvelous Jordan Family and Dunham, Astonishing Aerial Artists in Unbelievable Feats." In much smaller type than Sandow and the Jordans we read, "Directed by F. Ziegfeld Jr." The first initial and the Jr. remained Flo's billing on and off for most of his life.

Also of interest on Trocadero Vaudevilles picture art is the presence of a blond ballerina, a lovely young thing all in white giving her left hand to that white clown. This dancer holds the very center of this rich assembly, right down front, and she seems to be leading the way to Marilyn Miller, a combination of beauty, dancer, and heroine—the ultimate Ziegfeld Girl, as we shall see.

The eloquence of these illustrations was a key element of Ziegfeld's presentation, and Sandow became a national figure not only in news

stories but in the dissemination of posed studio photographs. In one series, Sandow poses in a full dress suit, rakish and seductive in his half-
smiles and the oxymoron of the gala torso at war with the stays and
encodings of Victorian dress. His elegance is hot. Women of romantic
inclination no doubt used the photographs to dream of Sandow in tête-
à-tête, perhaps in a restaurant's private room. Of course, most of the
Sandow shots found him in his business casual: as a Roman gladiator, as
Samson, or as "the Dying Gaul," stretched out on his side in nothing but
fig leaf and high-laced sandals.

Sandow even tried the movies, immortalizing his posing routine at
the start of the 1894 tour during a booking at Koster & Bial's Music Hall
in New York. William K. L. Dickson photographed Sandow on March 6
in the Edison Studios in West Orange, New Jersey, and if the resulting
film was no more than peep-show publicity in 1894, today it fascinates.
Sandow is martial yet alluring, antique but sexual, a show-off and a
mystery. He's Achilles. He's Olympian. One has to pull phrases out of the
book of myth just to take a reading of the man, and when Ziegfeld and
his troupe did finally reach San Francisco's Midwinter Fair, Ziegfeld
proposed a Labor of Hercules: Sandow would wrestle a lion into sub-
mission.

This is more Dancing Ducks of Denmark, because it was a hoax.
Worse, a scandal—so much so that, a generation later, when the *Follies*
toured the west coast, all anyone in San Francisco could talk of was "the
lion fight."

It started as a battle between two wild animals. The owner of a
menagerie[1] advertised a brawl to the death in which a grizzly bear was to
take on a lion named Parnell. The authorities stepped in to close this

---

[1]This man's name is given variously as Bone, Boon, and Boone, and he is most
commonly identified as "Colonel Daniel Boone." Surely someone has confused
Bone/Boon/Boone with the American pioneer Daniel Boone, who led the way along the
Wilderness Road through the Cumberland Gap and founded Boonesborough, Kentucky; surely others have carried over the confusion. That Daniel Boone could not have
been in San Francisco in 1894; he died in 1820.

ugly breach of the peace between man and beast. But now Ziegfeld leaped into his favorite place—the headlines—with a new proposal: *Sandow* would battle Parnell.

This was either crazy or a sham. It tells us that Ziegfeld was simply wasted in the world of curiosities rather than of artists. The Ziegfeld we will come to know lives in theatres, not the circus tent, and his cohort numbers avatars of talent on the genius level, not a piece of human sculpture whose activity sheet was a menu of boasts. Yes, Ziegfeld would leave the midway. But first he and his star had to endure the humiliation of the lion fight: because there was no fight to speak of. The genuinely dangerous Parnell was on site, slavering and roaring in his cage as the public filed into a tent especially erected for the event. But it was a lion named Commodore, not Parnell, that Sandow engaged in combat: ancient, exhausted, and indisposed, a real-life cowardly lion.

Commodore had been fitted with a muzzle and gigantic leather mittens, but they were unnecessary because the animal didn't charge Sandow even once. "There were murmurs of disapproval heard from all quarters," one reporter noted. Another wrote, "Some of the spectators yelled 'fake.'" What can one do to this sock puppet of a lion except to try bullying him into a tussle, if only in his self-defense? Some wondered if Commodore had been drugged, so limp was his performance. At that, what was Sandow doing in a cage with a lion in the first place? Sandow wasn't a warrior: Sandow was a thing of beauty.

It was an unmitigated disaster, the sort of thing that normally dissolves partnerships on the spot. Yet Ziegfeld remained Sandow's manager for two more seasons, in 1894–1895 and 1895–1896.[1] The two men were friends, it seems, able to absorb catastrophe. Unseasoned as he was,

---

[1] The theatre "season" today is no season in any real sense, defined arbitrarily by the timing of awards nights. In Ziegfeld's day, the season was defined *literally*, by weather, because most theatres closed for the two hottest months of the year. Further, most of the prominent stars shut down production in June, either to reopen in September or take on new work. Thus, the main reason why people went to the theatre—to enjoy a star performance—did not obtain during July and August. The summer was, by universal

Ziegfeld could teach Sandow a great deal about the marketing aspect of theatre, and Ziegfeld in turn collected physical-exercise tips that kept him trim for much of his adult life. The theatrical press— abundant in that day, when everyone above the rank of Hermit in a Cave routinely visited the playhouse—invariably referred to Ziegfeld and Sandow as "inseparable." They were thought more than manager and star: chums.

Still, the two decided to part company in the middle of their third season together. Sandow had married, and his English wife did not wish to live on the road or in separation from her husband. Then, too, Sandow had plans to turn his expertise into those how-to courses and Sandow gyms. Besides, once Sandow had toured, toured, and toured again, he had given his public all he had as a performer. Enduring vaudeville acts were made of song and dance or of comedy, easy to reinvest with new material. For all the merry splendor we see in Sandow's muscle show for Edison, he really was one thing only forever, like a statue. At that, the Edison people invited Sandow to return to West Orange in the spring of 1896 to make, this time, an appearance on the Vitascope. This new medium offered far greater exposure, taking Sandow out of the peep show and onto screens before an audience. It was all the rage in vaudeville, and "We believe it would result in a big advertisement for Mr. Sandow" is the key clause in the Edison letter to Flo at his favorite address in New York City, the Netherland Hotel, at Fifth Avenue and Fifty-Ninth Street.

When did Flo ever turn down an advertisement? Yet the film was never made, Sandow and his wife went back to England forever, and Flo toyed with a hundred options—a new vaudeville troupe, the management of Sandow touring the capitals of Europe, and so on. One thing was certain: he would never return to the Chicago Musical College. This

---

agreement, a time for the piquant offering that did without a star, or obscure placeholding titles catering to theatregoers too hungry to fast for sixty days. This was the recipe for the bill at the Casino the night Ziegfeld met Sandow: an oddity fit for the circus tent side by side with a dried-out old prune of a classic for devotees only.

created a lifelong rift between Junior and Senior, but a minor one. Considering that Flo was one of those Unavailable Men who love you when they can fit it into the schedule, Junior maintained solid ties with his family. Still, Chicago was now an episode in his past.

So, of course, was Sandow, along with three years of rootless cohabitation with a circus. Still, the experience taught Ziegfeld a lesson that he in turn would impart to others as he grew in power, as the theatre itself grew in this time, the Ziegfeld time. For all the Trocaderos' talents, all anyone really cared about was the headliner, Sandow. The press was centered on him, as was the excitement that sold out premieres and drew crowds of the curious to line the streets like petitioners in a hopeless case. The star defined the event.

Or no. The star *sold* the event. Contrary to what some writers tell us, the entertainment industry at this time was not entirely dominated by the big-name performers. The notable events were, yes: the managers' major productions, the New York or Chicago hits, the titles that so grandly reopened after the summer hiatus, eventually to be pasted into the archivist's scrapbook. However, many productions were make-dos, simply because there was a great deal of theatre but a finite number of star performers.

Flo decided that his fortune lay in the use of star attractions to sell his shows. His second favorite thing, now and forever after, was the management of unique talents; his first favorite thing was launching them from out of nowhere, as Flo had done with Sandow.

Now to find another of those exploitable lovely monsters to pitch to the public. In Europe, maybe? Sandow came from Europe, after all; that's what had made him new. It was time, too, for Flo to abandon vaudeville for legit, perhaps with a revival of some sure-thing older piece. Not one of those hammy cocotte burlesques like *Adonis,* Flo thought. Possibly . . . a farce? Something out of the Nate Salsbury handbook—remember the manager of *Buffalo Bill's Wild West*? Burlesque, by the 1890s, was a gray-haired old kook. Farce was youthful.

The form wasn't exactly a musical, though. Farce, in America at this time, was a more or less heavily plotted piece ready for the interpolation of song and dance specialties. For instance, Charles Hoyt's *A Parlor Match* (1884), one of the biggest hits in American theatre to that time. Its original stars, Charles Evan Evans and William F. Hoey, gave open runs in the big towns, split-weeks in the smaller towns, one-night stands in the sticks, and, if you were alive then, possibly played your living room at some point. *A Parlor Match* was so familiar to so many that reviewers had given up summarizing the plot because their readers knew the show cold.

For you youngsters: *A Parlor Match* uses the "buried treasure in the old house" theme to satirize spiritualism. During a seance, a large cabinet emits one "ghost" after another, each to present a specialty number or two. Thus the show's longevity: by the time the latest tour came to your town, a new group of specialists had been put into rotation, and back you went to catch the fun.

Evans played a bookseller and Hoey a drunken, scheming tramp named Old Hoss. Together they elaborated on their parts over the years till they were thought Hoyt's collaborators, and even in 1896, twelve years after *A Parlor Match*'s first night, the two remained national celebrities in this one title. Hoey had only recently made it a must-see all over again for a new interpolation, "The Man Who Broke the Bank at Monte Carlo." The song so defined Hoey's renown that whenever he entered a place where a band was playing, the conductor bid his men strike up the tune to cue in an ovation.

So here's an idea: what if Flo revives *A Parlor Match* with Evans and Hoey in a brand-new version for Broadway? And what if Flo discovers some new wonder talent to set the land agog during the cabinet scene—not just the usual specialty performer but someone . . . well, *special*? This will create what will turn out to be Flo's unstated theory of the guaranteed hit: something new made of old things. That is: retain the traditions but build around them innovatively.

We are now in the summer of 1896. Two events occur that will dominate Ziegfeld's future. One event was pure business: on August 31, 1896, in New York, three pairs of manager partners met over the festive table in the dining room of the Holland House Hotel, at Fifth Avenue and Thirtieth Street. There they consolidated their interests in a monopoly to control virtually all the important theatres in the country. Thus commanding the hardware, they would have the last word on the software, the plays themselves. If managers owned the entertainment industry, these six managers would own all the other managers.

Some of the six we have already met. One is Charles Frohman, who attended the meeting with his partner, Al Hayman.[1] It was the very prominent Frohman who did the actual producing; Hayman, seldom seen, provided the capital. Together they brought to the table prestige above all. Representing theatre chains in the west and midwest were Samuel F. Nixon and J. Fred Zimmerman. And, finally, bringing in the south and contracts with a host of important stars were Marc Klaw and the aforementioned Abraham Lincoln Erlanger. Like Mafia dons consolidating previously warring domains, these six men created the Theatrical Trust or, as it was generally known, the Syndicate.

As the chronicler is bound to point out, the Syndicate came into being as much to reform the theatre business as to govern it. The stage was living in a guiltless chaos of inefficient tour itineraries and even double- and triple-bookings as companies held on to safety contracts while secretly looking for better deals. The Syndicate organized playing schedules, but then it went on to impose a fascist unification. Anyone who defied their system was blacklisted, right up to the most resourceful managers and most beloved stars. The redoubtable Mrs. Fiske stood up to them and found herself performing in skating rinks. Mr. (Harrison Grey) Fiske, the editor of *The New York Dramatic Mirror,* ceaselessly denounced the Syndicate as "a hateful, corrupt and dangerous institution." The war was ugly, not least because all six of the Syndicate were Jewish; when *The Dramatic Mirror* termed them "a Shylock combination," it smacked of anti-Semitism.

---

[1] Al is often confused with his younger brother Alf, an important functionary in the Frohman production organization. The other main source of name confusion in theatre histories is the Aarons family, *père* Alfred E. Aarons and *fils* Alex A. Aarons, the latter of whom with Vinton Freedley produced most of the Gershwin brothers musicals of the 1920s.

An ambitious young manager like Florenz Ziegfeld Jr. would have no choice but to work with the Syndicate. It was fine for an established star such as Mrs. Fiske to perform in unexpected places: she already had a public, and they would follow her anywhere. But Flo was not only powerless but a stranger in town, in need of sound alliances, and he made the soundest possible, partnering up with Klaw and Erlanger themselves. If Charles Frohman was thought the least reprehensible of the Syndicate, Erlanger—who, ironically, looked like Frohman's twin brother—was a very tyrant of art. Like all fascists, he did it not because he had to, but because he loved to.

Yet it must be said that Erlanger's protection gave Flo all the enabling liberation he needed. Thus far we have seen nothing of Ziegfeld the artist. He has been Ziegfeld the opportunist and, somewhat, Ziegfeld the showman. He will evolve soon enough—but the evolution was unquestionably hastened by Flo's ability to slip into and out of the wolf pack as it suited him. Whatever it meant to the rest of the theatre world, the formation of the Syndicate meant a great deal to Flo.

The other important event of the summer of 1896 occurred when the Syndicate was still just a luncheon date on six men's calendars. Some weeks earlier, Flo and Charles Evan Evans went to Europe to find their bright new prodigy to create a fashionable craze in *A Parlor Match*. Like the formation of the Syndicate, this event is business, but business mixed with romance. Flo comes into his manly inheritance as manager and lover—the only two things he was throughout his life. He has become *Ziegfeld* now, as he finds his star in London and heads for his destiny on Broadway. The episode with Sandow recedes into the file of Forgettable Early Work; it is only at this time, with this new discovery, that Ziegfeld comprehends his theatre. Yet he does it through his characteristic vision of the stage as a place of erotic abandon. It is impossible to imagine what Ziegfeld's Broadway would have been like had he not started it with Anna Held: and this event is personal.

CHAPTER THREE

The Exotique

Étoile de Paris: so Ziegfeld first billed her—"Parisian Star"—because he wanted to decorate his first Broadway show with something you couldn't get in the neighborhood. She was beautiful, of course, but more than that: stylish. Foreign, too, but not just foreign. Sandow was foreign, with his German accent and high-pitched giggle, but Sandow's foreignness only made him alien. This one's foreignness would be the come-hither kind, intimately alien. She lived in perfect French—ideal for Ziegfeld's program, because everyone knew the French are sensual to a fault, and sensuality is what Ziegfeld was the manager of. This one won't be Sarah Bernhardt French, marching through Western Civilization on one false leg in plays that are frivolous in an uplifting way. This one would be frivolous in a frivolous way, in Naughty Postcard French.

Étoile de Paris! One might call Anna Held a professional Parisian, so avidly did she define herself in its myth and culture. Even after becoming one of America's outstanding theatre people and working almost solely in the United States, she still kept her house in Paris, a four-story *hôtel particulier* in the Faubourg St.-Honoré. Ritzy Anna, of *le tout Paris*. Yet it was said that she was but half-French, that the other half was Polish, that she was born in Warsaw. "Varsovie!" she echoes, in her memoirs. "Imagine me coming from a place like that!" Elsewhere, she put it more conclusively: "I was born in Paris. *Voilà*. That is settled."

Some said she was born in America. In 1956 *The New York Times Magazine* ran a picture essay called "Through Lautrec's Eyes," a series of drawings of French music-hall stars alongside their photographs. Anna was included, and her picture caption noted that "she came to Montmartre from Indiana." A reader from that state promptly wrote in to express incredulity. Anna Held "as a native Hoosier is almost beyond belief." Could *The Times* verify the statement? It could, or at least thought so: Held's birthplace had been drawn from the 1906 *Who's Who on the Stage*. And, indeed, so the old volume reads.

Indiana, to launch the saga of an orphan waif fit for a novel by Hector Malot! The daughter of a glover, Anna found herself without family when she was still in her teens. Somehow or other, she landed in England, working for the Yiddish theatre troupe run by Jacob Adler, founder of a thespian dynasty that made important history with New York's Group Theatre in the 1930s. Adler's Yiddish company played in four languages, so Anna functioned, we presume, in French and perhaps Polish, and was soon taking on leading roles. Still, it must have been a desolate existence for one so ambitious, for the fancy clientele of Anna's late father had inculcated in her a yearning to experience life among the *gratin*: "I learned to love money," she confides, "something without which no generosity, no *beau geste*, is possible here on earth."

Jewish stage tradition favors music theatre, and Anna noticed that lighter fare and song spots best endeared her to the public. She was now discovering her true *métier*: the music hall and caf'conc', the café concert where a discerning audience ate and drank while taking in the latest "speakers" of songs.[1] Anna was still in her teens when she was prominent enough to accept engagements all over western Europe—and she was only twenty when she made a rash marriage, to Maximo Carrera. He

---

[1] The French like music, but they *love* their language, and the words matter more. In their popular music, the performer is called the *diseur* or *diseuse* (literally, the "speaker"), and many a famous singer—Yvette Guilbert, for instance—had no vocal quality to speak of.

was middle-aged, Uruguayan, and noisy. But he was rich, and Anna did say she loved money, or simply the security it could bring to a life that had started in a state of vulnerability and hardship.

True, by the mid-1890s Anna was—if only for the moment—a successful artist of the popular stage. Her earnings did not yet make her town-house rich, however, and it must have been Carrera's share of his family fortune that ensconced Anna in Right Bank splendor. As usual with such marriages, the wife has to pay a price as well. "His moral nature was that of a conquistador," she wrote later. A true son of the rich, he "led a life of regularly scheduled excesses."

The main one was gambling—Ziegfeld's great flaw as well. That William Hoey specialty number about the man who broke the bank at Monte Carlo treats in a jaunty manner the plunger's impossible dream. In reality, he doesn't break the bank: he gambles till he has lost everything. And as French law made the wife responsible for her husband's debts, sooner or later Anna could lose everything, too.

So if Mlle. Held had married well, Señor Carrera had married better. Running through his inheritance and depending on his family's increasingly exasperated indulgence, Carrera could see in Anna a kind of emergency safe-deposit box for the time when he had gambled away his all. Yet he seems to have been no worse than the usual society parasite, demanding and reckless but relatively pleasant between tantrums.

Even so, Anna wanted her freedom. Rather than divorce, the Carreras simply evaporated on each other, going separate ways. Anna's took her, as always now, to some of the great stages of Europe, and it was at London's formidable and almost brand-new Palace Theatre of Varieties[1] in that August of 1893 that Florenz Ziegfeld caught Anna's act. He must have known instantly that she was what he needed: ravishing, sexy, and

---

[1]It was two years old when Anna played there, built as the Royal English Opera House by Richard D'Oyly Carte, manager of W. S. Gilbert and Arthur Sullivan. With the stream of classic Gilbert and Sullivan behind them, the two authors quarreled over money, and Carte inaugurated the new house, in 1891, with (Julian) Sturgis and Sullivan:

above all happy. She knew how to flirt and she knew how to dress, so men were fascinated and women attentive. When Anna appeared, a thousand pairs of opera glasses went up as if on signal; when she left, it was to warm and grateful applause. She was a natural, less in talent than in that ultra-French quality, *le charme.*

"A bright little comedienne," noted Harry B. Smith, who wrote a number of shows for her in her Ziegfeld period. "But her singing alone would never have made her reputation." Still, this was a time when many stars of vaudeville and the musical itself put over a number more through force of personality than vocal command. The musical's available history, with its Ethel Merman and Alfred Drake (not to mention the current generation of superb acting singers such as Christine Ebersole or Brian d'Arcy James) misleads us about the nature of popular music's performing styles around the turn of the century. Ancient recordings tell us that, excepting "comic opera" (i.e., operetta) and outright balladeers like Chauncey Olcott, musicals were filled with fakers and makeweights.

Anyway, Anna's material didn't require a lot of vocal tone. Her signature number, "Come Play With Me" (by Alfred Plumton and G. P. Hawtrey), is a slowly bouncing $\frac{6}{8}$ ditty with a narrow vocal range. Unlike the smash-and-grab theme songs favored by American women stars, the "Ta-Ra-Ra Boom-De-Ay" or "I Don't Care," "Come Play With Me" is shy and importunate. The verse opens a wistful flirtation:

> *I have not been here very long;*
> *As yet I'm quite a stranger,*
> *And so, to try an English song*
> *May seem perhaps a danger!*

Ivanhoe, a grand opera. Though it enjoyed an impressive run, Carte sold the theatre to new management, and it went over to music hall and revue (as the Palace from 1911; and it looks like one) till *No, No, Nanette* played it in 1925. It reverted then to musicals, and is still in such use today at the very center of London's theatre district, in Cambridge Circus. The theatre is currently the property of Andrew Lloyd Webber.

But the chorus grows a bit confident:

> *For I have such a way with me,*
> *A way with me,*
> *A way with me.*
> *I have such a nice little way with me,*
> *Do not think it wrong.*

This is Harry B. Smith again: "She sang mostly with her eyes and her shoulders." How else to present such coquettish frivolity? And note that, offstage, Anna was levelheaded and untheatrical. She was, in fact, generous, intelligent, and fair, and I'm guessing that some of that came across along with the eyes and the shoulders. Like many attractive women then and now, she made an act out of a personality that wasn't hers, and perhaps Anna had the ability to play "between" her act and her reality, giving her extra presence. I like a statement she makes, again in her memoirs: "Vivre sans le beauté d'un sourire, c'est aimer sans joie et mourir sans espoir." (To live without the beauty of a smile is to love without joy and to die without hope.) She sounds lovely.

On the other hand, who, Anna wondered, was this Florenz Ziegfeld Jr., with his nightly bouquets, even a diamond bracelet? He wasn't the only one sending flowers and jewelry backstage. Ha! I bar my door to this man! Finally, Ziegfeld had to bribe the house staff and rush Anna's dressing room. Oh yes, Monsieur the American manager? Oh yes, Broadway? A new version of this American classic, you say? A comic tramp? A cabinet scene? *I* come out of a *cabinet*?

But they do say that however much he looked like a tailor's assistant, and despite a very slightly nasal voice, Florenz Ziegfeld Jr. was as much a natural as Anna Held, and *his* act was Enchanting Women. Further, at some point in their discussion, Anna must have realized that an engagement in America would put an ocean between her and the bailiffs confiscating any Carrera ownings they could locate.

There was one hurdle: Anna was engaged for the coming season at the Folies Bergère, *contrat de travail*. No matter, the impetuous Ziegfeld replies—he'll buy out the Folies contract, and he'll pay Anna $1,500 a week for *A Parlor Match* in New York and on tour with a three-month guarantee. That was fabulous money compared to what superior yet not top-drawer music-hall talent earned in Europe; but Ziegfeld was offering to take Anna out of music hall. Having got off the Midway for vaudeville, Ziegfeld was now to leave vaudeville for the Big Time, The Street. A smart manager knows that you have to spend money to make money, but also: you move among the powerful to attain power.

Yes, they're such obvious rules—but then, why were so many managers in the Small Time for life? If such rules are truisms, why were most managers of the 1890s wornouts and never-made-its? The MGM backstagers with Judy Garland and Mickey Rooney are obsessed with the Big Time as an American Dream—as, even, the only one that counts. We call them babes in arms, but when Garland rips Gene Kelly's head off in *For Me and My Gal* with "You'll never make the Big Time because you're Small Time in your heart," she's leveling a moral judgment upon him that is all but terminal. This is post-Ziegfeld thinking; it took a Ziegfeld to establish first of all that entertainment comprises a hierarchy and that those on the bottom are wasting their lives. And Ziegfeld established it by building his management till it was absolutely at the top of the Big Time, gorging itself on that first American virtue, famous success.

So if Sandow was prelude, Anna Held is the first act in the play of Ziegfeld's legend. He was moving quickly toward the goal of his Broadway premiere when a speed bump arose: Édouard Marchand, manager of the Folies Bergère, reneged on his promise to accept a financial settlement in lieu of Anna's contract. With Ziegfeld already returned to America, Anna, concluding a date in Switzerland, simply crept out of Europe and arrived in Southampton, England to board the liner *New York* for the United States.

All the while, Ziegfeld bombarded the press with announcements, speculations, and crazy tales. To some theatregoers, the real story was the reunion of Evans and Hoey (as well as five others of the original cast) in their party piece. To Ziegfeld, that was the maguffin. The *story* was *étoile de Paris* Anna Held, told in headlines in every major newspaper in relentless detail, astonishing even for an era fascinated by the stage.

Marchand's impedient demands for Anna in his Paris boîte—when all New York awaits her!—was good for one entry:

SAYS HELD MUST NOT SAIL

Then there was the "saucy Miss Held" file:

TROUBLE OVER SONG BECAUSE SHE IS PRETTY

But lo,

MLLE. HELD IS COMING

And at last:

MLLE. HELD IS HERE

A human interest angle will address the ladies:

WHAT IS A COCKTAIL? ASKS FAIR ANNA HELD

and the men don't have to ask twice for their share:

NAUGHTY BICYCLE DRESS WHICH SHE MAY SHOW IN PARK

It was almost anticlimactic to read that Anna was reporting for anything so mundane as work:

REHEARSALS BEGIN

and, with next to nothing on what Evans and Hoey were up to (new gags? new songs?), *A Parlor Match* opened at the Herald Square Theatre on

September 21, 1896. The show had played tryouts in Boston, but Ziegfeld didn't let Anna step in till New York, for thrill insurance. And, at last:

ANNA HELD'S DEBUT
NAUGHTY, CHIC AND PRETTY, SHE SETS HER AUDIENCE WILD

" 'Oh! yes: she'll be the rage,' said everyone as she disappeared at last with a flurry of pantalettes" was the prediction of the *New York Herald*'s critic. Another wrote, "As a spectacle, Mlle. Held is a success." It's barbed praise; what does he mean by "spectacle"? Yet a third advanced what was to be the standard line on her singing: "Her voice is not as charming as she is, but it will do." There was one complaint, from Edward A. Dithmar in *The New York Times,* in his weekly Broadway roundup. He thought Anna "would not be a 'sensation' at all if the idea had not been ingeniously forced upon the public mind that she is inherently and delightfully naughty."

Ziegfeld managed not only the preparatory PR but Anna's first-night appearance itself. Keyed up because Anna had not yet performed anywhere in the country, the audience must have been disappointed to find her listed in the program for only "Come Play With Me." In fact, Anna had rehearsed a whole set; Ziegfeld planted a claque to call for encores. Apparently, he did not take the company into his confidence, and Hoey, who had an entrance right after Anna's scene, came onstage while she was still holding forth. Mastering the situation, Hoey grabbed a handy chair and sat facing Anna—"as if," she later wrote, "he alone was my audience." Indeed, she fell in with the stunt, directing her next solo right at Hoey, who of course responded with takes and "business" (as shtick was then called). The audience enjoyed it as an accidental first-night frolic especially for them, though for all we know Ziegfeld warned Hoey about the encores precisely to enable the accident and allow Hoey to improvise at leisure. In all, the famous cabinet disgorged such talents as Beatrice and Millie Tait, Grayce Scott, Annie St. Tel, the dancing Sisters Helene, and the Olympia Quartette. But the evening belonged to Anna Held.

She'll be the rage. To start with, she gave interviews without number and always had something quotable to share, despite her as yet rudimentary English. "I am never discontented, never envious" is one Held-ism. "I hate affectation. I am a democrat."

Better than interviews were events—actual, exaggerated, or wholly fabricated happenings to set tongues wagging. Certainly, Anna's attire was the talk of the womenfolk, because she invariably showed up anywhere dressed in full kit, looking like something that had just popped out of an Easter egg. There was particular emphasis on Anna's corsets, though all women and even some men wore them in this age, that of the "hourglass figure."

Her bicycle riding was an event, too, especially when she leaped off her wheels in midflight to aid a judge whose carriage was in the thrall of runaway horses. Yes, that was quite a story. Or what about an event that actually happened: Anna's kissing contest? As staged by Ziegfeld, Anna faced off with a willing opponent, an actor of guaranteed obscurity, so he could attract no interest with which to crowd her notices. How many kisses could Anna handle? She made it to number 156 before collapsing in a half-faint. (A doctor had been retained for safety's sake.)

Some of these tales mark Anna as an unnaturally bold member of her sex; that was Ziegfeld's point. He was a salesman, and his product was not just song and dance but the unnamable feelings of pleasure and stimulation that musical theatre create in us. To Ziegfeld, talent in a man was useful. But talent in a woman was sexy; and part of Anna's talent lay in the way she played at life, dared in life, adventured in it.

So the height of all this regulating of the media was the story of the milk baths, still spoken of today. Master promoter though he was, Ziegfeld couldn't think of everything himself, and he seems to have offered to make it worth one's while to dream up yet another fable that would prove irresistible to newspaper editors. A minor writer of this and that, Max Marcin, conceived the notion that Anna had a standing order with a dairy to deliver to her hotel suite forty gallons of milk a day—eighty on Sundays! This, of course, would be what gave Anna her lustrous skin tone, her Decline and Fall of the Roman Empire *volupté*.

Marcin even found a milk dealer to stooge for this nonsense, his name given variously as R. H., H. R., and H. B. Wallace, of 25 Patchen Avenue in Brooklyn. Unfortunately, Wallace was not warned about the tale's kicker: Ziegfeld was going to default on payment because the milk was sour. Imagine bathing in sour milk! So, as the story ended, Wallace was supposedly taking Ziegfeld to court.

It was all Marcin's fantasy, of course, though the press printed it—just as they printed Wallace's exposé. He had never delivered any milk to Anna, he said, and was outraged at the suggestion that he sold spoiled milk. Ziegfeld was delighted, because it is all but impossible to dispel a tale that allows people to believe the worst of a celebrity, impossible even with the truth. The question is not, Who has the facts? but rather, Who is persuasive? Anna had beautiful skin; besides, she was French. In her memoirs, she herself called this sort of thing "le P. T. Barnum système," curiously using French words in an English syntactical construction.[1] But Ziegfeld was no more than anticipating modern American culture, in which all public life is a form of theatre. If it's news, it's true, whether it's true or not. You call it lies. Ziegfeld calls it the script.

And he must be right, because, ever after, most people believed that Anna Held took milk baths. Actually, as she later revealed, her beauty-secret ingredient was Italian olive oil, three tablespoonful a day, taken internally, along with external applications as part of massage therapy. However, that was too sedate an explanation for the vivacious Anna. Many were the clerics, professional bluenoses, and other custodians of the American moral character who insisted on returning to the milk baths when inveighing against this hussy, this professional Jezebel.

And Anna did nothing to tamp down her saucy approach. On the contrary, for *A Parlor Match*'s post-Broadway tour she added a number called "The Contrebasse." After a verse in $\frac{2}{4}$, a waltz chorus pleaded with the string bass player not to seduce her with his alluring oscillations:

---

[1] The correct French would be "le système P. T. Barnum" or "le système à la P. T. Barnum."

Grâce, grâce!
Ma vieille contrebasse.
Quand tu scies ton armoire
Ca m'fait la froum, froum, froum,
Froum, froum, froum, froum.
Ferme les yeux, Grégoire.[1]

A Parlor Match's New York run was only five weeks, but it held the road for nearly six months. All the while, Ziegfeld was cutting out new PR jigsaw, here about the smallest dog in the world—Anna's, of course, a certain Chico—and there when a San Francisco paper claimed that the woman playing there as Anna Held was an imposter. Ziegfeld was suing, naturally. But the most fetching of all these stories was told in the spring of 1897, when Ziegfeld and Anna threw a dinner party at the Netherland Hotel, where Anna was living.

So was Ziegfeld. The dinner was when he announced to their friends that Florenz Ziegfeld Jr. and Anna Held were husband and wife.

---

[1] Mercy, mercy!/My dear bass fiddler./When you saw on those strings/It turns me wild with desire./Close your eyes, Grégoire.

CHAPTER FOUR

Étoile de Paris

That dinner party typified the kind of company that Ziegfeld intended to keep. Among those present was one of the first friends he had made in New York, James Buchanan Brady (the famous "Diamond Jim"), and the most prominent American musical-theatre actress of the day, Lillian Russell, soon to be one of Anna's closest friends. Some of those present may have known that Ziegfeld and Anna had already become intimate; some may have been wondering exactly where and when the marriage had occurred. Mr. and Mrs. weren't saying. This is not as surprising as it sounds, because Ziegfeld was an intensely private man, and as for Anna, this was the age in which A Lady Never Tells.

So away the two of them went on a sort of honeymoon in Europe, where Anna had her own surprise for Ziegfeld: his so to say stepdaughter, Liane Carrera. It was as much a shock to Ziegfeld as it is to you.

Liane Carrera! Was *she* the reason why Anna had married—not for money, but to legitimize her offspring with the Carrera name? But how did Anna regard this daughter who, thus far, was a secret? The existence of a little one could only compromise Anna's actressy presentations, saddle her airy spirit with mundane biology. But needy little Liane, parked in convent schools and the like, was not about to oblige with reticence. She was barely three years old in this summer of 1897, yet she was already nurturing a profound distaste for the man she believed had taken her mother from her. Indeed, she would be expressing herself on the matter soon enough.

The life of Liane Carrera is a saga in itself: that of the unwanted child who cultivates a fantasy that Maximo Carrera, Anna Held, and Liane would have had a wonderful life together but for the meddling, acquisitive Ziegfeld. It was that American who broke up the Carreras, who used Liane's mother to advance himself and make his fortune, who turned the lovely Anna from thoughts of motherhood. True, Liane would be invited to visit Anna and Ziegfeld in New York from time to time. But surely it was Ziegfeld who got Anna to discourage Liane from going on the stage herself when she was older—*yes!*—when Ziegfeld was lord of the realm and could have persuaded any theatre to star La Liane, building and guiding her as he had built and guided her mother. For did not Liane have cabaret in the blood? She had genetic rights to stardom!

Liane actually did go on the stage. She appeared as "Anna Held's Daughter" and played, it seems, somewhere between feebly okay and Get the hook! Still, even after she quit the theatre, Liane always thought of herself as Anna Held's Daughter: robbed of her just inheritance and living into 1988 as the proprietress of the tiny Anna Held Museum, in San Jacinto, California. And Liane did have her revenge, taking charge of her mother's memoirs to the point that Anna's biographer, Eve Golden, believes them untrustworthy to a great degree.

In any case, Ziegfeld and Anna were not in France in 1897 for family reasons, but rather to sample the styles of European musical theatre. Ziegfeld had seen enough of European popular art on his earlier trips to note how much more earthy and sexual it was, mirroring cultures that were franker than America's about bodily appetites. Even the English music hall delighted in jokes and songs replete with wicked double meanings—this at a time when American vaudeville was so strictly monitored that backstage signs warned one and all away from "cuss words," references to religion, and even commentary on divorce law.

Compare that with a typical English music-hall number of 1879,

"Tuner's Oppor-Tuner-Ty," by Fred Coyne and Harry Adams, for Coyne's use in his act. The number concerns Miss Crotchety Quaver, who maintains close relations with her piano tuner. As her boy friend tells us, the tuner was ever so thorough at "fingering the keys":

> *And first he'd tune it gently, then he'd tune it strong,*
> *Then he'd touch a short note, then he'd run along . . .*

The published sheet music cover shows Miss Quaver's boy friend surprising her and her dangerously French-looking tuner (he wears checked pants) at their exercise. The tuner is only touching Miss Quaver's shoulder, but the blandly suggestive lyrics and smirking puns make it clear what "tuning" is, especially when the boy friend abandons Miss Quaver for a more faithful maiden while taking up the art himself:

> *Now we're married, and all my doubts and my fears*
> *Are for evermore laid on the shelf,*
> *For if ever her instrument gets out of tune,*
> *I am able to tune it myself.*

Of all the cabaret capitals that Ziegfeld had visited, it was Paris that most intrigued him, with its revues combining unique performers, topical humor, and female nudity. True, this seems an odd blend: how does nudity relate to jests about government scandals or the doings of the fashionable world? Perhaps what held these shows together was less a theme than an attitude, a love-of-life embrace of whatever made the authorities nervous. In certain ways, the French Revolution never quite ended; the French revue, looking back on the past year's events, added an extra soupçon of liberation to public life, as much sexual as cultural.

New York had actually enjoyed a "review" (as it was spelled) of retrospective commentary in 1894, at the Casino, *The Passing Show*. The following year, the Casino presented a follow-up, *The Merry World* (1895). These two had none of the zany openness of the Parisian show, with its air of a primitive rite taken over by urbane wags. Nor did "review" catch on in an important way. If Ziegfeld had any thought of trying his own revue à la Paris, he would have had to postpone it indefinitely—or, in fact, for ten years, which, as we'll see, is what happened.

For now, Ziegfeld and Anna returned to New York for the 1897–1898 theatre season in a strong position. *A Parlor Match* had enriched Ziegfeld and made Anna's name, albeit in what was no more than a hyped featurette in everyone else's play. Now she needed a vehicle of her own.

The Broadway of that time ran from Fourteenth Street up to just south of Forty-second Street, counting about twenty-two playhouses. Booking jams were common, and shows occasionally had to extend their pre-Broadway tour with the hope that a latest opening would fail and close, freeing a theatre for a new engagement. This is one reason why we sometimes discover surprisingly short runs for well-received shows, even those destined to become perennials for a generation or two: the theatre manager had booked another title earlier, and—hit or not—his tenant had to leave.

The obvious solution to this problem was to build more playhouses. However, it was difficult to assemble affordable adjacent plots to create a suitable building lot along the existing stretch of theatre-district Broadway. After all, this was the very center of New York town, clogged with shops and hotels. "Broadway" had been gradually moving northward generation by generation ever since there was a "Broadway"—but no one wanted to venture into the area north of Forty-second Street. That neighborhood, known as "the Long Acre" (after the junction of Broadway and Seventh Avenue at Long Acre—today Times—Square), was undevelopable, primarily given over to the horse and carter trades, screaming with the blacksmith's clangor and stinking of manure. Worse, it was poorly lit at night and thus a magnet for the footpad and cutthroat.

And yet one manager saw possibilities in opening up the territory. He figured that, after one grand claim was struck, the Long Acre would be gold-rushed into a brand-new theatre district. The horse exchanges, saddle makers, and wheel- and wagonwrights would move elsewhere. The brownstones would cede place to theatres—a cluster of them, to welcome crowds to the area, creating the security that busy streets enjoy. The commercial infrastructure of restaurants and hotels would tag along, and the city authorities would maintain this important addition to the local economy, starting with street lamps.

So Oscar Hammerstein crossed the border, reaching the east side of Broadway between Forty-Fourth and Forty-Fifth Streets, and he raised not one but four theatres in a single building, one of the four partly in the open on the roof, for comfort in the warm-weather months. The structure was a veritable amusement village, for it included also a café and facilities for billiards and bowling.

Hammerstein called the complex the Olympia. It opened on November 25, 1895, just about a year before Anna Held made her New York debut. And now Ziegfeld proposed to join forces with Hammerstein in presenting Anna's first appearance as a star, title role and all. The work chosen was *La Poupée* (The Doll), a French piece of 1896 that had quickly crossed the Channel for a big success in London. And already, something is wrong.

La Poupée is the work of composer Edmond Audran, to the words of Maurice Ordonneau; the score's generical label, clearly marked on the title page, is "opéra comique." That is, the format of light opera, with spoken dialogue. Opéras comiques can be very light, medium light, or *Carmen*—but they are operas all the same, demanding voices at least as rich as those we hear in *The Student Prince* or *Candide*.

Anna's role in *La Poupée,* that of Alésia, takes in solos, four love duets, and ensembles, and Anna simply didn't have the vocal equipment to get through them.[1] As for the story itself: Alésia accidentally breaks one of her inventor father's animated life-size dolls and then has to substitute herself in its place in a marriage to a monk.

---

[1] A few writers state that Anna had appeared in *La Poupée* in Paris, but its entire run, during the fall and winter of 1896–1897, occurred during the run of *A Parlor Match,* when Anna was in the United States.

Yes, it's one of those crazy French things. *La Poupée*'s legacy-with-a-catch plot finds the young novice Lancelot forced to wed to save his bankrupt monastery, for he can inherit only if he takes a wife. Demure to a fault, the virginal hero plans to sneak around the catch by marrying a doll, but then he meets Alésia—the "doll"—and the monastery ends up one brother short. The work's best comic hook retrieves business from Jacques Offenbach's *The Tales of Hoffmann,* in which a mechanical doll occasionally runs down and has to be rewound. In *Hoffmann,* she is reanimated by a giant key in her back; Alésia has only to be tapped on the shoulder. In the Duo de la Séduction, Audran amusingly treats the doll chatter in a halting, jumpy line that suddenly cuts off at odd moments. But, of course, once Alésia is freed of her disguise, she and Lancelot enjoy a Duo de la Caresse to close in a sensuous waltz: the musical opposite of doll.

Ziegfeld must have been wild to present Anna as a doll because she could play the automaton to a public that knew only her natural vivacity. It would be a Broadway in-joke, expanding on rather than repeating Anna's *Parlor Match* success. And as the London version of *La Poupée* (translated by Arthur Sturgess) had fiddled with the score, perhaps Ziegfeld felt free to commission more fiddling to slim Alésia's music down to Held size.[1] Still, it's hard to imagine how Anna got around the doll's big set piece, the Air de la Poupée, "Je sais entrer dans un salon," which sets her off in a sequence of waltz, gavotte, minuet, and waltz again. Alésia is not a very high soprano role, and the range is narrow. Still, it demands a genuine singer.

In any case, *La Poupée*—the French title was used, without accompanying translation—did not rock the town the way *A Parlor Match* had done. The show opened on October 21, 1897, at the second-largest of the

---

[1]There is no record of *La Poupée*'s music as Ziegfeld and Hammerstein presented it, not even a listing of numbers in the program. For completeness, Richard C. Norton's *A Chronology of American Musical Theater* cites a *La Poupée* tunestack while noting that it is drawn from the libretto published in England, not from the Ziegfeld-Hammerstein production proper.

four Olympia auditoriums, the Lyric, which seated about 1,700. Was the place too grand for the diminutive and nuanced Anna? The production collapsed after 14 performances, provoking a lawsuit from Hammerstein and a countersuit from Ziegfeld. The official reason for the sudden closing was "bankruptcy proceedings," though it doesn't state whose. Oddly, a completely different troupe gave their own version of *La Poupée* later that season at Daly's Theatre, located as far south as the Olympia was north: five blocks below Herald Square.

The bankruptcy attendant upon *La Poupée* could easily have been *both* Ziegfeld's and Hammerstein's, for they were alike reckless overspenders, lifelong penniless millionaires. They often guessed wrong, too. Hammerstein was finding it impossible to keep his four stages occupied, and the upkeep was tremendous. For his part, Ziegfeld had erred in expecting Anna to burst forth as a queen of light opera. Anna wasn't an operetta soubrette. Anna was a cabaret bijou, an entertainer who performs her own material, not someone else's.

So Hammerstein lost the Olympia—all of it—and Ziegfeld lent Anna to the vaudeville kings (John) Koster and (Adam) Bial, who gave Anna the top star's traditional next-to-closing spot at their variety house on Thirty-Fourth Street. Here, as not in an operetta by Audran, Anna could develop her relationship with the audience, for instance by tackling a typical American genre, the so-called "coon song."

What could draw Anna further from her insinuating French "come play with me" than the cakewalking southern-dialect specialty, devoted to cataloguing imaginary events of black culture? Invariably sung by whites in blackface, these ditties told of being homesick for Dixie, of picnics and music-making, of the doings of Mr. Johnson (a buzz term for anyone from a cheating boy friend to the law), of the beauty of the Southland, especially in the vicinity of the Swanee River. A typical example is Kerry Mills' "At a Georgia Camp Meeting," written in 1899:

When that band of darkies began to play
Pretty music so gay
Hats were then thrown away.

Thought them foolish coons their necks would break,
When they quit their laughing and talking
And went to walking for a big choc'late cake.[1]

This genre was ubiquitous from the 1890s into the 1920s, and the main reason why is absurdly basic: it was easy to write. The lyricist drew on the themes listed above and the composer ragged. In fact, all the ethnic stereotype numbers were easy to write, which is why American entertainment was full of them. Whether black, Irish, Italian, or Jewish in theme, they came with prefabricated vocabulary and images, even musical hooks. "The Dublin Rag," interpolated into *Madame Sherry* (1910), virtually wrote itself, as Phil Schwartz gets into g minor with a droning "bagpipes" bass and Harold Atteridge's lyrics loot the Gaelic verbal storehouse:

"The Wearing of the Green" may sound so sweetly to your ear,
But wait until that tuneful Dublin shamrock tune you hear . . .

In a way, all of these minority-group numbers were coon songs, because they all treated their subjects to a parade of false clichés, isolating them as "coons": persons without dignity or rights. Their manner could be offensive even for the age, let alone today. Into a future Ziegfeld show, *The Century Girl* (1916), the singing duo (Gus) Van and (Joe) Schenck, specialists in the ethnic repertoire, slipped James Kendis' "He Likes Their Jukulele." This potent mixture united the craze for Hawaiian music with the Jewish theme:

When they celebrate they have a Jubilee.
Girls display their fancy straw and Jewelry . . .

---

[1]The music that accompanies these words, the song's entire refrain, can be heard in *Show Boat* during the Trocadero performance, as the dance that Frank and Ellie perform right after they sing "Goodbye, My Lady Love."

Lest someone miss the premise, the song sheet advises the vocalist to "Emphasize First Syllable In The Following Words—'Jubilee,' 'Jewelry,' 'Jupiter,' 'July,' 'Jukulele,' 'Junited [States].'"

The black coon songs themselves were absolutely ubiquitous, probably more popular than all the other types put together. Anna's first sample in this line was "I Want Dem Presents Back," and the staging that Ziegfeld commissioned for it was a sensation. The back curtain represented sheet music, the notes cut out so that chorus boys in blackface could poke their heads through and provide vocal support. Anna resisted the blackface makeup—an unusual deviation from the etiquette—but she was costumed to fill the eye all the same, perched in a basket carried on the back of an aged black man. At second look, one realized that Anna was in fact wearing the basket around her middle, the man's legs were her own, and the man himself was a *trompe l'oeil* appendage fixed to her waist.

Koster and Bial had engaged Anna for two weeks, but she was held over through the Christmas holidays to accommodate a box-office surge as she enlarged her core audience. This was how to "break" a new star, Ziegfeld knew from his Sandow period: churn up the PR but give the public satisfaction on-site. Thus, it will join the publicity machine and pass rave reviews on to friends. This went just so far with Sandow, because he could do two things only: one, be beautiful, and, two, perform idiotic feats of strength. When he tried to broaden his field with the lion fight, he had a disaster.

Anna, on the other hand, could, one, be beautiful; two, put a song over, which is more art than weightlifting; and, three, grow. She had an amazing facility in language, and was picking up English well enough to soar through the interviews that Ziegfeld continually arranged for her. She charmed everyone; Sandow had made many people uncomfortable in some incomprehensible way. Maybe it was simply because men, at that time, weren't supposed to be works of art. Sandow even got into fights in public; Anna was a peacemaker.

Still, the next time she headlined on Broadway in a story show, it had to be an Anna Held show, the right one, true Anna. *La Poupée* was her lion fight, and that must not happen again. For now, in February 1898, Ziegfeld sent Anna off on a vaudeville tour with her new act and an important addition to her reputation: her very own private railroad car.

It was a practical extravagance. For one thing, no star dared troop without this badge of membership in the club of success—and of course the furnishings and knickknacks gave reporters more content, yielding more column inches of PR. The private car wasn't just a luxury: it taught the public how to perceive you. Ziegfeld and Sandow had tried it in their last season together, and now Anna had her car, formerly the property (so said the PR) of Lillie Langtry. She, too, was a beauty whose precise endowment of talent was at times in dispute. And yet Oscar Wilde said, "I would rather have discovered Lillie Langtry than America," and Langtry was famous for having enchanted Edward VII of England. So Anna's railroad car was a case of fame by association.

Now Anna toured while Ziegfeld took a long look at Broadway to decide where he and Anna would fit in. The temporary separation from Anna could be thought symbolic, because Ziegfeld had to establish an identity separate from his management of Anna Held. The two shows they had done together were not Ziegfeld shows in any real sense. *A Parlor Match* had been around for so long that many didn't even realize that it had been revived. It was always there, like your front porch. And the imposing construction of the Olympia absorbed *La Poupée* in the grandeur that was Hammerstein. Anna was a Name; Ziegfeld was nobody.

The first thing he needed was a theatre of his own, to enjoy what that manager of managers Charles Frohman enjoyed: a shop window. In Ziegfeld's personal playhouse, he could display his style of ware, proclaim what the word *Ziegfeld* meant. A manager who freelanced, hopping from house to house, could never govern a public, a constituency of theatregoers who bought tickets to his shows *because* they were his. They did that for Frohman, and if Ziegfeld was going to compete with the Frohmans, he had to have an address.

Ziegfeld couldn't afford a theatre leasehold by himself, so he chipped in for one with a partner, William Anthony Brady. Twenty-five years old (and already the father of future actress Alice Brady), Brady was Ziegfeld's junior but well ahead of him in the business. The two men had something odd in common: both had managed good-looking athletes. Ziegfeld of course had his Sandow, and Brady managed James J. Corbett, a champion boxer who simultaneously maintained an acting career.

Sharing a stage with another manager was how Ziegfeld got into trouble with *La Poupée*. But Oscar Hammerstein was less a manager than a legend, a force of nature, and an assembly of theatres, relatives, and opera; there wasn't room in all that Hammerstein for a Ziegfeld. Brady would be easier to deal with, and the pair moved into the Manhattan Theatre, in a wonderful location on the west side of Broadway between Thirty-Second and Thirty-Third Streets, convenient to the carriage trade in their Fifth and Madison Avenue mansions. Opened in 1875 as the Eagle, it then became the Standard, hosting the first New York runs of Gilbert and Sullivan's *H.M.S. Pinafore, Patience,* and *Iolanthe,* huge hits in their time, from 1879 to 1883. Rebuilt after a fire, the house became the Manhattan Theatre, and it was then that Brady and Ziegfeld took over.

Their first co-production was *Way Down East,* opening February 7, 1898. This melodrama by Lottie Blair Parker, "elaborated" by the more stage-savvy Joseph R. Grismer, enjoyed something of an ultra-production, with real animals to establish the Maine farmland setting and a paper blizzard for the big moment when the unmarried young mother is forced out into the snow. (In his 1920 film adaptation, D. W. Griffith took it all to the edge, leading the helpless pariah, played by Lillian Gish, to a spectacular "ice floes and waterfall" climax that is not in the stage script.)

Way Down East's New York stand of 152 performances is deceiving: Brady forced the run without a single week in the black in order to tout the tour as "the great New York success." His hunch was that while New York had tired of Victorian-values art, the provinces would thrill to it, and indeed the piece became a road-and-stock favorite. When Griffith bought the rights, Brady held him up for $175,000, a monumental amount for a work that had worn thin over a generation. But then, Griffith thrilled to Victorian values, too.

Ziegfeld was not party to this transaction; nor did his name join Brady's on the posters during *Way Down East*'s years of touring. The two apparently shared the Manhattan Theatre and its program billing but put on plays individually—and with Brady busy with his *Way Down East*, Ziegfeld, it would seem, made the Manhattan his own. The next Ziegfeld-Brady "co-production" was *The Turtle* (September 3, 1898), a smash hit. *Mlle. Fifi* (February 1, 1899) was a semi-flop and *The Manicure* (April 24, 1899) a total flop. Ziegfeld and Brady parted company, and the Manhattan Theatre came under the management of Mrs. Fiske and her husband, in 1901.

This is just so much data. What interests us is how the all-American flavor of *Way Down East* suddenly gave way to three French farces on the usual French subjects—adultery, divorce, sneaking through doorways, and hiding behind screens. *The Turtle*, *Mlle. Fifi*, and *The Manicure* were literally French, all adaptations of shows that Ziegfeld and Anna might have seen on their annual European summers. In other words, even before Ziegfeld wielded power as a manager, he was discovering himself artistically as a manager, with a latent French taste in both themes and approach.

Anna's career suffered while Ziegfeld pursued his. She ended up in *The French Maid* (1897), an English musical by Walter Slaughter and Basil Hood. The latter was to enjoy a distinguished career as a librettist, not only with Slaughter but with such composers as Arthur Sullivan (on his last two works) and Edward German (on *Merrie England*, still occasionally heard today). *The French Maid*, on the other hand, was one of the era's less undying titles, based on the courtship of Suzette (the title part) by twin brothers, a gendarme, and the Maharajah of Punkapore. Suzette sounds like the Anna Held role, but Anna was on hand to supply specialty numbers while studying the Suzette, Marguerite Sylva. The plan was for Anna to become more secure in delivering English dialogue, and she did at length succeed Sylva as the French maid. Still, the engagement did nothing for her public profile. Anna was more in her element in her beloved Paris in the summer of 1899, when she won the top prize in the *Fête des Fleurs,* a parade of horse-drawn carriages festooned with flowers and driven along the boulevards and through the Bois de Boulogne.

Better than a tarted-up carriage was one of the new motor cars; Anna not only rode in them but drove one. This was astonishing for a woman at the time, an act of social defiance, something your scapegrace niece might do while the old folks grumped. Further, the autos themselves were at once temperamental, complicated, and perilous. Of course, Ziegfeld immediately put Anna's cars into PR rotation. There were two: one of the first of the new four-wheel De Dion-Boutons (earlier models were three-wheelers) and a Panhard "racer," which could actually break twenty miles per hour and introduced the modern transmission. Ziegfeld and Anna dedicated the autumn of 1899 to the granting of interviews on the pleasures of driving one's own roadster. There was even to have been a race between Anna and any and all comers—by road—to Philadelphia. This must have been another of Ziegfeld's fantastical flourishes. Given the crawling pace of those vintage autos, had such a race actually been held, the contestants would still be en route as I write.

In all this—the *Fête des Fleurs,* the new series of interviews despite a lack of career advancement, the automobiling—one sees in Anna someone who above all knew how to have a good time. Ziegfeld was obsessed with creating the kind of Chicago success that would place him in the almanacs: the businessman celebrity like those tycoons of meat and grain whose names were common nouns in the midwest. Anna, on the other hand, was not obsessed; Anna was enjoying herself. All that she and Ziegfeld had to do at this point was devise a show to implant the Ziegfeld trademark while allowing Anna's public to adore her fragile but nonetheless arresting talent to the fullest. The show would be French in atmosphere, surely, and would contain eccentric supporting characters (as in the successful *A Parlor Match*) rather than a chorus of monks (as in the unsuccessful *La Poupée*). As for the authors, why not approach the best? Why not, in fact, engage the two men who wrote the first classic American musical with an integrated score?

It is seldom mentioned today, but Reginald De Koven and Harry B. Smith's *Robin Hood* (1891) really is the launching title in a list that runs on to something like "*Naughty Marietta, Rose-Marie, The Cat and the Fiddle, Carousel.*" This is the classic line of comic opera/operetta/musical play, in which the score is the work of a single writing team dramatizing core material and relevant incidentals only: no specialties, no guest-spot whoop-de-do. Virtually all the outstanding titles of the nineteenth century were the work of multiple writing teams, and they doted on specialties. *The Black Crook, Humpty Dumpty, The Brook, Adonis, A Trip To Chinatown,* and other titles dear to the encyclopedist were vaudevilles with a plot.

Reginald De Koven was the unrivaled composer of American musicals in the 1890s. Victor Herbert would soon overwhelm him, and *Robin Hood* is known today mainly as the source of the dreary wedding anthem "Oh, Promise Me!." But when Ziegfeld called on De Koven for Anna's next show, our manager was setting out on a path that would lead to Irving Berlin, Jerome Kern, Sigmund Romberg, Rudolf Friml, George Gershwin, Richard Rodgers, and Vincent Youmans: most of the best composers in the business.

For his part, Harry B. Smith was the top musical-comedy wordsmith of the age. He was as well a native of Chicago. Smith even attended the same high school as Ziegfeld, albeit some years earlier. When Smith's sister took piano lessons, Smith met the senior Ziegfeld and actually did some press work for the Chicago Musical College.

It was Anna who got the idea for the new show: *Papa's Wife,* adapted from the French hit *La Femme à Papa* (1879). Composed by Hervé (the pen name of Florimond Ronger), *La Femme à Papa* was a vehicle for Anna Judic, a toast of Paris in the 1880s. Judic was as sleek and saucy as Anna, and a better singer. She made her reputation in Offenbach and had tried an American tour in 1885 in full diva kit, with fabulous salary and private railroad car. However, Judic was a one-off for all her success, a novelty not to be repeated—and she performed everything in French. Not only did Anna Held play in English: she now felt sound enough to triumph in the dialogue scenes, heretofore her danger zone. For the first time, Anna would meet Broadway on its terms.

Harry B. Smith thought the plot of *La Femme à Papa* needed a little thickening, and he added bits of another Hervé-Judic piece, *Mam'zelle Nitouche* (1883). Some Hervé was heard along with De Koven when *Papa's Wife* opened, on November 13, 1899, at the Manhattan Theatre. So the alliance with fellow manager William A. Brady had paid off after all, for now Ziegfeld had the use of Brady's playhouse without having to share manager's credit. There is, too, some anticipation of the Ziegfeld to come. "It was with this play," wrote Smith in his memoirs, "that Mr. Ziegfeld first revealed himself as a connoisseur of pulchritude. There were only sixteen girls in *Papa's Wife*, but they were all highly decorative and in their costuming economy was not considered."

Papa's Wife gave Anna another role playing footsie with her identity of the virgin harlot: a convent girl whom a young man more or less hires as "la femme à papa." She is to marry his gallivanting father to serve as a stabilizing influence. Of course, she is more truly *la femme au fils,* and the two young people end up together. As so often in 1890s musical comedy, the character content was largely supplied by comic eccentrics, here led by two veterans of *The French Maid* who would become regulars in Ziegfeld's early shows, Charles A. Bigelow and Eva Davenport. Another comic, George Marion, not only acted in the piece but directed it.[1]

Still, the evening depended entirely on Anna Held in her first tailored leading role, and Anna triumphed in the musical hit of the season, rivaled only by a Weber and Fields burlesque, *Whirl-I-Gig*. Ziegfeld capitalized on Anna's reputation as a motorist with a spectacular finale to

---

[1]Film buffs may start at Marion's name, for while he was a stage journeyman of no great account, he did luck into the role of Chris, the father in Eugene O'Neill's *Anna Christie* (1921). Filming his part in the first (silent) version, with Blanche Sweet, Marion made such a strong impression that he was tapped for the talkie, with Greta Garbo—one of the early sound film's classics and thus George Marion's legacy.

the first act: Anna driving offstage in an automobile. She also pulled off a nicely shaded tipsy scene—difficult to do in an age that avidly passed judgment on drinking women. *The New York Times* found the drunk scene "utterly lacking in the charm, the grace, the naiveté of Anna Judic" and dismissed Anna as "a music-hall singer who had taken on more than was good for her."

That was the standard line on Anna up to now; the other critics broke away to hail Anna's newfound gifts. Yes, she was in part a phenomenon of the PR talk shop. "The season before last it was Maude Adams," said one writer. "Last season it was Mrs. Carter, and now it is Anna Held."[1] Most reviewers gave Anna her due as an actress of skill as well as charm. "It will no longer do to treat Miss Held as a fad," said a reviewer during the Boston tryout of *Papa's Wife*. "She is worthy of serious critical consideration." And her English proved at last up to national speed. "I speak English so well," she now said, "I am no longer cute."

Papa's Wife played 147 performances in New York, then toured throughout 1900 (except during the summer) and into the spring of 1901. Taking no chances, Ziegfeld ordered up a second helping for Anna's next show: De Koven and Smith adapting another Anna Judic vehicle, with Charles A. Bigelow and Eva Davenport as the featured comics and George Marion supporting and directing, all as before. The new piece was called *The Little Duchess,* and its source was one of the biggest hits on the nineteenth-century light-musical stage, *Niniche* (1878).

Technically a "vaudeville-opérette," *Niniche* had a fully plotted script but a rudimentary score, thrown together at the last minute by the

---

[1]This is higher praise than the writer intended. Adams, Broadway's regular Peter Pan till—as we'll see—a Ziegfeld star attempted to succeed her, is on the short list of America's greatest actresses. Mrs. Leslie Carter was a socialite and beauty who stormed the stage by an act of will and began uncertainly. However, she scored a tremendous success in an adaptation of the French backstager *Zaza* the season before this was written. Note that Adams, Carter, and Anna represent a trio of managers—respectively, Frohman, Belasco . . . and the increasingly imposing Ziegfeld.

show's conductor, Marius Boullard. Judic played *Niniche* everywhere, and all sorts of versions were developed for other stars, usually with brand-new scores—though all editions had to include some equivalent for Judic's shocking entrance aria, sung in a bathing suit, "Mon Costume Est Si Collant" (My Suit Is So Tight). *Niniche*'s lead role is that of a Polish countess with a shady past in the Parisian demimonde. Rumor says she is the former sweetheart of a thousand gentlemen, the legendary . . . Niniche!

Where Smith had put two shows' worth of material into *Papa's Wife*, for *The Little Duchess* he seems to have pared away; a note in the program read, "Owing to the length of the performance the plot has been eliminated." Billed as "The Dainty Artistic Comedienne," Anna made her entrance in *The Little Duchess* in her own bathing-suit number, "A Dip in the Ocean." She also sang two coon songs, "What'd Yo' Do Wid de Letter, Mr. Johnson?" and "Chloe," a serenade. Its verse begins with a bit of scene painting:

> *By de river when night is dark,*
> *What's de music you hear dere? Hark!*

We go into ragtime for the chorus:

> *Chloe, I'm waitin' here in de moonlight,*
> *Waitin' alone for you.*

Note the lack of relation to Anna's character, a member by marriage (to a diplomat) of the Polish nobility and a quondam courtesan. Genre songs not only didn't have to "fit" into a show: they weren't supposed to. From our modern vantage, we know that the more faithful to character, the better the score, reaching great moments as early as the Wanting Song and as late as the Eleven O'Clock Number: "All I Need (Is One Good Break)" or "Rose's Turn." However, in 1899, only the best composers were valid dramatists, and there really weren't any best lyricists at all. Story numbers tended to the dutiful; it was the genre inserts that sparkled.

Besides the southern ditties, Held sang what was to become her own private genre, the Eyes Song. *The Little Duchess* offered two of these as well, "The Maiden With the Dreamy Eyes" and "Those Great Big Eyes." Anna enjoyed yet more genre in an Irish piece, "Pretty Mollie Shannon," in which she appeared as a boy in checked shirt, striped pants, jacket, flowing tie, and sailor cap. ("Dainty waltz song," the sheet music promised.)

That makes six numbers, Anna's entire *Little Duchess* tunestack, and one doesn't hear a word of story anywhere in them. Thus, Bigelow, Davenport, Marion, and the rest of the cast kept the plot pumped while Anna made visitations from the Planet Cabaret. She also put on a fashion show, in gowns constructed and accoutered to end an era: velvet, kid, ruffles, ropes of flowered lace, a very opera of attire topped by hats that looked like a weekend with Puss in Boots. She was often accompanied by a mini chorus line—the "girls" of musical comedy—who were also dazzlingly costumed, though of course not to challenge Anna. A note in the *Little Duchess* program called special attention "to the evening gowns worn in the 'Sadie Song,' embroidered gowns made by Maurice Hermann, from special plans secured by Mr. Ziegfeld in Paris, from the leading fashionable modists of the day, representing their latest creations."

Scene after scene of Dressy Ladies was a Ziegfeld innovation, and the form he was gradually inventing would also include at least one oddity per show. *Papa's Wife* had the automobile; *The Little Duchess* offered an all-girl fencing-school scene. Musicals of the day could be plain or pretty, but few were as elaborate as Ziegfeld's were getting to be as a rule. Another manager could have put on *The Little Duchess* for $25,000 and feel like a spendthrift; Ziegfeld spent twice that amount. It was all too much for the unnamed *New York Times* reviewer, who ignored the fencing novelty and complained that Ziegfeld was imitating others, if on a grand scale. The English import *Florodora* boasted that famous Sextet, so *The Little Duchess* countered with "two sextets, and in addition it has double sextets and quadruple sextets." A Belasco comedy called *Naughty Anthony* had scored "a mild sensation" when one of the girls in the cast removed her stocking. So, of course, "six girls do that in *The Little Duchess*." This writer also thought little of Anna. He allowed that she wears lovely jewelry, but he saw only "a little woman who has learned to roll her eyes and go through a varied number of mechanical motions."

Nonetheless, Anna had by now won over a public made of admirers, enthusiasts, the curious, and even just ladies in search of fashion tips. Remember, middle-class women didn't buy off the rack in those days; they employed dressmakers, and many inspected Anna through opera glasses in order to memorize the couture for their own personal knock-offs. Some may have been considering whether or not to try to go as far as Anna was believed to go in corseting down her waist size. In fact, Anna's cinching in gave her the standard advantage over nature, no more: from 20.5 inches down to 19.5, by her own report.

Anna's shows were now Official Broadway Events. *The Little Duchess* opened on October 14, 1901, at the Casino, the equivalent of the Majestic or Shubert today. Everyone who writes about Ziegfeld and Anna makes a port of call out of October 19, at the end of *The Little Duchess'* first week, because that night Anna broke the Casino's house record. A punctilious statement from the box office notes, as always, the weather ("good"), the percentage of tickets purchased ("Entire house sold out"), the scale, which was standard for the day ($2.00, 1.50, 1.00, and 50 cents for standing room), the applicable variations ("extra chairs"), and the previous record holders (Lillian Russell in *Princess Nicotine* grossed $2,265.50, and a performance of *Florodora* reached $2,290.50). Anna Held in *The Little Duchess* went to $2,303.00: "Largest house ever within the Casino walls."

After 136 performances, the show toured for the rest of the 1901–1902 season, and, after the annual Ziegfeld-Anna European jaunt, toured from October 1902 into May 1903: two full seasons in all. This was the size of a smash hit. Yet it was still Anna, not Ziegfeld, who profited in renown. Years later, first-night critics would so subscribe to the Ziegfeld Myth that they seemed to be reviewing one-man shows, emphasizing production over writing, even over star performances. At this time, however, Ziegfeld wasn't even mentioned in the notices. Theatre people knew that Ziegfeld and Anna were a team, and of course their public profile was that of husband and wife. In his personal relationship with Anna, Ziegfeld maintained the relationship he was to have with virtually all his women stars: sexual but paternalistic, even kingly. And Anna, we believe, responded with womankind's fatalistic Realpolitik, old as time: that's how men are, if they're worth having at all.

Yet of the two it was Anna who had the power. She earned the money; he could only arrange for that to happen. True, that would sooner or later make him a major manager—but the manager's world was about to become perilous. To the ingratitude of stars, the unpredictability of audiences, and the shortage of inspired writers one now has to add the ferocity of rival managers. For the most ambitious of the last group had entered upon a war for control of the theatre industry. No one who produced shows in America would be permitted to stay neutral.

CHAPTER FIVE

The War of the Managers

By the spring of 1903, the Syndicate—especially Klaw and Erlanger but most particularly "Honest Abe" Erlanger—was behaving as if corrupted absolutely by its absolute power. Syndicate rule had turned the stage into a Breughel of Judgment Day, for Erlanger didn't enjoy running American theatre as much as he enjoyed making American theatre feel the terror of being run by Erlanger. This of course created enemies eager to dethrone him. But there was no one for them to build an alliance with in any real sense, for Syndicate procedures instantly isolated rebels, closing every major hall to them and threatening those who supported rebellion with their own isolation.

It was not, at least, a perfect system. There was too much theatre for six men to control absolutely, and it was really only Erlanger who collected enemies like cigar bands. The other five of the Theatre Trust, even Marc Klaw, varied from bland partnership in Erlanger's regime to a certain guilty remove. Charles Frohman and Al Hayman got along with Erlanger, no more. His fascism made their work easier; but they were, let us say, essentially apolitical.

However, one of the odd generalizations of the American popular arts in the twentieth century is that the founding generation of businessmen gives way within a decade to a much longer-lived second generation of upstarts. In film, for example, the fanatically unadventurous WASP outfits monopolizing Thomas Edison's patents—American Biograph,

Essanay, Vitagraph, Kalem, and so on—evaporated in the face of the experimenting of Jewish immigrants accommodating D. W. Griffith, Thomas Ince, and other mavericks. In the music publishing business, the established publishers devoted to the story ballad and genre numbers were wiped away when Irving Berlin and Jerome Kern invented the American musical-comedy score in the 1910s, to be joined by Porter, the Gershwins, Rodgers and Hart—all for new imprints.

In the theatre, three very young men from upstate New York challenged the Syndicate and won. However, Lee, Sam, and J. J. Shubert didn't conquer the Trust by changing the art on them. The Shuberts weren't intending to discover new forms; they simply wanted to share the ones available.

At first, it appeared that the Shuberts and Erlanger's group might get along. Syndicate partners Nixon and Zimmerman even booked attractions into Shubert houses. Suddenly, for no apparent reason, Erlanger placed his chieftain's ban on the Shuberts—and here we have to step out of narrative chronology a bit, in order to understand just how personal the Syndicate-Shubert war became, and how it affected more or less every move that Ziegfeld made.

The personal in the matter inhered in Sam S. Shubert, the firm's poster boy and diplomat. Failing to create a peace with the Syndicate, Sam had to hurry to Pittsburgh when Erlanger moved to close that city's stages to the Shuberts, provoking legal action. Sam could have left it to deputies to argue for his team, but this was a crucial battle: if Sam defended Shubert interests every single time they were under assault and did so in person, Erlanger would surely give up fighting and go to treaty.

Rather than lose a day of work, Sam took a night train to Pittsburgh to present his motions in court the next morning. A freak accident occurred: Sam's train collided with the munitions wagon of an army transport, which smashed open the civilian car in a roar of fire. The lower half of Sam's body was so badly burned that he died the next day, May 12, 1905. The family was of course devastated—but none more so than Lee and J. J., who shared a peculiarity in that they hated all humanity except for one person. That person they loved: and that person was Sam. At a meeting among Lee, J. J., and Shubert organization honchos, someone put forth the suggestion that this tragedy was the conclusion of the war. They must now sell their holdings to Erlanger and seek another line of trade. After all, Sam had been the guiding spirit of the business, and Sam knew theatre. Only he could have lured the great Richard Mansfield into signing with the Shuberts when they were flybynights from the provinces. Without Sam's charming daredevilry, the Shuberts had no chance against the entrenched status quo. They had lost, and should make the best of it.

Lee Shubert, the oldest, was too morose to speak. But J. J., the youngest, now sprang up. This wasn't about theatres any more. This was about . . . Sell out to Erlanger?

"*Fuck Erlanger!*" J. J. shouted. "Fuck his *sons* to the *last* of their *days*! Fuck *Klaw* and *Hayman* and *Frohman* the faegele! So they killed Sam! *Did* they? So we take *their theatres* and *their plays* and *we kill them, too!*"

And so the Syndicate bought itself a sworn-to-the-death foe, and, at last, there was an Other Side for Syndicate haters to unite with. However, managers unwilling to take a side now had two contentious forces shouting, "Choose!" Before, if one made kowtow to Erlanger, one could thrive unmolested. Now, alas, to camp with Erlanger drew Shubert fire, and vice versa. It was a dangerous time in which to be a rising young manager, especially one with a star who could break the house record of the outstanding musical playhouse of the day. Sooner or later, the Shuberts would make an offer to Anna—and Ziegfeld would indeed be forced to choose.

Obviously, none of this could have been foreseen at the turn of the century, when Sam arrived alone in New York to launch the Shubert incursion. But see how quickly the business shifted around Ziegfeld; how slithery the assembling hosts. Sam established his beachhead at the Herald Square Theatre and signed Richard Mansfield. Erlanger was irritated. Then Sam took over that very temple of musical comedy, the Casino. Erlanger saw that it was not good. Then Sam nabbed the little San Francisco Music Hall, dubbing it the Princess, which was rather an

improvement over its recent names, the Jonah and Hermann's Gaiety.[1]
And Erlanger declared the war.

We are now back in real narrative time, as Ziegfeld and Anna return
from their vacation after *The Little Duchess* and the war becomes part of
Broadway geography. Thanks to Oscar Hammerstein's Olympia, the
theatre district was finally ready to move northward; the irrepressible
Oscar himself opened up Forty-Second Street between Seventh and
Eighth Avenues, street of streets! On the block's northeast end, Hammerstein built the Victoria (in 1899) and the Theatre Republic (1900).
Now, in October 1903, the Shuberts and the Syndicate deployed forces
on the same block. Across the road from Hammerstein's two houses rose
the Syndicate's New Amsterdam, a power playhouse with an air of
Medicis, of Rothschilds, big, beautiful, and unique.

And across the road from the New Amsterdam, nestled confidently
next to the Theatre Republic, rose the Lyric, owned by Reginald De
Koven but leased to the Shubert brothers. They opened two weeks be-
fore the Syndicate, with that classy Shakespearean and Shubertian star
Richard Mansfield as a young German royal enjoying college life, in *Old
Heidelberg*.[2] Then came the opening of the New Amsterdam, with a lav-
ish mounting of *A Midsummer Night's Dream* with Nat C. Goodwin as
Bottom, a rather grandiose bomb.

So the Shuberts and the Trust were facing off on Forty-Second
Street. *Choose!* Ziegfeld threw in with the newcomers—tentatively—
when he presented his first musical without Anna, *The Red Feather*,
which directly followed *Old Heidelberg* into the Lyric on November 9,
1903. If Erlanger should ask, Ziegfeld had an excuse: *The Red Feather's*

---

[1]This playhouse is not to be confused with the Princess Theatre of Kern, Bolton,
and Wodehouse. The Shubert Princess was down on Twenty-Ninth Street, the more famous Princess on Thirty-Ninth—and in any case not built till 1913.

[2]The play flopped, but the musical didn't: *Old Heidelberg* was the source of *The Student Prince* (1924), another Shubert production and the longest-running musical of the
1920s.

composer was Reginald De Koven, and De Koven owned the theatre. In fact, the De Koven-Shubert plan for the Lyric had been to alternate De Koven's shows with Mansfield's, taking in interim bookings as needed.

Clearly, De Koven was the muscle on this show, although Ziegfeld continued to apply his style of extravagant visuals and lovely ladies in splendid costumes. But didn't musical comedy always count on lovely ladies in splendid costumes? No, not always; and Ziegfeld had an eye. *The Red Feather* itself is one of the most obscure titles in this book; it seems to have left nothing behind, scarcely a photograph or song sheet. De Koven worked with lyricist Charles Emerson Cook and the successful playwright Charles Klein on an operetta narrative: in Romancia, the usual dashing army captain (George L. Tallman) courts a countess (Grace Van Studdiford) while chasing a bandit known as the Red Feather (Grace Van Studdiford). That's right: the countess is the bandit. The show managed to edge its way through a two-month run of undersold houses, but meanwhile Ziegfeld had unveiled his next Anna Held special, this time at a Syndicate house, the Knickerbocker.

The show was *Mam'selle Napoleon,* a musical version of a play that Ziegfeld and Anna had attended in Paris, Jean Richepin's *Mlle. Mars.* Anna had fallen in love with the title role, that of an actress of the Comédie-Française who saves her guardsman boy friend from the wrath of Napoleon. For prestige, *Mam'selle Napoleon* was presented almost as if it were Richepin's play in translation rather than a musical drawn from it, however closely. True, Richepin was a librettist of the musical stage as well as a playwright—but it was Joseph W. Herbert who wrote the book and lyrics, directing and joining the cast as well. As for *Mam'selle Napoleon*'s composer, once again Ziegfeld chose one of the best around, Gustav Luders. The name means nothing today, of course, but when Ziegfeld engaged him, Luders had enjoyed three hits in a row with his usual partner, Frank Pixley: *The Burgomaster* (1900), *King Dodo* (1902), and *The Prince of Pilsen* (1903), which was less a hit than a sensation. One of the few scores of the early 1900s still to be heard on radio into the 1940s, *The Prince of Pilsen* was virtually the music of New York when Ziegfeld started putting *Mam'selle Napoleon* together. Everywhere one went, one heard some version or other of the jaunty drinking song, "Heidelberg"; the dear little waltz, "The Message of the Violet"; a story ballad, "The Tale of the Sea Shell"; and the martial air for baritone and men's chorus, "Fall In."

Also important, *The Prince of Pilsen* solved a problem rife in this age, balancing musical comedy's silly fun with its romantic core even in the music. Too often, romantic shows dragged in jokes like a child pulling a yakking wooden duck; the fun shows were bamboozled by the mush. (This was partly why *The Merry Widow* scored such a penetrating success here, in 1907: its romance and comedy are perfectly blended in its two leads, comedians as well as sweethearts.) *Mam'selle Napoleon* would be especially challenging, a piece of somewhat serious emotional content, climaxed when Mademoiselle Mars conquers Napoleon with a stirring delivery of the tale of a mouse that aided an injured lion. Anna determined to present this to her American public in Richepin's original French, re-creating the moment when she fell in love with the play.

Presumably, the busy Joseph Herbert would find a way to bond the music with the comedy. But meanwhile, Ziegfeld put forth his most lavish production, fitting some of the chorus girls into Paris gowns and giving Anna her most ostentatious costume plot yet. She entered as Gainsborough's Blue Boy and hit some sort of apex in Napoleonic garb, complete with hand in coat and enigmatic smile. And she really did love this show. "One moment I am all emotion," she told one of the thousand interviewers attracted by Ziegfeld's drumming. "Another [moment] is all sympathy. And then again I am just gay, and I am Anna Held."

Ziegfeld hired a fine cast in support. Frank Rushworth (as Anna's vis-à-vis) and Arthur Lawrence (Napoleon) are nobodies today, but Ziegfeld was born with a nose for talent. When we reach the 1920s and names of at least minor note, we will see how suavely he filled the featured roles with performers gifted enough to captivate without tilting the stage away from the star. For instance, *Mam'selle Napoleon* appears to have marked the Big Break of future darling Bessie McCoy, in a featured part; we'll be meeting her again. The show's head comic was Frank Moulan, one of the most prominent of his kind in what would have been the Charles A. Bigelow role had Bigelow not become unreliable.

Unfortunately, manager Henry Savage claimed contractual rights to Moulan's work, and a court decision stripped Moulan from the show right after the first night, December 8, 1903.

But then, the critics stripped *Mam'selle Napoleon* of its future that same day, in reviews suggesting that Ziegfeld had schemed to irritate them with a coarse and infantile piece. All noted the show's visual beauty, using it as a paddle on Ziegfeld, Anna, and the striving Joseph Herbert: "Between gowns," one reviewer groaned, "the plot crept in."

Anna's fans kept the piece running for five weeks, and Ziegfeld imperiously ordered up a tour that lasted till April 1904, enduring rabbit punches from reviewers all the way to Montana. In all, *Mam'selle Napoleon* was without qualification Ziegfeld and Anna's first public disgrace. Ironically, it left something behind: because of the tremendous sales of *The Prince of Pilsen*'s piano-vocal score, Gustav Luders' publishers printed a *Mam'selle Napoleon* score before the show opened. Like the Shogun in *Pacific Overtures*, it is seldom seen.

It was a highly disappointing season for Ziegfeld, then, with two shows of little account opening almost back to back, in November and December 1903. However, at the end of that December, Ziegfeld's hometown suffered a calamity that had a tremendous impact on the American stage and everyone in it. Not since John Wilkes Booth shot President Lincoln was the theatre community so hated by those who have no use for theatre in the first place. What happened was an accident, yet it was treated by press and popular talk almost as an act of willful evil: the Iroquois Theatre fire of December 30, 1903.

It all started innocently enough, as Eddie Foy's extravaganza *Mr. Bluebeard* opened at the Knickerbocker in New York on January 21, 1903. This was Foy's second Bluebeard musical, a mixture of Arabian Nights and fairyland with the flavor of English pantomime—based, indeed, on an English original. It was as well a Syndicate show. Managers Klaw and Erlanger lavished on it a fabulous production, for extravaganza was by its nature spectacular. A cast of nearly three hundred and a capital cost of $150,000 made *Mr. Bluebeard* possibly the most expensive American musical to that time.

Another thing that extravaganza loved was a mishmash of story-book romance and vernacular comedy. Thus, side by side with "The Triumph of the Magic Fan" were such numbers as "The Beer That Made Milwaukee Famous," "Billy Gray, U.S.A., O.K.," and "Hamlet Was a Melancholy Dane." The inevitable coon song was a contribution from the tireless J. Rosamond Johnson and Bob Cole, "When the Colored Band Comes Marching Down the Street." Such hybrid entertainment was ideal for youngsters yet amenable to grown-up taste: a perfect family show, like two other extravaganzas of the same year, *The Wizard of Oz* and *Babes in Toyland*.

Though Eddie Foy was the sole star of the evening, he did not play the title role. Bluebeard (Dan McAvoy) is of course the villain; Foy played scalawags, not murderers. He was the heroine's father in his earlier *Bluebeard* outing, *Bluebeard Jr.* (1890), and now he was Sister Anne, in drag. A solid hit, *Mr. Bluebeard* closed in late May and set off on tour, to Pittsburgh, Indianapolis, Cleveland, and then Chicago, to open Klaw and Erlanger's 1,724-seat showplace for big musicals, the Iroquois.

At the usual holiday matinée before New Year's Day, in a house composed mainly of children, mothers, and aunts, a spark from an arc light set a piece of scenery alight, and, as the show played on, stagehands battled the flames unavailingly. This brand-new Klaw and Erlanger play palace had not been routined for emergencies: the fire exits were hidden by drapes and the windows roofing the stage house, to be opened in case of fire to let the heat escape, had been bolted down for installation in the new building and never unfastened. Worse, the asbestos curtain caught as it was lowered, turning the Iroquois auditorium into a flue. Hell roared out from the stage into the house, incinerating those who weren't already caught up in the panic of those trying to flee. Six hundred two souls died on site, followed by further casualties in the hospital.

The fire was seen not only as a disaster but an outrage, an enormity of Syndicate recklessness, Erlanger evil. The lack of adequate safety measures in the theatre's hasty opening sounded the note of "public be damned" that many heard in the very notion of Business As Usual when the business was Big. All over the land cartoonists drew Erlanger and the fire as culprits of terror; *Life* magazine showed him laughing as the Iroquois succumbed.

One good thing came out of the fire: expanded fire-code stipulations for every theatre in America. Another result was Erlanger's loss of authority, for his sense of crisis management was so undeveloped that his public reaction to the fire was virtually one great Gwaa-ha-ha! He was no less ruthless, then, after December 30, 1903: but he was less the unquestioned despot.

It was bound to happen, fire or no fire. The theatre was expanding so rapidly that the Trust would have found it impossible to monitor all the new managers, talent, contracts, and theatre realty constantly being brought into play. Most important to Ziegfeld, of all the theatre's forms it was the musical—Ziegfeld's form—that was growing most grandly at this time. He could not have been surer of his destiny if he had been Dick Whittington hearing Bow Bells, even if Ziegfeld has been slow thus far in discovering his style in the form. Not one of Ziegfeld's six musical productions has been an original save *The Red Feather*—and that was densely generic.

Further, none of the available kinds of musical interested Ziegfeld (though he was, for one reason or another, to get to them all at some point). There was extravaganza, throwing off the biggest hits, as we have seen. There was the farce with songs, revitalized by George M. Cohan. There was the star-comic vehicle with a comic-opera musical menu, like the aforementioned *Prince of Pilsen,* in which a big fat clown of a Cincinnati brewer visits Nice and gets mistaken for a prince while operetta people sing those Stein Songs and Messages of the Violet. Further, Victor Herbert was taking over from Reginald De Koven as Broadway's alpha composer, gamely sorting out the various genres by devising a different musical grammar for each.

However, Ziegfeld wanted no part of this. Cohan was so corny—and what is the point of raising one's curtain on a lovely place like Nice to spend time with a brewer from Cincinnati? As for Victor Herbert, Ziegfeld thought him ideal for ballet music, for that touch of highbrow. For pop music, you needed a taste of the carnival midway.

On top of that, Ziegfeld's addiction to high-stakes gambling continually weakened his financial position. Not only would he find himself short in the raising of essential capital: he at times tried to stiff his authors on their royalty payments. True, Ziegfeld did have an amazing ability to charm wealthy notables into backing him. Diamond Jim Brady wasn't just a friend but a contributor.

Yet Ziegfeld was reduced, in his next show, to co-producing once again, at that in the least Ziegfeldian of forms, burlesque. True, here was theatre's version of midway art—even if, at this stage in its history, burlesque wasn't even thinking of employing the likes of a Little Egypt. But burlesque was sloppy and cheap: the opposite of Ziegfeld. In fact, the mating of this man and this form came about only because Ziegfeld apparently wanted to get in on the entertainment business' story of the decade: Weber and Fields had broken up their act.

The parting half a century later of Dean Martin and Jerry Lewis was not bigger, for Weber and Fields were truly beloved (indeed, only known) as a duo. Their characteristic spin on burlesque, with its tastefully alluring (and fully covered) Weberfields Beauty Chorus, its *Forbidden Broadway*–like spoofs of popular hits, and its gala women headliners (up to and including Lillian Russell), was one of Broadway's talking points. Now that Lew Fields had abandoned Joe Weber and burlesque itself to produce original book shows, Weber needed a spicy breakaway in format. So Anna joined Weber's company for *Higgledy-Piggledy,* a title in the Weber and Fields tradition. (We've already mentioned *Whirl-I-Gig,* and other bills were, for instance, *Fiddle-Dee-Dee, Hoity-Toity,* and *Twirly-Whirly.*)

Perhaps to proclaim a new post-Fields Weber, *Higgledy-Piggledy* contained no parody of a current show. Instead, it told a brand-new story with a burlesque feel to it. The premise was that favorite trope, Americans Touring Europe; this time it was a mustard king and his more or less marriageable daughter. Weber of course played the father, one Adolph Schnitz. Harry Morris stepped in as the Fields (so to speak), playing the protégeur of a certain Mimi de Chartreuse—Anna's role, of course. The daughter, Philopena Schnitz, was Marie Dressler. Charles A.

Bigelow rejoined Ziegfeld in this comic-rich cast, a Weberfields feature. George Marion again directed and, just to make things confusing, someone named *Sam* Marion laid out the dances and performed some of them.

Everything lies in the execution, but Weber's execution was retro in every respect. Indeed, burlesque itself was retro, so much so that only Weber and Fields had been able to keep it vital in a major Broadway theatre. That theatre—the very one that Anna was now to play in—was a hideous firetrap that the Iroquois tragedy should have closed forever. (The city did force Weber to make certain structural alterations.) On top of it all, Weber and Fields had been strongly anti-Syndicate. Wouldn't Ziegfeld arouse Erlanger's ire?

Of course, everything was grand at the start, as always in the theatre: the first day of the "table read," the giving of gifts and passing of compliments, the nosh kiosk.[1] Woody Allen's period film *Bullets Over Broadway* catches this air of deceptive etiquette with a first day of rehearsals just as I describe leading on to all seven of the deadly sins, even a murder. For Weber and the Ziegfelds (as we might call them), it began with Anna's return from Europe with one hundred onlookers at the harbor. In a special ceremony, Ziegfeld presented Weber with, as Anna recalled, an "épingle de cravate ornée d'un énorme diamant" (a tie pin decorated with a large diamond). Weber declared himself delighted to be épinglé,

---

[1]The table read, a modern term, is simply the first traversal of the script by the entire cast, seated around a table. There was no such thing in Ziegfeld's day, in fact. If the manager thought it useful, the *playwright* would read his work to the assembled cast (and, for musicals, the composer would play the score). Most actors worked from what were called "sides": a booklet containing only their lines preceded by the last few words of their cues. This shows how perfunctory acting was expected to be in those days, but sides had the advantage of making immediately visible the size of one's part. Counting the number of "lines"—which really means the number of times one picks up a cue—is arbitrary, for a "line" may consist of anything from a single word to a Racinian tirade. Thus, in 1904, actors didn't boast of the number of lines they had, but the number of *sides*—that is, the page count of their role.

and all then set out in a hearty mood for their first season together, that of 1904–1905. And before three pages of sides had been turned, everyone was screaming at everyone else. A key moment, described by Anna herself, found Ziegfeld calling the dress rehearsal to a stop because of a set depicting the "pavillon d'Arménonville."

"That's not Arménonville!" Ziegfeld cried. "That's Hoboken!"

Weber agreed to have something else run up to Ziegfeld's satisfaction. But, really, who cared about the sets in burlesque?

The women's costumes, at least, were planned with some care, and Anna was very happy with her songs. Still, the atmosphere of burlesque was, quite simply, a self-destructive detour on Ziegfeld's way. Burlesque did not comprehend the visual idolatry that Ziegfeld was inventing, letting the satyr loose in the city. In burlesque, the men traded in hokum and the girls all had mothers. Burlesque was essentially about the one theatrical element that Ziegfeld didn't understand: jokes. The man had no sense of humor whatsoever. Eventually, he learned to trust the public to tell him by their laughter who was funny. This early in his career, in an environment hostile to what he loved, Ziegfeld was confused when he wasn't skirmishing with the penny-pinching Weber.

Ziegfeld would say, "Anna's role is too small."

And Weber would reply, "The lights on the marquee are too big. And cost plenty."

Neither Ziegfeld nor Anna seems to have foreseen the worst of it. Did you notice, two pages ago, who was playing the mustard magnate's daughter? Isn't any show with Marie Dressler in it going to be stolen by Marie Dressler, one of the most naturally funny comics of all time? "Never did sheer personality achieve a greater victory," said the unsigned review in *The New York Sun* of Dressler's entrance number, "A Great Big Girl Like Me." She sang it in a gigantic hat topped with three tons of lace that ran down either side of her head, meeting in a knot around her neck to surge down her bodice to her knees. "On came the festive Marie," *The Sun* went on, "and in less than half a minute the house was in roars of laughter."

Higgledy-Piggledy opened on October 20, 1904, and by October 21

Ziegfeld and Anna realized that they had ventured far out of their comfort zone. Worse, Weber now proposed to add a parody to the show after all, spoofing the season's comedy hit, George Ade's *The College Widow*. George Marion had directed that one, too, so he was game, and the tale of a lass wooing a football hero to get him to play for her father's college promised Weber an easy goof. [1] Unfortunately, he left very little room in the burlesque for Anna. *Higgledy-Piggledy* ran 185 performances, toured, then played a two-week return in late summer of 1905, a solid hit. But by the time the spoof, called *The College Widower* (with Weber in the "Jane" role), made the evening a double-bill, Ziegfeld and Anna had terminated their association with Weber.

So the Ziegfelds had had two bad seasons in a row and Ziegfeld as manager was still in an early evolutionary state. However, one week after *Higgledy-Piggledy* opened, something momentous occurred on the New York theatrical scene: the opening of the subway, on October 27, 1904. This was not the beginning of rapid transit in Manhattan, for elevated railways ran up and down Second, Third, Sixth, and Ninth Avenues. However, even short hops were interminable, and the conditions were grimy. Most people took the horsecar.

The subway, however, was going to be truly popular, and it stood to influence the way people regarded the geography of Manhattan in the way it singled out Forty-Second Street as the island's central east-west thoroughfare. This first subway line, the Interborough Rapid Transit, chugged uptown from City Hall to Grand Central Depot, turned west along Forty-Second to Broadway, then cut north to fork at One Hundred Fourth Street and end in the Bronx at Mott and Bailey Avenue stops.

As the quaint terminology implies, Grand Central Depot was not the present structure, but an older one that had been modified and enlarged

---

[1] Those readers who find Ade's plot strangely familiar are right: *The College Widow* was the source of *Leave It To Jane* (1917), the most frequently revived of Jerome Kern's Princess musicals.

several times. Its location at Fourth Avenue (as Park was then called) above Forty-Second had been chosen because city authorities banned the steam-engine train below that point, to control pollution. This was in the 1850s, when much of the area above Forty-Second Street lay empty.

By 1904, however, real-estate development had crossed the border. As we know, there were already four theatres on Forty-Second Street between Seventh and Eighth Avenues; by 1920 there would be eleven, with some twenty others opened on the four cross streets to the north. The *New York Times* tower had arisen, too, on the absurd triangle created by the numbered street and the two intersecting avenues; Longacre Square had been renamed Times Square earlier in 1904. And the new IRT subway stop at that location, anticipating more business than at other stops on the route, was made the hub of the entire line.

Thus, Forty-Second Street and Broadway—the very center of the theatre district—was made the very center of New York life. A brace of luxury hotels sprang up, notably the Astor in 1905, right in Times Square itself. At that, a survey in 1910 set New York's tourist population at something between 100,000 and 200,000 souls a day—and theatregoing was presumably on their itinerary.

Further, fancy restaurants catering to those oathed to leisure and the breaking of sumptuary laws were already in place, as infrastructure of the late-night carousing that theatregoing encouraged. There was Reisenweber's, Maxim's, Bustanoby's, Café dell'Opera, Shanley's, Churchill's. As I've said earlier, they were called lobster palaces, as if pashas dined there; they might well have done. Rector's, the most famous of the lot, cost half a million dollars to build in 1899, unheard of for an eating establishment—but then, Rector's was about more than eating. All heads turned to inspect each arrival pushing through the revolving door: this was where the American *dolce vita* learned how to Make an Entrance. In a Belasco production of 1909, Eugene Walter's *The Easiest Way*, Frances Starr played an actress who is destroyed when her fiancé deserts her on learning of the compromises that actresses sometimes make to survive. Starr underwent something of a mad scene, then collected herself and prepared to compromise anew. "Doll me up,

Annie," she told her maid as the audience gasped. "I'm going to Rector's to make a hit, and to hell with the rest!" So the pasha was dining with chorus girls.

And Diamond Jim Brady with Lillian Russell; and opera singers with their entourages, flattering and wheedling; and the Count of Soigné with a divorcée considering life on the wicked stage, for example, Mrs. Leslie Carter, leaning toward the count to ask, through artfully trembling lips, "Would they like me, do you think?" And Ziegfeld with Anna. It took the building of a subway to do it: but Broadway now had its unique and heady world in which to prosper on gossip and fame while accommodating the larger audience that could take the IRT to the theatre. By day, the area throbbed with "the profession": actors hurrying to rehearsals or waiting on the street to make contacts. By night, the place lit up as the Great White Way, and manager Charles Dillingham introduced Broadway's first moving electric sign down on Thirty-Eighth Street at the Knickerbocker, for *The Red Mill* (1906), illuminating the arms of a "working" mill. Yes: and in their offices across Forty-Second Street from Klaw and Erlanger in *their* offices, the two surviving Shuberts, Lee and J. J., pursued their family vendetta against the Syndicate. It was all for Sam, as the Shuberts built theatres and corralled performers and hated Erlanger as Erlanger had never been hated before.

In particular, the Shuberts tried to draw into orbit any important member of the theatre world not already a Syndicate satellite, and while Ziegfeld and Anna were licking their wounds after their two recent flops, the Shuberts came calling. In the spring of 1906, Lee Shubert telegraphed Ziegfeld in Europe:

HAVE GREAT PLAY SUIT HELD CAN PUT IN REHEARSAL
IMMEDIATELY ARE YOU INTERESTED

Ziegfeld was extremely interested. It had been some eighteen months since he had opened anything, hit or flop. Worse, his gambling addiction had led him into an appalling situation in Biarritz: he had squandered all he had and signed promissory notes for a great deal that he hadn't. Now he planned to invite the worst sort of scandal and flee his responsibilities altogether. There is, after all, such a thing as bad publicity, and welshing on a bet in dinner clothes will create it. The rules for gentlemanly behavior were stricter in those days, and no casino would admit one after such a caddish stunt.

So Ziegfeld was broke and shamed—but his deeply superstitious nature must have noted one arresting possibility in the Shubert offer. The Casino was now a Shubert house, and the record that Anna had set during the run of *The Little Duchess* still stood. Wouldn't her reappearance on the same stage reinform their luck?

For her part, Anna dreaded having to bail out another gambling addict with her own money, and as Anna was the apparent Mrs. Ziegfeld, she was liable by French law to make good on his debts. So Ziegfeld and Anna, in Paris, were very eager to depart for home. Replying to Lee Shubert, Ziegfeld said:

IF FOR CASINO INTERESTED SHOW YOUR CONFIDENCE CABLE ME
TODAY THOUSAND DOLLARS WILL SAIL SATURDAY

A thousand dollars? Shubert made a counteroffer of a few hundred dollars for travel expenses, but Ziegfeld was Ziegfeld. He so loved telegraphing that he had a special bulk discount deal with Western Union, and he would have enjoyed negotiating back and forth with Shubert by cable till they had all but produced the Casino show itself. However, Alfred Baulant of the Biarritz casino was stalking Ziegfeld legally, and he had to get out of Europe. He did hold out for his thousand:

MY CABLE STATED ONLY TERMS ON WHICH I WOULD SAIL AT
ONCE ANSWER TODAY OR TOO LATE

and Shubert gave in:

CASINO OPENS SPRING PLAY MOTOR GIRL GREAT STAR PART
SALARY HELD ONE THOUSAND DOLLARS FIFTY PERCENT PROFIT

I MAKE PRODUCTION IF TERMS SATISFACTORY I WILL CABLE
MONEY

Had Ziegfeld won? Lee Shubert's "I make production" meant that *The Motor Girl* would be just another of the girl-title musical comedies so popular at the time, with scores off the rack, standard jokes, and décor cannibalized from whatever had closed on the road during the previous season. You knew the plot before the curtain went up: *The Girl and the Wizard, The Girl From Dixie, The Girl From Paris, The Girl From Montmartre, The Girl and the Bandit, The Rollicking Girl, The Hurdy Gurdy Girl, The Girl At the Helm, The Kissing Girl, The Yankee Girl, The Sweetest Girl in Paris, The Wall Street Girl, The Charity Girl.* At least *The Motor Girl* hung out an amusing hook in that Anna was the only musical-comedy star known for a love of automobiles.

Ziegfeld may have felt that he could handle Lee Shubert. He cabled assent, and he and Anna sailed home on Shubert money. However, Ziegfeld couldn't handle Abe Erlanger, who had been engaged in mortal combat with the Shuberts since Sam's horrible death the year before. The doom that every manager sought to avoid was now Ziegfeld's: he could choose his enemy, the Syndicate or the Shuberts.

Ziegfeld chose the Shuberts, perhaps because Erlanger whispered an offer or two into Ziegfeld's ear. We have no evidence of it—but Ziegfeld now became intimately partnered with Klaw and Erlanger in ways beneficial to all, but to Ziegfeld especially.

However, across Forty-Second Street at the Lyric, the Shuberts, notorious for their own cheating and conning, were all but berserk. Not only had Ziegfeld taken their money on what appeared to be a false promise: he kept the money they had advanced him. Of course, though we speak of "the Shuberts," we mean either Lee or J. J., for each operated within his own milieu and virtually never communicated with the other. They were two different producing outfits united by an accounts ledger. Still, to the outside world they were an unshakably united entity: the Messrs. Shubert, as they billed themselves. And the Messrs. as such took Ziegfeld to court to recover the thousand dollars while Erlanger looked on, making glad little noises. He hoped they'd all lose. The Shuberts did in fact prevail, though it took a few years, and they so hated Ziegfeld now that when Lee swore that no Ziegfeld show would ever play a Shubert house, he actually meant it. He held to it for almost twenty years, giving way at last for business reasons only.[1]

Meanwhile, Anna's new show was presented in a recent Klaw and Erlanger acquisition, the old Broadway Theatre. Built in 1888 and seating 1,800 when most playhouses held 1,000, the Broadway stood on the southwest corner of Broadway and Forty-First Street, too far north in 1888 but now, in 1906, extraordinarily central. With its five stories of brick and stone and its American flag on top, it looked like a gigantic all-American firehouse. Yet it was there that Anna played her most Gallic outing yet: *A Parisian Model*.[2] Setting aside *Higgledy-Piggledy*, which was really a Joe Weber and Marie Dressler piece, *A Parisian Model* was Anna's first original. The storyline was familiar even so, using the legacy-with-a-catch premise: heroine stands to inherit a fortune on the condition that she not reveal its source, so of course her boy friend (Henry Leoni) thinks some lascivious protégeur has expressed his gratitude. Piling cliché upon Pelion was Ziegfeld's most constant comic in his Anna period, Charles A. Bigelow, getting into the usual loony disguises: a Hispanic, Paderewski, a drag bit. In fact, the stereotypical minority figure, the high-class celeb, and a woman were de rigueur in musicals when the jester went masquerading.

Don't blame Ziegfeld. The one element in the musical that resisted evolutionary development was its plotting, because there were no innovative book writers.

Yet.

---

[1] *The Motor Girl* finally came to light at the end of the 1908–1909 season, at the Lyric, with Georgia Caine as the sister of a champion racing-car driver who dons his clothes and wins for him. Written by third-rate composer Julian Edwards and two nobodies, the show lasted 95 performances, then vanished forever.

[2] Thus in the program and on some of the sheet music. Most sources restyle the title with a definite article as *The Parisian Model*.

Besides, the Parisian setting and the "artists and models" atmosphere gave Ziegfeld a lot to work with. Along with the by now customary Harry B. Smith for book and lyrics was composer Max Hoffman for the plot numbers, with rather a lot of interpolations by others. Along with Anna for her blend of coquette and cutup and Bigelow for his grotty pranking was Gertrude Hoffman, a dancer who also did impersonations. (She was Max Hoffman's wife; apparently, they came as a set.) An arresting new addition to Ziegfeld's atelier was Julian Mitchell, an antecedent of the modern director-choreographer and already the veteran of a rich history that included the spectacularly long-running *A Trip To Chinatown* (1891), a lot of Victor Herbert and Weber and Fields, and both *The Wizard of Oz* and *Babes in Toyland*. Mitchell was nearly deaf, which would seem to militate against his getting much choreography done. On the contrary, only star dancers like Gertrude Hoffman created their art in reaction to the appointed music. The dancing master of the ensemble—Mitchell, in this case—worked out the "combinations" more or less independently of musical accompaniment, to a counting system he then taught to the chorus dancers. Deaf was not a problem.

Mitchell was gifted and Anna a delight, but what made *A Parisian Model* unique in Anna's catalogue was Ziegfeld's exploitation of that bohemian aura. A co-producer was listed along with Ziegfeld, Frank McKee; he was presumably the show's banker, as Klaw and Erlanger were not yet capitalizing Ziegfeld's ventures. But this was a Ziegfeld production from top to toe, in fact the most Ziegfeldian production yet. One Caroline or Catherine Seidle or Sidle (the names appear thus variously in programs) designed the less important costumes, as she had for *The Little Duchess* and *Higgledy-Piggledy*. But Landolff of Paris styled Anna and Ziegfeld's pet showgirls, used primarily to dress the stage during Anna's numbers.

These included the expected Eyes Song, "I (just) Can't Make My Eyes Behave." Oddly, the equally expected coon song was given to not Anna but Henry Leoni: "I Want You Ma' Honey." However, during the run Anna was given a specialty, "Won't You Be Ma Teddy Bear?" in which Anna danced with two children, both in teddy-bear garb. More enduringly, Anna's third-act duet with Leoni, "When We're Married," was replaced by a song occasionally heard today, "It's Delightful To Be Married." Anna herself got lyricist credit, to the music of two composers, Henri Christiné and Vincent Scotto, originally published as "La Petite Tonkinoise" (The Little Tonkinese Girl). A buzz of snappy innocence, the new lyrics conjure up the maidenly minx that enchanted Anna's public:

> *It's delightful to be married,*
> *To be, be, be, be, be, be, be, be, be, be married.*
> *With a house, a man, a family,*
> *You should be happy like a bumblebee.*

Charles A. Bigelow had his establishing number, "I'm the Man (They Talk About So Much)," and he and Anna enjoyed a Kiss Duet that kept changing its title. But what really put *A Parisian Model* over were its production numbers, which give us Ziegfeld at his most audacious. They could not have been thought up by Smith or Hoffman or even Julian Mitchell. They were too risqué for musical-comedy journeymen to have conceived, as with those society ladies getting their hands on Sandow's muscles. This is neither Syndicate nor Shubert thinking: it's Chicago World's Fair thinking, Broadway with a midway plaisance.

The highlights of *A Parisian Model* comprised a little crash course in Ziegfeld 101. First of all was "I'd Like To See a Little More Of You," an interpolation by Will D. Cobb and Gus Edwards. The song creates a staging pun: we see a great deal more of the chorus girls than was ever possible before, for after entering the set of "A Sculptor's Studio" in long robes, they each took a post behind an artist's easel and dropped their robes, revealing bare shoulders and legs. Were they nude? For a few moments, the audience was scandalized and incredulous, till the girls came out from behind the easels: in strapless gowns, their skirts tied above the knee. What a relief! Still, wasn't the suspense enjoyable?

The second of Ziegfeld's coups was "La Mattchiche," using the old spelling for the Brazilian tango in quick two-step rhythm that became popular in the 1910s as the Maxixe. Ziegfeld's twist was to assign the dance to Anna and . . . Gertrude Hoffman in short hair and men's clothes! This was beyond ribald, beyond wicked, and the moment it started 1,800 pairs of opera glasses rose to 1,800 pairs of eyes—more and more an audience habit at a Ziegfeld show.

The third and most elaborate of Ziegfeld's inventions became ubiquitous in the early Hollywood musical: a song lyric creates the concept for the ensuing dance. We take this for granted now, as when Busby Berkeley expands "By a Waterfall" into an aquacade or "Lullaby of Broadway" into a parable of dangerous Manhattan nightclubbing. However, before *A Parisian Model,* dances didn't observe the verbal content of the songs they accompanied. Dances were self-governing expressions, unrelated to anything.

Ziegfeld makes his little history in *A Parisian Model*'s opening scene, "Callot's Dressmaking Establishment, Rue de la Paix, Paris." Here Anna presented her first number, an early example of the Heroine's Wanting Song. This staple of the Golden Age musical eventually gave us such differently pointed numbers as *Brigadoon*'s "Waitin' For My Dearie," *Gypsy*'s "Some People," and *Rags*' "Children of the Wind." It's the moment that opens a show's beating heart to the public, inviting it to share in the adventure emotionally.

True, the Anna Held kind of heroine doesn't wish for romance or stardom or independence. Anna Held wishes to be the best-dressed woman in the world; her Wanting Song is "A Gown For Each Hour of the Day." In a masterpiece of quick-change subterfuge, Anna got into and out of six superb costumes while dancing through and around a line of showgirls in their Landolff creations.

Add to this trio of innovations a Bells Number—the girls rotated on a platform while shaking their legs to ring their bell anklets—and a roller-skating finale with sixty skaters. Thus, *A Parisian Model,* unlike *Brigadoon, Gypsy,* and *Rags,* was a staging rather than a composition, an *experience.* Unlike those later shows, *A Parisian Model* cannot be revived even as a curiosity, because Ziegfeld and Anna didn't decorate its content. They *were* its content. To look at it from another angle, imagine trying to extend *Gypsy*'s original run by adding in a dance for Ethel Merman with two teddy bears and a song with Merman's new lyrics to a French tune.

A Parisian Model enjoyed a long and confident tryout, doing turn-away business from the first—the certain mark of a performer who commands a lock audience. Ziegfeld himself was still Anna's inferior in the public's perception, but this show in particular won notice for consistency of style from those who notice such things. What Ziegfeld and his cohort had made was very nearly new in form: musical comedy but racier than musical comedy—in fact, a blend of book show and Folies Bergère, the American genre liberated by *volupté*. The Bells Number was just so much rococo, and the teddy bears were surely enchanting. But the girls behind the easels who Might Have Been Nude were very bold, and Anna's onstage costume changes in "A Gown For Each Hour of the Day" verged on indecency. True, the audience didn't see much: but surely the stagehands did. And "La Mattchiche"! That . . . that cocky love dance between two females!

Clearly, *A Parisian Model* was headed for notoriety, and, to Ziegfeld's immense satisfaction, the headlines broke into warp speed even before the New York opening. The occasion was the Jewel Robbery, comparable to the milk baths in terms of PR—and to this day no one knows whether it, too, was a fake. En bref: Anna's satchel containing her life savings of jewelry and money was stolen from the company train on the Baltimore-to-Cleveland leg of the tryout, in late October 1906. By the time the police report was made, journalists were everywhere, quizzing the troupe and chasing the two lead players, tearful Anna and coldly-in-command Ziegfeld.

It was a stunt: so everyone said. But "Our houses are full anyway," Ziegfeld alibied to the press. "We don't have to stoop to such things."

All sorts of false stories were generated on top of the *real* false story. Or was it? The police felt that Anna, at least, was absolutely innocent of any PR finagling; about Ziegfeld they were less certain. The public was enraptured, not least with descriptions of the stolen jewelry, in all sorts of shapes but always marrying diamonds and rubies or sapphires and emeralds—rings, necklaces, a "corsage piece," and Ziegfeld's lucky emblem, an elephant, in pearl with diamond encrustings. "They were rare trinkets," Ziegfeld explained. Yes, indeed.

The case dragged on with a few rather theatrical leads: "a small, ferret-looking sort of an individual" and a gray-haired man had been seen making a sinister exit from the train at the time of the robbery, for instance. But POLICE BAFFLED, the headlines announced.

At least Anna and Ziegfeld got to spend time with his family in Chicago. His parents and siblings don't figure importantly in Ziegfeld's life story, but he was in his own way a loving son, and Anna adored Ziegfeld's francophone mother. Perhaps it made her feel less an orphan to converse in the language she loved with a woman she could address as Maman.

At last, as *A Parisian Model* neared its New York premiere, the jewels were recovered. Or perhaps only some of them were; the newspapers dealt in versions. In one, Ziegfeld, sworn to secrecy, was to take two adjoining rooms in a hotel never to be named. In one room, he was to place a ransom payment. In the other, he was to wait. A door slams, Ziegfeld springs into the hallway . . . no one! He returns to the first room. The money is gone, but the satchel sits there instead. Yes, there is the jewelry. But everything negotiable, from cash to notes, has vanished.

Is it Liane or Anna who states, in Anna's memoirs, that she believed Ziegfeld had conned her for starting money for his next projects? "Une histoire assez suspecte" is how the memoirs describe the adventure in the two hotel rooms. Anna lost, we read, not only money, but "confiance en Flo."

However, *A Parisian Model* had been doing standing-room-only business since it started its tryout. Ziegfeld had to be flush (at least till the next time he gambled). Could this have been a PR scheme that ran awry? Would Ziegfeld have risked losing Anna's jewelry, which—again, depending on the version—was worth between thirty thousand and three hundred thousand dollars? (Anna herself made it twenty-eight thousand, along with thirty thousand in cash.)

At any rate, now Anna had Something To Wear on *A Parisian Model*'s opening night, November 27, 1906. "Clothes and scenery constituted a large part of the performance," one critic groused; everyone else loved it. Some even noted that, indeed, the show appeared to inaugurate a new breed of musical comedy. Anna was "a Lorelei set to music," as one wrote, speaking for almost all. But more: the entire show matched her very being, breath for breath. It was carefree, mischievous, seductive. *A Parisian Model* took a very free look at the human appetite. It was—more than one writer used this word—"insinuating."

"It's the most immoral spectacle ever put on a stage!" So said the Reverend Madison J. Peter. It was "La Mattchiche" that most offended him, with Anna's "contortions and advances toward her partner." This was nothing less than "pandering to the animalized and depraved passions of a sin-slaved public."

How Ziegfeld must have loved that, and how he must have loved Anna then. Fame is the second virtue, but looks are the first, and there is no third. Anna and *A Parisian Model* had finally put Ziegfeld over. He was not yet truly famous outside the thespian community, but his management was top in class. The show ran 179 performances in a theatre the size of an opera house, toured through 1907, and even returned to New York in 1908, for three final weeks.

Best of all, Anna kept on being wonderful, beautiful, compelling. She really did seem to wear a gown for each hour of the day when out in public, and was one of the most painted and photographed of women. She attested to Pozzoni's Medicated Complexion Powder because, as Ziegfeld must have explained, Pozzoni's company would print her homage with a full-color portrait sure to hold the eye.

There had been French stars in America before Anna, but none as well liked till Maurice Chevalier. Even among the more naturally American leading ladies of the time, Anna might share first place but never be overtopped in popularity. Lillian Russell, first of them all, was now in her Later Phase—still important, but dated. Fritzi Scheff, who made a career out of a single role, Fifi in Victor Herbert's *Mlle. Modiste* (1905), was more a singer than a personality. Marie Tempest had given up on musicals in 1900, and Edna May, the first American to thrill London, remained more the West End American than a Broadway fixture. Elsie Janis was a tomboy hoyden, *hors de concours*, and Julia Sanderson and Christie MacDonald came along after Anna, in the 1910s.

There was Marie Cahill, very prominent at this time. But as a tough Irish broad who sopranoed her coon songs and had a lot of problems getting along with colleagues, she seems the opposite of Anna. Perhaps the closest to Anna in overall style was Fay Templeton, American and basic in appeal but a rampaging, sexy kitty when the mood struck her. Still, in the very year of *A Parisian Model*, 1906, Templeton was in George M. Cohan's *Forty-Five Minutes From Broadway* as the Mary with the Grand Old Name and just this side of going nun.

In short, Anna had no superior and, really, no equal. She was at the top and had taken Ziegfeld there with her as a kind of prince consort, walking a few paces behind. If he had indeed created a form of musical, it was one only Anna could use. Sooner or later, Ziegfeld would have to devise an entertainment bigger than a Sandow or an Anna: something starring Florenz Ziegfeld Jr.

And in the summer following *A Parisian Model*'s first season, Ziegfeld discovered the pattern of entertainment that was to make his name as the manager of the age—of all time, even. As always with Ziegfeld, it consisted partly of what others had introduced, what talent scouts and writers threw into his path, and what he himself invented. Altogether, it essentialized the musical's past while creating its future.

So grand. Yet it started simply because Klaw, Erlanger, and Frohman had taken over Oscar Hammerstein's Olympia complex, and Erlanger wanted something dandy for the summer of 1907 to put the roof-garden theatre to use. This was when Ziegfeld officially went into business with the Syndicate, no doubt because they were impressed by his huckster skills, his track record, and his union with the ever more bankable Mademoiselle Held. Erlanger invited Ziegfeld to come up with something suitable, and Anna said to Ziegfeld something like, "Why don't you give them a revue like the ones we love in Paris? Those satires on all the doings of the season? The people? The jokes? It would be so chic, Flo. The Parisians know how to laugh, yes? Americans, they are so afraid to laugh at themselves. You will teach them, Flo, yes? With *compère* and *commère* to narrate and please? And music and girls, Flo, yes? Just as they do in Paris?"

CHAPTER SIX

Ziegfeld's Revue

The "roof garden," popular from the 1890s into the 1920s, anticipated the modern nightclub in its combination of theatre and restaurant, in a quasi open-air setting. In those days before air-conditioning was generally available and noiselessly efficient, most theatres closed in the summer. It was not only because of the warm weather: the stars, well paid for the ten months of the season, wanted the summer months off. With auditoriums dark and producing no revenue, theatre owners sought to attract a public to an alternate space on top of the playhouse structure (usually "open" just enough to let the breeze waft in), serving food and drink and, in the informal atmosphere, offering the lightest of entertainments. There was more often than not a selection of whatever was hot in vaudeville at the moment, but there were also attempts to try something special. The first black show to dare Broadway, a short piece entitled *The Origin of the Cake Walk; or, Clorindy* (1898), played the Casino Roof.

The roof theatre that Oscar Hammerstein set atop the Olympia covered the building to its extremities, topped off with its own roof but open at the sides. There were typical theatre seats in the center, benches at the sides for overflow, and a sort of Dutch village on an upper level at the rear. The whole thing was airy and happy, and Ziegfeld must have hated it. This was the innocent amusement garden that folks like his parents would enjoy, a place of guiltless fun. Ziegfeld liked his pleasure guilty.

When assuming control of the Olympia, the Syndicate had renamed the Music Hall the New York Theatre, so Ziegfeld's venue would be the New York Theatre Roof. That didn't quite suit the show that Ziegfeld had in mind. He redecorated and renamed the place the Jardin de Paris, and asked Harry B. Smith to come up with a script for a topical revue in the manner of the Folies Bergère in Paris; Julian Mitchell, with three colleagues, would direct. Smith admitted to history that the idea for this American *Follies* was Anna's, then added in the aside that Ziegfeld "apparently considered the French revues rather stupid affairs."

Then why do one? Describing with exasperating vagueness the conception of this first entry in a series that would reproduce itself almost annually for over twenty years, Smith mentions that prototypal American revue of 1894 at the Casino, *The Passing Show*; he also mentions Weber and Fields. Perhaps Ziegfeld had in mind the *French* format played in the *American* style. That is: a host and hostess guiding the public through a retrospective of some of the more colorful names and events of the preceding year, in the songs and jokes that Americans would respond to. "Another one of those things in three acts" was the program billing for the new show, as if nobody knew what kind of show it was.

Certainly, nobody knew what kind of score a *Follies* demanded; Ziegfeld simply asked rather a lot of writers for numbers—eighteen different bylines for music and lyrics, counting numbers added during the run. "Music [meaning the songs in this case] by everybody" was the credit line in the program.

The title owed nothing to the Folies Bergère. It was Smith's, from a newspaper column he wrote in his youth in Chicago. "Follies of the Day" it was called; this would be "Follies of the Year." Ziegfeld, extremely superstitious yet partial to the number thirteen, wanted a thirteen-character title, so the new piece was called *Follies of 1907*[1] when it opened at the Jardin de Paris on July 8 of that year.

The *compère* and *commère* were Captain John Smith (David Lewis)

---

[1]There was an English revue tradition as well, dating back to *Under the Clock* (1893). Coincidentally, that title, too, came from a newspaper column, in the London *Times* entertainment listings. Note that Ziegfeld's name was not attached to the *Follies* as yet.

and Pocahontas (Grace LaRue), because the three hundredth anniversary of the Jamestown colony had inspired a fair the previous spring. The show's first set was, indeed, the Jamestown Exposition Grounds, though the itinerary of modern life taken by Smith and his sweetheart took the public to a train station and thence to New York for looks at Enrico Caruso's so-called Monkey House Trial, a parade of Gibson Girls at the beach in bathing attire, the Metropolitan Opera House's *Salome* Controversy, and other points of note in and around New York.

Already, we see how topical *Follies of 1907* really was. Caruso had been arrested on the charge of molesting a woman in the Central Park Zoo the previous November, barely a week before the opening of the tenor's fourth season at the Metropolitan. The case was a sensation, for Caruso was literally the Tenor of the Day and the Met a bastion of the propriety of high art.[1] The Gibson Girl, less sensational but omnipresent in the culture, was artist Charles Dana Gibson's rendering of young all-American womanhood. As for *Salome,* Richard Strauss' opera from Oscar Wilde's play threatened Met propriety even more than Caruso's legal troubles. At least, that was the feeling of the Met's board of directors, which forced general manager Heinrich Conried to cancel the production after a public dress rehearsal and a single performance. Wagnerian soprano Olive Fremstad was the Met's Salome, a fine singer also noted for her acting, and her love scene with the severed head of the Baptist rocked the house. "Strange, inexplicable, complex, psychic" was the report in *The Sun.*

---

[1]It would be an offense to the memory of this greatest of singers to leave the matter there, for Caruso was in fact the victim of a hoax. He was found guilty (and fined only ten dollars), but the accusing woman had vanished, the cop who arrested him was a loudmouthed loon previously charged for making a false affidavit in a comparable case, witness testimony was contradictory, and the deputy police commissioner who pursued the case was forced out of office. A former chief of police called Caruso's arrest "an outrage" and his conviction "based on no evidence at all." When the tenor made his first appearance of the Met season a week later, in *La Bohème,* the audience greeted him with a cheer.

The question asked of Ziegfeld and his cohort was: How to style the commentary on these topics? Weber and Fields Dutch carousing? Something higher in tone? Wit, even? There had been little sustained spoofing of current events thus far in the musical—burlesque's spoof, of course, was limited to literary works or the latest shows. *Follies of 1907*, however, offered not only the themes cited above but versions of President Theodore Roosevelt, Mark Twain, Andrew Carnegie and John D. Rockefeller, and even the professional censor Anthony Comstock.

In the event, everything was turned into musical comedy: a little of every style from low to high, zany to ironic. The Caruso trial showed up as a comedy sketch with crazy operatic interpolations, and the Gibson bathing beauties sang, danced, and paraded around. There was no nudity or even the suggestion of it this early in *Follies* history, and the Gibson girls—in white with men's black ties—showed skin only in bare arms and a slightly low-cut bodice. Given the direction the *Follies* would take in good time, it is almost shocking to realize that this first view of Ziegfeld's Beauties was little more than the chorus line had been showing in burlesque for two generations. Burlesque also popularized sexy drag, and one of the girls was dressed as a man in a white suit with a straw hat.

The number itself was Alfred Solman and Paul West's "The Gibson Bathing Girl." She was tintyped in Annabelle Whitford, distinguished by a black bathing suit without the tie. Although this first *Follies* had no stars when it opened, Whitford was arguably one of the most *seen* young women of the day: she is the girl doing the Butterfly Dance in an early kinescope that was introduced in peep shows, projected onto screens in nickelodeons, and is glimpsed yet today in documentaries on early cinema.

The chorus was billed as "Anna Held Girls," and Ziegfeld, for one, counted fifty of them. Anna herself did not appear because she was still on the road with *A Parisian Model*. Besides, established stars like Anna did not appear in roof shows, especially this modest one, which cost an unusually generous $13,000 but got very little advance attention.

Truth to tell, the closest this *Follies* came to celebrity prominence lay in its heavy complement of impersonated "guest stars." The *Salome* takeoff presented not only those dueling impresarios Hammerstein and Conried but two versions of Salome herself. First, Emma Carus, a belter built like a valkyrie, presented a coon version in "(Come down) Salomy Jane." Then, wearing the same costume as Carus, Mlle. Dazie performed her notion of the Dance of the Seven Veils. This of course accorded with strict opera practice, wherein the singing Salome always made herself scarce while a dancer took over. But Ziegfeld provided an extra treat: a man suddenly ran down the aisle to shout that the cops were raiding the joint, and a squad did indeed heave into view. It turned out that they were part of the show, and immediately joined Mlle. Dazie in a kickline.

Some of my readers may have recognized the name of Emma Carus, famous for having introduced Irving Berlin's first huge hit, "Alexander's Ragtime Band." That lay some years in the future, however, and it may be that Ziegfeld regretted not having invested more heavily in name power, for at some point during the run Nora Bayes was brought in. No attempt was made to integrate Bayes into the doings; she simply came out and sang the kind of things she always sang, such as "Meet Me With Bells and Spangles On."

There was already a certain amount of that "just do it" entertainment in the show anyway. In between the topical commentary was . . . well, anything. So Carus sang the dashing Bowery waltz "Mother's the Boss At Our House" while LaRue sang "I Don't Want an Auto," whose refrain insists, "I think I oughtn't auto any more." And Mlle. Dazie performed her "Doll Dance" and later a "Jiu-Jitsu" pas de deux with one Prince Tokio.

At least, Mitchell kept it all lively, bringing the Anna Held Girls into the aisles at one point, all but unheard of then. And the show did prosper, moving from the roof setting to play two weeks at the Liberty Theatre, a Klaw and Erlanger proscenium house on Forty-Second Street. The New York run totaled 70 performances, followed by two months in

Washington, D.C. and Baltimore, a New York return for a week at the Grand Opera House,[1] then more touring, for a month in Philadelphia.

So *Follies of 1907* was a hit: the kind that doesn't count. It came into being in the summer, when no one is paying attention to Broadway. The show wasn't even reviewed as a Broadway attraction; it was noticed on the vaudeville page. And that's how Ziegfeld's few detractors saw it years later, when the *Follies* got big: vaudeville meeting you with bells and spangles on.

However, right from the start the *Follies* defined how revue breaks with vaudeville: in the concentration of topical humor; in the sophisticated view of man's appetites (because the Met couldn't run *Salome* but the *Follies* could); in an attempt to employ some of the lead players throughout the evening, giving it some unity; in the overall theme (as the Captain and Pocahontas learn what is latest in their land); and, yes, in bells and spangles. Ziegfeld doesn't know what his *Follies* is yet; he has to experiment. As well, he must find more of those exploitable new stars that he loves to spring upon an unsuspecting public: *Follies* stars that he can trademark. He'll need trusted associates wise in scouting talent. He likes the look of things, so he'll need genius designers—and songwriters, of course, more expert than the eighteen ham-and-eggers of *Follies of 1907*. Unfortunately, while Ziegfeld is ready to tune the new music, there are no new musicians. Note that Irving Berlin, the first of the Golden Age songwriters to appear, hasn't even produced "Alexander's Ragtime Band" yet.

Meanwhile, Klaw and Erlanger had their own new star for Ziegfeld to exploit, a Danish blonde named Adeline Genée, who had made a big

---

[1]This amazing playhouse was built in 1868 at a strange address, the northwest corner of Twenty-Third Street and Eighth Avenue. This was woefully off the Broadway track, which centered on Union Square. Opened as Pike's Opera House, it actually did start with opera, but ran through virtually every form of theatre before going over to the movies during the Depression. What amazes is its longevity: it was still "in the business" when it was nearing its hundredth birthday, and wasn't demolished until 1961. Some of my readers may have been inside it: yet when it was inaugurated the Civil War had ended but three years before.

success in England. Genée was a superb mime and dancer, but she couldn't do anything but mime and dance, so Ziegfeld had to figure out how to build a story show around a protagonist who would do little more than look passionate and have a ballet every so often. Such a limited talent would surely have better suited the *Follies,* in the Mlle. Dazie manner. But apparently Klaw and Erlanger wanted a book show; revues were as yet unfamiliar in form, difficult to sell. Besides, *A Parisian Model* proved that Ziegfeld could create a smash out of, one, a European star; two, a big budget; and, three, imagination—though, all through Ziegfeld's life, they underrated the imagination and called it "taste."

Genée's vehicle was called *The Soul Kiss,* billed as "a musical entertainment" because, once again, no one knew what the thing really was. Harry B. Smith wrote the book and lyrics, to the music of Maurice Levi and rather a lot of others, and Smith got his plot angle from a newspaper interview with a spiritual medium. This woman, the inventor of the titular "soul kiss," told of exchanging one "with my affinity in the planet Neptune." At such a time, she said, "I close the doors, throw myself on a couch, my soul goes out from my body to meet him and I experience a billowy ecstasy." Madame gave classes in acquiring the technique: "The complete course of instruction," she warned, "is $300.00." Strange, inexplicable, complex, psychic.

But so far, so good, because at least *The Soul Kiss* has the sound of a sexy show, and Ziegfeld knows how to sell that. Klaw and Erlanger gave him the New York Theatre itself, not the roof, and *The Soul Kiss* opened on January 28, 1908 to play 122 performances, a fine showing. Smith had concocted a fantasy in which J. Lucifer Mephisto (Ralph C. Herz) bets a million dollars that an ingenue (Florence Holbrook) cannot keep her sculptor fiancé (Cecil Lean) faithful for a year. And how can she, when The Dancer (our own Adeline Genée) tempts him with—yes!—the soul kiss!

This must be the most unintegrated musical Ziegfeld ever put on, because just when the story would get interesting, la Genée put her personal spin on it all with a danceretta. She entered very late in Act One, after the title song, to initiate the public in "The Dance of the Soul Kiss."

Later came "Grand Ballabile" (Italian for "ballet"), "Pas de Fascination," and "Danse de Chasse" (for a hunting scene, with real hounds). Then, too, the score had few plot or character numbers. The singing duo Collins and Hart got "A Quiet Sunday in 1920," and Cecil Lean led the men in "Those College Yells." Further, the show found a place for a medley of Harry Lauder songs, though the Scots singer's material hardly suited a tale set in France. Also out of place was an Italian stereotype specialty, "Since My Mariutch Learned the Merry Widow Waltz." And of course there were the Girls, dressed in one number as replicas of Ethel Barrymore, Mary Garden, Maude Adams, Maxine Elliott, "Madame Nazimova," Ethel Jackson (New York's merry widow in the Franz Lehár show, which opened before, played through, and closed after *The Soul Kiss'* entire run), Anna Held, and even George M. Cohan, in drag. "The clothes are so fine," noted *The Times,* "that each girl wears as little as possible, perhaps to keep expenses down and perhaps for other reasons."

The real Anna Held launched her European summer early, because on April 23, 1908 Maximo Carrera died of complications brought on by diabetes. Anna now had to take charge of Liane, fourteen years old and hungry for family, or at least a mother, especially a famous-actress mother. As we know, Liane dreamed of going on the stage herself. Anna had fallen into it out of sheer survival; Liane may have seen it as a way of solidifying the bond with Anna. It in fact created tension between them.

Ziegfeld stayed behind, readying his second *Follies,* which opened on June 15, 1908, again at the Jardin de Paris. And again Harry B. Smith wrote the script, Julian Mitchell led the staging team, and the songs flew out of a cornucopia of writers led by Maurice Levi. This time *compère* and *commère* were Adam and Eve, but Nora Bayes, Mlle. Dazie, Grace LaRue, Annabelle Whitford, and the comic team of Harry Watson Jr. and George Bickel were all held over from 1907.

In fact, *Follies of 1908* was arguably the most cautious piece ever mounted: almost a replica of the first *Follies.* After 1907's Charles Dana Gibson Girl, 1908 offered a number entitled "The Nell Brinkley Girl," Brinkley's drawings of blond charmers being almost as familiar as Gibson's portraits. Annabelle Whitford was again the Girl of the moment, and the inexhaustible Mlle. Dazie again did nothing but dance, peaking in "Danse Harlequinette." Nora Bayes sang more Nora Bayes songs, all by Albert Von Tilzer and Mr. Bayes, Jack Norworth: "Nothing Ever Troubles Me," "Since Mother Was a Girl," and "You Will Have To Sing an Irish Song."

These were the three pillars, one might say, of the vaudeville diva, historically interesting to us because Ziegfeld's popularization of revue would bring more and more of these talents into rotation on Broadway. Pillar Number One was the personal number, the "me" song, which was to permeate popular music on stage and screen as singers used their songbook to create persona—Sophie Tucker, Al Jolson, Bing Crosby, Frank Sinatra, Lena Horne. Pillar Number Two is the cultural commentary, on how times have changed Since Mother Was a Girl. Pillar Number Three is the ethnic stereotype, the only one of this trio to fall out of usage as minorities became humanized as individual personalities. True, that would take a good two generations to accomplish. So the usual *Follies* spoofs treated *The Soul Kiss* and *The Merry Widow*—but note that the latter offered "Merry Widows of All Nations" in versions Spanish, Bowery, "Dutch," Irish, and coon.[1]

Indeed, *Follies of 1908* was so studied a continuation of what *Follies of 1907* began that its only originality lay in the institution of a Big Hit Song, notably lacking in the first *Follies*. The number was "Shine On, Harvest Moon," written and sung by Bayes and Norworth. For some reason, the title became a kind of theme song for the *Follies* as a series, especially in later years when the words *Ziegfeld Follies* became a summoning term for the height of showmanship. Ziegfeld even used "Harvest Moon" nostalgically in the last *Follies* that he himself produced,

---

[1]Everyone must be getting sick of this word, but it was standard usage in the theatre of the day, and to euphemize is to falsify history with candyspeak. Let us instead look forward to the growing racial sensitivity in the 1920s, when, almost overnight, "coon" was retired in favor of the more neutral "Lenox Avenue style," after a Harlem thoroughfare.

twenty-three years after this one. No wonder: it was his first classic. (Anna's numbers, though popular when new, never caught on in the long run.) Oddly, by the time Ziegfeld invoked the spirit of the *Follies* with the old number, a new *Follies* theme song held sway by popular acclaim because it cut more closely to what the *Follies* represented: Irving Berlin's "A Pretty Girl Is Like a Melody."

While *Follies of 1908* outran its predecessor to a total of 120 performances, including moving downstairs for the final weeks into the New York Theatre itself, Ziegfeld joined Anna in Paris. Then they took Liane back with them to America. They had been living for some time in the Ansonia, one of the first of the really big apartment buildings to distinguish Manhattan's Upper West Side, at Broadway between Seventy-Third and Seventy-Fourth Streets. The Ansonia was popular with theatre people and musicians because of its heavy walls, which encouraged late-night partying or practice sessions at the keyboard. Further, the rooms themselves varied in shape from square to circular, and they could be reconfigured to create one's own unique layout. (The building is as popular as ever today.)

Whatever attempts Ziegfeld, Anna, or Liane might have made in creating a family unit, the three were less a family than a bohemian couple with a resentful child in tow. Liane did not want to be Ziegfeld's daughter, and Anna did not want to be Liane's mother. She was not cold or ungiving to the girl—and yet. Liane was, like it or not, an encumbrance, and she did nothing to make an awkward situation bearable. Worse, the press would find out about Liane sooner or later. Ziegfeld could start stories, but even he couldn't stop one, and Liane was a beaut of a story: the Broadway star's guilty secret, pent up in French convents while maman tries on the latest hat.

Actually, Liane was now pent up in an American convent: Miss Comstock's School, top-okay for young ladies of rank. Liane was a day student, but as she got home, Anna was busy preparing to make a public appearance, for in the kind of life Anna had made for herself, an actress is never truly offstage.

Then there was the new show. This one was called *Miss Innocence*, Ziegfeld's joke on Anna's notoriety. This time Anna would play someone more like her daughter, sheltered and unworldly (and, we should note, cut off from her parents), then suddenly brought out into the great world. Harry B. Smith, by now something of a Ziegfeld family retainer, wrote the book and lyrics, to the music of Ludwig Englander. The latter was not up to Ziegfeld standard, a dependable second-rater who was probably recommended by Smith, Englander's most constant partner.

Miss Innocence's fanciful plot began as its heroine, also named Anna, left the School of Innocence on the Isle of Innocence in the Mediterranean Sea. A picaresque, the show took Anna to Paris, to Vienna, into the air *over* Paris, to "A Studio on the Rhine," thence to the "Land of Peach Blossoms." All this wandering around—not to mention the innocence—was a real departure for an Anna Held show. True, the script had its ribald side; critic Channing Pollock griped about "the atmosphere of the Tenderloin." And of course there were the eyes and coon numbers, both interpolations: Egbert Van Alstyne and Harry Williams' "I Wonder What's the Matter With My Eyes" and J. Rosamond Johnson and Bob Cole's "I Have Lost My Little Brown Bear."

Indeed, much of *Miss Innocence* was sung in novelty interpolations. Ragtime had been the rage of musical comedy since just before 1900, and *Miss Innocence* offered Melville J. Gideon and E. Ray Goetz's "Oh! That Yankiana Rag." Anticipating to an extent the New Dance Sensation of the coming decades, the "Yankiana Rag" tells how "Those tunes from Dixieland and Yankeeland" thrill Parisians irresistibly onto the dance floor:

Look up into my eyes, ma belle Cherie,
Soul kiss, and glide with me, my own baby;
Honey bug, throw yourself away,
Whenever the band starts in to play . . .

Note that Goetz combines French with American slang and plugs the title of Ziegfeld's *The Soul Kiss* while Gideon authenticates the music with quotations from the public domain. Like Irving Berlin in "Alexander's Ragtime Band" three years later, with its evocation of bugle call and "Swanee River," Gideon empowers his ditty with a taste of anthem: just before its dance break, the "Yankiana Rag" jumps from "La Marseillaise" to "Yankee Doodle."

Julian Mitchell was directing once again, and dance numbers like this one were his meat. Even so, the Ziegfeldian surprise and delight peaked when Anna and a navy lieutenant (Leo Mars) took a spin in an airplane. The craft resembled a Wright Brothers contraption without a front engine, set above the stage in front of a backdrop of the Paris skyline. "In My Flying Machine" was the number, quickly replaced during the run by the more romantic "We Two in an Aeroplane," another Van Alstyne-Williams contribution.

Miss Innocence opened on November 30, 1908 at the New York Theatre, thus keeping Ziegfeld in the Klaw and Erlanger camp for the fifth consecutive title. "Easily the most elaborate production in which Miss Held has appeared," said *The New York Times,* singling out the "Yankiana Rag" as "particularly snappy." But then, the score was so full of fetching interpolations that all of them were encored on opening night, in the fashion of a day that could hear theatre music as it was meant to be heard only in the theatre during a performance.

"The most elaborate production" is praise indeed, considering how prodigiously Ziegfeld had already been spending on Anna's shows. Besides the scenery, there were the costumes, almost preposterously flattering even for the chorus. As for Anna herself, women stars were supposed to dress to catch the eye, but Mademoiselle's hourglass couture with its "nuns went blind in the sewing" lacy inflections really took the cake. One of her favorite accessories for photo ops at this time was a sable coat made of 110 pelts. The thing was so voluminous that when Anna wore it she looked like the interior of an Indian hunting lodge. So it wasn't a question of simple theatrical illusion anymore: this was a women's hard-on contest. When *Miss Innocence* played Philadelphia, one newspaper headline read ANNA HELD'S 'DIAMOND GOWN' CHALLENGE TO PHILADELPHIA SOCIETY. The article ran a sidebar, FACTS ABOUT DIAMOND GOWN.

These included "Made in Paris," "Designed by Miss Anna Held," and "3,000 diamonds used in its creation."

Anna could afford it. Ziegfeld's gambling was forever ruining him, but Anna was a millionaire, and now that Maximo Carrera was dead she could bank her salary in France without fear of legal attachments or of Ziegfeld's laying claim to it. Indeed, he entreated. If he had to get his backing from Klaw and Erlanger, they would all but ransom the profits. Yet Anna would not give in, and it created a wedge between them. He was her husband second—first, he was a manager. Even this early, when the *Follies* was a little summer thing, Ziegfeld occasionally made visionary statements about wanting to change the look of the musical, purge it of its cute recipes, fill it with sharp sudden swerves into the untasted. Like the protagonist of a Hollywood bio, he was telling people what his life was going to mean.

This seems odd, because most of the time Ziegfeld said little of a personal nature. To Anyone. About Anything. He was the theatre maker as poker player. You don't discuss the hand you're going to play: you play the hand.

Another of the Ziegfeld legends pops up here, telling us that, shortly before *Miss Innocence*'s opening, Anna discovered that she was pregnant and that Ziegfeld imposed upon her a kitchen-table abortion. There's an account of this in Anna's memoirs—but, remember, the angry Liane edited them, amending and, for all we know, inventing as her agenda demanded. She hated Ziegfeld and always sought to blacken his character. Then, too, she may have thought of herself as an abortion-rescue baby, in the way that her mother neglected her: as if it was only Maximo Carrera's intervention that persuaded Anna to bring the child to term.

It is true that Anna could not in any practical way rehearse and open *Miss Innocence* knowing that, sometime during the New York run or the tour, the production would have to be canceled. Stars were not replaced in shows in those days; when a star abandoned a role, the show closed. Even if Ziegfeld would have been willing to replace Anna, who else could play her part? Try to imagine the original staging of *Gypsy* suddenly threatened with the loss of Ethel Merman and someone piping up with, "I hear Benay Venuta's free."

Further, the tale that Anna-Liane tells is like an old show boat melodrama, with Ziegfeld as the Heavy Father. "I kept Liane close to me," we read, "as if her presence protected me against the evil spells that I sensed were all around me." I hear garlic works well, too. Ziegfeld is of course on hand to utter menaces—"exiting stage left," Eve Golden notes, "and all but twirling his mustache."

Every writer hears Liane's fine hand in this episode, because Ziegfeld didn't menace women. Ziegfeld loved women; he loved Anna Held. Had he arranged for an abortion, it would not have been in their apartment, but in the most hygenic surroundings, one of those private hospitals that women of means resorted to, in the Gloria Swanson manner. Further, Anna identified as a Catholic even while living in irreligious independence. She would never have considered an abortion, or submitted to one even under coercion. The Ansonia would have been roused to break down the apartment door if such a thing had occurred.

The union of Ziegfeld and Anna was in trouble, even so. It was probably because of his inability to focus on anything besides his work, but there was as well his constant exercise of the manager's *droit du seigneur*. It exasperates the little woman; but then Ziegfeld's work *was* sex, in a way. It hasn't yet been revealed as such, but he is approaching the point at which his shows function partly as bordellos of the visual. One might almost say they were mounted so Ziegfeld can enjoy the pick of his cast, then show you why he's so happy: isn't she something?

The next one, they all say, really, really was. After a date with her, you were less adroit in the workplace, less attentive at home, and dreaming awake.

About her.

CHAPTER SEVEN

The Wonderful Tart

Miss Innocence, like *A Parisian Model*, was a tremendous hit, lasting 176 extremely well sold performances in New York. On its last night, in May 1909, Abe Erlanger himself took the stage during the curtain calls to bestow upon Anna a gold loving cup in token of the loveliness of her ticket-selling power. One wonders what Oscar Hammerstein thought of this bit of Broadway news, for he not only had a bomb with Ziegfeld and Anna but lost his theatre—and here were Ziegfeld and Anna making a hit on the stage of that very theatre. And for the Syndicate, no less!

After the summer vacation, Ziegfeld reopened *Miss Innocence* in New York, then swept the show off for a tour. It is not unfair to say that Anna had become the biggest musical-comedy star on Broadway. But for how much longer? "I hate to acknowledge that I am near the end," she told an interviewer. "But I must obey Mr. Ziegfeld, and he says that next year is the last."

What? With the public at her feet? With Ziegfeld secure because he has Held and the Syndicate has him? Or did he mean, by chance, that next year is the last of their personal association?

Because Ziegfeld had fallen for a beauty again. Her name was Lillian Lorraine, and like all of Ziegfeld's "special" girls, she was a performer. There was a symmetry in that, because when Ziegfeld fell for you he put you into his next show. Starred you, even. True, starring Lillian Lorraine posed a certain challenge, because her lack of talent was so complete it was almost innovative. She could not make up for it with personal magnetism, because she had the content of a confetti cannon. All that Lillian could command was her looks—but these were of the order that gives a sixteen-year-old from a penniless San Francisco background the confidence to come to New York: because the stage makes a place for the Lillian Lorraines.

It does so, in fact, even when they are destructively unreliable and apt to get involved with enraged loons. When Lillian stays too long at a party, gunfire breaks out. Escort Lillian to Rector's and suddenly a strange mad bull of a man will come charging up out of nowhere to start smashing you in the face. Consider: only three years before Ziegfeld met Lillian at an audition, Harry Thaw shot Stanford White during the second act of another roof show, *Mamzelle Champagne* (1906), over who had power rights to Thaw's wife, Evelyn Nesbit.

Lillian Lorraine was a Nesbit: supremely beautiful jailbait, unworldly yet experienced: Cleopatra as a virgin. Anna Held was, variously, the Doll, Papa's Wife, Miss Innocence: aspects of womanhood. Lillian was one thing only: Miss Heavenly Trash. Sex with her, one imagined, was a cross between rock-a-bye baby and a cage match.

Ziegfeld tested his still vulnerable reputation when he set Lillian on stage. He actually featured her in five editions of the *Follies,* but her inability to fake talent was worse than her simple lack of it. She just didn't belong on a stage: she only looked as if she did. Lillian didn't even get her legend right, goofing up on the first rule of that great American celebrity type, the doomed beauty: Achieve scandal, stay thin, die young. Lillian lived till 1955, the pinup as frump.

First of all, Lillian got two spots in *Miss Innocence*—a number of her own called "My Post Card Girl" (with a girls' chorus to back her up) and an ensemble called "Three Weeks With You." (During the run, the first number was replaced by "Shine On, Harvest Moon" from *Follies of 1908,* possibly because it's an especially easy number to get through.) And while Ziegfeld always insisted that his shows tour with their entire original New York cast, Lillian didn't tour with *Miss Innocence* because Ziegfeld had Plans. He also had no tolerance for unprofessional behavior, so Lillian's approximate sense of responsibility was bound to create tension. It is worth noting that all of the other major women performers whom Ziegfeld promoted affirmed the sense of obligation to the public that was hardwired into the theatre of that age. From Anna Held and Fanny Brice to Billie Burke and Marilyn Miller, the customer was boss not because he was a tyrant. Because he came to see *you*.

Lillian was now to be graduated from *Miss Innocence* and "Follied," in the third edition. Still at the Jardin de Paris, this latest *Follies* unveiled its incarnation of 1909 on June 14, setting the format in stone. It would begin to evolve soon enough, but the 1907 and 1908 *Follies* dictated the format of 1909. Author of book and most of the lyrics: Harry B. Smith. Composer of most of the music: Maurice Levi. Chief director: Julian Mitchell. Singing star with specialty spots: Nora Bayes, for the third time, with husband Jack Norworth at her side, as in 1908. Dancing specialties: Bessie Clayton, Mitchell's wife. Spoof targets: James M. Barrie's *What Every Woman Knows*, a recent Frohman hit at the Empire for Maude Adams, and Oscar Hammerstein's Manhattan Opera Company, with a burlesque of *Lucia di Lammermoor* and Bayes stalking in for "Mad Opera House." *Compère* and *commère*: Greek gods, with Annabelle Whitford as Venus, Mae Murray as Cupid, a Psyche, and three other girls playing Apollo, Cupid, and Adonis in drag. Annabelle Whitford's "cartoon girl" spot: The Christy Girl, later replaced by "The Brinkley Bathing Girls," which combined the seaside attire used in 1907 with the Nell Brinkley reference of 1908. Special Effect Number: "(Going up, up, up, up) Up in My Aeroplane," in which Lillian Lorraine rode out over the audience in the latest in Ziegfeld's line of real-time automation stunts. Gala Production Number: "The Greatest Navy in the World," set against a harbor backdrop with the girls wearing headgear representing battleships. In a blackout stippled with follow spots on the hats, the public saw, in effect, navy cruisers massing on the water, a sensation.

Discovery: Lillian Lorraine, of course. But there was also Sophie Tucker, at this point in her career a blackface singer, well ahead of her days as a mistress of ribaldry and the gender war. Still, the talent spoke freely, and Ziegfeld gave Tucker her chance—but a performer war broke out when Nora Bayes heard Tucker. Bayes threatened to walk if Tucker's exposure wasn't cut back, and Ziegfeld had to comply, for Bayes was his PR insurance.

Tucker was left with a single spot, "Moving Day in Jungle Town." Into an African setting came President Theodore Roosevelt, billed only as "A Mighty Hunter," to surprise those browsing the program before the show began. Kermit Roosevelt accompanied his dad while animals scampered about in confusion. Then the Jungle Queen (Tucker), in blackface, stepped forward for the number.

It's a wild one, a kind of terrorized march. Nat D. Ayer's music and A. Seymour Brown's lyrics are humdrum when not amateurish—and yet. Like so many early *Follies* numbers, the song *as a whole* is wacky fun on a novel subject. The verse, keyed most unusually in the minor, paints a picture of frozen terror:

All the beasts and birds, too scared for words,
Kept very still.
Each one was afraid of this great man,
Who'd come to kill.

But the chorus breaks into panic and ragtime in the major key:

Run, you lions and tigers, run, run, run.
Here comes Teddy with his gun, gun, gun.

Resenting Tucker's success even in that one number, Bayes took both husband and songs out of the show after only a month, leaving Ziegfeld to bring in Eva Tanguay, a singing star as big as Bayes. Tanguay, famously the "I Don't Care Girl" (for her signature song), was in fact more of a treat than Bayes, for the latter performed in a strict stand-and-deliver style while Tanguay threw herself all over the stage, prancing and whirling and crashing to the floor. In any case, Tanguay not only came into the *Follies* with her own tunestack but took over as the Jungle Queen, so Tucker was out of the *Follies* almost as soon as she was in. It was a rare case of Ziegfeld's mishandling a major talent, and though Tucker later became as big as Bayes and Tanguay put together, she never worked for Ziegfeld again.

Although it ran only 64 performances, *Follies of 1909* would appear to be the best *Follies* thus far, because Ziegfeld and his staff were finally working out the technical kinks. Ziegfeld liked his art lavish, as we know, but elaborate sets could take six or seven minutes to set up and another six or seven minutes to strike. The standard solution to that problem was to cover a set change with a solo or duo down front "in one" (that is, before a traveler curtain to hide the stagehands' activity). But how many times in an evening could one so impoverish a *Follies*?

Ziegfeld had in mind a show that kept on turning into something else, sweeping the public into a wild dream with only the intermission as a rest stop. "Let the acts and the stunts and the features follow one another as swiftly as the cars of a train," Ziegfeld said at about this time. That was the energy of the surprise, as when, clapping at the end of a number, you were startled by a new sight: Nora Bayes and Jack Norworth as little kids in a playroom, the set built out of scale to size them down to dainty. Norworth, in a sailor suit and Fauntleroy wig, rode a rocking horse and Bayes, carrying a dolly by one leg, sucked a finger. Their number was "I Wish I Was a Boy and I Wish I Was a Girl," and the moment it ended Ziegfeld wanted you rushed right into the next crazy picture. He filled his shows with talent so he could not merely please but bowl you over with it; recovery periods after each sequence would allow you to catch your balance again. And lest you turn aficionado and revisit the show with the confidence of having collected it already, Ziegfeld would jolt you with new sketches, new songs.

For example, at one point Lillian got a hit song, "By the Light of the Silvery Moon," even easier to sing than "Shine On, Harvest Moon" and one of the few tunes of this age that is still heard today.[1] Like the previous

---

[1]Gus Edwards and Edward Madden wrote "By the Light of the Silvery Moon," but for some reason writers have lately been crediting it to Irving Berlin.

"Moon" number, it's about a couple sparking, as Madden's verse clearly establishes:

Place: park.
Scene: dark.
Silv'ry moon is shining through the trees.
Cast: two.
Me, you.
Sound of kissing floating on the breeze . . .

When the refrain bounces in with the title line, the authors create the perfect hit, simple to pick up and fun to whistle. Ziegfeld must have plugged that one to death, you think? Actually, he dropped it into the show during the run, took it out before closing night, and seems not to have reinserted it for the tour. This was the energy of delight: its elusiveness, its love of teasing. The audience may be the boss of talent, but no one is the boss of Ziegfeld.

Except Abe Erlanger. During *Follies of 1909*'s tryout, at the Apollo on the Boardwalk in Atlantic City, Ziegfeld heard that rival managers Lee Shubert, with his chief of press, and Lew Fields, with his wife, Rose, were in the house. Abe Erlanger was, too, and it was probably he who told Ziegfeld to eject Shubert. The Apollo was a Syndicate house. Syndicate managers didn't enter Shubert houses; what was a Shubert doing in the Apollo? Looking over the talent to steal them out from under us? Throw that Shubert bastard out of the place!

Ziegfeld first sent the Apollo house manager to ask Shubert to leave. He refused, and Fields took Shubert's side. They paid for their tickets, and they're not leaving.

Ziegfeld himself now appeared in the aisle, affirming that Shubert must go. Fields, Ziegfeld said, could remain. Fields averred that the entire party was staying, and by now a Scene was in play in front of the entire orchestra, who were avidly following events.

Two stagehands came down the aisle at this point—sent, we presume, by Erlanger, who must have been enjoying his dream of dreams, watching the whole thing from the usual backstage peephole. And Erlanger won, for Rose Fields became so uncomfortable that Lee Shubert, in a rare courtly gesture, took himself and his press officer out of the Apollo.

"There was a spirited skirmish between the rival theatrical camps . . . tonight" ran the report in *The New York Herald*. Note that the reference to the two sides in the managers' war needed no explaining: every theatregoer knew that the Syndicate and the Shuberts were engaged in a struggle for control of the American stage. We note as well that a New York newspaper was covering Ziegfeld's out-of-town opening: the *Follies* was by now major news.

The immediate consequence of the incident was an intensification of the Shuberts' hatred of Ziegfeld. Well . . . Lee Shubert's hatred of Ziegfeld, for J.J. Shubert hated Lee even more than the Shuberts hated Ziegfeld. The event also created a strange-bedfellows partnership between Erlanger and Joe Weber, for Erlanger decided to feud with Lew Fields, and a tasty deal with Fields' former partner would cook the pie up nice and hot. However, the main reason this story lives on is because historians love to name the Shuberts' press officer: A. Toxen Worm.[1]

That summer, Ziegfeld and Anna ended their attempt to make a family with Liane Carrera. Fifteen years old by then, Liane returned to Europe with Anna to continue her schooling there, though the girl visited Anna in the United States from time to time.

As Anna wound up the *Miss Innocence* tour, Ziegfeld apparently spent the entire 1909–1910 season planning *Follies of 1910*. But this show turned out to be an important document in the evolution of Ziegfeld's art, with the first appearances of genuine *Follies* personalities. Thus far, the *Follies* has run on good-enough talents or stars without any real membership in the *Follies* club, but the year 1910 gives us two players

---

[1] A Dane, Worm was the ideal Shubert employee, viewing the world with the acrimony that also characterized the Messrs. Worm was known as the Great Dane because of his gigantic girth. A bit slimmer and he could have been Victor Herbert's twin.

who were to become genuine ornaments of the office: Fanny Brice and Bert Williams.

Both were comics and singers, but the kind that transcend such literal transcription. They were jesters with an emotional reality: tortured characters somehow or other bearing up, stereotypes universalizing themselves. Both sang coon songs, because the form was still immensely popular, but Brice's forte was the lament of various Jewish girls. True, a French number became her theme song: "My Man," "created," as the French express the first performance, by Mistinguett in *Paris Qui Jazz* at the Casino de Paris, in 1920. Still, Brice seemed more characteristic in "Second Hand Rose" and "Rose of Washington Square," and she eventually assembled a pride of "Rose" numbers. Cole Porter even wrote her a "Hot-House Rose," though Brice never sang it.

Williams, too, excelled in lament, though *his* most characteristic numbers were less about black culture than the difficulties in being human. Consider Williams' theme song, "Nobody," with lyrics by Alex Rogers to Williams' own music:

> *When life seems full of clouds and rain,*
> *And I am filled with naught but pain,*
> *Who soothes my thumping, bumping brain?*
> *Nobody!*[1]

Both Brice and Williams were also adept in situation numbers. Brice's, again, were more consistently ethnic, painting tiny novelettes of

---

[1]Sharp ears will have detected a resemblance to *Chicago*'s "Mr. Cellophane," a deliberate reconstruction of Williams' style. Much of *Chicago*'s score is built on such references; other subjects include Eddie Cantor ("Me and My Baby"), Helen Morgan ("Funny Honey"), Marilyn Miller ("A Little Bit Of Good"), Ted Lewis ("All I Care About"), and Sophie Tucker ("When You're Good To Mama"), all of whom were major Ziegfeld stars or, like Lewis and Tucker, worked for him at some point. Any survey of early-twentieth-century entertainment cannot avoid celebrating Ziegfeld; it is our first warning about how great a shadow he will cast.

working-class life in the "Rose" songs or enthusing at the possibilities on integration into the racier aspects of the national culture, as in "I'm a Vamp From East Broadway." The joke lies in the juxtaposition of the typical Bricean yenta and the latest red, white, and blue fad—politics, the arts, even Pentecostal redemption, in "Soul Saving Sadie (from Avenue A)." It was Brice's performance of yet another Salome takeoff, Irving Berlin's "Sadie Salome, Go Home," in a touring burlesque show that recommended Brice to Ziegfeld (even if he planted stories that he discovered her peddling newspapers). It was that juxtaposition again, Sadie of the neighborhood turned into Richard Strauss' headline diva.

The bad news was that, when Ziegfeld summoned Brice to his office, she had just signed a contract with a minor-league manager. The good news was that precocious Fanny had set her name on a document at the age of seventeen, a year below the legal limit of consent. So she was freed to abandon burlesque for the *Follies*, a very nearly indescribable jump in professional prestige.

Burlesque—I repeat for emphasis—was not lubricious in 1910. Burlesque was cheap. It was going on the stage without leaving the neighborhood; the *Follies* would take Brice to Broadway. Forever after, she loved to tell how excited she was to walk out of Ziegfeld's office right at the center of the Great American Theatre at Forty-Second Street and Broadway, for Ziegfeld was now so close to Klaw and Erlanger that he did business where they did, in the New Amsterdam Theatre building.

Fanny on Broadway! Fanny drunk on the euphoria of success! Wandering through the theatre district, she waved her *Follies* contract like a banner at passersby, banging it around, turning the pages—"Look who's with Ziegfeld! See where it *says?*"—and sharing the news that, indeed, would change her life. Brice stopped friends and strangers alike; she showed off her prize to Irving Berlin five times.

Bert Williams, on the other hand, had already played Broadway, in all-black shows, with his partner, George Walker, and Walker's wife, Ada Overton. But no black had ever had a lead role in a white show like the *Follies*. Racial segregation was strictly observed in the theatre of the early

1900s. A black ensemble might on rare occasions share the stage with a white ensemble; this had occurred in the Harrigan and Hart *Mulligan Guard* shows from 1878 to 1885. But "sharing" consisted of a clear demarcation of space between the races, situated on opposite sides of the stage. Further, black characters in white shows were played by whites in blackface makeup—an overstated look with greasepaint highlighting for comic roles and plain burnt cork for serious roles. This rule apparently held till 1919, when Charles S. Gilpin, soon to be Eugene O'Neill's emperor Jones, played a small part in John Drinkwater's *Abraham Lincoln* in his own color. Even so, the use of blackface persisted into the early 1930s—and, in 1910, a manager who violated the unlegislated racial regulations too provocatively might see his show closed by the police for inciting to riot.

So while Ziegfeld could risk casting Williams, that actor's participation in *Follies of 1910* lay in solo work or taking the stage with men only. Very pointedly, Williams did not appear simultaneously with the women in the show—at least, not in *this* Follies. Indeed, it was reported that Williams had asked for a clause in his contract "protecting" him from having to perform with (white) women; historians have speculated that this was another of Ziegfeld's PR fabrications. There might even have been such a clause—again, for the purposes of PR, it is said. However, isn't it more likely that Ziegfeld's plan was less to get attention than to deflect the wrong kind? Wouldn't Ziegfeld proclaim this contractual segregation in order to still the dark mutterings of reactionaries?

To see how cautious Ziegfeld had to be yet how daring he also was, consider an editorial that ran in the Messrs. Shubert's weekly house organ, *The New York Review,* in 1912, when Williams was fully integrated into the *Follies*:

> *White people even in the north are revolted by the commingling of negro men and white women on the stage. The idea certainly is revolting to self-respecting Caucasians and its continuance will undoubtedly bring widespread discredit upon the theatre. No one is particularly astonished, however, that Ziegfeld is the one manager*

who exploits this condition on Broadway. It is in line with his policy
of going to lengths to [sic] which no others would demean themselves.

So the Shuberts called it sensationalism; it still took guts, and surely some sort of belief that talent created its own regulations. Ziegfeld wanted his beauties classic and his performers original. The Girls were every wonderful girl you ever dreamed of; the stars were new in look and sound, in the way they moved and the things they spoke of. Sandow was German and Anna Held French; now Ziegfeld could bring black and Jewish identities into his mixture. And that is just the word: the *Follies* is going to run on genius crazies who come from places unlike your own.

Again, it's that surprise. The delight lay in the very different shades in the Williams and Brice humor—his wan victory in discerning all mankind's abuse of Nobody, her dizzy role-playing. Ironically, Ziegfeld himself *still* had no sense of humor and let the public's hearty response to these inveigling novelties tell him that they were ideal for the *Follies* mixture.

As the years passed and Williams and Brice became *Follies* regulars, songwriters sought to create for them specialty numbers like the ones the two had already introduced—Brice's "Rose" songs, for instance. Williams tended to commission his own material, much of which, like "Nobody," he collaborated on himself. However, he called on Will E. Skidmore and Renton Tunnah for one of his funniest novelties, "(If you want to spread joy, just) Pray For the Lights To Go Out." The verse starts, "Father was a deacon in a hardshell church," but the holy work of the Baptist congregation blurs into a good old Harlem rent party. The lights fail, and a sister who "felt religion coming on" provides the chorus:

Throwed up both hands and got way back,
Took two steps forward and balled the Jack . . .

This sort of sexual double-meaning, later popularized in the songs of Bessie Smith and early Ethel Waters, runs directly counter to the predicaments of Fanny Brice's characters. They were fanciful, a Becky in the ballet. Williams' people were basic: they come to pray, but at the first opportunity get up and, uh, dance.

Thus, in 1910, the *Follies* begins for the first time to evolve in both form and content. This fourth *Follies* surpassed its predecessors above all in the Williams-Brice energy, so different from what mainstream entertainment was used to that some found it difficult to acquire the taste. Abe Erlanger got there, but he made it the hard way, starting with the dress rehearsal before the Atlantic City tryout, when he ordered Brice to clean up the diction in Joe Jordan and Will Marion Cook's "Lovie Joe."[1]

This tale of a guy from Birmingham who "can do some lovin' and some lovin' sho'" was pure coon song in not only its particulars—Birmingham was a key location in these dialect numbers—but its language: "An' when he starts to love me I jes' hollers 'Mo'!'" After Brice finished, out of the darkness of the auditorium came the voice of Erlanger: "Will you please sing that chorus over and pronounce those words 'sure' and 'more'?"

Why was Erlanger making an issue out of a feature of a genre that had been crowding the stage for a decade? We have the account from Brice herself, in a serial interview in *Cosmopolitan* magazine twenty-six years later, and, as she recalled it, Erlanger was objecting to the dialect because it was vulgar. He wasn't questioning the ersatz quality of the art: he just didn't want it in a Syndicate production till its vulgarity was corrected.

----

[1]The number was published thus but appeared as "Lov*ey* Joe" in the program; such discrepancy is extremely common in these years. Songwriters were not necessarily consulted when the program data was readied for the printer, though their publisher of course deferred to them on the wording of the song sheets. Ironically, these contradictory titles for a single number could be created at exactly the same time, for musicals departing for their first tryout date were ordering the tunestack listing in the program and bringing out their first two or three song sheets simultaneously. This is why so many shows have sold music for numbers that got dropped on the way to New York, from *Lady, Be Good*'s "The Man I Love" to *Do I Hear a Waltz?*'s "Perhaps," and from *Leave It To Jane*'s "Why?" to *The Apple Tree*'s "I'm Lost."

"Where do you think you are," Erlanger went on, and this is a tell: "*in a burlesque show?*"

The italics are mine, because Ziegfeld was in fact bringing the attitudes of burlesque onto the top level of the theatre world—doing, as they would put it in the 1920s, the uptown lowdown. Coon songs were of course not new to Broadway; we've seen Anna Held make them elemental in her songbook. But the Syndicate's *Follies* was supposed to be too "sophisticated" for the degradations of pop. At least, Abe Erlanger thought so. However, Ziegfeld's notion of "sophistication" was the literal one. "Adulterated," says Webster. "Complex." A blend of the available arts.

What truly astonishes us is the confidence that Brice showed in standing up to the man who owned Ziegfeld and the *Follies* combined. Remember, there was no union protecting actors in 1910; one could be fired for anything at any moment, especially for defying the regime of Abraham Lincoln Erlanger. And yet, as—one imagines—the entire house froze in awe, Brice stepped downstage to inform Erlanger that she lived on the edge of Harlem and could swear to the authenticity of the pronunciation. "I can't sing [these numbers] any other way," she told him.

"*You're out!*" Erlanger shouted. "No one says 'No' to me on my stage!"

Ziegfeld could intercede this much: Brice would not be going to New York with the rest of the company, but she could at least play the week in Atlantic City. However, once the curtain rose on Brice, she razed the roof, dialect and all—as, indeed, Ziegfeld might have anticipated—and Erlanger rehired her. In a famous anecdote, when Brice finally gains the wings after a number of encores of "Lovie Joe," Erlanger shows her his battered straw hat.

"See," he says. "I broke this applauding you."

Better than that, "Lovie Joe" was moved up to the first spot for the New York opening, all but admitting that Brice's illuminations on the human condition were just shocking and wonderful enough to start off Ziegfeld's unpredictable *Follies*.

As for Bert Williams' role in *Follies of 1910,* though he would eventually prove one of Ziegfeld's best sketch comics, his debut *Follies* gave him only one speaking bit, in a boxing takeoff as Jack Johnson. Williams' other spots were all vocal solos, such as "I'll Lend You Everything I've Got Except My Wife" and, in a foray into black-attitude commentary, "White Folks Call It Chantecler, But It's Just Plain Chicken To Me."[1]

Ziegfeld was still billing the chorus as "The Anna Held Girls," and in 1910 Anna legitimized this stretch of the imagination by making her sole appearance in a *Follies*: on film. Halley's Comet had just come round again in its seventy-six-year orbit, and, as the *Follies* doted on current events, Anna appeared as a comet and Harry Watson as the earth. It was all over in fifteen seconds. For once, Ziegfeld didn't exploit the event for PR, letting the public receive it as another of those *Follies* surprises.

Lillian Lorraine was in the 1910 *Follies*, too, mainly for "Lillian Lorraine's Swing Song," also entitled "Swing Me High, Swing Me Low," by Victor Hollaender and Ballard MacDonald. Photos of these early *Follies* shows reveal a genuinely antique look, and this bit of Fragonard run amok is an example. A kind of trellis of flowered swings offered a line of eight mounted girls with Lillian at center, her swing perched higher than the others. As the girls sang and propelled themselves into the air, they threw little bouquets into the audience while bells attached to the swings caroled away.

––––––––––

[1]*Chantecler,* a barnyard parable by Edmond Rostand in which the actors are costumed as animals, had its premiere in France, in early 1910. As the latest play by the author of *Cyrano de Bergerac,* the living playwright of choice among many of the greatest European actors from Sarah Bernhardt to Coquelin *aîné, Chantecler* was major news. Coquelin himself was to play the title role, but he died during rehearsals, adding to the play's fame. (Lucien Guitry, father of Sacha, took over.) Now Charles Frohman enters the scene: infatuated with the play, he bought it for his own particular star . . . Maude Adams. The notion of this fairytale enigma bucking and strutting about in rooster costume made *Chantecler* headline matter. As Frohman's brother Daniel put it, "Never, perhaps, in the history of the American stage was the advent of a play so long heralded." Thus, even though *Chantecler* did not play New York till January 23, 1911, *Follies of 1910,* which opened on June 20, could nevertheless assume that its audience had collected all the information necessary to enjoy Ziegfeld's spoof of the Rostand, which turned his "human" comedy into a cockfight.

That was the public Lillian. The private one was living in the Ansonia, kept by Ziegfeld in a flat one floor below Ziegfeld and Anna. This was not a fling with the help, but a full-fledged affair with a demanding and irrational woman who probably guessed that Ziegfeld was no longer in love with Anna. It gave Lillian the rights of an autocrat, and she exercised them. Years later, after Ziegfeld's death, Billie Burke looked back on this episode from the vantage of the official Widow Ziegfeld and the perspective of one of the few human beings who truly knew this impossibly private man. And Billie said, "Of all the girls in Flo's life, I think I was most jealous of Lillian. I believe he loved her."

The last sentence is incomplete. Does Billie mean all his other women were dalliances—that Lillian was the love of his life? Or simply that he loved a number of women, but Lillian the most?

Certainly, Lillian stood out as the one without the stardust. Anna, Billie, and Marilyn Miller were Ziegfeld stars because the public sought out their company. Lillian was a Ziegfeld star because he kept putting her in his shows.

And now she made it into her third *Follies* in a row, *Ziegfeld Follies of 1911*, opening June 26 at its habitual roof venue, the Jardin de Paris. Note the change in title: for the first time, the show was not just the *Follies* but the *Ziegfeld Follies*, his invention. Fanny Brice and Bert Williams returned, comic Leon Errol joined the company, Bessie McCoy took over the lead dancer's spot, and the Dolly Sisters[1] dollied.

The 1911 *Follies* maintained the *Follies* structure. This year, the season's hit shows under irreverent inspection were *The Pink Lady* and a "morality play" with music called *Everywoman*, which modernized the

---

[1]Hungarian to a fault, twins Roszika and Janszieka were possibly the first of the frontline sister acts, a staple of American entertainment in the 1920s, 1930s, and 1940s. Later sister teams primarily worked as close-harmony singers, like the Boswells or the Andrewses, but in earlier decades sisters were charmers who also sang, danced, and made colorful marriages. They were a feature of the *Follies* in particular, right up to the Collette Sisters in the last *Follies* of Ziegfeld's lifetime.

medieval classic *Everyman* and changed the protagonist's gender. As always in theatrophile New York, even those who had skipped *The Pink Lady* and *Everywoman* knew enough about them to enjoy the burlesque, which—in burlesque's time-honored tradition—got a lot of the girls into drag for both spoofs. This proved especially naughty in the takeoff on *The Pink Lady,* a Parisian concoction on the escapades of an unknown thief with a new idea: he steals kisses.

The elaborate "Everywife," billed in the program as "a symbolic play in four scenes," actually made some history. Its mocking of the original's play high-toned allegory was to be expected, with the *Follies* version set in "Yesterday, Today and Always," and characters such as Everyhusband, Rhyme, and Reason. Leon Errol played Drink, and Bert Williams played Nobody, after his signature song. But here is where the history comes in: this was the sketch in which a black man was integrated into the white Broadway musical.

As we've noted, Williams' first *Follies* appearance found him obligingly out of view—a veritable Nobody—when women were on the stage. And Ziegfeld "got away" with his mixed-race casting through this diplomatic nicety. But the whole thing was ridiculous anyway, because whether or not the audience could see Williams on stage with white women, Williams was sharing a theatre's backstage with white women. So what was the public being spared? "Enough!" cried Ziegfeld (we suppose), and "Everywife" definitively placed Williams on stage in the company of Ziegfeld Girls. From then on, Williams was a full-fledged member of the *Follies* ensemble—which led to, among other ineffective complaints, the Shubert brothers' attack previously quoted.

As for the *Follies'* inevitable New Dance Sensation, that spot introduced "The Texas Tommy Swing," and the expected sequence drawn from the world of the cartoon artist was modeled on Tad Dorgan's Daffydils, a Sunday-page collection of loony puns and rebuses. Jerome Kern worked for Ziegfeld for the first time in this sketch, to the words of Bessie McCoy herself, "I'm a Crazy Daffydil," the confessions of a high-energy scatterbrain:

If a story's read, is a whistle blew?
Warden, quick! Cell Thirty-two!
I'm a crazy daffydil.

Irving Berlin returned from *Follies of 1910,* giving Brice "Ephraham Played Upon the Piano" and Williams "Woodman, Woodman, Spare That Tree!"—both collaborations with Vincent Bryan.

By far the major event of *Ziegfeld Follies of 1911* was a sketch for Williams and Errol that went over so well that the two improvised business and new lines till the scene lasted—if the house proved appreciative—for twenty minutes. In a set representing the construction site of the new Grand Central Terminal, Williams played a redcap and Errol a commuter who for some reason is circumnavigating the very heights of the ironworkers' girders high over the New York skyline. Signs read "160 foot drop" and even "288 foot drop," and Williams keeps dropping then retrieving (by rope) the hapless Errol. All along the way, the pair indulge in vacuous conversation, as when Williams explains that he gave his three children Bible names: Hannah, Samuel, and Iwilla.

> ERROL: Iwilla? I don't remember that name in the Bible.
> WILLIAMS: Sure 'tis. Don't you 'member where it say, "Iwilla, rise"?

At length, Errol takes his most drastic fall yet, but a dynamite explosion on the site hurls him skyward as Williams looks on:

> WILLIAMS: There he goes, now he's near the Metropolitan Tower. If he kin only grab that little gold ball on the top . . . 'Um, he muffed it.

Blackout.

As to why Ziegfeld's name was finally set into the title with that magical word *Follies* in 1911: he was becoming too useful to the Klaw and Erlanger concern to be treated with condescension. There is evidence, for example, that one reason why *The Pink Lady* was such a smash was that Ziegfeld applied his Touch. It makes sense, for *The Pink Lady* was rather like the shows that Ziegfeld had put on for Anna. True, the new show's score, by Ivan Caryll and C. M. S. McLellan, was far more integrated than the Held scores; the authors even wrote their own interpolation, "By the Saskatchewan," when a catchy, irrelevant tune was called for. Still, the Parisian setting and the interaction of the *monde* with the *demimonde* gave the show a Ziegfeld-and-Anna feel. Of course, Klaw and Erlanger would invite Ziegfeld's participation; of course, he would accept. *The Pink Lady* enchanted buffs of the romantic-comic musical just as *The Merry Widow* had, and while Klaw and Erlanger gave Ziegfeld no name billing on *The Pink Lady*, they had to give him something: the words *Ziegfeld Follies* at last.

For all that, though still technically a roof show, the *Follies* had become too prominent for the outdoors. This much Ziegfeld had done for the revue as a genre: it was no longer vaudeville by other means but A Real Musical. After one more year, the *Follies* would open in a proscenium house. One year after that, it was to play the New Amsterdam, the most prestigious booking in the American theatre.

Anyway, hadn't Ziegfeld given the Syndicate prestige, in his own way? All Broadway knew that those pesky Shuberts had been principally (though silently) involved in the launching of the New Theatre, Broadway's first repertory company, with gala names and concepts—E. H. Sothern and Julia Marlowe in Shakespeare, Marie Tempest in *Vanity Fair*, Maurice Maeterlinck, John Galsworthy, Arthur Wing Pinero, even a play about Beethoven with complete musical illustration. True, the whole thing went crash after two seasons, but it was undeniably classy— the one thing that, according to Abe Erlanger, the Shuberts weren't supposed to be. The *Follies* didn't have Sothern and Marlowe or Beethoven, but it was successful—and, for all its edgy eros, it had a corner on class. "Ziegfeld has exquisite taste" would become a cliché (even if a lot of his comedy was low). But what Ziegfeld really had was an air of worldliness in his mixture, an awareness of intelligent things. One had to be up on the doings of the great world to follow the jests of the *Follies*; everyone knew about Halley's Comet, but not everyone could place *The Pink Lady* or *Everywoman*. And while Ziegfeld came to feel that his book shows should appeal to the widest audience possible, the *Follies* was always to be something of an elite item. The riffraff might buy tickets, but it didn't necessarily have access.

As Anna was still touring *Miss Innocence* in the 1911–1912 season, Ziegfeld readied musicals for other performers for 1912. Eddie Foy headlined in *Over the River* in a co-production with Charles Dillingham; Lillian was in this one, too. Returning to the work of Charles Hoyt, the author of Ziegfeld's first Broadway show, Ziegfeld by himself put on *A Winsome Widow*, based on Hoyt's *A Trip To Chinatown*. This already was a "sort of" musical, another of those farces-with-songs, one of which was "After the Ball." *A Winsome Widow*, however, was a *Ziegfeld* musical, stuffed with just about everything *but* "After the Ball." The gigantic cast included Leon Errol, the Dolly Sisters, and Mae West; the chorus girls played "Bowery Boys," "Troubadors," and "Hockey Boys"; and the finale featured ice-skating on real ice. *A Winsome Widow* had as well Frank Tinney, a blackface comic notorious for the at times dangerous quality of his improvisations. On opening night, during Tinney's monologue, two women got up to leave, and Tinney indicated them with "There goes the sewing circle," drawing upon himself *grrr*s of disapproval from the audience.

Over the River and *A Winsome Widow* were both hits—the *Widow* was a smash—but all was not well at the Ansonia. *Miss Innocence* had finally closed for good, and Anna, back from the tour, now had to deal with the elephant in the apartment one floor below: Lillian. On the other hand, one could always count on Lillian to seize the opportunity to screw up a good thing, and in March 1912 she evaporated from *Over the River* to elope with one Frederick Gresheimer. Why? Well, in the style of entertainment-world news that titillates rather than informs—a style that Ziegfeld invented, Walter Winchell popularized, and is now threaded into the fabric of American culture—Lillian told all to reporters. It seems that she was on the beach at Atlantic City the summer before, and Gresheimer "was in his bathing suit and looked perfectly grand." Gresheimer offered to teach Lillian how to swim, and "in five minutes he had me paddling around like a little tadpole."

That sounds like a double-meaning laugh in a *Follies* sketch. Gresheimer turned out to be already married, but even after ironing out that kink he turned out to be one of those Jealous Husbands: the kind that attacks Ziegfeld physically when Gresheimer spots Lillian and Ziegfeld having dinner in one of the Times Square lobster palaces. And *that* sounds like something out of Weber and Fields.

A heterosexual male with a powerful libido can delight in a woman, as Ziegfeld did Anna Held. He can love a woman, as Ziegfeld did Billie Burke. He can make a woman the star of the age, as Ziegfeld did Marilyn Miller. But he can also get so damn-it-to-heck hot for a woman that he'll risk everything for a date, and that was Ziegfeld's relationship with Lillian Lorraine.

So, on April 14, 1912, Anna served Ziegfeld with divorce papers, naming Lillian as co-respondent. And that is real life.

CHAPTER EIGHT

The Wife

There was one problem: Ziegfeld and Anna had never married. That soirée at the Netherland Hotel in 1897, when the couple announced that they were Mr. and Mrs. Ziegfeld, was simply an efficient way of eliminating questions about their legal status. They didn't want to marry and they didn't want to be haunted by Talk, so they balled up the mystery and batted it away. After all, they *were* Mr. and Mrs. Ziegfeld, in their own fashion, and by 1912 they were married by common law. That slowed up the divorce proceedings by a few months, but on January 9, 1913 Anna Held was unmarried legally, culturally, and professionally.

Was she really headed for retirement, as she had earlier claimed? Anna was a headliner at her height, and managers vied to sign her. She would have been out of place in the new style of urban American dance musical comedies that clustered around the prototype revealed in Irving Berlin's *Watch Your Step* (1914). But Anna was perfect for the soft-grained yet sexy "European" musicals following *The Merry Widow*, especially adaptations from French comedies such as *The Pink Lady*. *Oh! Oh! Delphine* (1912), by *The Pink Lady*'s aforementioned Caryll and McLellan, was the smash of its season just as *The Pink Lady* had been of its. Note that *Delphine* had a female lead that cried out for Anna: the wife of an obsessively jealous husband whose pet parrot squawks "Oh! Oh! Delphine!" whenever Delphine thinks of another man. The look of crazed suspicion on the husband's face as the bird told on Delphine was just the sort of wacky audience-pleaser that Ziegfeld emphasized when Charles A. Bigelow was cutting up in Anna's shows; and the setting, a high-style resort where Brittany meets the sea, was ideal Anna territory.

Yet it was as if Anna had divorced the theatre and Ziegfeld together. Along Broadway, folks generally sensed that Ziegfeld had grown restless and that Anna could not function without him. Still, she put her typical Parisian face on it all, *blasée, cocasse.* "It is quite lovely being single," she told one of her favorite and most supportive critics, Alan Dale. "I don't want any more marriage—yet." As for Ziegfeld, "I am sorry for him. He is so used to managing me."

And yet, as the uninformed observer saw it, Ziegfeld and Anna were enjoying a gay divorce, for the two were constantly seen about, he so intent on her that, some swore, he was courting as if they had just met. It must have been a deep alliance, for right at this time Anna haled Ziegfeld into legal session in the matter of a $3,000 debt, and she won, and it didn't slow up the postmarital waltz by so much as a measure. Could it be that divorce did not matter to them because marriage hadn't mattered—that these two were simply beyond the constraint of convention? Had destiny not issued the summons that makes lives into legends, Ziegfeld would have been running the Chicago Musical College and Anna would have been the Widow Carrera. But then, the art that changes art is not made by the adherents of convention.

Whatever Anna was to do with her career, Ziegfeld at least was thriving as he curated his revue. Modern theatregoers prefer the book show as a form, but Ziegfeld flourished in revue because of its amorphous nature. Book shows had to perform certain tasks at certain times, such as updating the love plot. What if there was no top-drawer love song handy? Revues, on the other hand, could do anything they wanted.

As he readied his sixth consecutive *Follies,* strengthening his position with Klaw and Erlanger, Ziegfeld moved permanently from the roof to the parquet. Still in the former Olympia building, Ziegfeld took over its second-biggest proscenium house, the Music Hall, renamed the Moulin Rouge for *A Winsome Widow.* It was there that *Ziegfeld Follies of 1912* opened, on October 21. The autumn opening seemed to announce that the *Follies* could no longer be thought of, in the parlance of the day, as "one of those warm-weather things."[1]

Interestingly, just when Ziegfeld might have dug into the rut of success, he was tinkering. The 1912 *Follies* began with a shock all the more electric because it occurred not in the informality of a roof space but in a "real" theatre: some of the ticket buyers suddenly got up to fight with each other about what sort of show they wanted to see. They were *Follies* cast members, of course—but one realized that only after the first few anxious moments. Opera buffs may recall Syergyey Prokofyef's *The Love For Three Oranges,* which begins much the same way. However, in that work the disputants are on stage and singing to the conductor's beat, unmistakably part of the composition. In the 1912 *Follies,* the arguments simply sprang up out of nowhere with real bite to them, perfect faux-naturalism. And note that Prokofyef's opera wasn't premiered till 1921, nine years after this *Follies.*

It was a good one; they were all good at this time. Bert Williams and Leon Errol led the drolls; their big sketch this year found Williams as a cabbie and Errol a rider, the horse played by the usual two men doing loony things with their legs. The hit tune was "(And then he'd) Row, Row, Row," given to Lillian Lorraine. She also got "Daddy's Got a Sweetheart and Mother Is Her Name," an odd choice for the real-life vamp who had only just broken up Daddy's marriage. The number introduces a crucial breakaway in *Follies* style in its authors, composer Dave Stamper and lyricist Gene Buck. Still in their twenties, they would renovate *Follies* song style, contributing more numbers to the series than any other team, right to Ziegfeld's last entry, in 1931. Also, Buck in particular would prove invaluable, with a view of the musical that comprehended

---

[1]This thinking lasted for a single season only, as June really was ideal *Follies* time. With Broadway slowing up at season's end, Ziegfeld could seize a monopoly on PR. Then, too, he could draw the attention of the "crust" just before they set off on their vacations: a last night out in their finery before Europe and the resorts. This gave the *Follies* tremendous cachet as "society's favorite show," and so on—an important boost to the reputation Ziegfeld intended to make for himself, as we'll see.

Ziegfeld's vision. Buck could thus scout for new talent of the Ziegfeld kind: not just gifted performers but those who suited Ziegfeld's unusual taste.

At the same time, Ziegfeld lost his book writer, Harry B. Smith. Finally tiring of the endless waits in Ziegfeld's outer office trying to collect the royalty checks he was owed, Smith made himself unavailable for future Ziegfeld assignments. It was a momentous break: Smith was Ziegfeld's outstanding link to his past in not only the first *Follies* and Anna's shows but in their shared Chicago background. Yet Ziegfeld may have found it useful to allow Smith his liberty, for Smith was of an older Broadway and Ziegfeld was creating a newer one. Smith went blithely on in countless jobs, but he insistently favored the old style of comic opera and its descendant, operetta, and after parting company with Ziegfeld he made precious little history.

Lillian Lorraine departed the Ziegfeld outfit as well. She didn't quit, and it wasn't Ziegfeld who fired her: it was good old Abe Erlanger. Lillian's habit of showing up late for rehearsals for the new numbers that were constantly being slipped into the *Follies* finally led Erlanger to override Ziegfeld once more. However, Lillian was no Fanny Brice, and she stayed fired. No one knows exactly when Ziegfeld and Lillian ended their affair. But her life and career now took her to other places—vaudeville, for instance, where she had a huge hit with "Daddy Has a Sweetheart." She even made a return to the *Follies,* in 1918. It was not a perfunctory appearance; Lillian was featured in many numbers. Her tour de force was a duet with Will Rogers, "Any Old Time At All," staged as a dressy bit to play shy cowboy Will against pert glad-rag doll Lillian. Still, the year 1912 marked the end of Lillian's importance in Ziegfeld's offstage life.

Ziegfeld Follies of 1913 reclaimed the end-of-season opening, on June 16. More important, this *Follies* gave Ziegfeld an outstanding promotion, from the Moulin Rouge to the greatest playhouse on Broadway, the New Amsterdam Theatre: so Ziegfeld's siding with the Syndicate against the Shuberts had paid off in rare coin. Even so, that managers' war now felt as irrelevant as stereopticon slides as the theatre expanded and evolved beyond the grasp of even the most powerful combine. Indeed, old-timers had to run to keep up with the newcomers these days.

But Ziegfeld's personal headache had returned, in the form of Liane Carrera. Anna brought her daughter back from Europe after the summer of 1913 to the usual pyrotechnics as the *France* docked in New York Harbor under what must have seemed like the personal supervision of Anna's new manager, John Cort. There was a fabulous floral display; clucking and freaking as Anna's zoo of tiny dogs careered down the gangplank; reporters, photographers, and process servers; and dear little Liane telling everyone in sight that she, too, was going on the stage. "Aren't the flowers beautiful?" she added. "Mama paid a fortune for them, because she's a star and a star must appear to be loved." All right, Liane didn't use those exact words, but she was turning into a professional pain in the neck even to the people she liked. Imagine a picnic. Anna packs the sandwiches. Ziegfeld orders the pastries. Liane invites the ants.

Now to a great event of 1913 that vastly affected several lives important to us: the New Year's party at the Sixty Club, in the Hotel Astor. Three of Ziegfeld's four great loves were there, although the first two, Anna and Lillian, were cut to one when Lillian picked a quarrel with Ziegfeld early on and went stomping off somewhere. Marilyn Miller, just fifteen, was too young to have attended, though in some six months she was to make her Broadway debut as a Shubert star. Billie Burke came in late, on the arm of W. Somerset Maugham, in whose play *The Land of Promise* she had opened a week before, on Christmas Day.

This was a costume party, and Ziegfeld had arrived earlier in his standard goofy getup, a tramp costume given him by *Follies* comic Harry Watson Jr. That much of a concession to the evening's masquerade Ziegfeld was willing to make—but, he thought, silly outfits belonged on actors, not managers. So, at some point, Ziegfeld found an opportunity to slip off to change into tails, making quite a contrast to the pastel colors of everyone else's fantasy dressup. Anna, for instance, had come as the Empress Josephine.

As Billie recalled it, she and Maugham joined the swirling revelry at about two o'clock on the morning of January 1, 1914. They took their gala time parading down the ballroom's grand stairway, and suddenly Billie noticed a man staring at her from the floor.

"He had a Mephistofelean look," she later recalled. "He was slim and tall and immaculate" but also shameless in his attention. Whether by accident or design, Maugham did not say hello or introduce him to Billie; the two men must have met, but they moved in very different circles.

Now for a theatrical twist, as Ziegfeld "produces" his first night with Billie Burke. These theatrical parties often fall under the control of some bon vivant who wants everyone having a good time on his terms only—you know the sort, who takes over the floor to call out the Rules of the Dance like some eighteenth-century fop in a wig with a big bonking stick. "Ladies' choice!" they gleefully carol. Or "Castle Walk!" This evening, the selected number was the Paul Jones.

This was a sort of "change partners" walkaround, the men in an outer ring moving clockwise and the women inside moving in the opposite direction. At the sound of a whistle, you had to stop and partner up with whoever was next to you. Somehow, every blow of the whistle found Billie with her "Mephistofelean" admirer. (He had bribed the bandleader, of course.) Billie admitted that, all at once, she found herself "desperately and foolishly falling in love with this strange man" as the two of them danced a string of Paul Joneses together.

It was growing dangerously late on a school night—New Year's Day commonly found theatres giving special holiday matinées—and Billie's manager, Charles Frohman, had sent a minder to keep his vivacious young star in harness. Frohman's deputy was Victor Kiraly, who kept pointing to his watch and singing out, "Matinée tomorrow! Matinée tomorrow!" Yet Billie danced on with her new beau—who was, by the way, noted for his stepping. She still had no idea who he was. Then someone passed them and called out, "Why, hello, Flo."

Billie didn't include it in her recollections, but she must have done a take. Incredibly enough, she had been a major Broadway name—and a

Syndicate star, at that—for six years without ever meeting Florenz Ziegfeld Jr. Every so often today, one hears someone or other imagining Ziegfeld as a heavily accented European, barking out directions in Kantian sentence structure full of word mix-ups. Back then, that someone was Billie. She had always connected the name Ziegfeld with the picture of "a dour man with a beard."

Now everything fell into place. The dark beauty costumed as Napoleon's *belle amie* who was stalking Ziegfeld and Billie with "enormous jealous eyes" must be Anna Held. And Ziegfeld himself was . . . well, perilous! He was "*cavalier* about women," as Billie had often been told. But she was smitten, that fast: "Even if I had known then precisely what tortures and frustrations were in store for me during the next eighteen years because of this man, I should have kept right on falling in love."

Unlike Ziegfeld's other three principal loves, Billie is very familiar to us today. Anna Held and Lillian Lorraine left nothing behind, and Marilyn Miller's three films are not known to most viewers. But Billie made many movies in the 1930s, including a few prominent ones as well as the title that all Americans are raised on, *The Wizard of Oz.*

Unfortunately, these films disguise the Billie who fell in love with Ziegfeld on New Year's Eve in the Astor Hotel ballroom, for she had two distinct and even contradictory careers. Billie of the movies is a sharp comedienne playing a prattling human doily, usually a society scatterbrain. However, Billie the Charles Frohman star was someone else entirely—younger, obviously, but keen, bold, and vivacious in a red-hair-and-blue-eyes coloring.

Performing ran in her blood. Her father, William E. Burke, was a circus clown, and, though American, Mary William Ethelbert Appleton Burke was raised in England because her father played Europe. It was Billie's mother, Blanche, who put her on the stage.

"She doesn't want to," said her father. "She hates it, she is shy and retiring, you will ruin her." That was the dialogue as Billie remembered it. She herself didn't really have an opinion about going on the stage, even after seeing Sir Henry Irving and Ellen Terry in Sardou's *Robespierre* at the Lyceum in 1899. This was normally a benchmark experience in the life of a girl with a creative destiny ahead of her, datum for many an interview in later years. But Billie was unmoved. Undeterred, Blanche arranged for Billie's debut in a music hall in Birkenhead, doing imitations and the usual coon songs.

"Let's 'ave it a little louder, dearie!" someone called out.

No matter: the same thing, more or less, happened to Ethel Barrymore on her debut. Blanche Burke clearly knew something that others didn't about her daughter's potential, for she got Billie to the West End in a musical called *The School Girl* (1903). This was a major event: co-produced by George Edwardes and Charles Frohman and starring Edna May and Marie Studholme. Best of all, its music was the work of Leslie Stuart, composer of the biggest hit of the day, *Florodora* (1899).

True, the eighteen-year-old Billie had a smallish role, that of Mamie Reckfeller. But she got to lead an ensemble number, "My Little Canoe," one of many attempts by Stuart and others to crack a knockoff of *Florodora*'s Sextet, "Tell Me, Pretty Maiden." Technically one of those ubiquitous coon songs, in dialect, "My Little Canoe" starts with a strolling vamp like the Sextet's, and it moves from one melodic cell to another, ever changing key, in the Sextet's manner. Billie was in charge of the verse, as the girls and then the boys made reply over a barcarolling orchestra:

BILLIE: Mamie, if you've nothin' else to do,
Ma Mamie girl,
I'm goin' to give an invitation
GIRLS: For to come along o' me
BOYS: In my little canoe . . .

At the refrain, syncopated for that touch of ragtime, everyone mimed paddling down a river:

Mamie, I've a little canoe.
Room for me, my Mamie, and you.

. . .

And when I've told my worries to you,
Then we might canoodle, Mamie, we two.

Billie had to rehearse it in secret and did not perform it full out till the dress rehearsal: because May or Studholme would likely have claimed it for themselves. Indeed, they tried to, even that late in production. The managers held fast, however, no doubt pointing out to Edna May that at least Marie Studholme wasn't singing it and vice versa. (May won out in the end, for she took *The School Girl* to New York, where "My Little Canoe" became Edna May's big number, and that's *that*.)

At the show's London opening, "My Little Canoe" enjoyed a sensation, and Billie was made. It could happen like that in those days. She continued to work in England, but now that she had come to Charles Frohman's attention, she was ineluctably bound for Broadway, for Billie was Frohman's favorite kind of performer: a classy young woman. Frohman duly brought her over, in 1907, to play opposite John Drew at the Empire in *My Wife,* and it was a running joke in the Ziegfeld household that Ziegfeld had seen her in it in the company of Charles Dillingham and that the two discussed how much more a really driving manager might make of her. Ziegfeld made no move to steal Billie from Frohman, however, because Ziegfeld was enmeshed in the Klaw and Erlanger side of the Syndicate, of which Frohman was a fully protected officer. Erlanger would never have allowed it.

We may be certain that Victor Kiraly told Frohman that Billie spent New Year's Eve in rapturous dancing mode with Ziegfeld, and Frohman must have hit the ceiling. He didn't like his ingénue stars to marry, and, more than that, Charles Frohman hated Florenz Ziegfeld Jr. *Hated* him. Frohman despised the kind of shows Ziegfeld put on, with all that Anna Held froufrou and the sex craziness. Frohman didn't enjoy surprise and delight: there was too much jagged and unpredictable in it. Too much adventure. Frohman liked creamy theatre, rich, thick, and settled. Frohman's theatre was your theatre. Ziegfeld's theatre was *his* theatre, teaching you new ways to be entertained.

Besides, doesn't Ziegfeld eat young actresses for dinner? Even the Shuberts don't riot around so.

Courting Billie, Ziegfeld invested in the usual flowers and candy, but on the Ziegfeldian level. The flowers, for instance, "were delicately and smartly boxed in a cone shape," Billie later reported, "and they formed a tiny Colonial bouquet, showing the utmost taste and care in their selection."

Wow. Try to resist a man who knows not only flowers but Colonial bouquets. Predictably, Ziegfeld made no attempt to get Frohman on his side. In fact, he made no attempt to get Billie on his side: he worked on Mama. And Blanche Burke loved Ziegfeld. He was the first of Billie's beaux to win her approval.

There was this as well: Ziegfeld was a manager who, though successful, was still going places, full of talk of the things he would make the theatre do. Frohman was the most successful manager in the business, but Frohman was fat and happy and going nowhere. Billie enjoyed being a Frohman star, but she nourished ambitions, and Blanche made it clear that it was Ziegfeld who could fulfill them.

For his part, Frohman warned Billie not to entertain the gallantry of this most dangerous of men. In his characteristic telegram speech pattern, Frohman gave Billie her options: "That Ziegfeld. No good. No good at all, Billie. No Ziegfeld. Or no Frohman. Billie chooses. American theatre is looking on, my dear."

Billie chose Ziegfeld. "Something weakened within me every time he proposed," she said. So at first, it seems, she was resisting. Nevertheless, "desperate and unlikely things are almost certain to take precedence over judgment and caution." Then, putting it philosophically but also with almost poetic simplicity, Billie says, "It does not matter that you think things through with the utmost logic. . . . Possibly this is a provision of Nature in the make-up of women. A time comes. They fall in love. I fell in love with Flo Ziegfeld."

Frohman's final contribution to this controversy was to observe, most inaccurately, that Ziegfeld couldn't produce worth a damn.

Ziegfeld's reply was "Did you ever see Frohman eat oysters?"

Before Billie could make the fatal step of marrying Ziegfeld, Frohman paid a visit to Burkely Crest. With him was Alf Hayman, by then Frohman's right-hand man (again: not Alf's older brother, Al, who backed theatre but didn't participate in managing actresses). Blanche called Billie with "I think there are two detectives downstairs. Named Frohman and Hayman."

When Billie came in, the men behaved like a pair of Shuberts, pushing and controlling.

"He is still in love with [Lillian] Lorraine," said Alf Hayman.

"He still sees Anna Held," said Frohman.

Billie stood up to them. She later recalled the scene taking place in the sunroom of the great house, in which a dozen birds in cages overlooked a billiards table. The two men toying with the billiard balls, whirling them along the table. The cockatoos and parrots cawing their warnings.

"Both these women live at the same hotel," Hayman told Billie, referring to conditions at the Ansonia, where Ziegfeld had virtually stacked Anna on top of Lillian as Don Juan schedules a double feature on Saturday night. "With the birds screeching and those balls knocking against the table," says Billie, "I defended Flo and I defended myself."

Their cautions about Ziegfeld's liberal love life unavailing, the two men played what they hoped was their ace: Frohman really would act upon his threat to drop Billie from his roster if she married Ziegfeld. In fact, Frohman didn't only object to Billie's choice of husband; Frohman objected to husbands, period. Frohman liked maidens, because Frohman's art was the opposite of Ziegfeld's. Frohman preferred straight plays to musicals, light rather than broad comedy, and characters who were fond rather than appetitive. No wonder his favorite play was *Peter Pan*.

Frohman and Hayman's threat at once confused Billie and meant nothing to her. She was not under their control in the matter of romance—but was this true romance or a show-biz fantasy? As women of that day sometimes did, Billie decided to test Ziegfeld: she would give him a Final Good-bye and see what happened.

And that's when gambler Flo played his ace. "Let's talk to your mother," he suggested.

That sewed it up tight. Blanche Burke was sick of Frohman and a little in love with Ziegfeld herself. Moreover, Billie had been married to her career long enough.

"I think Flo will be a wonderful husband," Blanche told her daughter, "and I think you will be a very happy girl."

Ziegfeld and Billie decided to elope—not behind Blanche's back, but behind Frohman's. Billie was playing the title role of Frohman's latest production, Catherine Chisholm Cushing's *Jerry*. It was two weeks into the run, a Saturday; Blanche picked Billie up at the Lyceum Theatre after the matinée to escort her to the meeting place, Sherry's Restaurant. Billie was in such an emotional uproar—because nice girls didn't elope and Frohman girls, remember, didn't marry at all—that she tried to back out at the last minute. However, she was unable to reach Ziegfeld to cancel, because he had smartly foreseen all hazards and kept himself incommunicado. He had counted on Billie's good old-fashioned upbringing: nice girls keep appointments they can't cancel.

Some sources tell us that Ziegfeld's parents were in the wedding party; this is not so. Ziegfeld, Billie, and her mother comprised the group that crossed the Hudson to Hoboken. The ceremony was lightened by the parson, who was confused by both communicants' names. Thus:

"Ethelbert," he asked Ziegfeld, "do you take this woman to be your wife?"

"I do," said Billie.

Parson much confused. But going on:

"Florence," he said, turning to Billie, "do you take this man to be your husband?"

"I do," said Ziegfeld.

"Say who?" asked the parson—or words to that effect.

Some newlyweds cruise the Atlantic or float along Venice's Grand Canal. Ziegfeld and Billie (and Blanche) took the ferry back to Manhattan; Billie thought it quite the most romantic postlude, in its own strange way. She recalled "a little man with a concertina" playing "Neapolitan love songs in counterpoint with the lapping wavelets of the

Hudson and the mellow hoots of the tugboats." And Ziegfeld—next to her at the ferryboat railing, responding to her vulnerability at this hour of rebellion and surrender, this changing of managers and pleasing of Mama, this sudden maturity after a career of playing adolescents, tomboys, and Jerrys—asked, like a leading man in a play, "Is my wife happy?"

It was Saturday, April 11, 1914. Billie had to return to the Lyceum for *Jerry's* evening performance, but at least she and Ziegfeld had the rest of the weekend in which to improvise a honeymoon. The press ran the story on Monday, and Frohman, incredulous that one of his stars had actually flouted his control, executed a revenge. The punishment fit the crime: Frohman put man and wife asunder by closing *Jerry* to send it out on tour. Thus, Billie was forced out of New York just when Ziegfeld was extremely occupied there with rehearsals for *Ziegfeld Follies of 1914,* which opened at the New Amsterdam on June 1. If Frohman could not close the marriage altogether, he could at least depress its opening weeks. That was his final statement on the matter, and he broke with Billie forever.[1]

Returning from the provincial circuits at last, Billie took up housekeeping with Ziegfeld at Burkely Crest. Anna learned of their union not from Ziegfeld but, like the general public, in the papers. She was surprised and utterly crushed. Anna knew that Ziegfeld bedded other women, but she had somehow been planning to be the only woman whom Ziegfeld actually loved.

Perhaps Anna had been misled by how much concentration Ziegfeld had given her, virtually building his career around the eight shows they had done together. However, the Anna Held shows were not

---

[1] There is every reason to believe that the ever unrelenting Frohman would have kept Billie frozen out had he lived another forty years, and he might have: he was barely middle-aged when Ziegfeld and Billie married. However, the very next year Frohman made his annual trip to London, on the last crossing of the *Lusitania.* According to a survivor, who saw a crashing wave carry the unjacketed Frohman into the ocean, he met death with the same stubborn dignity with which he had lived.

about Anna Held in the fullest historical consideration, because Ziegfeld's shows were about reopening Western Civilization's conversation between the sexes.

It was, of course, a conversation held entirely in pop. The higher arts deal in abstractions: Leonore rescues Florestan. Pop art deals in realities: Florestan fucks Leonore with the rapt clarity that explodes society's cautions, demolishes religion, schools, banks, the press. Ziegfeld says, Only one thing is true. Everything else is cosmetics.

CHAPTER NINE

The Golden Age of the Follies

The first intimate thing that Billie learned about her husband was that he wore long underwear almost all year long.

Well, naturally any son of Chicago would have adopted the practice from youth, as insulation against the frosty wind racing in from the prairie or over Lake Michigan. Of course, in Ziegfeldian fashion, Ziegfeld wore only the spiffiest of long johns—tailored silk in a delicate shade of peach, as if designed for the *Follies*.

But "No, no, no, no, no," we imagine Billie tut-tutting as she wrests them off him. "You're not on Lake Michigan any more."

So Ziegfeld gave up his union suit—but not his long working hours. Not his hectic mornings getting out his telegrams, charging up his telephone calls, and piling up his production notes. Billie was flabbergasted. After Charles Frohman's eccentrically lean approach to the making of theatre, with his avoidance of paperwork and sentences so stingily minted that they skipped subject and verb to cut to the object, here was a manager who reveled in descriptions, questions, observations.

But then, Ziegfeld was a micromanager at a time when theatre was well-nigh machine-made. Musicals, in particular, were manufactured, and at top speed. There were no deliberations, no "development," no masturbating workshops. The manager commissioned writers to create, technicians to frame, and performers to illuminate work that could play its first public performance three months after the manager said, "Go!"

Moreover, managers didn't only put on plays. They also guided the careers of artists under contract. Not to a specific work: to the manager himself.

Billie's manager was now Ziegfeld, and he wanted to put her in the movies. D. W. Griffith's *Birth of a Nation* (1915), Thomas Ince's *Civilization* (1916), and other road-show features were introducing the skeptical American middle class to the movies' bona fides as entertainment. Cinema was only just breaking. It had more than a taste in it of the World's Fair midway that Ziegfeld had put behind him, and it was a new form, which made him both wary and intrigued. Besides, Ziegfeld demanded for Billie—and got—the highest salary yet paid to a movie star: $40,000 for five weeks' work, on *Peggy* (1915). Even more lucrative was a serial entitled *Gloria's Romance* (1916).

This was a Chicago project, for the Randolph Film Corporation of that city, made partly on capital from the *Chicago Tribune* for the rights to publish weekly installments of the film's action. Just as movie serials oblige the public to buy multiple admissions to follow each next chapter, the print series sells newspapers. Jerome Kern composed the "soundtrack," played live in those silent days by a symphony orchestra; the composer himself conducted on opening night, at Charles Dillingham's Globe Theatre (today the Lunt-Fontanne). Big-budget Hollywood frequently made itself at home in Broadway's finest parlors: *Birth of a Nation* (1915) played at the Liberty Theatre, only a few doors west of the New Amsterdam on Forty-Second Street.

Though Ziegfeld was not involved in the production of *Gloria's Romance*, it showed a Ziegfeldian high-stakes finish. Even the scenarist, Rupert Hughes, got $25,000, a phenomenal amount. Oddly, the whole thing came about by chance: the *Chicago Tribune*'s circulation manager, Max Annenberg, ran into Ziegfeld in Times Square, and the two Chicago "old boys" walked up Broadway as they chatted. Ziegfeld was on his way home to the Ansonia, and Annenberg came upstairs with him. There he saw a photograph of Billie on the grand piano and immediately opened negotiations for *Gloria's Romance*. These ended at $150,000 for thirty weeks' work, a truly unforgettable deal for the mid-1910s.

Yet it turned out in the end that the serial format's popularity had died for a time, and *Gloria's Romance* bombed. Strangely, this did not hobble Billie's movie career, and she went on to a slew of titles for Paramount in the second half of the decade: *The Mysterious Miss Terry, The Land of Promise, Let's Get a Divorce,* and *The Misbehaving Widow* among others.

Back in New York, Ziegfeld was tending the 1915 *Follies.* The series continued commercially powerful, producing each season's biggest opening night, a bragfest of celebrities dressed to thrill, even in the warm weather, and the area in front of the New Amsterdam awash with oglers and mounted police.

And yet. While the delight remained an essential element, the surprise was getting rare. Professional complainers could not resist noting the way the best sketches and numbers in earlier *Follies* had been finding echo in later ones. Was Ziegfeld developing a unique format or simply perpetuating one? For instance, why did every Bert Williams–Leon Errol *Follies* include a sketch in which Williams played an underdog making a fool out of Errol, encoring 1911's Grand Central Station scene in different settings?

Errol was all over the 1915 *Follies,* directing as well as performing. But Julian Mitchell returned to co-direct what was to prove the most revitalizing *Follies* in the entire series: for the surprise was back in the form of two artists who took control of the *Follies'* visual side. This pair, arriving simultaneously by sheer coincidence, were to prove almost as authorial as Ziegfeld himself. It was in *Ziegfeld Follies of 1915* that these two—bickering over whether the music of his colors might drown out her tender little sighs, or whether his lighting suited her dark secrets—created the Look of the *Follies.* They were Joseph Urban and Lady Duff Gordon, and they quickly became the bullet points in the revue's résumé—the first *Follies* thing you remembered for as long as you lived. Urban created the sets and Lady Duff Gordon the costumes, but it was more than that. Together, they made Ziegfeld's last argument that his shows were the top shows. It was as if he discovered the land called *Follies*: but they drew the map.

In his collaboration with composer Dave Stamper, Gene Buck enriched the *Follies* with hit tunes and fillers. However, Buck really made his salary as a talent scout, for it was Buck who brought Joseph Urban to Ziegfeld's attention. A Viennese architect who also directed and designed opera productions, Urban left home after a scandal and lived itinerantly, oddjobbing in theatres till he landed, improbably, at the Boston Opera. On Broadway, Urban was asked to design the sets for Edward Sheldon's *The Garden of Paradise* (1914), an adaptation of Hans Christian Andersen's *The Little Mermaid*. "From the ocean depths to . . . sun-kissed shores," *The Dramatic Mirror* noted, "back to the cave of the Sea Witch under the sea; to the royal palace of the King of the Blue Mountains; to the Queen's Bower of the airy, sunny Southland, the wonderful Queen's garden and the scene of the bridal feast," Urban physicalized the abstract world of romance.

It was Urban's Broadway debut, yet he was already being called a genius, because he was both artist and technician, a master of styles from *pointillisme* and children's book illustrations to Japanese woodblock and *trompe l'oeil* perspectives. For one sequence in the 1915 *Follies*, Urban painted a zeppelin flying over London, the top half of the view dominated by the lightest of aircraft, almost a vast bumblebee, and the city itself a panorama as solid as a roomful of toys. To combine intimate and epic was Urban's delight, so that, as the lights came up on the next set, one gasped at once at the grandeur of detail. Thus, evoking Paris for Fanny Brice's "My Man" in the 1921 *Follies*, Urban placed the singer, as a pathetic apache, on a quay beside the Seine, with the skyline shining in a yellow haze dominated by the Eiffel Tower. At least, that is what one saw at first: a split second later, one realized that this charming postcard view, even all Paris, was overwhelmed by a gigantic dull gray bridge. Of course, this only underlined the sense of helpless isolation that Brice brought to the song, as a woman victimized by a heartless force that she thinks of as love.

An Englishwoman, as her name suggests, Lady Duff Gordon is the opposite of that lonely little thing singing "My Man." Here was a being who knew how to run her own life despite the interloping of men. Just for starters, she survived the *Titanic*; by 1915 she was in America to expand her dress-designing business. Her colleagues saw themselves as couturières for gentlewomen in an etiquette of reticence. One did one's work; one was admired, recommended. But Lucile, Lady Duff Gordon's user name, saw herself as designer to the stars on the American plan. One created excitement; one was exclusive, famous.

Lucile did everything uniquely, raiding Broadway for her studio models and discovering young women in unexpected places. The best of them would be renamed, in her own style, mononymously, then presented with the flourish of a chaperone at a debutante's ball. Kathleen Mary Rose was a teenager executing menial tasks in Lucile's salon when Lucile performed her usual *My Fair Lady* transformation, rechristening the girl Dolores. A haughty name for a haughty sprite; and soon enough Dolores emerged in a spotlight to prowl Ziegfeld's stage in a spectacular peacock outfit with pailletted feathering almost completely surrounding its wearer. None but Lucile could have designed the peacock getup, and none but Dolores could wear it. Ziegfeld paid this outstanding showgirl an incredible $500 a week for her peacocking; and Lucile knew joy.[1]

Dolores' peacock bit was not actually part of the *Follies*, per se. In 1915 Ziegfeld created a miniature *Follies* on the New Amsterdam roof, the *Midnight Frolic*. A fall or winter offering, the *Frolic* allowed *Follies*-goers to elevator upstairs after the show, relaxing with food and drink to take in another hour or so of entertainment. This was the era of the dance, in which civilian couples would emulate the stars by trying out the latest steps: this was how the [Harry] Fox Trot got started. The band was already playing when the *Midnight Frolic*'s ticket holders came in, and the band played long after the show had ended, making this the first

---

[1] Dolores' hypnotic turn along a bare stage remained so intense a memory that Stephen Sondheim's *Follies* (1971) raised its curtain on a revival of the moment, preserved for my readers in this book's frontispiece. Lucile, too, got a look-up in a seventies musical. She was spoofed as a male dress designer, Madame Lucy, in *Irene* (1919), revised in 1973 for Debbie Reynolds' Broadway debut. George S. Irving played Madame Lucy.

nightclub. Eddie Cantor called the *Frolic* "the supper club of the Four Hundred" because of the concentration of social rajahs. There was a balcony, but the floor was available to VIPs only. Especially appealing was Ziegfeld's use of a restaurant layout instead of auditorium seating, allowing dressy show-offs to make an entrance as gala as that of Dolores.

The bill of fare at the *Frolic* favored fish and fancy chicken, but there was as well Filet Mignon Cocotte or Grisette at $2.75, Spaghetti Ziegfeld at $1.50, and, for the tourist from El Dorado, Cold Lobster Mayonnaise, price discreetly unquoted. As always in such establishments, it was the bar that cleaned up—so of course Prohibition killed the *Frolic*, which held on only through 1922. Still, while serving as a mint for Ziegfeld and the ever more shadowy Klaw and Erlanger interests, the *Frolic* gave Ziegfeld an ideal audition venue: unproved talent could be hired for the *Frolic*, then graduated to the *Follies* if they killed. Eddie Cantor made his New York debut in this way, in the 1916 *Frolic*, and his great moment— his *Follies* passport, one might say—gives us a kind of How the Fox Got His Tail story.

Cantor's spiel was what was known as a "nut act": loony, fast-moving, and unpredictable. At his music, he'd come racing out, and even before hitting his mark he'd be telling the audience that they were bound to like him because he'd been up all night writing new material.

"Yes," Cantor would say, "it's a fresh act!" The public tittered in anticipation of some gag as Cantor added, "Why . . . it's the freshest act on the stage today!" And "Yes, it is!" he'd sing out.

Three beats. Then, in his unique delivery of humble proclamation: "Eddie Cantor, fresh from the Bronx!"

And the public would roar as Cantor sailed into the act proper. Now, on this particular night of his Ziegfeld debut, strolling among the tables, Cantor produced a deck of cards and asked for a little assistance from those assembled. He handed out a card each to the most distinguished-looking gentlemen in view, and they just happened to be William Randolph Hearst, Diamond Jim Brady, and Ziegfeld's sometime manager partner Charles Dillingham. Asking the three to hold their cards high so the other spectators could see them, Cantor then went on with his characteristic business that alternated braggadocio with cringing terror as the runt who conquers bullies by baffling them with neighborhood lingo. Hawaiian numbers were the rage of the mid-1910s—even Jerome Kern wrote one—and Cantor closed with a neighborhood version, perhaps "Since Sammy Learned the Hula." Starting offstage to his applause, Cantor suddenly Remembered Something, and turned back to the three gents, still standing with their cards on high.

Retrieving the cards with merry thank-yous, Cantor staged another fake exit as the audience laughed. It's a good thing Hearst laughed, too. Returning yet again, Cantor solemnly announced how important success was for him: "Mother needs me now that Dad's gone."

They waited for the punch line. Actually, there were two: "With good behavior, he may be out in ten years" was the first, and the second was "When you work in a bank, you just can't take home samples."

The next morning, Ziegfeld sent Cantor a wire: ENJOYED YOUR ACT YOULL BE HERE A LONG TIME. "Here" meant downstairs at the *Follies,* the grandest booking on Broadway. And that's how the fox got his tail.

By this time, Ziegfeld's roster of star comics was complete: Bert Williams, Fanny Brice, Leon Errol, W. C. Fields, Will Rogers, and now Cantor, the last to join the *Follies,* in 1917. Other prominent comedians were on-site, such as the brother and sister team of Johnny and Ray Dooley, Ray playing bratty kids with such réclame that it became a *Follies* thing, to be taken over by Fanny Brice as Baby Snooks much later. And one star comic, Ed Wynn, did appear in two *Follies*. This was not enough, however, to make him a fixture of *Follies* style.

What Ziegfeld created with "his" core jesters was a reflection of melting-pot America. The Australian Errol and the Philadelphian Fields were the default setting, Williams contributed the lore of the black ghetto, Brice and Cantor that of the Jewish working class—and Rogers added in an unexpected "ethnicity" as the cowboy. Counting only shows that Ziegfeld produced himself, this sextet forms a kind of *Follies* comics dream team at the revue's height of influence, as witness their *Follies* appearances:

Bert Williams   1910, '11, '12, *out because of illness*, '14, '15, '16, '17, '18, '19
Fanny Brice   1910, '11, *out because of a misunderstanding*, '16, '17, '20, '21
Leon Errol   1911, '12, '13, '14, '15,
W. C. Fields   1915, '16, '17, '18, '20, '21
Will Rogers   1916, '17, '18, '22, '24
Eddie Cantor   1917, '18, '19, *out because of union militancy*, '23, '27

Note that the 1916, 1917, and 1918 *Follies* feature at least one representative each of the black, Jewish, and cowboy humors, just when the *Follies* had taken on Joseph Urban and Lucile to become more or less a national institution. Its look was sophisticated New York, sly and strange—but the comics gave the *Follies* a new Americanness.

Year after year, Ziegfeld retained the summer opening from the show's roof days, and each *Follies* would play New York for about five months, then tour out the season. The tour was ambitious, traveling beyond the northeast into the midwest and sometimes the west coast as well—and Ziegfeld would drop any artist, even one of the stars, who refused to tour. America's *Follies* was New York's *Follies*: wherever you lived, you saw the show that Hearst and Brady and the rest of the Big Time saw. Ironically, almost never did Ziegfeld star a name on a *Follies* poster. Ziegfeld's *book* shows had stars. The *Follies* starred the *Follies* itself.

For all the importance of the comedy, it is odd to report that, even now, Ziegfeld still had no sense of humor whatsoever. He could pass a sharp, dry remark: but he never *heard* anything funny. He didn't have to: the public told him what was funny by its laughter. W. C. Fields had honed his pool-playing act over the course of a long career till it played itself; Will Rogers changed his script daily, reviewing the headlines as he turned rope tricks. Or: Bert Williams' gift as a mime was so rich that when he "played" a hand of poker, one saw the other gamblers in his reactions; the very table came to life. On the other hand, Eddie Cantor's was an athletic performance, tossing off a tune with such giddy éclat that he simultaneously pranced and clapped his hands and, while scampering into the wings, pulled out a handkerchief to wave. In other words, the *Follies* comics ran a little variety show of their own, some rehearsing their material as if polishing a diamond and some rushing on to invent bufoonery on the spot.

Cantor got his start in the latter way, improvising his way to center stage in a piece called *Canary Cottage*. It was 1915, a time of "bedroom" comedies: more naughty than erotic, though still somewhat daring. *Canary Cottage* was a bedroom musical, about men hosting cuties at a house party when wives and fiancées burst in. The star was Trixie Friganza; Cantor was slightly featured in a blackface role, as a chauffeur. He had two no more than okay songs and nothing-doing dialogue—yet every time he tried to ad-lib a joke Friganza had it cut.

Finally, Cantor learned the lesson taught to Billie Burke in her Edna May musical, the one with the Canoe Number: don't let the star know how good you are before opening night. For the San Diego tryout, Cantor seemed the humble supporting player. Then he unloaded everything he had for the Los Angeles premiere.[1] With Friganza now helpless to intervene, Cantor tossed off new lines and effected all sorts of loony doodads such as juggling and throwing his voice. He even dared to ridicule Friganza, a woman of ample proportion. As she made an exit dressed in white, Cantor cried, "My God! A milk wagon!"

The next performance was a matinée. As Cantor entered the theatre, he was redirected to Morosco's office, a few blocks away. There, Morosco told him, "What you did last night is the most unforgivable thing that can happen in the theatre. Now, you go back to the matinée and do everything you did last night, exactly the same way."

And more: when Friganza told Morosco, before the entire company, "This amateur goes or I am leaving," Morosco replied, "We intend to keep Eddie Cantor for the run of the play." And, as so often in the theatre, the star made peace with the upstart; she even hired him to compose

---

[1] The show's producer, Oliver Morosco, was based on the west coast and treated New York as no more than a tour date. He did join with the Shuberts to build a Broadway house, named for himself, on Forty-Fifth Street. It was demolished (with the Helen Hayes and the Bijou) to make way for the Marquis Hotel.

a set of ad libs and doodads for her own use. Thus, temperament recognizes star talent.

By the time *Canary Cottage* reached New York (launching the Morosco Theatre, in fact), Cantor had left Morosco for Ziegfeld. But we see Cantor's style already fledged: the script is no more than a model, to be personalized and crazied up. To the wry, practiced expertise of W. C. Fields and the artfully unstudied patter of Will Rogers, Cantor was electricity without a grounding wire, giving everything he did an impulsive energy. Today, we are used to seeing shows that are very carefully amended in rehearsals and then "frozen" shortly before the opening. In Cantor's day, audiences enjoyed a touch of danger, of unpredictability, in their Broadway.

Unlike Cantor, Fanny Brice was a long time in placing her style and persona. Some things worked well for her, like the aforementioned "Sadie Salome, Go Home." But too much of what she did in her early years was miscellaneous, even anonymous. This was why she and Ziegfeld parted company between the 1911 and 1916 *Follies*: after a solid debut in the 1910 edition, Brice found herself relegated to subordinate status in 1911, quite without the distinctive numbers that inspired her. Cantor's fidgety high jinks could lift virtually any uptempo tune, but Brice sang best in character: and, thus far, she hadn't established one.

The separation from Ziegfeld must have been wrenching for someone plucked from the obscurity of burlesque. But somehow or other Ziegfeld came to the conclusion that—in this very early stage of her career—Brice wasn't right for the *Follies*. Years later, trying to explain the problem, Brice claimed it was a case of faulty communication. When Ziegfeld finally confronted her, she told him—and these are her own words as she recalled them—"You never sent for me. I thought you had lost confidence in me."

"Was there so little friendship between us," he replied, "that I had to send for you like any actor?" And then: "You belong here. [That is, in the *Follies*.] You'll always belong here."

This was in either 1912 or 1914, yet Brice did not return to Ziegfeld till, as I've said, 1916. She could easily have rejoined the *Follies* sooner, for she was not under contract to rival managements for long. Freelancing between vaudeville and legit, she even took a role in the post-Broadway tour of the first Princess Theatre show, *Nobody Home* (1915). Perhaps it took some time for Ziegfeld to "place" Brice, in songs and sketches keyed to her gift for at once ennobling and satirizing the aspirations of Jewish girls assimilating into American Culture. As if to emphasize the rediscovery of Fanny Brice, Ziegfeld created suspense by withholding her entrance into the 1916 *Follies* till the second act. This gave her dominion over an evening that boasted also Bert Williams, W. C. Fields, and Will Rogers, not to mention Ina Claire, Marion Davies, and Ann Pennington.

By this time, the *Follies* had evolved considerably from the format of its early years, when Brice had joined the outfit. *Compère* and *commère* were gone, along with the evening-length "review" of the previous year. Gone as well was the svelte casting plan of a star or two, a few discoveries, and various minor functionaries. No, the *Follies* had become an all-star show, grand but lively, colorful and crazy, sweeping from comedy to song to the Girls and back.

Often, Ziegfeld combined the three in one sequence. True, this had been the practice from the start, but on a modest scale; now they collaborated in self-contained one-act musicals. For instance, *Ziegfeld Follies of 1916*'s second-act curtain rose on a spoof of Russian ballet. (Diaghilev's Ballets Russes had visited New York earlier that year.) *Les Sylphides* and *Le Spectre de la Rose* were guyed, but the main object of the fun was *Scheherazade*. Because Michel Fokine's curious choreography using Rimsky-Korsakof's symphony had included a great deal of mime as well as dance, W. C. Fields and Bert Williams both got into Ziegfeld's version. Capping it was Brice's summation in a Stamper and Buck number, "Nijinsky," in the language and accent of a kid from the ghetto. Another extended sequence took the *Follies* to Hollywood for a fixture of the day, celebrity imitations. Everybody did them. Ina Claire presented her Geraldine Farrar, Ann Pennington her Mary Pickford . . . and Brice was Theda Bara, in evil-vamp black for "I'm Bad."

Still, the best Brice of all was unveiled in "Becky Is Back in the Ballet," a number she brought to the 1916 *Follies* from her recent vaudeville bookings. A clodhopping waltz, "Becky" introduces another of Brice's Roses, whose mother, in a spoken patter section, encourages her to dance when company comes: "Do for mama the dying duck like Pavlova!" Becky's mother urges, meanwhile assuring the guests, "For that I paid two dollars a lesson." And "Look out, darling, look out you don't break your technique!"

Such numbers gave Brice leverage in balancing her act with Cantor's. She portrayed the Jewish archetype in a somewhat incomprehensible world, while he treated the fears of the milquetoast archetype in an entirely hostile world. Her only enemy was humiliation; his enemy was other men, all bullies. Oddly, while both played Jewish, she put on an outrageous accent and he spoke plain English while making constant references to Jewish culture. A typical Cantor number would rhyme (Lawrence) "Tibbett(s)" with "kibitz," but in Brice's territory Becky is back in the *ballet*: out in the Christian's world of audiences in evening wear, gloved hands condescending to applaud the most abstract of European arts. Cantor's reference point is opera, but his model, we notice, is American. Lawrence Tibbett even became a movie star. Brice's model is Pavlova: unknowable, beyond Hollywood, and probably anti-Semitic.

This was exactly the richness of mix that Ziegfeld wanted: even his Jewish stars were unlike each other. And, of course, part of that Ziegfeldian surprise and delight lay in the all-American audience at the New Amsterdam enjoying but also being startled by the new ethnic humor. Yes, they already knew Weber and Fields. But Weber and Fields were Jewish only in their "Dutch" accents. Their content was most often working-class guy things—playing cards or the etiquette of the saloon. Cantor and Brice were breakaways. They showed how it felt to grow up with Old Country parents in a new country where performers elucidated art that was at once autobiographical yet irrelevant to them—those idiotic mammy songs, for instance. In a rare moment of rebellion, Ziegfeld's first *Follies* star, Nora Bayes, decided to get personal with "Has Anybody Here Seen Kelly?," which she first sang in *The Jolly Bachelors*

(1910). The usual Irish number, "Kelly" sounds the query of a wee dar-lin' lass separated from her husband on a visit to New York. But when Bayes got to the umpteenth repetition of the title line, she threw in a fake error: "Has anybody here seen Levi—I mean Kelly?," as if ridiculing the ethnic masquerade that *Follies* comics in particular were going to make unnecessary.[1]

This, Ziegfeld might have said, is how a nation like ours takes its en-tertainment, scanning the whole of its citizenry for unique attitudes and experiences. Ziegfeld's favorite, to be sure, was Will Rogers, arguably the closest in attitudes to the *Follies* audience. True, his résumé took in ex-perience in Wild West shows, which made him unlike just about every New Yorker except Ziegfeld, who, we remember, may have logged some experience with the Buffalo Bill company. Remember, too, that Rogers was of three-eighths Cherokee blood, which made him even more ex-otic than Williams or Brice.

Rogers was comparable to Fields in that he was on hand mainly for sketch comedy and his solo act. (On rare occasions, Rogers turned up in a musical number, as already with Lillian Lorraine, and usually for comic effect.) So Rogers and Fields lacked the versatility of Williams, Brice, Cantor, and Errol, who took part in the music as well.

But Ziegfeld liked it that way. Later, revue would cherish all-around performers like Clifton Webb or Ethel Waters, who could take part in the entire show, unifying it smartly. The *Follies,* however, always had a place for the singer who only sang, the dancer who never spoke. Furthermore, the solos by Fields and Rogers or, say, the singing duo Van and Schenck were used to keep *Follies* playing tempo up to speed while the stage-hands, behind the traveler curtain, readied the next Joseph Urban vista.

---

[1] *The Jolly Bachelors* was produced by not Ziegfeld but Lew Fields. However, the Kelly-Levi joke, in reverse formation, made its way, over fifty years later, into a sort-of Ziegfeld show, *Funny Girl* (1964). When Fanny Brice, as Private Schwartz From Rock-away in a Military Number, nears the rhyme for "red, white and bluish," she starts a line as "I tawk dis vay becawse I'm" and suddenly veers into "British," complete with soigné John Bull accent.

These spots "in one" were small only in the physical sense. The talent was large, even hypnotic, in Rogers' intricate rope tricks during his monologues on current events, or in baritone Gus Van's bravura plastique next to tenor Joe Schenck's self-effacing piano playing. Audiences would stare at him for minutes, waiting to see if he'd ever glance down at the keys.

The solos were crucial as well because they could fit almost anywhere in the program, thus easing the rearrangement of the playing order during the famous twenty-four-hour dress rehearsal. This was when Ziegfeld made his final decisions, cutting numbers back or deleting them altogether while moving everything around. Dress rehearsals of musicals were chaotic as a rule, but there was no chaos like *Follies* chaos.

Came then the tryout week at Atlantic City's Apollo Theatre: more chaos, but less frenzied, even languorous chaos. And at last the New York opening, with the grandees, the cops on horseback, the masses of onlookers. *Follies* first nights were the biggest on Broadway; they say that cast members taking their places for the first number could feel the public's eagerness right through the New Amsterdam's house curtain. To Bert Williams, who was living in an oppressive culture, playing the *Follies* meant making major history in defeating oppression. But to someone like Fanny Brice or Eddie Cantor from the neighborhoods, or like W. C. Fields, who came up from homeless poverty, playing the *Follies* meant more than you had Arrived. Playing the *Follies* meant you were Staying.

The revue conveyed a sense of responsibility on its chosen. Brice taught this to Cantor when they first met, rehearsing the 1917 edition. As a veteran of the Ziegfeld style, she warned him out of his *Canary Cottage* showboating. Nobody stole the *Follies*—not with so many great performers in view. "Theirs was a camaraderie I didn't know existed," Cantor later recalled. "I had never heard of it before [and] I never have seen it since. They were a family and they wanted the *family* to be a hit. They helped each other."

Indeed, after Nora Bayes hounded Sophie Tucker out of *Follies of 1909,* we know of no major incidents of prima donnas targeting colleagues who were simply going about their lawful occasions. Watching Cantor pull off a "vaudeville bow"—a trick salute designed to provoke extra cheers—Brice warned him to lose the practices of the Smalltime.

"This is the *Follies*, kid," she told him. "The *top*." Cantor got it. "Here, she showed me, you wanted reserve and poise."

Perhaps because he was himself the child of immigrants, Ziegfeld made it a personal mission to integrate his Broadway ethnically. Perhaps because Chicago was so mixed in its population (albeit primarily in Scandinavian, German, and Polish subgroups), Ziegfeld thought it natural to Americanize with a miscellany. Perhaps Ziegfeld simply liked the way his mishmash of jesters stirred the *Follies* pot. Whatever his motivation, Ziegfeld's art reflected the cultural drift from America's slow-moving nineteenth-century rural raconteurs to the urban enfants terribles of the early twentieth century. And Ziegfeld it was who, so to say, *invented* the entertainment industry into show biz: because the edgy, sexy, wisecrack art that he concocted still rules today.

CHAPTER TEN

The Century Shows and the Ziegfeld Girl

By just about 1916, the Shuberts were the masters of Broadway. Not only had they conquered the Syndicate, but there was scarcely any Syndicate left. With Charles Frohman dead, his partner, Al Hayman, retired, to die two years later. Nixon and Zimmerman gave up as well, leaving only Klaw and Erlanger, already dissolving their union in bitter recrimination and legal action that lasted well into the 1920s.

Broadway's very geography now sang Shubert, for the Messrs.' real estate laid claim to not only The Street itself, at the Winter Garden (opened in 1911), but also amid the hub of activity of Forty-Fourth and Forty-Fifth Streets, in two large houses for big-ticket attractions, the Shubert (1913) and the Forty-Fourth Street (1913), and, co-investing with independent managers, in the more concisely built Booth (1913), Broadhurst (1917), Plymouth (1917), and, we already know, Morosco (1917).

The battle between the Shuberts and the Syndicate had been a holy war among atheists, because it was not about theatre but about control, about power. And while the Shuberts could be as ruthless as the Syndicate in certain of their dealings, now that they had prevailed they were willing to live and work in peace with rival managers. Except one.

The reason Lee and J. J. continued to regard Ziegfeld as their mortal enemy lies only partly in his duplicity when they tried to star Anna Held in *The Motor Girl*. It was also only partly because the *Follies*, the *Midnight*

Frolic, and various one-time-only Ziegfeld diversions so insistently played the New Amsterdam Theatre and Roof, flaunting Ziegfeld's alliance with the monstrous Erlanger. It was mainly because the Shuberts had built the Winter Garden to rival the New Amsterdam and as a home for their own Shubert *Follies* annuals: and it all seemed so simple, but it turned out not to be.

The Shuberts chose the Winter Garden site (covering nearly the entire block bounded by Broadway, Seventh Avenue, and Fiftieth and Fifty-First Streets) most immediately because the lot was already assembled. There was thus no need to create sneaky front companies to negotiate with various small-holdings owners, not to mention the usual holdout at the very end, asking for millions. In fact, the lot already hosted a building, the Horse Exchange. Though it was still in operation, it had to be as moribund as the blacksmith and the buggy; perhaps its owner would make the Messrs. an interesting deal. Then, too, rather than build from scratch, the Shuberts need no more than convert the interior. Best of all, the result would house a wide, rather than deep, auditorium with a vast stage capable of hosting pageants with set changes at Ziegfeldian quickstep tempo.

So surely the Winter Garden was intended to dominate as Erlanger's New Amsterdam had done—to pull the very meaning of "Broadway" up from Forty-Second Street to the north, proclaiming the Pax Shubertiana. This never happened. Broadway stayed put, with the Winter Garden standing alone for a good twenty years.[1] Worse, the revues that the Shuberts mounted failed to challenge the *Follies* no matter how many stars or discoveries (the preferred variety: they came cheaper) they hired or how carefully they copied Ziegfeld's format. In all, the Shuberts found Ziegfeld worse than treacherous: inimitable.

On the other hand, Ziegfeld himself was trying to drift away from his Syndicate connections, going into partnership with Charles Dillingham

---

[1]A few playhouses did dare the side streets above, say, Forty-Sixth Street, but Broadway proper lay empty of theatres except for the cinema built in 1924 that, some years later, became today's Broadway Theatre.

at the Century Theatre for a new series of revues. Dillingham was known mainly for "family" musicals, and the Century was a three-balcony palace of spectacle on Central Park West, near the main entrance to the park. This was twelve blocks north of even the Winter Garden—as far from Abe Erlanger's New Amsterdam as one could get within the Broadway milieu.

Setting up as the Century Amusement Corporation, Ziegfeld and Dillingham refurbished the house and announced their first attraction: *The Century Girl*. How was this to be different from *The Ziegfeld Girl*, which Ziegfeld had, more or less, been putting on since that first *Follies*, in 1907? And when Ziegfeld and Dillingham followed *The Century Girl* with *Miss 1917*, what themes, formats, attitudes did this new series unveil?

Simply put, the Century revues were to out-*Follies* the *Follies* with one caution: less brinkmanship in the revelation of beauty. There would be fewer showgirls wearing little more than lighting, but a heavier complement of musical-comedy talent than even the *Follies* had. More stars! More set-and-costume dazzle! And no unreconstructed gleanings from vaudeville or copycat sketches. The Century revues would be the best time you ever had on Broadway.

And *The Century Girl* veritably was that. For the songs, the producers—we can use the word, for it was coming into use at exactly this time—hired the two best writers of the day. This would presumably create the best score of the day: half Irving Berlin and half Victor Herbert (working with Henry Blossom, the best lyricist before 1920 who was not P. G. Wodehouse).

The staging staff was typical 1910s Ziegfeld: director-choreographers Edward Royce and Ned Wayburn, with Leon Errol directing the sketches, Lucile designing the gowns, and Joseph Urban painting his by now routinely breathtaking sets.

Excellent, of course. Untoppable. And the cast was astonishing: headliners Hazel Dawn (as charm heroine), Elsie Janis (the impish heroine), and Marie Dressler (the ravishing frump heroine). Comics Sam Bernard (for "Dutch" fun), Frank Tinney (for blackface fun), and co-director Errol. Singing duo Van and Schenck and dancing duo (James) Doyle and (Harland) Dixon. The typical Ziegfeld sister act in Marion and Madeline, the Fairbanks Twins. And heading the showgirl contingent was Vera Maxwell, known as "the most beautiful woman in the world." But weren't they all?

The format was simple, even excessively so: there was no format. The usual town topics took hits, with yet more burlesque of the Ballets Russes from Leon Errolovitch, Marie Dressleroff, and Harry Kelloski (Harry Kelly). Nevertheless, *The Century Girl* was, as Channing Pollock put it, "all-star vaudeville against a backdrop of supreme spectacle."

This observation needs to be relished in context, because even at the Palace, vaudeville's temple, there was no such thing as all-star vaudeville. There was tank-town vaudeville, top-circuit vaudeville (as for the Keith or Orpheum outfits), or big-ticket vaudeville, as at the Palace. All of them started their programs with lesser acts, rose to good acts (the first of these just before the intermission), then proceeded to the best acts available (which varied from merely enjoyable in the tank towns to the Heaviest Names in Show Biz at the Palace). But nowhere in American entertainment was there all-star vaudeville till *The Century Girl*. Pollock thought it not only "out-Follies the Follies" indeed, but that it "out-hippodromes the Hippodrome," a reference to the most colossal variety house in America. Thus, Frank Tinney, whose characteristic moment it always was to abandon whatever set piece he was involved in, amble down to the footlights, and rattle on about anything at all, took *The Century Girl*'s opening night as his chance to confide to the audience: "Dillingham and Ziegfeld, they says to me, they says . . . 'Frank! If we do the business we *should* do, we won't lose more than two thousand dollars a week!'"

The Century Girl was a smash, opening on November 6, 1916 and running 200 performances. Frank Tinney was of course right in that the heavy running costs demanded near-capacity houses—and the out-of-the-way theatre precluded much walk-in business. As we know, subway riders could get out at Times Square and fan out to shop for their fun. They were unlikely to reach Columbus Circle without having bought tickets at one of the forty-odd box offices along the way. Down on Forty-Second Street at the New Amsterdam, Ziegfeld never had had to extend himself; the Century Amusement Corporation was going to have to hustle.

"Charles Dillingham and Florenz Ziegfeld Jr. offer their second annual revue" was the billing as the pair tried to out-century the Century with *Miss 1917*. Wayburn, Urban, and Lucile (along with seven other couturiers) were again on hand, and, to the lyrics of P. G. Wodehouse, Herbert now co-composed with Jerome Kern. The cast was, if possible, even castier than *The Century Girl*'s had been: the once again Weberless Lew Fields; the just-emerged star soubrette Vivienne Segal; the beloved "Yama Yama Girl," Bessie McCoy;[1] singing couple Elizabeth Brice and Charles King; dancing couple George White (a future producer himself, to be Ziegfeld's rival as lord of the *Scandals*) and Ann Pennington; dancing single Irene Castle; Marion Davies; Van and Schenck: a complete ballet company under the Metropolitan Opera's dancing master, Adolf Bolm, to open Act Two with "Falling Leaves: Poem-Choreographic";

---

[1]McCoy introduced one of the biggest song hits of the early-twentieth-century musical, "Yama Yama Man," in Karl Hoschna's *Three Twins* (1908). Dressed in harlequin pajamas with gigantic fluffy buttons and a clown's cone hat, McCoy pranced her way through this ragtime novelty about a bogeyman who terrifies "ev'ry little tot at night." The verse creeps about in the minor key, then flares into the major for the exuberant chorus—an outstanding newfangle where most songs came off the assembly line. McCoy's performance became one of the sights of the age, and she greatly saddened her public when she retired to marry the intrepid war correspondent Richard Harding Davis. After his death, in the spring of 1916, she returned as Bessie McCoy Davis, making her first reappearance on Broadway in this very show for the Kern-Wodehouse "The Old Man in the Moon." Marked "light and shimmering," this dainty piece tells how the sly old dog came down to monitor the hostilities in Europe and side with the U.S., which had been over there for seven months. Later in Act One, when McCoy reprised "Yama Yama Man" in exact re-creation, one critic wrote, "The house literally rose to her." Ginger Rogers revives the number, pajamas and all, in *The Story of Vernon and Irene Castle*.

and Vera Maxwell again with such other notable beauties as Peggy Hopkins Joyce, Lilyan Tashman, and that peer among peers Dolores. As if that weren't enough, the rehearsal pianist was George Gershwin.

Miss 1917 was so gigantic that it couldn't go out of town for a tryout. Worse, it had to postpone its opening twice. Yet the premiere still lasted from eight o'clock to midnight—an hour too long by *Follies* standards. Here's Channing Pollock once more: "The most wonderful of shows, the most glittering and gorgeous, the glorification of girl, the harmonious blending of art and nature."[1]

Miss 1917 made a lasting contribution to the history of revue in its amplification of the last sequence in Act One into the evening's showpiece. The imposing first-act finale had become a *Follies* hallmark—but in *Miss 1917* Ziegfeld exhilarated it as something so splendid that it became the rule in all good-sized revues. Whether as a production number (in, say, *The Band Wagon*'s working carousel and cast in full yodel kit for "I Love Louisa"), burlesque (*Two's Company*'s "Roll Along, Sadie," a takeoff on *Rain* with Bette Davis as Sadie Thompson), or, as here, a collection of songs illustrating a concept, the big number before the intermission ran through revue's apogee in the 1920s and 1930s, its retreat in the 1940s, and its eclipse in the 1950s.

Virtually the last third of *Miss 1917*'s first act presented a self-contained salute to the tunes of bygone Broadway. Kern and Wodehouse in their best form wrote the framing number, "The Land Where the Good Songs Go," a long-lined ballad in the style that Kern would develop into his unique blend of European operetta and Tin Pan Alley. As various soloists and groups stepped forward, the music that had been the songbook of a generation was given encore, with the added kick that each singer was made up to resemble the star who first introduced the number.

So Marion Davies appeared as Edna May for "They All Follow Me,"

---

[1] Note Pollock's "glorification of girl" five years before Ziegfeld started promoting the *Follies* with the phrase "Glorifying the American Girl."

the Salvation Army heroine's Tambourine Number from *The Belle of New York* (1898), with its stirring refrain of "Follow on! Follow on! When the light of faith you see!" Cleo Mayfield and her Summer Time Girls presented Blanche Ring's specialty from *The Defender* (1902), "In the Good Old Summer Time." Van and Schenck did not attempt to pose as Marie Cahill for "Under The Bamboo Tree," from *Sally in Our Alley* (1902), but this is when Bessie McCoy reclaimed her own "Yama Yama Man," and, as noted, the audience leaped to its feet in gratitude. "Dinah" and "Sammy" (from *The Wizard of Oz* [1903]) also clocked in on an already exhaustive review.

Then came Vivienne Segal's spot. At a rehearsal, Victor Herbert helpfully recommended a Fritzi Scheff specialty, his own "Kiss Me Again." Segal would make a lovely Fritzi Scheff. Jerome Kern quickly made a countersuggestion: a Julia Sanderson specialty, *his* own "They Didn't Believe Me." Segal would make a darling Julia Sanderson.

Segal decided she'd rather be lovely, and chose to render the Herbert. After an interval of intense geschrei, Herbert prevailed, and while the touchy Kern might have nursed a grudge against both Segal and Herbert, *she* went right into Kern's *Oh, Lady! Lady!!* the next year, and two years after that, *he* composed the Big Ballet in Kern's *Sally*. Besides, Kern's "Toy Clog Dance" brought down that first-act curtain, as the entire company hoofed all the way up a stage-filling staircase into the flies. So if Herbert won the geschrei, at least Kern won the finale.

Miss 1917 was the most expensive musical to that time, at a cost of $300,000. It may have been the greatest revue to that time as well: and it bombed. Opening on November 5, it struggled through 48 performances—six weeks—before giving up; and the Century Amusement Corporation folded in bankruptcy.

No one today knows what happened. True, the score was surprisingly underpowered, but all that vocal talent made it sound great. Then, too, the production opened at a $3.00 top, unusual then. But it was not unheard of—Dillingham habitually went to six or even seven dollars for his Montgomery and Stone shows. Another problem was the long running time, although after the first few nights, parts of the program began to disappear, including Castle, White, Brice, King, and the ballet troupe.

Perhaps the problem was too much Ziegfeld, too much revue. Remember, the *Follies* was always on, faithfully every year since 1907. Why make the trek to the West Sixties for a faux *Follies* when the real one was playing down in the theatre district?

But now we should consider The Girl. Who *was* Miss 1917? In the show itself, it was Marion Davies—but who was Ziegfeld's girl, show biz's girl, America's girl? Why was The Girl the musical's essential, and who was she?

Nobody, said Ziegfeld's detractors. It was all done with strings. Beauty? It was the way he dressed them, undressed them. It was the walk, the lighting. Critic George Jean Nathan, smart enough to know better, claimed that Ziegfeld "can take a various assortment of them, most of whom naturally or in other hands wouldn't be worth a second glance, and with that peculiar cunning of his convert them into what appear to be lovely and glamorous creatures."

Don't be ridiculous. Ziegfeld simply had the best taste on Broadway: in hot. He chose lovely and glamorous creatures to begin with, and his "cunning" was no more than atmosphere—for instance, in what became a *Follies* feature, the tableau. This was arranged by society scion and artist James Ben Ali Haggin Jr., who, joining Ziegfeld's outfit in 1917, dropped his first name and the Jr. to suggest a personage of the mysterious East, arriving by flying carpet to edge the *Follies* into yet bolder sexual statement. In fact, while Ziegfeld's lighting could simulate nudity, the Ben Ali Haggin Tableau literally featured nudity, legally possible as long as the women did not move.

In such Haggin Tableaux as "The Triumph of Love" or "A Kiss in the Dark," the traveler curtains would part, every man in the house would whip out his opera glasses, and, much too soon, the curtain would close out the scene. That of "The Triumph of Love" was a Venetian gondola manned, so to speak, by women in medieval dress, with a few swimming maenads in the water, apparently nude but facing upstage. "A Kiss in the

Dark" offered baroque maidens, framed in an oval, attendant upon a Strephon and Phyllis. This tableau was presented in two "views": first the couple adoring, then the couple embracing.

Whatever one's fancy, one had to admit that these were genuine beauties. It wasn't a walk or lighting: it was the *girls*. Photographer Alfred Cheney Johnston also came on board around this time, to change entirely the use of photographs for PR exploitation. Earlier, *Follies* girls were seen in ensemble shots or, like other Broadway performers, posing in a kind of go-everywhere stance suitable for general use. Johnston caught Ziegfeld's girls with his camera the way Ziegfeld caught them with his *Follies*: in racy shots with a blatant come-hither, and costumed as fully or lightly as on stage. Johnston shot some of his subjects completely nude—but the public was not aware of this. What it saw of the Johnston showgirl was what it saw onstage at the New Amsterdam: artistic and glamorous, a model of young womanhood even if she was in effect an extremely classy version of the playing cards produced for inspection in railroad smoking cars.

The Ziegfeld Girl. It was an age of Girls—the Gibson Girl, the Nell Brinkley Girl, all those *Girl* musicals we've mentioned—and what of the D. W. Griffith Girl, another signature of the age? Griffith at first selected Mary Pickford as the tintype, but shrewd Little Mary was as much businessman as girl, headed for bigger things than Griffith samplers. So he turned to Lillian Gish, Girl for life. Little Mary was dauntless; the Griffith Girl must be tender and helpless, the subject, one suspects, of unspeakable fantasies. In *The Nation,* Joseph Wood Krutch analyzed the use of girls in the various twenties revues that sprang up in imitation of Ziegfeld, finding in them the equivalent in "a democracy [to] what troupes of dancing girls were to kings." Worse: "These spectacles possess in a mild way something of the same charm which the audience in a Roman amphitheatre perceived when it [looked down on] Christians driven in to the lions."

Unlike Ziegfeld, Griffith did not dare touch *his* Girl, lest her holy innocence be contaminated. He despoiled with art. To gaze upon Gish in, say, *Broken Blossoms* (1919) is to discern the most chaste but also the most victimized of women, the craven subject of a brutal father with no champion but another victim, albeit a male. Alfred Cheney Johnston's camera roved freely through show biz, taking down not only those Girls but Lynn Fontanne, Scott and Zelda Fitzgerald, and John Barrymore tenderly holding baby Diana. And, indeed, Johnston got to both Lillian and Dorothy Gish. They look subdued but not intimidated. However, had Johnston's eye penetrated to Lillian's inner Griffith as it registered the inner Ziegfeld of Drucilla Strain, Hazel Forbes, the Fairbanks Twins, and other Ziegfeldiennes, he might have snapped her in her *Broken Blossoms* "smile." It's a famous moment: the little prey pushes up the corners of her mouth with her fingers, then freezes the look with eyes a-shriek in despair.

That was the Griffith Girl. The Ziegfeld Girl knew brutal men, but only on her way to divorce court, where—as her, shall we say, colleague Ivana Trump later put it in *The Ex-Wives Club,* she didn't get even: she got everything. Ziegfeld girls were thought by the public to lead the charmed lives dear to the evolving media culture of headlines and fiction. Their day job, like everything else in their life, occurred at night, when they would glide across a stage dressed in original sin. The rest of their time was taken up by men with nothing better to do than be handsome and give jewelry of fabled cost.

So the Ziegfeld Girl *de résistance* would be Peggy Hopkins Joyce. This despite her having appeared in only two Ziegfeld shows, *Miss 1917* and the *Follies* of that year. Essentially a showgirl, Joyce nonetheless managed to swing a line or two in a sketch. This made her impossible backstage. "A girl should always be superior," she observed in her uniquely detached vision, "when she has a speaking part."

Though she was nominally in show biz, Peggy Hopkins Joyce in fact appeared in almost nothing but scandals. She was much courted, often married, and very famous. If one couldn't say precisely what she did, one knew what she believed in: material gain through the exploitation of her beauty. Such a credo was the natural offspring of the mating of Ziegfeld and Broadway, and that was the Ziegfeld Girl: the upwardly mobile harlot. "Why be beautiful if you can't have what you want?" Peggy Joyce asked. Another Joyceism: "Hunger certainly makes you think about things."

She was very quotable, because her vapidly greedy worldview led her to phrase the most cynical deductions as if she were reading from Old Mother Hubbard. Something about this beautiful and rapacious adventuress struck everyone as essential to the age. Peggy Joyce neither defined nor redeemed her times; she helped color them in, no more. Yet she was symbolic of something, for Anita Loos seized upon her as the model for Lorelei Lee in one of the fiction bestsellers of the 1920s, the gold digger as cultural icon. "Ziegfeld Girl" and "gold digger," in fact, were synonyms for something new in the world, women who Achieved by becoming serial brides. "I can't marry everyone," Peggy finally wailed.

But she could—everyone rich, at least. The Ziegfeld Girl collected jewelry as if it were stamps or matchbooks, and while you went camping or to the shore, she went to Europe, France (as Lorelei puts it). Fanny Brice enjoyed a number in the 1920 *Follies* poking fun at the real source of it all—the *Florodora* Girl.[1] Singing "I Was a Florodora Baby," Brice framed a lament that took her far from her Roses and Beckys. Still, as the old saw cuts it, you can take Brice out of the neighborhood, but you can't take the neighborhood out of Brice. "Five darn fools got married for money," she complained, but "*I* got married for love!"

Of course, *she* could say that: Brice was the *Follies*' seriocomic in residence, to use the old show-biz term for, among other things, a woman talent who doesn't get the boy. The Ziegfeld Girl got the boy for reasons your mother didn't consider when she got your father, because Ziegfeld was an iconolater of women with power. Not Lillian Gishes: goddesses. The sort of women husbands had been dreaming about when they woke up guilty.

---

[1] There were actually six of these, the original female half of the *Florodora* Sextet, "Tell Me, Pretty Maiden," when the English show came to the Casino Theatre, in 1900: Daisy Greene, Marjorie Relyea, Agnes Wayburn, Margaret Walker, Marie L. Wilson, and the enchantingly named Vaughan Texsmith. They all married millionaires, founding a legend that the Ziegfeld Girl inherited.

If a lot of marrying was written into the activity sheet, so, all too often, were tragic outcomes. Power did some of these women no good whatsoever. The astonishing Dolores used it wisely, taking from Ziegfeld what she needed, marrying well, and leaving public life forever. But note that, if Dolores remains *the* Ziegfeld Girl in purely visual terms, her name does not come up in discussions of the lives of Ziegfeld Girls.

No, *then* they speak of the Dolly Sisters. A set of twins like so many *Follies* cuties, Roszika and Janszieka even had Ziegfeld Girl names: Rosie and Jenny *Dolly*! They logged their first tabloid marriages early on. Rosie married rich but Jenny married show biz, taking young leading man Harry Fox to husband. By 1917, aged twenty-five, they were "the million dollar Dollies" in a film of that title—and they seemed so, remarrying and being seen in importantly frivolous European places and dressing as if life were a stage and amassing the usual jewelry collection.

But what good is a happy Ziegfeld Girl? Don't the classics tell us that beauty bears doom? The Dollys' saga ended grimly—one of them hanged herself—but also according to the rules. Were these women paying for the crime of being blessed with attention? Are jealous gods driving them crazy? This is why Ziegfeld's chroniclers never know what to do with Lillian Lorraine. She seems to have ended up unhappy, or at least frustrated by the lack of attention. But she kept on living.

Some say that Lillian was Ziegfeld's choice among his Girls. But he was possibly even more involved with Olive Thomas, everyone's favorite among the doomed because of a ghastly but also mysterious death a few weeks short of her twenty-sixth birthday. Thomas' background was standard up-from-rags, her rise to riches occurred before she was twenty, and she married famous. Like so many other Ziegfeld Girls, she participated but little in Ziegfeld's art: two *Frolics* and a *Follies*. Thomas won her prestige in Hollywood, after leaving Ziegfeld. Yet her epitaph read, in all the papers, FOLLIES GIRL DIES IN PARIS.

Born in 1894, Olive Duffy began in Pennsylvania, in a poor family made even poorer when her father died, in her youth. Upon her mother's remarriage, renamed Olive Van Kirk, she had to leave high school to sell over the counter in a women's-things store. At sixteen, simply to get out of this drudgery, Olive herself married one Bernhard Thomas. Somehow or other she evaporated out of the union and made her way to New York, caught Ziegfeld's eye, and immediately became what in Renaissance days was termed a "favorite."

"I began to hear disturbing news" is how Billie puts it in her memoirs. Indiscreet friends told her "interesting anecdotes about yachting parties," which is about as euphemistic as a lady can get. One thing we can say about the Ziegfeld marriage: there were no elephants in the living room. Ziegfeld kept plenty of secrets, true—but everything that Billie heard she brought right out into the open in "a thorough-going fit of blazing, red-headed jealousy. I sulked, wept, and wailed."

As we're about to see, she did a good deal more than that. For his part, Ziegfeld was his provokingly quiet self, smoking a cigar and trying to reassure her with one loopy lie after another.

"Look, Billie," he told her, "you can't believe all you will always hear about me and various girls."

But Billie didn't want bland calmyoudowns and alibis. She wanted a fight. At length, Ziegfeld would utter one insultingly false statement too many—and that, Billie disarmingly recalls, "was my cue to tear the draperies off the windows and throw the chinaware."

That was how the Ziegfeld marriage worked. Billie didn't let unvoiced antagonisms knot her up and corrupt her home. She *spoke*.

This time, however, after the smoke cleared, Ziegfeld had the last word, in a curious statement that was more clever than true. "The trouble with you, Billie," he said, "is you always pick the wrong girl."

But Billie was right in picking Olive Thomas. Olive was the kind of woman every man wants; that in itself may be the definition of the Ziegfeld Girl. Certainly, none of Ziegfeld's rivals in the Girl business could select them with Ziegfeld's eye. There was no such thing as a George White Girl, an Earl Carroll Girl, or a Messrs. Shubert Girl. Maybe Ziegfeld never touched Thomas—but he cultivated a soft spot for her and a hatred for the man who, he enjoyed thinking, took her from him and destroyed her.

This rival wasn't another producer. He wasn't even a man but rather a kid, like Olive. And he was the younger brother of that other kind of Girl from Ziegfeld's kind—the president of the club of independent women, Mary Pickford. Olive Thomas' great love and murderer—to hear Ziegfeld tell it—was that toothily grinning all–American boy Jack Pickford.

Thomas had launched her film career in the east, and, arriving in California in 1917, landed at Triangle, the studio of Thomas Ince, Mack Sennett, and D. W. himself. It was a magical time to break into the movies, for the middle class, finally discovering this alternative to theatregoing, was veritably gobbling movies up. One could attract a gigantic public overnight, and Olive did so, leaving Triangle for the intensely ambitious Myron Selznick. The son of pioneer mogul Lewis Selznick and brother of future mogul David O. Selznick, Myron was so young that his mother had to sign the contracts for Selznick Pictures.

Among them was *The Flapper* (1920), a rare Olive Thomas title that has survived, to give us a look at one of the Girls in her full truth: but the evidence is inconclusive. Playing a spirited schoolkid who tries the sophisticated life in a crush on an older man on an overnight in New York City, Thomas is charming but hardly a dream beauty. Alberto Vargas painted her seminude and Ziegfeld hung the picture on his office wall: an open scandal in the form of art. It suggests an American Garbo; Selznick's flapper is anything but. Returning from the big city, Thomas dresses like Tosca (complete with tasseled staff) and sophisticates about, but she seems no more special than the other young ladies of silent Hollywood. Then, too, the black-and-white photography fails on Thomas' most alluring feature, her dark violet-blue eyes. Is it possible that Ziegfeld's stage management really did turn the ordinary into the spectacular, as so many opinion makers wanted to believe? In any case, Thomas was a smash in the movies, with access to Hollywood royalty: Queen Mary, Prince Jack, Princess sister Lottie, and the dowager empress Mrs. Pickford, terrifying to a fault.

Olive and Jack were made for each other, for she was starved for fun and he was fun. Like her, he was physically beautiful, possessed of a wish to charm, and a natural in the movies. There the resemblance ended.

The ex-gingham clerk from Charleroi, Pennsylvania was still getting used to the fast life, while Jack, twenty (to Thomas' twenty-two) when they wed, was already one of the most dissolute figures in Hollywood. "The gayest, wildest brats who ever stirred the stardust on Broadway" was the verdict of Frances Marion, the scenarist who wrote *The Flapper*. "They were much more interested in playing the roulette of life than in concentrating on their careers."

You know what happens now. No sooner has the honeymoon ended than the quarreling begins. When Ziegfeld and Billie fought, it was to clear away the clutter of dishonesty: at least, that was Billie's intention. When Thomas and Pickford fought, it was part of their joyride in the painted hearse to hell. It was in Paris, in 1920; after one such fight, that Thomas mistook for either drinking water or sleeping pills a bottle of bichloride of mercury tablets: poison. It was never explained how such a mistake could have occurred; Ziegfeld held that Pickford had lured his wife into his world of ecstatic pharmacopeia and she was in such a haze that she might have mistaken anything for anything else. Another theory saw Pickford as having infected Thomas with syphilis—the mercury tablets were used at that time to treat the disease. Perhaps a devastated Thomas wanted to kill herself: the tablets were properly used topically, not ingested.

Pickford, utterly devastated himself by Thomas' action, insisted that it was nothing more than an accident in the dark. The Paris police came to the same conclusion. However it happened, Thomas lingered in agony for days, then died. The perfect Ziegfeld Girl.

Of course, that is really the tabloids' Ziegfeld Girl, the doomed beauty who leaves us so early that her copy never gets stale. However, for all his emphasis on the loveliness of very young women who did literally nothing more than show up in the *Follies,* the *Midnight Frolic,* and, later, Ziegfeld's many book shows of the 1920s, what he really loved was talent—theatre talent, especially. Of Ziegfeld's four great life's loves, Anna, Billie, and one yet to be named were performers above all. Only Lillian Lorraine was not of their class; and even Lillian must have counted *some* performer's gifts or Ziegfeld would never have given her so many important musical numbers.

In fact, the true Ziegfeld Girl was, whatever happened to her in the end, an entertainer of delight, the kind of thing today's show biz lacks. We still have great talents, but we've run out of that blend of charm, warmth, and eccentricity that marked Golden Age notables. Whether as Ziegfeld's Fanny Brice or, later, someone like Mary Martin; in Ziegfeld's Will Rogers or, say, Robert Preston, these stars were, like F. Scott Fitzgerald's rich, different from you and me. They were brilliant performers, yes: but they enlightened as well, working the data of life into a magic. They were artists. One might even call them freaks, but one means it as a compliment.

And the ultimate Ziegfeld Girl, now to be named, was just that sort of magician. An astonishing dancer, she could sing and read lines but also lent a fetching sense of humor to everything she did. She, too, was a beauty, a little odd up close perhaps but possessed of a radiance to fill the New Amsterdam. She is the fourth of Ziegfeld's loves, the most gifted musical star of her era, and she may have been the one Ziegfeld Girl whom Ziegfeld could not win over sexually.

Chroniclers take it for granted that he did so, but there is no evidence. Theatre people of that age assumed that there was bound to be a door fee when the still relatively unknown ingénue was offered entrée into the *Follies*. But this one had both a sexual appetite and a strong sense of self, and she would have had no patience for the importuning of the nasal-voiced old guy whose office was a brothel. Mere Ziegfeld Girls paid that price; this Girl paid in talent. When it came to importuning, she responded to chorus boys only. In a way, she was her own Ziegfeld, and her name, as you must have guessed, was Marilyn Miller.

CHAPTER ELEVEN

The Dazzler

Marilynn Reynolds, born in 1898, started out in show biz—as did many future stars—in a family act in vaudeville. A native of Evansville, Indiana, Miller had two older sisters, an older brother, and a performer-manager stepfather named Caro Miller. He was unfortunately one of those strict-discipline grown-ups who forgets what it was like to be young and treats kids as unruly impediments to the execution of his will. This seems to have activated a rebellious chip in Miller's personal computations. She loved freedom and hated authority, which explains the approach-avoidance nature of her later relationship with Ziegfeld, one of the most controlling of producers.

That unusual first name was an agglutination of Mary and Lynn, Marilynn's maternal grandparents. Raised in the wings of vaudeville houses, Marilynn looked on as siblings Ruth, Claire, and Edwin appeared with Caro as the Four Columbians. But when Edwin fought back against Caro's punishing rod and the act became the Three Columbians, Marilynn made her debut as a surprise baby Columbian.

She was a sprite all her life, youthful and happy but also one of those natural talents that needs seasoning and practice but no lessons. No one had to show her how; she knew how. The dancers of early-twentieth-century show biz worked out their own steps, combinations, acts—a blend of instinct and stealing from one's betters. There weren't a lot of choreographers around, but there was a great deal of what we can call unethical public domain.

At some point, Caro Miller expanded the act to include his wife and, officially now, little Marilynn. They were the Five Columbians, and the star of the act was on her way to discovery. She could do everything, including the celebrity imitations so much a part of stage work at the time, and she was shockingly young—still fifteen when she signed for Broadway. Lee Shubert saw Marilynn in London and decided to put her into the Messrs.' annual revue, *The Passing Show,* in the 1914 edition. We've already had a sample of the underage contract when Myron Selznick did business with Olive Thomas, and now Caro Miller signed Marilynn's Shubert papers. (This will presently be music to Ziegfeld's ears.)

Marilynn's Shubert deal took her into three *Passing Show*s and two other titles, yet they did not put Marilynn over. It was the Big Time, yes. But Shubert revues were constipated hodgepodges, vaudeville with a Broadway face. Over at Ziegfeld's, the *Follies* offered the most effective showcase in the industry; no other producer made the help look so good. In Olive Thomas' movieland, so the story goes, one Ziegfeld Girl who had just arrived in Hollywood met another Ziegfeld Girl in the middle of shooting a film, and Miss Famous told the newcomer, "If the boss telegrammed me today, I'd be in New York tomorrow."

So Marilynn's Shubert years, 1914 to 1918, were better than vaudeville in the material sense but short in career enhancement. "The Winter Garden Company present their annual summer review [*sic*] *The Passing Show of 1915,*" the hoardings cried, naming the authors as composers Leo Edwards, William F. Peters, and J. Leubrie Hill and wordman Harold Atteridge but omitting the central credit, "In pathetic imitation of Florenz Ziegfeld Jr." It seemed so easy: attend the *Follies* five or six times, "steal everything but the ushers" (as J. J. liked to put it), and put on the same show with different performers and different material.

Yet even with young Marilyn's fizzy charm, the Jewish comics Willie and Eugene Howard, John Charles Thomas (the Roscoe, for those who know Sondheim's *Follies*), a Russian ballet troupe, and a Hawaiian sextet to feed the hula fad, *The Passing Show*—this one, any one—was a bit of a dirge. Yes, there were the spoofs of the latest plays, which Ziegfeld had appropriated from burlesque and were now regarded as essentials in any smart revue. *The Passing Show of 1915* spoofed three of the previous season's straight plays, Edward Sheldon's artily la-di-da *The Song of Songs*; *Trilby* (1895), revived with its original Svengali, Wilton Lackaye; and George Bernard Shaw's *Androcles and the Lion,* with Willie Howard and Arthur Hill, respectively, in the title roles.[1] Isn't that like Ziegfeld? the Shuberts might have asked. Yes. But all the rest of the comedy centered on the Howards, whereas Ziegfeld filled his stage with clowns playing off each other's different styles. The Howards were two of the same thing.

There was another problem: J. J.'s relentless attempt to pull off a Ziegfeld by sticking posing showgirls into everything—solo songs, sketches, production numbers. It was the despair of the *Passing Show* creators that, late in rehearsals, J. J. would appear and start Ziegfelding. Alas, the bargain-basement Shubert touch lumbered his Girls with not the creations of Lucile but stock finery from the warehouse, so familiar from other Shubert outings it could be called historic. Ziegfeld's Dolores would materialize as the Peacock Girl and the house would instantly go quite, quite still. But let a Shubert version enter and the house would murmur, "There's the beaded number from the last eighteen Casino shows."

The Passing Show of 1915 cast Marilynn as First Love, to dance in the ballet sequences, imitate the popular comedian Clifton Crawford, and sing and hoof in three solo spots. It's a snazzy program—till one hears the solos. "Small-Town Girlie" tells how modern life has reached the country, as "Ev'ry one-horse town has a village clown and a midnight cabaret." But it's a dim little ditty, and "The Trombone Man" is worse, too raucous for a heroine and with inane lyrics that one never heard at

---

[1] A curious in-joke informs this casting, for Hill played the lion in the original production of *The Wizard of Oz* for several years in New York and on tour. He was more or less beloved in the role, in fact: the favorite actor of a generation of children whose first show this was.

the New Amsterdam. Worst of the three is "Any Old Time With You," a bomb of a number. No: a dud.

It wasn't simply that *The Passing Show*s had poor scores, nor that Shubert writers never matched snappy *Follies* novelties like "Moving Day in Jungletown" or "The Broadway Glide." The *Follies* was a whirlwind of the unexpected. *The Passing Show* was a mudpuddle decorated with the beaded number from the last eighteen Casino shows.

So, of course, Ziegfeld stole Marilynn from the Shuberts and, of course, she wanted to be stolen. It was logical the way destiny is logical, because while both Anna and Billie were limited as musical stars, Marilynn had the potential to inhabit a story show so absolutely that she could well become Broadway's greatest heroine. This one might hold a show in the modern sense: in the way Ethel Merman, Mary Martin, and Gwen Verdon held shows. Anna was wonderful in her giddy folderol, but those were very old-fashioned concepts by the time Ziegfeld and Marilynn crossed paths; and Billie was no one's idea of a variety diva. Marilynn could *enable* Ziegfeld, provide the human material for something no one had tried before: state-of-the-art musical comedy in the Ziegfeld manner. That is, the dependable old ingredients made novel by the application of surprise and delight. At stage center would be the Cinderella, hoofing and toe-dancing, singing a break-the-heart anthem and projecting as much carnal knowledge as saucy innocence. At stage right and stage left, the comics, one quaint and one sleazy. Joseph Urban, Lucile, Dolores, Jerome Kern teamed with Victor Herbert again . . . but we're leaping ahead of the history. First, Ziegfeld has to liberate Marilynn of her entanglement with the Shuberts.

A squad of Philadelphia lawyers couldn't break a Shubert contract, but the first thing a Syndicate manager learned was the art of the loophole. Marilynn seems so young—nineteen going on twenty as we speak. She must have been—what?—fifteen or sixteen when she signed with the Shuberts. Who set his name on the paper? Caro Miller, the stepfather? But was he Marilynn's *legal guardian*?

Well . . . actually . . . no. Miller had never legally adopted Marilynn. As her stepfather, he naturally assumed that he held legal status in taking responsibility for her professional undertakings.

In fact: he didn't. Only through adoption could he have been granted such rights. So Marilynn's Shubert contract evaporated—doing it to the Shuberts again; delicious—and Ziegfeld put Marilynn into *Ziegfeld Follies of 1918.* They had to ride over one little speed bump along the way, for Ziegfeld disliked cute spellings in performers' names. Cute *names* per se were fine (although for every Vanda Hoff or Drucilla Strain there were ten Betty Martins). But those two *nn*s looked like an error. Ziegfeld asked nicely, Marilynn said no, and he went into a nag about it that lasted five years.

We sometimes read that Ziegfeld only liked established stars, but we have seen him creating his stars as a rule, from Sandow on. Virtually all the longtime *Follies* headliners were nobodies or so when Ziegfeld hired them—Brice, Errol, Fields, Rogers, Cantor. (Bert Williams, ironically, is the exception; his fame extended even to white audiences who had never seen him onstage.) Not till Ziegfeld's last few years, when success was mysteriously eluding him in show after show, did he take on, for his book musicals, talents that had already won their star—the Astaires, Evelyn Laye, Bert Lahr.

In 1918, however, Ziegfeld owned Broadway, and he filled his *Follies* with *his* people: Cantor, Fields, Rogers, Ann Pennington; leading showgirls Dolores and Kay Laurell; drag zany Bert Savoy with his straight man, Jay Brennan; the Fairbanks Twins; Lillian Lorraine in her last *Follies* of all; Marilynn, as we know, and the song-and-dance man she fell in love with and was to marry, Frank Carter. There were stars out front as well for the opening, on June 18, the sixth *Follies* to play the New Amsterdam. The crush took in Ethel Barrymore, Laurette Taylor, George M. Cohan, Irving Berlin (in uniform), novelist Rex Beach, professional vamp (and, she claimed, reincarnation of Cleopatra) Valeska Suratt, and the evening's official hostess, Billie Burke Ziegfeld, whose arrival at something like 8:28 signaled to the conductor to strike up the overture.

By now, the public knew what to expect of the *Follies* except when it didn't. For instance, Savoy and Brennan simply presented their usual act, in which the former camped and minced about while the latter fed her lines. A sketch set in patent attorney W. C. Field's office offered assistants Cantor and Carter and zany inventors Harry Kelly and Gus Minton going through familiar motions. Yet more familiar was the scene in which Cantor is forced into some sort of physical humiliation, reacting with his hundred different whines and fainting spells. Here, it was "The Aviator's Test." Will Rogers' lariat-cum-patter act was a cliché by now, even if Channing Pollock thought Rogers "more than a monologuist," dubbing him "a talking Thackeray."

But the opening was a knockout, as the curtain rose on a dark stage that eventually lit up on a revolving ball with Kay Laurell perched on top. As the "Spirit of the Follies," she did little—in fact, nothing—more than look fabulous as other girls came on as Follies of Speed, of Dance, and so on. It was the latest of Ziegfeld's solutions to the problem of how to start a show whose only subject was itself: whose existence depended on its being the greatest show on earth, regularly once a year.

More surprise and delight arrived in a Mirror Number, "When I'm Looking At You." Lillian Lorraine sang it, then, in typical Ziegfeldian "pun" fashion, the title created the visual, as Marie Wallace, in the "mirror," pretended to be Lillian's reflection while the two Fairbankses doubled each other as well.

And what of Marilynn? Her outstanding turn was another show-biz impersonation, this one of Billie Burke! "Mine Was a Marriage of Convenience" was the number, a reference to Billie's latest show, a revival of Sydney Grundy's *A Marriage of Convenience* by actor-manager Henry Miller. Note that the *Follies* continued to require a high cultural I.Q. of its public, with at least a glancing knowledge of the theatrical calendar.

"There is no use advising you to see the *Follies*," wrote our *Follies* guide Channing Pollock. "You *will* see it. Everybody does." That is, everybody enough to fill the New Amsterdam for the typical four months or so, followed by the tour to reach a more national everybody. And it was still Ziegfeld's rule that the entire original *Follies* company must hold together till the show closed on the road, sometime in spring.

Indeed, when Will Rogers wanted to skip a few afternoons to take in the World Series, Ziegfeld moved the matinées to Friday and Monday rather than disappoint ticket buyers. After all, the *Follies* was art, to be protected from compromise and humiliation. This was also good business management. "You know, Bill," Ziegfeld wrote him by letter, "there isn't anything I would not do for you, but you must realize we have an enormous organization, enormous expense, and with the [spectacle] necessary now with The Follies it takes a year to get our production [i.e., capitalization] back. To give matinees without you in them *would be absolutely impossible.*" Besides, as always Ziegfeld discerned in all this a PR opportunity: "I think we can get a good story through the dramatic column[s] . . . owing to your desire to see the Games I agreed to this, so you know what high esteem I hold you [in]."

One wonders if the *Follies'* everybody took in Anna Held, Ziegfeld's most prominent castoff and, though only forty-five in 1918, something of a relic. The picture hats and intricately evolved gowns suddenly seemed *so* last century. Worse, Ziegfeld's emphasis on above all American youth as the frame of female beauty appeared to dismiss Anna herself.

She had been very busy in the last few years nonetheless. Her final show with Ziegfeld, *Miss Innocence,* had opened as far back as 1908, when the *Follies* was still a roof show. Besides performing in vaudeville, Anna had made war work in France a personal crusade. She spent countless hours consoling the wounded in French hospitals, and even saw another of her beloved automobiles, a Renault touring car with ice box and fold-down table, requisitioned by the French Army for use by officers reading maps in the field on that handy table. After the war, Anna gave many a lecture across the breadth of the U.S., telling of the suffering of *les poilus,* the French enlisted men, of the slaughter of the thousands, of the gassing. "You must go!" she told American men, the husbands, sons, and brothers of her fan base of women. "All must act together!" In another part of the forest, her memoirs, she cried, somewhat gruesomely, "Suivez-moi, jeune homme! Mon sourire et mes yeux ensorceleurs vous conduirons peut-être dans l'autre monde." Follow me, young man! My enchanting eyes and smile may well lead you into the beyond.

Follow Me was the title of Anna's next show. It opened on November 29, 1916, four months and a week before the U.S. entered the war, but this was no Preparedness Musical. Anna did insist in slipping one "message" speech into the proceedings, denouncing war even as she still fervently hoped that America would get into it. Otherwise, *Follow Me* was typical Anna fare, set in Paris and offering the star as a flame of cabaret.

There were two Eyes Songs in this one, Anna's "Oh, I Want To Be Good But My Eyes Won't Let Me" and—this sung by her co-star, Henry Lewis—"What Do You Want To Make Those Eyes At Me For (When They Don't Mean What They Say!)."[1] Anna should have been ready for those tricky senior roles, yet she showed up, as ever, in her hourglass figure and *passéiste* wardrobe. Other musical-comedy heroines were kitting out in the trim new styles, even in street clothes in the famous Princess shows. Anna continued to dress as if for the Second Coming. She even borrowed Lucile from Ziegfeld to rig up the first version of the peacock outfit that Lucile would redesign for Dolores in the 1919 *Midnight Frolic*.

It sounds expensive, so Anna must have paid for the costume herself, because the producers of *Follow Me* were the Shuberts. Incredibly, Anna had gone over to the enemy. The Messrs. must have plied her with blandishments; they did talk of naming their next theatre after her, as they had done for Maxine Elliott, Nazimova, and Julian Eltinge.

There was to be no Anna Held Theatre, but *Follow Me* was a hit, and Anna embarked on a tour. The first year of full-out American wartime, 1917, saw Anna and *Follow Me* in Oregon, Canada, Washington, D.C., at Fort Dix, and thence to California. There Anna began to weaken, visibly suffering and occasionally canceling performances when she was too fragile to move. She was spelled at times by that obsessive Anna Held Jr., Liane Carrera. Liane's blurb was ready: "I was doing Anna Held's songs and dances as though I had been doing them all my life."

---

[1] Amusingly, the latter number is one of the few associated with Anna that my readers may actually have heard sung on a Broadway stage. A collaboration of (this is the sheet music billing) Joe McCarthy, Howard Johnson, and composer Jimmie Monaco, "What Do You Want To Make Those Eyes At Me For" was interpolated into the Harry Tierney-Joseph McCarthy *Irene* score when that piece was revived for Debbie Reynolds, in 1973.

The tour called off, Anna was brought back to New York, to her residence at the Savoy Plaza Hotel, on Fifth Avenue and between Fifty-Eighth and Fifty-Ninth Streets. Doctors diagnosed her ailment as multiple myeloma, a rare blood disease that was untreatable at the time. In the popular imagination, Anna's problem was corsetitis: she had killed herself with field expedients in the name of beauty. Nameless surgeries to slim the hips, quack prescriptions, fad diets, and, yes, the Anna Held strangle-the-waist corset. All nonsense. Anna was told that she had a few months to live, and we presume that she and Ziegfeld must have met at least one last time. Unfortunately, while most of Ziegfeld's professional life is documented, his personal life confounds inspection—and there is as well his terror of being around death. He habitually sent the most imposing sympathy wreath to a funeral while failing to make an appearance himself.

That year's *Follies* was in its fourth week when Anna died, on August 12, 1918. She was laid to rest in the Gate of Heaven Cemetery in Mt. Pleasant, New York, in a plot purchased by Anna's lifelong colleague and friend Lillian Russell. The stone is grandiose: an arch bearing Anna's name framed by two mourning seats. I have not given Anna's age in this book because she herself never gave it once she had entered upon the world stage. However, Anna's grave finally dispelled the mystery, giving her birth year as 1872. Anna, we now know, was five years younger than Ziegfeld, forty-six when she died.

She was wife, instructor, and pupil, and, we think, the first to see what potential this man had as an artist. What a marriage: Paris and Chicago! Even: gentlewoman and hustler. Ziegfeld made enemies wherever he went; Anna befriended everybody. In her own strange and continental way she expanded American art to comprehend other arts, thus to enrich it. She was a beautiful woman, a lovely personality, and a creative force, and she gave up Ziegfeld as much because she had no more to teach him as because those Ziegfeld Girls were wrecking their relationship.

Billie felt the same way about the Girls. But one Ziegfeld Girl had nothing to do with Broadway—and this one not only didn't threaten Billie's marriage with Flo but sealed it. In the midst of death is life: Patricia Burke Ziegfeld, born at Burkely Crest on October 23, 1916.

A typical Ziegfeld "formal": sitting and serious in a three-piece suit. Many later shots find Ziegfeld less magisterial, but he almost never smiles.

Ziegfeld's Early Stars

The Great Ziegfeld:
A Photo Essay

Sandow, the first Beautiful Male in show-biz history. Anna Held **(overleaf)** was the Beautiful Woman....

Held tended to overdress, but her hourglass symmetry and *charme* made her one of the musical's biggest stars.

A magazine cover finds her in full gala, a cross between Rapunzel and the Coty Girl.

This is the nearest Anna got to the everyday; she might be off to the grocer's.

Stars of the Follies

If Bert Williams was the philosopher and Will Rogers the satirist, Eddie Cantor was the *Follies'* resident hysteric. We find Cantor outside the stage door during a wartime *Follies* matinee, in his habitual blackface.

Ziegfeld's greatness lay not only in star-stuffed packages but also in brilliant supporting talent. Dancer Carl Randall and singer Emma Carus embody the type, though they appeared in different *Follies* editions, she in 1907 and he in 1915, 1916, and 1920. Randall played one of the musical's most famous characters, the subject of *Show Boat*'s "Bill." (The song was written for *Oh, Lady! Lady!!*, in which Randall was Willoughby "Bill" Finch.) Note the period hairdos. Randall revels in pomade, and a thousand spiders went blind spinning Carus' top.

The Dolly Sisters need no caption anchoring. But Fanny Brice **(overleaf)** offers a tell. . . .

Costumed for the 1910 *Follies* (albeit without the matching hat and umbrella), Brice anticipates Irene Sharaff's *Funny Girl* designs. However, note that Brice is in show dress yet offstage. This is because newspaper reproduction was so primitive that backgrounds distracted. So producers urged the White Studio photographers and Van Damm (actually the married team of George and Florence Van Damm Thomas) to include these character shots in their key sheets. At times, one can see the wainscoting of a hallway in the Thomas' Fiftieth Street apartment.

Ziegfeld's Family

The woman Ziegfeld fell in love with, Billie Burke, as a Charles Frohman star: the fine young lady **(above)** and the hoyden **(below)**. Not till Ziegfeld became Billie's husband and manager was she to try out other, less limited roles. Later, she found her vocation in Hollywood inventing The Billie Burke Type: a comic who doesn't know she's funny.

Ziegfeld, Billie in a trendy cloche hat, and daughter Patricia in 1925. Note that Ziegfeld still isn't smiling.

No Ziegfeld scrapbook is complete without Alfred Cheney Johnstons, here of Drucilla Strain, Gladys Glad, and Ann Pennington.

"Penny" was a dancing star, and we are glad to see Gladys, in her *Rio Rita* kit, creating a Rio Grande air with music. Drucilla, however, doesn't do anything but look fabulous: the truest Ziegfeld Girl of all.

Follies sheet music (**facing page**) typically featured a Ziegfeld Girl for the core numbers. Interpolations, issued by various publishers, were adorned with tintypes of the introducing singer. Yet how Greatness provokes imitation!

Ziegfeld's Rivals

Hitchy-Koo (**above**) art is stolen from that of *Follies of 1910* (unseen here; but note *Hitchy-Koo*'s composer, Cole Porter). Meanwhile, *The Passing Show* is dull, the *Scandals* energized, and the *Vanities* a limp *Follies*.

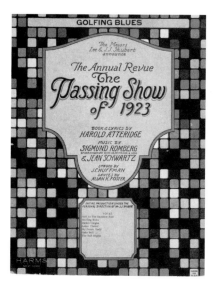

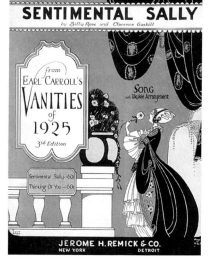

Ziegfeld's Book Shows

Norma Terris and Howard Marsh in *Show Boat.* Rehearsing *The Parson's Bride,* Marsh needs no script (parked under his knee) for "Miss Lucy, will you be mine?" *Rosalie,* like most twenties musicals, is boy meets girl, boy loses girl, boy gets girl. But *Show Boat,* the unique twenties musical, is boy rehearses with girl, boy loses girl, boy gets girl twenty-three years later.

Marilyn Miller as Rosalie.

Farewell

We view the northwest corner of Broadway and Forty-Fifth Street in 1936, when MGM's Ziegfeld bio played the Astor Theatre. Today, this is the site of the Marriott Marquis Hotel. (Sharp eyes will pick out the billboard of the Bijou Theatre, one of three playhouses demolished in favor of the new structure.) Four years after his death, Ziegfeld still overlooked Broadway. He does so yet today, and *that* is greatness. Ziegfeld is smiling at last.

CHAPTER TWELVE

Known Throughout the Land

So it seems that the Prince of Wales was at the *Follies* one night. Eddie Cantor was in the cast, and the prince made it known that he would like to hear Cantor render "That's the Kind of a Baby For Me." The number was from the 1917 *Follies,* and this was *Follies of 1919,* but a first-division celeb such as the future king of England could do that kind of thing in those days. The entire show was put on hold while Cantor came out to announce the interpolation to the public, and someone ran down to the New Amsterdam basement to find the orchestra materials in the 1917 trunk. Needless to say, whoever was deputizing for Ziegfeld on-site got a press release ready for the morning editions.

Meanwhile, on stage, Cantor was doing what most comics of Ziegfeld's era did very well: charming the public with a change in the program, exclusively for them on that night only. Seeing the music being distributed to the players down in the pit, Cantor neared the end of his spiel with "I've been asked not to mention the fact that a distinguished member of British royalty is with us tonight."

To be sure that the audience got it, Cantor gazed directly at the prince, who was next to his American hostess, Mrs. Cornelius Vander-bilt. This set off a buzz in the auditorium, as all those who knew that the prince was in town told the two or three who didn't. "But I want him to know," Cantor went on, "that if he leaves New York without seeing the Bronx, he'll be sorry all his life!"

And as the orchestra ripped into the intro, the prince leaned over to Mrs. Vanderbilt and asked, "What are the Bronx?"

The tale records something of the unpredictable excitement of Ziegfeldian revue, that mixture of expertise and improvisation that show biz used to thrive on. The duller revues plonked along night after night in a state of frozen adequacy; the better revues *breathed*. It kept everyone—performers and public alike—on his toes with a touch of wariness that we might call "hit sweat."

This air of "anything can happen" seems to have been most surely felt in this 1919 *Follies*, partly because it was stuffed with improvisers and also because it was considered the best of all *Follies* experiences then and later. But that is exactly what Ziegfeld planned on: a greatest of all *Follies*, to put Marilynn over as Broadway's Heroine, thus to herald his coming return to the story musical with the greatest of stories, the Show of the Age starring Marilynn Miller.

A storm of notes, telegrams, letters, and telephone calls revealed Ziegfeld's immediate plan: a modernized *Follies*, the surprise and delight to be refitted in state of the art. The format was not changed, but its look and sound was lighter and faster. The same old comics and cuties were on hand along with Cantor and Marilynn: Bert Williams, Van and Schenck, the Fairbanks Twins, John Steel. With Fanny Brice sidelined by pregnancy, Ziegfeld discovered Ray Dooley, a comparable seriocomic, in the Irish line; Dooley came complete with brother Johnny and husband, Eddie Dowling. The three were ideal *Follies* talents: versatile, to supplement the ones who only sang or danced.

They were twenty-somethings as well, and Marilynn was young, and the *Follies* itself, suddenly, was young. Following the newest style in revue, the core tunestack came from a single source, Irving Berlin, who with Jerome Kern was leading the first generation of all-American songwriters. True, grandfather Victor Herbert was writing the show's Big Ballet. But Herbert was the dean of music, sheer prestige. Berlin and Kern were wisenheimers; you heard it in *their* music, which avoided Big Ballet as a rule. Yet for all the sass, this was the loveliest of *Follies*, a Marilynn *Follies*. As Louis R. Reid wrote, in *The Dramatic Mirror*, it was "as sensuously beautiful a . . . *Follies* as has ever made the name of Ziegfeld known throughout the land."

Premiering on June 16 at the New Amsterdam, *Ziegfeld Follies of 1919* began with the usual incantatory prologue, in this case "The Follies Salad," in which the usual tenor sang cheers to eight girls who ambled in at intervals of eight measures of time, each costumed as a salad ingredient, from lettuce to paprika. (The Fairbanks Twins were salt and pepper.) But it was not that suave lambkin John Steel who brought them on: instead, Eddie Dowling did the honors, no doubt with the tiniest hint of whimsy. Eros, to Ziegfeld, was no laughing matter, true. But as long as the girls didn't fiddle with their costumes, he didn't care what the tenor did.

A salad of art and sex: the *Follies*. One reason to first-night Ziegfeld's annuals was to be among the first to report on them; in 1919 everyone was talking of a Ben Ali Haggin tableau called "Melody Fantasy and Folly of Years Gone By." A medieval study, it offered Simone D'Herlys as Lady Godiva on a great white steed and dressed in nothing but a headband and her locks.

Stunning. The usual solo spots before the traveler curtain gave Eddie Cantor (in blackface, in Act One) and Bert Williams (in Act Two) typical Ziegfeldian moments of ethnic reverberation. This was timeless *Follies*; the up-to-date 1919 *Follies* spent most of its time on Prohibition.[1] Both Cantor and Walker devoted at least one number each to it, in Cantor's "You Don't Need the Wine To Have a Wonderful Time (While They Still Make Those Beautiful Girls)" and Williams' "The Moon Shines on the Moonshine."

---

[1] We should address a popular confusion about exactly when the issue of a legally dry America rose to the fore of revue's topics menu. The Volstead Act, which many think of as synonymous with "Prohibition," was not passed (over President Wilson's veto, by the way) till October 28, 1919, when the 1919 *Follies* was in midrun. However, the Volstead Act simply outlined the enforcement procedures for Prohibition, which had become law in the Eighteenth Amendment to the Constitution, ratified on January 29 of 1919, to take effect a year later. Thus, *Follies of 1919* had nearly six months in which to ready its commentary.

Interpolations from the usual suspects brought in the latest dance craze in the Dollys' "Shimmy Town," gave theme to Joseph Urban's dike-and-windmill Dutch study in "Tulip Time," and emphasized the fresh breeze of Marilynn in "Sweet Sixteen." But Irving Berlin really did control this score. Never one to ignore a dance craze, he covered Prohibition as well in "You Cannot Make Your Shimmy Shake on Tea"; opened Act Two in a seraglio with "Harem Life" and "I'm the Guy That Guards the Harem"; and gave the *Follies* what is now regarded as its anthem, "A Pretty Girl Is Like a Melody." The most literal of Ziegfeld's pun-stagings, the song introduced the parading Girls as great classical melodies, here one by Mendelssohn, there one by Massenet. That team player John Steel would be indispensable in this one, the ultimate Roscoe in the most rhapsodic of salutes.

We of today take all this for granted, because the format has been wallpaper in American culture for four generations, most notably in Hollywood musicals and latterly for comment and satire. In 1919, however, it was not only novel but, in its loony way, stimulating, a union of lovely music and lovely Girlflesh, as if the two very different sensualities formed a logical bond. Who but Ziegfeld would "hear" a sashaying beauty in Offenbach's *Tales of Hoffmann* barcarolle? It's the Chicago Musical College and the Chicago World's Fair midway come together in transcendent revision.

By now, as we already know, the last spot in Act One was bound to be the Greatest Production Number Ever Seen, and *1919* really had one, a minstrel show on risers covering the width of the New Amsterdam stage. While the stagehands pushed the construction into place, Van and Schenck, Eddie Dowling, and John Steel quarteted before the traveler on a medley of minstrel standards. Then the curtains parted on the whole shebang, with the entire cast in place against a color scheme of silver, white, and pink. Cantor and Williams were the "end men," Mr. Tambo and Mr. Bones, George LeMaire served as the Interlocutor, and each of the other stars took a specialty. Berlin splashed the scene with "I'd Rather See a Minstrel Show" and, retrieved from his all-soldier revue, *Yip Yip Yaphank* (1918), "Mandy," with Marilynn presenting the straight version and Ray Dooley dooleying it. The sequence was such a spectacular exhibition that few critics noted that the minstrel show itself was by 1919 a dead form that refused to rest in peace, and Ziegfeld's end-of-days revitalization left such memories that many a movie not only tucked in a minstrel bit but—especially at MGM—retained Ziegfeld's stepped setting.

Among *1919*'s incidental pleasures was a comedy sketch called "A Saloon of the Future," again with showgirl impersonations, now of soda pop, fruit juice, and such, and Marilynn offered "A Syncopated Cocktail." Victor Herbert's ballet was set in the circus just so Marilynn could enter on a big white horse, an effect so thrilling that Charles Dillingham unapologetically stole it for *his* Miller vehicle, *Sunny,* six years later.

The other set-piece dance was a drugged-out pas de deux laid in an opium den where the featured dance team of Maurice and Walton—Miss Maurice costumed just this side of the law—displayed the dos and don'ts of pharmaceutical *volupté.* In the next generation of revue this would be an above all Artistic Highlight; in 1919, it was one of those guy-throws-chick-around things, immediately followed by the Dooley kids in a burlesque version.

Yet another bustle of stagehands was fronted by a before-the-curtain sequence, now for Van and Schenck. When the stage was ready, Ziegfeld unveiled a finale devoted to the Salvation Army. Showgirl Jessie Reed embodied the spirit of the corps, and there was just time for some more Irving Berlin, in "My Tambourine Girl" and, patriotically, "We Made the Doughnuts Over There."

Then the curtain hit the floor and the audience cheered. Yet it was almost too great a thing, this particular *Follies,* too rich a meal: all dessert. Ziegfeld called it "the best [show] I have ever produced," but what was he producing? They called them "girl and music shows" then; how basic a term for such sophistication of elements!

We don't want to get too filled with academic helium when deconstructing the *Follies,* but Ziegfeld's French Chicago of a Broadway recalls Friedrich Nietzsche's theories about ancient Greek theatre. He saw modern art as fragmented, with tragedy here and farce there, where the

Greeks liked their Apollonian and Dionysian served together, distinct but bonded in a not entirely coherent engagement of reason and ecstasy. Such art is not supposed to make sense: it is supposed to reflect human existence: a jumble of the demented, the rational, the idealistic, and the incomprehensible served in music and mystery and followed by jokes. Isn't that Ziegfeld's recipe for *Follies*? As if in Greece, he created a community of playmakers and playgoers who knew what to expect yet kept getting surprised. It was old Athens in the New Amsterdam. And no one could describe precisely what it was, because, to pick one example, a series of showgirls dressed as salad ingredients—even if Eddie Dowling was grinning a little—doesn't make any sense.

What held the *Follies* together was abandon. These were events defined by their own disruptions, by Ziegfeld's juxtaposing of typical fare (such as Prohibition jokes) with Lady Godiva (Good heavens, is that girl naked? . . . too late to be sure, as the curtains close the view up tight). It was Chicago as a musical, the Art Museum next to the Trocadero cabaret, that very American notion of Make Your Own Rules at a Seconds-To-Go Tempo. *The Ziegfeld Chicago of 1919.*

So Marilynn got her showcase as Broadway's new princess. However, she proved less accommodating than other Ziegfeld Girls, and had married defensively just before rehearsals for the 1919 *Follies* began. Worse, she chose as her bridegroom a man who was everything Ziegfeld was not— young and handsome and easy. A song-and-dance talent of promise with an extremely magnetic personality, Frank Carter was himself a Ziegfeld Boy, the juvenile of the 1918 *Follies,* hired for *1919* as well. Marilynn and he had actually met even earlier, as touring vaudeville teens, but now, suddenly, their romance thickened like plot in Sardou. Neither was the old-fashioned type, and they had become lovers long before they eloped, carefully hiding their liaison from Ziegfeld. Passive technicalities in Maryland's marital laws made the state the quickie marriage capital of the Western World, and in May 1919, just about a month before the 1919 *Follies* opened, princess and beau jaunted down to a friendly parson and came back Mr. and Mrs. Carter.

Ziegfeld immediately fired Frank from the *Follies* and, in one version, threatened to blacklist Marilynn out of show business if she quit to follow Carter. This seems unlikely, even for a man as obsessed and frustrated as Ziegfeld must have been, because no one with Marilynn Miller's talents would be out of work for long. Besides, wouldn't his worst enemies, the Shuberts, have snapped her up again? Wouldn't they co-star her with her husband, throwing back together whom Ziegfeld put asunder? A tantalizing revenge lay in such billing. Imagine the marquee:

The Messrs. Shubert

present

MARILYNN MILLER and FRANK CARTER

in

LOVE FOREVER

In the event, the old-school manager Henry W. Savage (the man who produced Broadway's sensationally successful production of *The Merry Widow*) signed Carter for the pre-Broadway tour of *See-Saw*, by Louis Hirsch and Earl Derr Biggers. Carter had the lead, opposite Dorothea McKaye; by coincidence, secondary roles went to the entry-level Guy Robertson and Elizabeth Hines, later to be signed for the greatest roles they never played, Ravenal and Magnolia in the original *Show Boat*.

For her part, Marilynn had no intention of going back to the Shuberts, or to anyone else. She nursed a very powerful grudge against Ziegfeld for separating her from her husband, but she was ambitious and realistic in the way that genius performers have to be. Adele Astaire, an exact contemporary of Marilynn (they were born barely a week apart) and comparable to her in most ways, gave up the stage for love when she was at the height of her drawing power. However, most of the theatre's great women stars gave up love for the stage, employing such field expedients as business marriages with gay men or passionless unions that provided little more than someone to host soirées with.

Marilynn knew that her destiny was entwined with Ziegfeld's: in the the-atre, not the bedroom. Ziegfeld seems to have known it, too, treating Marilynn with a deference he would never have shown to the other Girls in his employ. Indeed, Ziegfeld never stopped trying to wheedle Marilynn out of her sexual autonomy, more and more as their professional relationship prospered and she seemed the ultimate Ziegfeld Girl in the better sense: the greatest showman's greatest attraction. Propounding the glamour of her talent, Ziegfeld himself made her so tantalizing that he was sick with need, Pygmalion besotted with his creation.

So Sardou's curtain goes up on Ziegfeld/Scarpia scheming to score Marilynn/Tosca while destroying Frank Carter/Cavaradossi. It will be an act to remember—but something else happened first. The Strike.

Ziegfeld Follies of 1919 was in its seventh week when, on August 6, the fledgling Actors Equity called the first walkout in its history. It was a confusion of managers vowing to carry on with understudies, compa-nies dissolving under show-must-go-on stars, and legal questions and injunctions till, eventually, nearly every theatre was empty. Ziegfeld tried to keep the *Follies* open with legerdemain, claiming that he was not a member of the Producing Managers' Association, the target of Equity's action. This was plausible, as Ziegfeld was more generous than other managers, paying higher salaries to the chorus people.

However, Eddie Cantor was a star with the attitude of a grunt, a so-cially conscious union militant. If the actors were to win fair treatment, Equity had to show power. It could not do so unless Broadway went dark. And nothing could turn the lights out more eloquently than the closing of the *Follies*.

Cantor couldn't shut the *Follies* single-handedly, but he could pre-vail upon his colleagues to strike with him. The Shuberts would throw anything on stage and call it a show; indeed, they did just that in the first days of the action. But there could be no *Follies* without stars.

The strike inadvertently invented a substitute entertainment, for spectators would come to the theatre district to watch the doings on the street in the late-day sunlight as show after show posted the refunds notice. On August 11, at the end of the strike's first week, when its success was still in doubt, a huge crowd collected on Forty-First Street, at the New Amsterdam's stage door, to watch as arriving cast members were served with legal writ prohibiting job desertion. Cantor, Bert Williams, Eddie Dowling, the Dooleys, Van and Schenck, John Steel, and Marilynn all received their papers as the public looked on—and words spread from man to man: "They say Ziegfeld himself is in the house!"

Think of it! The man who had given them something no Shubert—or any other producer—could have given was asking them to play. Cantor owed his stardom to Ziegfeld, Williams his historic role as the racial integrator of Broadway.

But Cantor was adamant, however torn. It took him two days to talk others around, including some of the chorus people. On August 13, 1919, the New Amsterdam, too, put up a refunds notice, and Ziegfeld stood to lose his entire investment of $182,000.

Starve them back! the producers cried. Sue them to death! the Shuberts helpfully advised. Ironically, among the very few attractions running on various technicalities was a Ziegfeld title, that year's *Midnight Frolic*, because roof shows were cabaret rather than theatre. In any case, the actors withstood all attempts to dislodge them from their position, and the strike ended in Equity's unqualified victory after exactly four weeks.

Everything reopened, curtailed rehearsals were set back into motion, and unemployed actors once more made those rounds of producers' offices that we glimpse in early talkies. However, like the death of Sam S. Shubert fourteen years earlier, the strike created certain personal animosities. One of these involved Ziegfeld, as we shall see.

Marilynn Miller, at any rate, did not strike the *Follies*—astonishing evidence of loyalty from Tosca to Scarpia. How better to declare independence from this insistent, adulterous suitor than by jilting the *Follies*? But then, Marilynn was ambitious. To everyone else, the *Follies* was Ziegfeld. To Marilynn, the *Follies* was her stardom. There was a *bonne bouche* for her as well when the first new poststrike musical opened: Frank Carter's show, *See-Saw*, on September 23 at the Cohan Theatre, two weeks after the *Follies* reopened. Mr. and Mrs. Carter were once again companions, as Ziegfeld fumed and schemed.

He had more on his mind than that: his imitators. We already know about the Shuberts. They had been copying the *Follies* on and off since 1908, only a year after the first *Follies,* in a Casino revue aptly named *The Mimic World.* Apparently, it was to be billed with the subtitle *Follies of 1908,* but Ziegfeld somehow got wind of it and threatened to sue. Still, if the Shuberts couldn't use the magic word, they could still loot the format, and they kept on doing so, inaugurating in 1912 their annual, *The Passing Show,* and, in the mid-1920s, the less-well-known *Artists and Models.*

It was not till 1919 that Ziegfeld first endured a concentration of competition, and the next few years would see yet more. For the first time in its history, the *Follies* would be running concurrently with others of its more or less exact kind: *The Passing Show of 1919* and two new titles destined to go annual, *Scandals of 1919* and the *Greenwich Village Follies.*[1]

As for the Shuberts' own personal revue, *The Passing Show of 1919* offered an impressive roster of performers, including two who were to go over to Ziegfeld, Mary Eaton and Charles Winninger. It even had a hit number, "I'm Forever Blowing Bubbles." However, as we noticed when *The Passing Show* was doing nothing for Marilynn Miller, the shows as wholes were lame. Ziegfeld's writing and technical cohort were the top; the Shuberts' were third-division. Ziegfeld got the best because he paid the best; the Shuberts were tightwads. Critics routinely excoriated *The Passing Shows* for their shabby look even when the sets and costumes were new. Channing Pollock got the number of the entire series

---

[1] There's that word again; and Ziegfeld pounced. Then it was discovered that there had been a London *Follies* in 1906—a year before Ziegfeld's. The word, so to say, was out. To complete the tale, the ever Ziegfeld-hating Shubert organization immediately became the little Village show's *protégeur,* hauling the production uptown to the Nora Bayes (the Forty-Fourth Street Theatre's roof) and even opening a few of the later editions at the Messrs.' "second" flagship, the Winter Garden.

when he called the first of the line "as exciting and amusing as the clatter of dishes in a cheap restaurant."

The *Scandals*, however, offered a genuine challenge to Ziegfeld's *Follies* hegemony. They were the brainchild of George White, a former Ziegfeld dancer—but White and his sometime partner, Ann Pennington, were not of the languid ballroom genre of pas de deux. These two were mad, stamping, thrill-a-second whizzes, and White ran his shows in that style. As with *Follies of 1907*, White opened shop with *Scandals of 1919*; not till 1920 did he unveil *George White's Scandals*. And by then the format was set: dancier and more tuneful than the *Follies*. White didn't follow Ziegfeld. He passed him at ninety miles an hour.

George Gershwin and B. G. De Sylva were the house team till Gershwin broke away to write book shows with his brother Ira, whereupon White teamed De Sylva with composer Ray Henderson. Henderson already had a lyricist, Lew Brown, and he wasn't giving him up. So the three combined as De Sylva, Brown, and Henderson, the screwiest byline in the whole 1920s—and they gave White better music than Gershwin had done.

Of all the revues of 1919, only the *Greenwich Village Follies* could claim surprise and delight as elemental in its style, albeit on a miniature scale. If Ziegfeld's *Follies* managed to connect as both sophisticated and lowbrow, the "other" *Follies* was arty, even weird. A typical Ziegfeld moment, in *Miss 1917*, offered Bessie McCoy Davis' reprise of "The Yama Yama Man," to an ecstatic house. Remember? The gigantic theatre, the first-nighting swells, the classic number. A typical *Greenwich Village Follies* moment offered the same performer in "My Marionette" as a life-size puppet on strings. It was charming, but a little creepy; and the audience would be less ecstatic than soigné and bemused.

Or take the matter of Prohibition. Every revue twiddled it, but only the *Greenwich Village Follies* came up with the delicately sneaky "I'm the Hostess of a Bum Cabaret," envisioning a drinking establishment floating in the ocean in observance of the three-mile limit of legal safety. The unique *Greenwich Village* number was the show's hit, "I Want a Daddy Who Will Rock Me To Sleep," whose verse puns on titles of the "bedroom" comedies so popular in the 1918–1919 season. As at Ziegfeld's place, one had to be up on one's Broadway simply to monitor the references. Then, most unexpectedly, this apparent comedy number went into a melting ragtime lullaby in the chorus—possibly the only melting ragtime lullaby ever written.

Most important, the design of costumes and show curtains made the *Greenwich Village Follies* Ziegfeld's deftest imitator. And yet who exactly was his rival in this matter? The producing credit line for the *Greenwich Village Follies* said simply, "The Bohemians (Inc.) present."

Two other revue series were introduced a bit after 1919: Irving Berlin's *Music Box Revues* (in 1921) and Earl Carroll's *Vanities* (in 1923). The Music Box shows, written to inaugurate the eponymous theatre that Berlin built with producer Sam H. Harris, compared to the *Ziegfeld Follies* in expense and taste; the *Vanities* aped *Follies* eroticism. Interestingly, while the excellent Music Box genre proved exhausting to maintain and ended after four entries, Carroll's idiotic *Vanities* went on forever. A Broadway joke claimed that the *Vanities* did turnaway business: Ziegfeld's. (Those who couldn't get into the *Follies* bought tickets for Carroll's show.) In fact, the *Vanities* really was the nearest of all revues to the *Follies*—as near as a rubber tire is to the Colosseum in Rome. Carroll did what Ziegfeld did with no instinct for comedy, no eye for beauty, and—despite extensive experience as a composer-lyricist—no ear for music.

Among Ziegfeld's many several influences on show biz, his popularization of revue is perhaps the most significant. Far more than the book musicals of the day, revue let loose a refreshingly "dangerous" cultural energy, resistant to authoritarian views on race and sex, on who controls the public dialogue on what life is like. This energy began immediately to enliven the book musical, which matured to the point of being able to make more than passing remark on such issues as race relations and corrupt war lobbying within a decade of *Ziegfeld Follies of 1919*.

Meanwhile, Ziegfeld was also controlling a private dialogue on what Marilynn's life would be like. Now our hero seems not unlike a cloak-

and-mustache villain as he plots to keep Mr. and Mrs. Carter apart. Foiled again: the tour itineraries of her *Follies* and his *See-Saw* hit a crossing in Ziegfeld's hometown of Chicago at the same time, in the spring of 1920. Newlyweds again, Marilynn and Frank had a look at a Packard automobile—a custom model with so much hat and cane about it that Marilynn fell in love with it and Frank bought it for her. He arranged it on the sly, having the dealer tattoo the doors with both their initials.

Not long after, the *Follies* reached Philadelphia as *See-Saw* closed its tour in Wheeling, West Virginia; Frank was going to drive the Packard up to present it to Marilynn. The surprise took another form, however, when Carter had an accident on the road. His passengers were un-harmed, but Marilynn, racing down to what she had been told was Carter's convalescent hospital room, learned that he had died in the crash. Now she knew the truth that all stars of that day had to learn: the manager always wins.

What passed between Marilynn and Ziegfeld directly after Carter's death is unknown. There is no question that, in the long run, she treated him thereafter with impatience and resentment at best and outright contempt when riled. It was as if Ziegfeld was now the only man Mari-lynn hated and Marilynn the only woman Ziegfeld feared—this even as he readied "her" show. It was to be an essential, even epochal, musical comedy: newest in style but oldest in soul. Again, Ziegfeld was not gen-erally an innovator in what a musical does. He was an innovator in how a musical does it. The Girl. The comic. The songs. The look of beauty, fa-ble, gold. To put it one way, if Ziegfeld were still in charge of Broadway, the concept musical would not exist, Stephen Sondheim would be writ-ing *Topper* scripts, and Hal Prince would be teaching driver ed. To put it another way, if Ziegfeld had decided to revive *The Black Crook* for Mar-ilynn Miller, it would have been so spectacular an experience it would be running yet.

In the event, the show that Ziegfeld prepared for Marilynn ran an amazing 570 performances, with another 600 or so on the road. This combined run of three years is especially noteworthy given that the production played only the biggest houses in every venue, from Boston to Chicago. (Further, a twenties version of the modern-day "bus and truck" tour, licensed to play the small time, added a fourth year to the total.) No open-run offering sold out in those days, but this one came close, and it remained many theatregoers' favorite musical experience even after *Rose-Marie, Show Boat, Of Thee I Sing,* and *Anything Goes.* One reason was the star, who was the first song-and-dance woman who could carry a full-size show not just on vocal allure or charm but sheer locomotive talent. Another reason was that *non pareil* Ziegfeld staff, with Jerome Kern here and Lucile and Joseph Urban there.

A third reason was Ziegfeld. The gods of theatre once foretold that a sweetheart would provide the warmth, a jester would supply the holiday, and music would redeem a heartless world. The people called it musical comedy. And the one that Ziegfeld produced for Marilynn Miller was the biggest hit Broadway had ever seen.

CHAPTER THIRTEEN

Ziegfeld's Masterpiece

Something had been happening in the musical for a generation, but especially in the previous five or six years, and Ziegfeld—possibly by instinct rather than analysis—had figured it out. To simplify: a revolution in the conceiving of musicals had begun to reject the exotic settings, gone-fishing character development, and anthology scores that had prevailed. What we might call the New Musical favored contemporary American settings, sensible characterization, and unified scores by a single writing team.

Samples of the old style would include our old friend *Adonis* or, say, *The Wizard of Oz*, with its countless interpolations. Or all those European stories, from *The Prince of Pilsen* to *The Pink Lady*. Or the impossible stories, as with *High Jinks'* perfume that turns folk into erotic daredevils or *Robinson Crusoe Jr.*, in which Al Jolson played Crusoe's chauffeur. Or every show that Ziegfeld put on with Anna Held.

The New Musical was, for example, *The Only Girl* (1914), *Going Up* (1917), *Irene* (1919), *Mary* (1920), and, most famously, the Princess Theatre shows of Jerome Kern, Guy Bolton, and P. G. Wodehouse. These works discarded the wizards, princes, and pink ladies. *Mary* was so "ordinary" that its hero is a guy who builds houses, and the Princess piece *Leave It To Jane* (1917) is a college musical. Who will win the Big Game?

Kern, Bolton, and Wodehouse, we may recall, were already Ziegfeld alumni, Class of (*Miss*) *1917*. Ziegfeld applied to them for his next show—because he wanted something in the New style. True, this style was generally modest in scale and played by ensembles rather than stars. But that can be finessed. Do the boys have something for Marilynn for the 1920–1921 season?

"Well . . . ," says Kern, or Bolton, or Wodehouse. "There is *The Little Thing.*"

Ziegfeld heard that, all right; it *sounded* like Marilynn. "What's *The Little Thing?*" he asks.

And the trio starts reeling it out. It's set in New York City, in a boardinghouse. It's an actor's home, so there's plenty of atmosphere and opportunities. Vaudevillians, artistes of the opera, thespians, eccentrics, zanies . . .

Ziegfeld: "Who does Marilynn play?"

The heroine is an orphan waif. A foundling.

"Her name is Sally Rhinelander," says one of the three. The surname is a well-known Manhattan telephone exchange. "Because she was found in a telephone booth with a Rhinelander number."

Ziegfeld considers. "So she's Sally in Our Alley," he says. The boardinghouse setting and the old song.[1]

"Sally wants to be a dancer," says one of the three authors. "And one of the boardinghouse tenants is an old woman who used to be a dancer herself."

"Make her a man," replies Ziegfeld. "No one wants to look at an old woman." And now, warming to it: "Yes, he's the star comic. And Sally wants to dance in the *Follies*. First, she charms society. The finale is her debut—a ballet spot!"

I imagine the skeptical Kern saying, "An orphan waif charms society?"

----

[1] Sally and her alley comprised a very popular image of a working-class sweetheart, Sally being one of those plain names that tended to incite George M. Cohan to compose an ode, and the alley referring to the lane behind brownstones or row houses where working-class children played. Marie Cahill, one of musical comedy's biggest stars, popularized the phrase in *Sally in Our Alley* (1902). Further, Maude Adams interpolated that show's title song into *Peter Pan*; and "Sally in Our Alley" became a national catchphrase.

"In disguise," says Ziegfeld, invoking one of the sloppy traditions that the New Musical wanted to eradicate. "She's Princess Herzegovina or something."

Kern, Bolton, and Wodehouse trade looks.

"*The Little Thing*," says Ziegfeld, trying it on his tongue. That will have to change, for all its winsome charm; there's nothing little about a Ziegfeld production. Then, briskly: "Let's hear the songs."

They repair to the nearest piano, where Kern plays through the numbers written before the *Little Thing* project was abandoned. The songs include one that Wodehouse is keen on, "Church 'Round the Corner," because New York's Little Church Around the Corner is where he was married. It may well be that Kern took the occasion to play two titles written for *Zip! Goes a Million*, which had recently closed during its tryout—"Look For the Silver Lining" and "Whip-Poor-Will," extremely winning ballads. Indeed, the former is so essential to the history of the musical of the "good old days" that Kander and Ebb used it as the template for Mary Sunshine's spoof hymn in *Chicago* (1975).

However, the lyrics for these two songs were by B. G. De Sylva, not Wodehouse. Uncomfortable at being thus overshadowed, Wodehouse returned to England and expressed by mail his anger at having to share the stage with another lyricist. Kern replied with guns blazing: so Wodehouse was now out of the production. Clifford Grey replaced him, and yet another interpolation added Anne Caldwell to the lyricist credits. Moreover, while Kern composed the tunestack, Ziegfeld hired Victor Herbert for that ballet spot at the show's climax. To have two composers and four librettists was antithetical to the New Musical's aesthetic. But then, so was Ziegfeld. At heart, the New Musical *selected* its materials, economized. In Ziegfeld's theatre, one amassed materials, extravagated.

There was one miscalculation, when Ziegfeld decided to call the show *Sally of the Alley*: because it was very like but still different from the Cahill title. No sooner did the PR releases go out than the press was confusing the one with the other and inventing variations. What is worse for business than a confusing title?: and during the tryout Ziegfeld shortened it to *Sally*. It was a New Musical in the old style, or even an

Old Musical with a New feeling. There is nothing older in musical comedy than the Girl and the Comic, and while *Sally* does enjoy a Boy Meets Girl, Sally's primary relationship is with the funny older man who enables her inner Cinderella.

Years later, Ziegfeld told *Time* magazine that there were "three themes for musical shows—Sex, Adventure, Romance." He didn't single out the comic theme because, to Ziegfeld, musicals were made of comedy. In fact, he decided to set *two* jesters alongside Marilynn. One shared top billing with her: Leon Errol. Another, Walter Catlett, had the third major role. Ziegfeld had actually promised Eddie Cantor the co-starring spot in the Marilynn show, but that was when the 1919 *Follies* was in rehearsal—before Cantor had led the *Follies* stars out on strike.

This was one of the few feuds that our man Ziegfeld actively engaged in. Normally, Ziegfeld didn't feud. Others feuded with him—many, many others. But Cantor's disloyalty baffled Ziegfeld, outraged him. He had treated Eddie like a son, given him stardom, *put him in the Follies!* Renounced by Ziegfeld, Cantor found himself signing with the Shuberts. They, too, hated strike ringleaders, but they hated Ziegfeld more.

So Ziegfeld gave Marilynn Miller his version of a Princess show, a spectacular candybox of talent with all those *Time* magazine elements in place. The romance inheres less in Sally's winning a society boy with the Social Register name of Blair Farquar (Irving Fisher) than when her talent takes wing at the society party and finally soars in the Butterfly Ballet at the *Follies*. It's Girl Meets Ziegfeld. And note that, while *Sally* played the New Amsterdam, its last act takes place on that very stage: in the capital theatre of the land of show biz, where Klaw and Erlanger ruled. Really, it's Girl Meets Syndicate.

But here's more that's New: the firm of Klaw and Erlanger was legally dissolved at this very time, the fall of 1920. Thus, when *Sally* finally opened, on December 21, Broadway itself had become New—liberated from the Trust but also, just now, ready to receive Eugene O'Neill, the Lunts, and "jazz." *Sally* was a part of it: in his *New York Times* review, Alexander Woollcott wrote that, "as you rush to the subway at ten minutes to midnight," it is "not of Urban nor Jerome Kern, not of Leon Errol, nor even of Marilynn Miller that you think first." Instead, he held, "you think of Mr. Ziegfeld. He is that kind of producer."

How much producing makes one an auteur? Ziegfeld had commissioned *Sally* from writers known for *writing*. And they wrote a mostly solid story, about a girl who rises from nothing to thrill the world: the Marilynn Miller Story, in effect. Friends assist, but she makes it through self-belief—already a lesson that musical comedy loved to teach. Oddly, *Sally* concentrates on this theme while the heroine is charming society in that disguise: most herself when least herself. In the end, she wasn't Princess Herzegovina, but Madame Nockerova, the fabulous Russian ballerina.

So here's adventure as well, as Sally the foundling sweeps into a Long Island garden party in her drop-dead white-fur creation by Lucile and a careening Russian accent. Ziegfeld, Kern, and lyricist Grey devised for this sequence one of the greatest song-and-dance inventions of the age, "Wild Rose." It's a simple concept: Madame Nockerova flirts with the men's chorus. Yet it achieves liftoff in a way nothing of its kind had done before.

The number is another sample of Ziegfeld's Apollonian-Dionysian use of theatre to express beauty by crazing it up. First, the men rhapsodize over Marilynn till she goes into the refrain proper ("I'm just a wild rose . . ."). It's harmonically primitive, using only three chords till the final cadence. But it starts, momentously, on the sixth tone of the scale, a confusing sound just as the disguised Sally confuses these men. At the same time, the purity of the melody establishes Sally's security: she knows she's hot.

Now a patter section (Sally: "I'm frantic, romantic, excited, delighted . . .") draws the answering men into a big choral sound, while the orchestra bashes out the refrain fortissimo, the violins saw wildly away above, and Ziegfeld's dancing doll takes the theatre apart. Kicking and twirling in and out of the line of men as they march around, playing with her feathered fan, she shows the audience how it feels to star in your very own Ziegfeld show. At one point, every night, Marilynn would appear to pick out one ticket holder in the vast house and wink at him. "She wants *me*!" a thousand men rejoiced.

"Wild Rose" anticipates the salute-the-heroine number of the Big Lady Show of the Gower Champion era—"Hello, Dolly!" or "When Mabel Comes in the Room." However, *this* lady had to earn her adulation in a physical workout that spills elation over into abandon. It shatters received etiquette—what previous heroine ever got so wild on stage?—to create new etiquette. Yes, Sally is excited, delighted, as she sings. But she's getting into ritual, into the historical mystery of theatre, when mere entertainment turns into something as big as myth.

Maybe *Sally* wasn't written or Ziegfelded as much as it was Marilynned: the Ziegfeld Girl as the electricity running through the cables of musical comedy. Yes, she was elfin and so very young—twenty-two on *Sally*'s opening night. She was as well one of those genuine beauties who never takes the same photograph twice. She was even—for Ziegfeld's theatre has alarming power—a luscious specimen for the collector of fantasy.

So this is where the sex comes into the matter. Marilynn was a wild rose, all right: and, unlike the others, one who would not be plucked.

"Hello, you lousy son-of-a-bitch," she said when Ziegfeld brought his five-year-old daughter backstage after a matinée. Patty had been so entranced she hadn't wanted to leave the theatre after it ended.

Ziegfeld introduced the girl to his star. "You've heard me talk about Patricia, haven't you?" he said.

"To the point of nausea," Marilynn replied, working the cold cream and wipeaways at her dressing table.

After awkward hellos between Patty and Marilynn, Ziegfeld tried to smooth the scene down. "Is something bothering you?" he asked his star.

"You know goddamn well what's bothering me. It's this piece of crap you call a costume. I've told you a thousand times that it weighs a ton, and as far as I'm concerned you can just take it and shove—"

"This is the first show Patty has ever seen in her life!" Ziegfeld quickly put in. "The very first!"

Marilynn simply leapt the hurdle. "For the last time," she said, "I want to know what you're planning to do about this fucking costume."

Frantically, Ziegfeld threw out a bit more about Patty's first theatre trip as he edged the child toward the door. Marilynn continued to hector him about the costume, an elaborate wedding outfit she wore for *Sally*'s short final scene at that Little Church Around the Corner. Ziegfeld urged Patty to say good-bye, made Marilynn an empty promise to talk about the costume later on, and started to get the heck out of there.

Now Marilynn rose, holding the cold cream jar. And she was *mad*. She wasn't going to talk about the costume later on. "We'll damn well talk about it now," she announced. She was actually moving toward them when Ziegfeld closed the door behind him and Patty, just in time to block the cold cream jar, which Marilynn threw at him to splinter to bits against the door.

"It's different back here, isn't it?" said Patty. "It's like it has nothing to do with the play we saw out front."

That's a smart kid. In fact, she was possibly speaking more about the humdrum, unbuttoned backstage atmosphere than about Marilynn's behavior. But the point is relevant even so. *Sally* had everything to do with Marilynn's talent—so much so that both "Look For the Silver Lining" and "Wild Rose" were pitched in E Flat in order to climax on the upper limit of Marilynn's soprano, an F. ("So always *look* for the silver lining . . .") But *Sally* had nothing to do with Marilynn's *character*. Sally makes it on the optimism that essentializes her self-belief. Marilynn made it on guts. Like everyone who came up the hard way in vaudeville, she knew that survival meant getting tough when crowded, and Ziegfeld really crowded her. He was the man who, more or less, fired Frank Carter to death but also the only producer in town who perfected his art. His fifteenth consecutive *Follies* cost $250,000—five times what it cost Charles Dillingham to produce *Good Morning, Dearie,* that season's outstanding big book musical, and probably ten times what it cost the Shuberts to put on that season's outstanding little book musical, *Blossom Time.*

Ziegfeld Follies of 1921, which played the Globe (today the Lunt-Fontanne) because *Sally* was still packing the New Amersterdam, was one of the best in the series. The ethnic mix was a bit limited that year, with nothing more exotic than Fanny Brice (although this entry gave her her two classic solos, "Second Hand Rose" and "My Man"). In fact, this *Follies* went downright middle-American with the only appearance in the series of Raymond Hitchcock, a specialist in the folksy, slow-moving humor that urban runabouts like Eddie Cantor were driving out of business. Hitchcock was actually one of Ziegfeld's rivals, for he had been putting on his own annual variety show, *Hitchy-Koo,* since 1917.

The *Follies* material was particularly good this year. The sketches included one very strange item in which Brice, Hitchcock, and W. C. Fields were to imitate Ethel, Lionel, and John Barrymore in *Camille*—except the Barrymores are indisposed tonight and understudies are going on, so Brice, Hitchcock, and Fields had to imitate Barrymore imitations. One never saw anything that layered in a *Passing Show.*

But something was missing: Marilynn. Yes, Ziegfeld offered his public Mary Eaton, who like Miller was a blond all-arounder who could handle ballet as well as tap. This was no minor virtue in a Ziegfeld heroine, for he thought ballet prestigious in the way that Victor Herbert's ability to write cello concertos and operas as well as musicals was prestigious. Or perhaps Ziegfeld was simply saluting his father and the Chicago Musical College, bringing High Art to his public.

Even so, this 1921 *Follies* assigned to Van and Schenck "Sally Won't You Come Back?" which lists the natural pairings that bond all life. There's "the earth" and "sunshine," for instance. There's "flowers" and "dew." "Woods" and "birds," "song" and "words." . . . "And the alley can't do without you." The implication is that Sally of the Alley has become so central to Ziegfeld's art that he cannot put on a show without her.

Eddie Cantor called her "Lumpy." It's like something dreamed up for a Hollywood bio: gooey. Marilynn Miller was the opposite of gooey. But she did finally give in to Ziegfeld. Not in bed: on the marquee. Dropping that pesky second "n," she became the headliner we know today: Marilyn Miller.

Then, immediately, she changed her name again, marrying for the second time. She chose a lulu of a husband, as offensive to Ziegfeld as possible. It was Jack Pickford, the man who poisoned Olive Thomas. Well, that's what Ziegfeld thought, wasn't it? Frank Carter was now avenged.

Ziegfeld responded with PR assaults on Pickford in a kind of Broad-

way versus Hollywood brouhaha, for Marilyn and Jack had married at
Pickfair, sacred shrine of Little Mary and Doug Fairbanks. Marilyn was
the nymph and Jack the satyr, but Ziegfeld was Cassandra, warning of
disaster to an unlistening public. And what was Billie, who knew how
passionately "interested" in Marilyn her husband really was?

The trouble with you, Billie, is you always pick the wrong girl. Lillian, Olive, one of those Dolly Sisters? By now, Billie knew it was Marilyn. But how does one confront a husband over an infidelity he is unable
to commit?

The manager doesn't always win, after all. Marilyn would not be
managed, and that's why she liked Jack Pickford. Like her, he knew that
the point of being lovable is to jam a lot of life into your day and never
go to bed hungry. Like the Ziegfelds, the Pickfords fought a lot. Billie
fought because she hated Ziegfeld's inconstancy; Marilyn fought because Jack fought, because love is fighting, because the sex after is so
good. These two were kids. Billie and Ziegfeld were grown-ups. Parents.
Billie never seriously considered divorce because she wasn't going to
subject Patty to the insecurity of a fatherless upbringing, but at least she
could throw the $20,000 diamond bracelet that Ziegfeld gave her right
across the room in a fury. I don't want your money, you lout. I want you
to respect your vows.

That was never a problem at Mr. and Mrs. Pickford's, for Marilyn's
vow was to her career, and Jack never took an oath in any real sense. He
was a figure common to the film world then, a slacker avant la lettre, getting by on charm and the authority of his sister. His every day as Marilyn's
husband was a slap in Ziegfeld's face, not only for the obvious reason but
also because Ziegfeld loathed show-biz people who had no talent. To
Ziegfeld, Jack was a murderer, an interloper, and, worst of all, a phony.

And so, making the very sensible assumption that Ziegfeld would be
even more impossible than before, Marilyn played out *Sally*'s tour and
then ended her relationship with Ziegfeld. Sally really left the alley this
time. She threw Ziegfeld over for his closest rival as producer, Charles
Dillingham.

CHAPTER FOURTEEN

Daddy Has a Sweetheart and Mother Is Her Name

By the early 1920s, Ziegfeld had so consummated his format in revue that he could only repeat himself. The surprise and delight still held place, as when, in the 1919 *Midnight Frolic*, on the New Amsterdam roof, the closing number started with Frances White in "The World Is Going Shimmy Mad." White was gradually joined by Fanny Brice, W. C. Fields, Ted Lewis, Bert Savoy and Jay Brennan, the rest of the cast, the stagehands, and even the waiters, all caught in the grip of the shimmy.

Still, there is little to distinguish each new *Follies*, each new *Frolic*. That resonant *Follies* subtitle, "Glorifying the American Girl," is worth noting as having been coined for the 1922 edition. And Prohibition's closing of the *Frolic*'s lucrative bar sales led Ziegfeld to give up on the series (but for a lone last try in 1928) after the 1921 entry.

Besides, Ziegfeld was busy producing in a new genre—new, at any rate, to him: the Billie Burke Comedy. Straight plays were not his forte, but that's an understatement. He had no interest in them whatsoever. To Ziegfeld, all theatre was—to repeat the phrase of the day—"girl and music shows." And, as for comedy, he wanted to hear audiences roaring, not letting off pleased chuckles. Still, he was Billie's husband and therefore Billie's manager, so Florenz Ziegfeld Jr. was choosing and presenting the plays of Billie Burke.

These turned out to be a genre new to everyone, for Billie had long wanted to break out of the straitjacket of type that Frohman had kept her in: Billie the mischievous hoyden. "I am longing to get something I can branch out in and be an actress [in]," Billie told *The Chicago Record-Herald* three and a half years before she had even met Ziegfeld. Describing her Frohman career as a mandate to "bob my curls about . . . and wear pretty frocks and wrinkle up my nose," Billie stated, simply, that now she wanted "to act."

Ziegfeld locked his players into type no less than Frohman—but in musicals. He had so little experience in the "other" stage that he was happy to encourage Billie's ambitions. Rival manager Arthur Hopkins held the rights to Clare Kummer's *The Rescuing Angel* (1917), but this was the work Billie chose in which to present the new improved Billie Burke, as a woman torn between a rough man and a gentle man. So Ziegfeld had to co-produce once again.

He was solely in charge of Billie's next show, by her old friend W. Somerset Maugham, *Caesar's Wife* (1919), once again involved with two men. In between these titles, Ziegfeld put on a straight play without Billie in the cast, for reasons that no one can explain. *By Pigeon Post* (1918) was an English war play, an all but ubiquitous genre on Broadway at this time, not to rise to its exhibition title, R. C. Sherriff's *Journey's End,* till 1929. *By Pigeon Post* failed, but then so did the Kummer and Maugham pieces.

Ziegfeld now turned to Booth Tarkington for Billie's vehicles—a sage choice, as Tarkington had a gift for creating unique women in his fiction. (Think of how much Katharine Hepburn got out of Tarkington's *Alice Adams*.) Tarkington was an accomplished playwright as well, and like many others he wrote a script hoping to lure the spectacularly unearthly Maude Adams back to Broadway, *The Intimate Strangers*. In a "Note on the Heroine," Tarkington called her "elusive," explaining that her style is based on "a friendly and even tender mockery, and yet a wistfulness": which is Maude Adams to the core. "We know her and yet can never know her."

It tells us how well Ziegfeld supported Billie's aspirations that he got her a Maude Adams role; and how accomplished Billie was to have been able to play it—at that under Tarkington's (unbilled) direction. Indeed, while Ziegfeld once more had to suffer producer partners in Abe Er-langer and Charles Dillingham, it was Tarkington who brought Alfred Lunt into the production. Lunt had made Tarkington's *Clarence* into a smash two years earlier, and he must have been a jolt to Billie after her years of playing opposite the likes of John Drew and C. Aubrey Smith. (Though Billie did play an old Dumas title as *A Marriage of Convenience* with the redoubtable Henry Miller, under Miller's management, in 1918.) Conversational to a fault, *The Intimate Strangers* has no plot. Even its premise seems cockeyed: a woman of great charm so engages a grouchy guy (Lunt) that he marries her even though he can't tell how old she is.

What? But there were plenty of such works then, lacking reality and drive while reveling in that love of language that the French call Mari-vaudage. The sheer adult grown-up maturity of it thrilled Billie, not least in her no-frills entrance. There was no hubbub, no stage-whispered "Here she comes now!" Billie simply walked into the set of a near-empty railroad station:

> BILLIE: (over welcoming applause) I think maybe I could be *more* sensible if the news turns out to be of *my train*. Could you stand its being about my train instead of yours, Mr. Ames?
> LUNT: (a little stiffly) If mine came you'd be relieved of *me*.
> BILLIE: Yes, so I should.

It's rather flat after the pillow fights of Billie's Frohman era, but *The Intimate Strangers*, a hit of the 1921–1922 season, led to Billie's second Tarkington, in the title role of *Rose Briar*. Billie was growing and Ziegfeld was growing, but most of all Broadway was growing: seven other works had their premieres on the night *Rose Briar* opened, De-cember 25, 1922: a Christmas present to the public. This time, Billie played a cabaret star, which gave Ziegfeld a chance to slip in some mu-sic. Jerome Kern composed a song to Tarkington's lyrics, "Love and the Moon (are traitors, they say)." Once again, we note that, contrary to re-

ceived wisdom on Ziegfeld's poor ear for music, more often than not he
hired the best.

Rose Briar's plot found Billie enlisted as co-respondent for a divorce
case involving the man she herself secretly loves. An adulteress? Charles
Frohman would have cast Billie as *Peter Pan*'s crocodile first—but one of
the bonds in Ziegfeld's marriage with Billie was made of his affection for
her as an artist. He loved her in true romance, yes. Yet he also loved the
theatre's unique talents, as I've said, and he thought Billie was one of them.

So did Frohman, perhaps, but only as long as you *never doubted his
judgment* and *never defied his commands*. Back in 1915, after Frohman's
death, when Billie first contemplated trying the movies, she learned that
the Frohman Organization was going to pursue the Frohman tyranny
even after his death. Frohman's assistant, the younger of the two Syndicate Haymans, sent Billie a directive by wire:

IF YOU SIGN UP WITH PICTURES BEFORE WE SEE YOU AGAIN WE
WILL NOT CONTINUE WITH YOU FOR ANOTHER SEASON

Before she met Ziegfeld, Billie might have caved in to such bullying, but
Ziegfeld gave her confidence. Listen to the new Billie:

ANY MORE IRATE TELEGRAMS FROM YOU AND I WILL SIGN
IMMEDIATELY

Billie herself noted this evidence of "considerable development in me."
Alas, Hayman had learned his managing skills from the despotic
Frohman:

WE WILL HAVE NONE OF OUR PEOPLE IN PICTURES AND THIS
MEANS YOU

And that was how Billie was freed of men ordering her around. For
at length she and Ziegfeld realized that his expertise and her talent

created incongruent agendas, and (as we'll shortly see), she left contracted management altogether to freelance.

It was a lovely marriage, then, even with all the fighting. (For Ziegfeld will cheat, and Billie has to say something about it.) There was a lot of personal *there* in it, a lot of discovering and teasing. Billie was very amused to learn how much Ziegfeld pampered himself of a morning. He used not only every article available to the well-dressed man but rather a lot of those available to women. "He had quantities of delicate bath powders which he used with a large swan's-down puff," Billie later wrote, "leaving the bathroom . . . looking as if Gaby Deslys . . . had used it."[1]

On the other hand, when Ziegfeld traveled he just threw things into a bag. It was comparable to his habit of pulling some thrilling jeweled bijou out of his pocket without a presentation speech or gift box: more of that surprise and delight. Ziegfeld's life was like Ziegfeld's *Follies*: tons of preparation but a seat-of-the-pants performance with an immediacy that was intended to shock. His life had the excitement of his shows.

The Ziegfelds lived all over the place. Camp Patricia, named after their daughter, was the roughing-it getaway, on an island Ziegfeld bought in the lake district of the Laurentian Highlands in Canada, north of Montreal. For a man who loved luxury, Ziegfeld was surprisingly eager to spend a vacation without a speck of it. True, there were a lot of buildings at Camp Patricia, from the main house to guides' dormitory, with a full staff from trained nurse to chef. However, there was no telephone, an astonishing sacrifice for a producer who couldn't pass a Bell company booth without spending an hour giving notes to the authors of his next seven shows. In his days with Anna Held, Ziegfeld's time off was a tour of Europe. With the American Billie, Ziegfeld went native, grew a beard, and cooked rustic fry-'em-ups of eggs, tomatoes, corn, and beans. Then, too, Ziegfeld thought to reclaim his youth as an amateur marksman by getting in some hunting.

---

[1] Deslys, a Shubert revue star at the Winter Garden, embodied the Parisienne en grande toilette in the 1910s, much as Anna Held had done in the previous generation.

Billie forbade it. "I will not have this lovely place turned into an abattoir," she said, as their Canadian guides shrugged.[1]

The Ziegfelds even hosted guests from New York—Irving and Ellin Berlin, Rudolf Friml, Wunderkind costume designer John Harkrider, all officers of Ziegfeld's art, presumably to consult with the boss on those next seven shows. But most guests preferred invitations to the Ziegfelds' other regular vacation spot, Palm Beach.

Ziegfeld and Billie fell in love with the Florida resort when she was filming that serial *Gloria's Romance* in 1916. The very social, very expensive Palm Beach was not only the opposite of Camp Patricia but the opposite of all the other famous resorts of the day—Newport, Bar Harbor, Southampton, Saratoga. They were where society liked to call itself "well off." Palm Beach was *rich*. It was sinful as well. Sporty blue-book bachelor Alexander Phillips, a regular and a hit at most society vacation spots, had little success at Palm Beach. Asked why, he replied, "I did not drink and I had no wife to exchange."

It was a younger resort than most, exhibitionistic because it had no reputation to uphold. Elsewhere, divorce was hush-hush, a scandal; in Palm Beach it was what you had for breakfast. The very locale had the feeling of a Ziegfeld set, and Joseph Urban himself designed the Bath and Tennis Club (in 1926). Urban designed also the ultimate Palm Beach "cottage," Barbara Hutton's Mar-a-Lago, so expansive that it had its own golf course. As with everything else in Palm Beach, it reflected the belief that showing off was good taste. It was like Versailles, only grand. Harry K. Thaw—the man who murdered Stanford White in real life and *Ragtime*—took one look and said, "My God, I shot the wrong architect."

Naturally, Ziegfeld felt at home here. Palm Beach was a Chicago of social resorts, where the wealthy and powerful don't try to pretend that

---

[1]Billie actually said this on an earlier outing, when the Ziegfelds tried living wild in New Brunswick province in eastern Canada. Still, Billie sternly maintained her ban on the murdering of innocent animals at Camp Patricia as well.

they're anything else, where the go-getter is too industrious to limit the doing of business to business hours. It would have been a dire offense to talk shop in Newport, but Palm Beach accommodated the man of affairs. Business was a party and a party was business. The conference with Jerome Kern, Guy Bolton, and P. G. Wodehouse that led to the creation of *Sally* was held not in Ziegfeld's office in the New Amsterdam Theatre but during a weekend in Palm Beach. In the more regal places, house parties were about manners. Palm Beach had no manners, and house parties were about Guest Stars. No, not Kern, Bolton, and Wodehouse: Walter Chrysler Jr., son of the automobile tycoon. He was there that weekend, too.

Remember when Ziegfeld's millionaire friends were folk like Diamond Jim Brady? Those days seem so refined; weren't they wearing bustles then? The times of American life were catching up with Ziegfeld's ideal of a discordant show biz, astonishing with the melting-pot variety of its jokes, the speed of its finesse, the sex always happening. This is the Jazz Age, when the word *jazz* itself meant everything new that the authorities didn't approve of: from crazy dance steps at petting parties to the spiel of a grinning con man. There were jazz lawyers, jazz dinners, jazz motorcars. Like Tarzan's "Ungowah!" jazz meant everything and nothing.

The word was supposedly derived from black slang for the central appetitive act, which tells us how forward and defiant the jazz "movement" intended to be. It was like saying "fuck" to your father. Suddenly, everything was new, from music to morals: and Palm Beach was the jazz resort. The rector of the Groton School, the Reverend Endicott Peabody, called Palm Beach a "den of iniquity." He might as well have been speaking of the *Follies*—though, after the Reverend Madison J. Peter's assault on Anna Held and *A Parisian Model,* Ziegfeld's shows were never threatened by censorship even when other shows were. And yet which was more subversive—the mixed-race romance in Eugene O'Neill's *All God's Chillun Got Wings* (1924) or the next-to-naked Ziegfeld Girl, who Got Away With It simply because the *Follies* sparkled with class? O'Neill was art. Everyone knows how dangerous (and powerless) art can be, so *All God's Chillun Got Wings,* though not closed, was harassed. No one thought to harass the *Follies,* because the *Follies* was a musical (and a big municipal money-earner, with powerful friends). And everyone knows that musicals aren't art.

We must not forget to look in on the Ziegfelds at home at their permanent address, Burkely Crest. Originally the Kirkham Estate, it lay to the north of New York City in Hastings-on-Hudson, an easy commute to Broadway yet distant enough to pass through the suburban to the genuinely rural. Billie bought it for her mother and herself when a Frohman star, and it was, as they say, an idyllic place, peaceful above all. Orderly.

So of course, after Ziegfeld married Billie it became an eccentric place. Was that, at heart, the Ziegfeld Touch: not his famous extravagance in the best of taste but rather the liberation of one's inner nonconformist? Because once Ziegfeld appeared on the scene, the residents of Burkely Crest began to improve the grounds in unusual ways. Billie's mother, for instance, cultivated "an inexplicable mania"—so Patricia explained in her memoirs—"for Japanese teahouses." The estate was spacious and filled with nooks created by little groves of trees, and, everywhere she noted one, Grandma Burke would raise a teahouse. "If there happened to be any water nearby—a duck pond, or just a marshy place along the trees—she would put up a Japanese bridge, too."

One of the first things that Ziegfeld noticed about the grounds was the Kirkham playhouse, a dingy little box built for some unknown little girl of the nineteenth century. It lacked everything, so Ziegfeld had his *Follies* set builder, T. B. McDonald, erect a five-room *palazzetto* with a working kitchen.

Then there was the swimming pool, a good idea unless you ask Joseph Urban to design it as if for an aquatic number in the *Follies*. Urban created a statue of an ancient Greek ephebe holding a fish that fountained out a stream of water right in the center of the bathing area. And just in case someone figured out how to do laps while avoiding the statue, a canoe floated on the surface of the water.

Billie, who must have realized at some point that she was surrounded by loons, ran the household from one of those fabulous theatrical desks crammed with papers, lists of things to do, a ton of memorabilia and framed photographs, cameos, leather stationery files, fan mail, and sheet music (in the pre-1920s extra-large size) of "If You Would Only Love Me," by Jerome Kern and John Crook, from Billie's biggest Frohman hit, Arthur Wing Pinero's *The "Mind-the-Paint" Girl* (1912). Thus, each participant contributed something unique to life at Burkely Crest.[1] It was like the *Follies*: an amalgam of warring styles and attitudes coming together in off-kilter unity.

As animal lovers, the Ziegfelds kept a menagerie. There were dogs, of course, but over a dozen of them, along with donkeys, lambs, an extremely ornery little buffalo family, birds of many a feather, and even a baby elephant named Herman. Free to roam the grounds at will, Herman once barged into the main house in search of Uneeda biscuits. Typically, every hour or so he would visit a back door giving onto the kitchen and proffer his trunk to Delia, the maid, for a Uneeda or two. On this occasion, Herman surprised Patty in mid-biscuit and trunked the cookie right out of her grasp. Exasperated, Patty went deeper into the kitchen for another, and Herman went right after her.

Remember, this was a real-live elephant. A cub, yes, but an *elephant*, complete with a jeweled howdah designed, of course, by the faithful Joseph Urban. There was also an elephant boy, one Henry, but neither he nor Delia could persuade Herman to go back outside. He was after Patty, the mistress of the Uneeda biscuit, and as Patty retreated up the back stairs, Herman started up after her, got stuck, and began to trumpet and stomp.

Oddly, with all the staff on hand, only Ziegfeld appeared, in his dressing gown, on the landing. Taking in the baby elephant crazing away, Delia in consternation, and Patty looking innocent, he spoke. With one of his professional cohorts—Gene Buck or Eddie Cantor, say—

---

[1]Despite Billie's having renamed the place, Hastings locals continued to call it "the Kirkham Estate" for some time. Eventually, it became "the Burke Estate," and remained so into the early twenty-first century, when the house and outbuildings were demolished and the land broken up for redevelopment.

Ziegfeld might have raised his voice. However, as always with the ladies, Ziegfeld maintained a respectful tone.

"Patty," he said, "you're not supposed to bring Herman into the house."

Many are those who say that the *Follies* peaked in 1919. Later editions prospered, true enough. In fact, not a single *Follies* in Ziegfeld's lifetime lost money. But it may be that the show had become something of a windup toy, autonomous once the plans were set into motion. It was still delightful, but considerably less surprising. However, with *Sally* established as the greatest musical comedy of all time, Ziegfeld decided to turn his attention to the book show in a way he had never done before. The Anna Held vehicles tended to a sameness of format; now, in the 1920s, Ziegfeld was to instruct an assortment of titles, with different kinds of stars in different kinds of formats from the zany to the romantic-heroic and even one "all American musical comedy."

Where to go after *Sally*? The obvious option was another Marilyn vehicle, but she was with Dillingham now. Of all Ziegfeld's *Follies* stars, the one most certain to carry a story show was the versatile Eddie Cantor; unfortunately, Cantor, too, had a "but," as he was still with the Shuberts for his union-boosting during the strike.

As it happened, Cantor wanted to get out of revue and into a book show just when Ziegfeld wanted to do this book show with Cantor. But who makes the first move to end the feud? It was 1923, and Cantor was touring in the Shuberts' *Make It Snappy* while *Sally* was still on *its* post-Broadway tour. By chance, they ended up playing across the street from each other,[1] and one critic's blurb was ready: "Eddie Cantor at $3.30 a seat is a better entertainment value than Marilyn Miller and Leon Errol at $4.40." Cantor took out a full-page ad in *Variety*, reprinting the remark as a signal to Ziegfeld, who then telephoned Cantor. And the new Cantor show was on.

---

[1] In St. Louis in one version, Chicago in another. Cantor himself told both versions.

There was one problem: the heroine. That collaboration of Sweetheart and Comic that we read in *Sally*'s headliners' billing directly above, at $4.40 a seat, was Ziegfeld's idea of a perfect show. But with Marilyn gone, Ziegfeld had no one of Cantor's stature to, so to say, Sally him up with. He had only the aforementioned Mary Eaton. So Cantor's name stood alone above the title, with Eaton strongly featured under it, in the "musical comedy of Palm Beach and Golf," *Kid Boots*.

Opening on December 31, 1923 at the Earl Carroll Theatre, *Kid Boots* immediately placed itself as the latest smash. It was no *Sally* because it was silly rather than touching and enthralling. But it was the biggest and most colorful of the season's hits, and by far the funniest. A Broadway legend held that someone—Ziegfeld? Gene Buck? the show's director, Edward Royce?—caught sight of Cantor in a loud oversampling of the typical golfer's kit, from tam-o'-shanter to knickers and stockings, and cried, "I see a show!" And, indeed, Eddie Cantor in whoop-de-do golfing drag is the essence of *Kid Boots*: Eddie adventuring among Ziegfeld's Palm Beach country-clubbers.

The themes under discussion in the William Anthony McGuire-Otto Harbach book will be class and money, because Boy (Harry Fender) is penniless while Girl (Mary Eaton) is gentry, promised to Other Boy (John Rutherford) because he's rich. Boots (Cantor), too, has a girl friend, a wisecracker (Marie Callahan). Yet the romances are barely a throughline in a piece loaded with self-contained Eddie Cantor business: giving a putting lesson to gigantic Jobyna Howland, a massage therapist; being roughed up on her table; getting into revue-sketch sequences of mischief; and of course slipping into blackface for the interpolated eleven o'clock number, "Dinah."

And "Dinah" just might be the most interpolated number of all time, because it not only makes no attempt to slip into the plot but actually *wants* to look excrescent. It's offered as entertainment at a country-club shindig, preceded by a club functionary announcing, "And now I have the extreme pleasure of introducing Mr. Eddie Cantor of the *Ziegfeld Follies*." This is a startling non sequitur after some three hours of Cantor's having enacted the role of Kid Boots. But then,

Ziegfeld loved self-promoting product placement. We've had a few instances already, as when *Sally* triumphed at the *Follies*. However, others were starting to use Ziegfeld as a summoning term for Big Broadway. In First National's movie *Polly of the Follies* (1922), Constance Talmadge snagged a millionaire after making a hit in the *Midnight Frolic*; Ziegfeld himself was a character, played by Bernard Randall. *Variety* called Joan Crawford's first film, MGM's *Pretty Ladies* (1925), "devoted primarily to plugging the Follies." A few of Ziegfeld's stars were impersonated, Ann Pennington played herself, and Bernard Randall repeated his Ziegfeld.

Most prominent of all was Cosmopolitan's *The Great White Way*, which appeared a few months after *Kid Boots* opened. Cosmopolitan was William Randolph Hearst's outfit, built around his personal prima donna, Marion Davies. She was a former *Follies* star, and he was one of Ziegfeld's most formidable allies. Is it possible that *The Great White Way*'s release was timed to give *Kid Boots* a PR spike as a Davies-Hearst salute to "their" Ziegfeld? The film told of a romance between a boxer and a musical-comedy girl who reaches apotheosis in the *Follies*. It sounds like a Marion Davies role, but *The Great White Way* featured Oscar Shaw and Anita Stewart. Davies played the 1936 remake, *Cain and Mabel*, opposite Clark Gable. Note that *The Great White Way* did not simply invoke the *Follies*: it documented it with the casting of Ned Wayburn as himself, complete with backstage *Follies* scenes filmed in the New Amsterdam. Whether to present theatrical ambition or its successful fulfillment, how better than to say "Ziegfeld," say "Follies"?

Of course, some of the magic in those words had more to do with presentation than with content. Examining the structure of *Kid Boots,* for example, one is amazed that Ziegfeld will produce *Show Boat* in only four years, for *Kid Boots* is entirely lacking in originality. Nothing in the Harry Tierney-Joseph McCarthy score matches *Sally*'s "Look For the Silver Lining." None of the production numbers challenges the whirlwind appeal of "Wild Rose"—or, for that matter, Anna Held's automobile and aeroplane songs. There is no surprise in *Kid Boots,* and the delight resides exclusively in one's enjoyment of Eddie Cantor. He himself tells us that, in the middle of the *Kid Boots* rehearsals, Ziegfeld wanted to junk the whole thing.

"Eddie, let's call it off," says the boss. "The show's no good. Before we go to the expense of costumes and sets—"

And Cantor immediately rips into a unique pitch: he performs *Kid Boots* in miniature for Ziegfeld. "I gave," he later reported, "what I'll always consider the best performance of my life."

Ziegfeld must have enjoyed Eddie Cantor, too, for he relented; it's hard to see what worried him in the first place. Yes, the songs are lame—and the effervescent "Dinah" was not to be added till the Pittsburgh leg of the tryout, much later. Still, *Kid Boots* is above all a comedy musical. It doesn't need a good score; it needs Eddie Cantor.

Look at how purely functional everything else is—the opening chorus, for example, defining the setting of the Everglades Club with a lack of definition that is almost inspired. The club is a place "where sweethearts wander," we learn. "Where hearts grow fonder." Good, I was wondering.

While we await the manifestation of Cantor, the principals get scene-and-aria check-ins. The gossip columnist (Harland Dixon) gets "Social Observer," sabotaged by a gabble of chorus responses. "Tactful" they call him. What, a gossip columnist? He's also "smart." No, wait: some call his work "blackmail." Others sing, "It's art." That's kind of cute, actually. Dance, encore, exeunt.

Is it Cantor yet? No, it's the lovers' turn. Hero Tom and heroine Polly let us in on their mésalliance, then get into "When Your Heart's in the Game," which at least mentions golf, giving the lyrics show context.

Still, we're relieved when Cantor comes on, frantically jumping around. The chorus ad-libs "What's the matter?" stuff, and Eddie gets his first line: "I bought a second-hand watch—if I don't do this, it won't go."

After a scene-and-song with the caddies—all black, by the way, an unusual racial integration for that early in the 1920s—Cantor reaches his first set piece, Jobyna Howland's putting lesson. The master at work:

CANTOR: (patiently, to keep the public off guard) What did you go around in?

HOWLAND: A blue skirt and a brown sweater.

CANTOR: No! No! (wheedling) I mean the score. The number. (Emphasizing this ramp-up so the audience won't miss the punchline) What did you make it in?

HOWLAND: Oh! Seventy-one.

CANTOR: (Impressed, to build the joke) Seventy-one. Why . . . that's *phenomenal.* (Three beats. Then:) And the second hole?

Kid Boots proceeds in that tempo, as the plot keeps giving way to drawn-out comic bits. Finally, a golfing contest settles the romance: the winner gets Mary Eaton. Twist: the wrong Boy wins! Double twist: a crooked ball and switched golf bags throw the contest to the Right Boy. Time for one last jest:

MARIE CALLAHAN: Boots, do you really love me?

CANTOR: The show is almost over, and you want to start a fight!

A hit of this size, built on the reconciliation of strike enemies Ziegfeld and Cantor, sentimentalized the producer. Sitting alone with his star in a Chinese restaurant after the triumphant out-of-town opening, in Detroit, Ziegfeld told Cantor that from now on he was in an exclusive club: he could call the boss "Flo" or "Ziggy." That same night, Ziegfeld jotted down figures and, echoing Frank Tinney's jest in *The Century Girl,* told Cantor, "I just figured—if we sell out every performance. I'll only lose twelve hundred dollars a week."

That's two-thirds of Ziegfeld the producer: the idolator of talent and the spendthrift showman. The last third was Ziegfeld the obsessive sender of telegrams, especially unnecessary or very long ones. Was it to create his myth or simply to empower his dicta that he would send a telegram to a star in his dressing room . . . *from the box office of that very theatre?* During *Kid Boots'* post-Broadway tour, Cantor received twelve pages of Western Union from Ziegfeld, still intent on refining a show that was already a hit. Says Cantor, "The whole message [was] such a jumble of ideas" that he made no attempt to address any of them, responding with a single word:

YES

Ziegfeld fired back with an argument:

> WHAT DO YOU MEAN YES? DO YOU MEAN YES YOU WILL TAKE
> OUT THE SONG OR YES YOU WILL PUT IN THE LINES OR YES YOU
> WILL FIX THAT SCENE OR YES YOU HAVE TALKED TO THOSE
> ACTORS

And Cantor wired back

NO

There's a fourth third to Ziegfeld the producer: the cheat in the payment of authors' royalties. A strong supporter of the performers, often paying more than the going rate, and, after 1919, more than scale, Ziegfeld economized by stiffing the writers. We have seen Harry B. Smith drift out of Ziegfeld's ambit for that reason, and Ziegfeld inadvertently killed off the outstanding composer of the American stage thus while *Kid Boots* was still playing in New York.

The usual solution to the problem of Ziegfeld's failure to pay what he owed you was to wait for him out in his office. Richard Rodgers, after wasting three hours, used the leverage of the Dramatists Guild, which had the power to pull every top-level writer from Ziegfeld's employ. A word on the matter to the receptionist, and, says Rodgers, "the doors to Ziegfeld's office flew open and the producer came out with his arms outstretched and a broad smile pasted on his face." Ziegfeld didn't even pretend to find out what Rodgers wanted; he knew. A bookkeeper was produced, followed by "checks to Larry [Hart] and me for whatever amount was owed us."

Alas, when the great Victor Herbert was given *his* three hours to fritter away in Ziegfeld's office, in May 1924, Herbert lost patience with this producer who keeps a Metropolitan Opera composer waiting like a hungry actor. Jumping to his feet, Herbert ignored the secretary's frantic warning, barged into the sanctum, and there discovered Ziegfeld glorifying an American girl. Scandalized, Herbert suffered a heart attack. And died.

While Ziegfeld spent these years trying to build Mary Eaton into the new Marilyn Miller, the real Marilyn was learning what stardom was like after Ziegfeld. It would likely be a less adventurous time, for her new manager, Charles Dillingham, was no revolutionary. In early 1924, when Marilyn signed with him, Dillingham had just ended his nine-year direction of the Hippodrome, a spectacle house whose aesthetic combined *Uncle Tom's Cabin, Ben-Hur,* and the circus. Further, Dillingham's moneymaker in the 1920s was Fred Stone, whose vehicles kept alive the moribund form of fairytale extravaganza.

In fact, Dillingham was the ideal producer for Marilyn. In the musical, the only other big-spender manager was Arthur Hammerstein, and he specialized in operetta. For musical-comedy Marilyn, Dillingham could create in the form she thrived in. Better yet, Dillingham had lately been working with Jerome Kern, *Sally*'s composer and the emerging senior genius of the story score.

There is bitter candy in this box, however, for Ziegfeld must have been in despair at not only the loss of access to Marilyn but the loss of her to his sometime partner. Other producers were rivals, even foes, but it was Dillingham with whom Ziegfeld tried to start a new kind of revue at the Century, Dillingham in whom the wary Ziegfeld could almost confide. They were friends; Billie always liked to recall that it was Dillingham who first told them about Palm Beach.

All Broadway was wondering what Dillingham would invent for Marilyn; but inventing takes time. With Marilyn under contract and drawing a weekly paycheck, Dillingham had to put her into something immediately.

But what?

And then he had a brainstorm. Marilyn was the elfin tomboy, wasn't she? Girlish and chaste and a bit farouche, right? A musical-comedy Peter Pan . . .

The rain in Spain stays mainly in the plain.

Of course! Marilyn as Peter Pan—the first American since Maude Adams to dare the role on Broadway! A musical version? Well . . . no. James M. Barrie would never allow that. Anyway, *Peter Pan* has some music built into it, a few incidental vocals and some dance bits. Jerome Kern would surely compose new songs as needed, but the rest of the score would be the John Crook originals used in London and New York. The original sets, too! If only Barrie would say yes!

Barrie did, with the encouragement of Basil Dean, who had seen Marilyn as Sally and was to direct the production. As for Marilyn's readiness, she felt secure with the two dances awaiting in Crook's music, because while other performers could outsing her, her dancing was incomparable. As for acting, Marilyn would make no attempt to imitate Maude Adams. Audiences found Adams mesmerizing; the Empire, when Adams played there, went so quiet one could hear the lint accumulating in men's trouser cuffs. It was delicate acting, unknown to the musical. Marilyn was used to Ziegfeld scale, where gala talents tore themselves up to thrill the New Amsterdam, a much larger house. So Marilyn would be a bold and outgoing Peter, defying her own personal Captain Hook; and we know who that was. What a pleasure, though, for theatregoers, who now took their kids to *their* first *Peter Pan* while enjoying Marilyn's first new part since *Sally* had opened, four years before.

Was this why Ziegfeld announced that his next book musical would star Billie Burke and open simultaneously with *Peter Pan*? We note even the same scan that one hears in the Barrie title: *Annie Dear!* versus *Peter Pan*. Based on Clare Kummer's *Good Gracious, Annabelle* (1916), *Annie Dear!* faithfully retold the story of a romantic young woman fleeing her bearded goon of a cowboy groom before their wedding. She hides out in the last place an uncouth westerner is likely to find her: amid Society on an estate on Long Island. Annie is working there as a maid. Guess who else is there—but without his beard, so she doesn't recognize him and he wins her over. Wedding as planned.

The project was chosen partly because Billie had already filmed *Good Gracious, Annabelle*—and partly, it would appear, because

Ziegfeld wanted to set his wife into competition with his ex-star. Both, now, would open in musicals at the height of the season, in late fall— and *Annie Dear!* was to peak in a fantasy sequence entitled "Little Boy Blue's Search for the Crock of Gold at the End of the Rainbow," in which Billie would dress as Boy Blue and actors would don animal getups and be adorable. What James M. Barrie play does that remind you of?

Ziegfeld had another angle: five or six minutes of girls in drag is sexy fun. Three hours of it is irritating, a waste of woman. No doubt it worked for Maude Adams, who had an innocence that was downright spooky. Marilyn's innocence conveyed a subliminal erotic power that would never work in Barrie. Billie would triumph over Marilyn; Ziegfeld would overwhelm Charles Dillingham.

A lot of *Annie Dear!* worked reasonably well. In structure, it was or-dinary. By this time, musicals were experimenting with new ways to bring up the curtain, to avoid those deadly opening choruses. *Going Up* began with a book scene set to music, as the telephone girl in a country inn gossips with the guests; *Mary* began with a lone male voice singing "The Love Nest"; *The Student Prince* began with a quartet of servants.

But *Annie Dear!* strikes the same old poses, albeit using Ziegfeld's conceit of plugging his own shows. The opening chorus consists of the-atregoers lined up outside a ticket agency, disappointed because there's nothing for *Kid Boots* or the *Follies*. One character knows "a friend of a friend of Flo who'll see we see the show!"

At least, there was Billie's singular charm in her establishing number, the title song, in which she gave voice to musical comedy's most tradi-tional instruction. "There are just two things to go after," she sang, "one is love—the other is laughter." She had some good lines, too, as when asking where the estate is. Someone says, "Rock Point, Long Island":

ANNABELLE: (pleased) Oh, that's where all the fashionable robberies take place.

The support counted the dependable comic Ernest Truex as Billie's society boss and, as her fiancé, Marion Green, a terrible singer who for some reason specialized in operetta. But the casting was not a problem: the author was. As the originator of the material, Clare Kummer, an occasional songwriter, wanted to be *Annie Dear!*'s sole author: book, music, and lyrics. Ziegfeld brought in others to "help," and most of the music was Sigmund Romberg's by the time *Annie Dear!* opened, on November 4, 1924, at the Times Square Theatre.

Marilyn's Peter Pan bowed in just two days later, at the Knickerbocker, and it proved a disaster for its star. As Ziegfeld had foreseen, no one believed Marilyn as a boy. However, he was in the middle of his own disaster, for Kummer stubbornly resisted his attempts to strengthen *Annie Dear!* by invoking Dramatists Guild privilege. The show closed after 103 performances, and while *Peter Pan* lasted three weeks longer, it was only because the piece itself is a perennial. Dillingham gave it a stunning production, to be sure, but Marilyn was now suspecting that Ziegfeld really deserved his reputation as *the* genius in the presentation of talent.

On the other hand, Ziegfeld's W. C. Fields vehicle, *The Comic Supplement of American Life,* went over so poorly that it closed on the first date of its tryout, starting on January 9, 1925. The only Ziegfeld show not to meet a Broadway opening date, it played Newark's Shubert Theatre, so we can at least note that the Shubert-Ziegfeld war had officially come to an end. Certainly, the Shuberts had taken Broadway from the Syndicate and could afford to be conciliatory. In fact, while Abe Erlanger was still active—he built a theatre bearing his name on Forty-Fourth Street as late as 1927—the Trust as such had evaporated.[1]

The Comic Supplement took the form of a musical version of the "funny papers," as a series of loosely unified sketches with "book, lyrics, and ballets" by J. P. McEvoy. Often a newspaper reporter but primarily a facile writer-for-hire, McEvoy turned out everything from greeting-card

---

[1]Erlanger's Theatre was renamed the St. James in 1932 and is, of course, still in use. Theatregoers who venture into the downstairs lobby can, at this writing, examine a leftover sign giving the credits of the Erlanger's first attraction, George M. Cohan's *The Merry Malones,* featuring the Dandy himself.

verse to fiction. But it takes know-how to write even lame song lyrics. Worse, Ziegfeld hired as composers the distinctly third-division Con Conrad (who nevertheless won the first Best Song Oscar, for "The Continental") and the unheard of Henry Souvaine.

No doubt Ziegfeld hoped the grumpily festive Fields would simply rise above the score and make the evening out of his unique fun. The producer was about to commission musicals centering more on story and score than on stars, but in the mid-1920s he still saw shows as giftwrap around a sweetheart or comic. It was as if he lived by that line in *Annie Dear!*: "One is love—the other is laughter." While he braced himself for Charles Dillingham's Big Marilyn Show—which was bound to be an imitation of *Sally*—Ziegfeld tried another star-comic vehicle. This one was for Leon Errol.

Louie the 14th is a great title. It sounds like a hit; it sounds *zany*. Like *Kid Boots,* it gave the star the liberty of the stage, filling in around him with conventional easy-do whatnot. The show's title reveals the plot: demobilized in France after the Great War, gauche Louie ends up as the fourteenth guest at a posh dinner to soothe a superstitious host.

Ziegfeld, a superstitious host himself, put together a gala piece, making up for *The Comic Supplement*'s gaffe of a score by hiring Sigmund Romberg (working with lyricist and bookwriter Arthur Wimperis) for his first credit after superb work on *The Student Prince* (1924). Joseph Urban and Edward Royce were on hand, as ever, and Ziegfeld thought up a brilliant PR coup in buying up the gold dinner service of the defunct imperial Russian family, to be used on stage during the dinner scene. More: a Cordon Bleu chef served upon that xanthic plate a real-life banquet instead of the dyed potatoes and other ersatz commonly used in theatrical eating scenes.

Billie seems to have been the only person along Broadway who hadn't heard that the Romanofs' dinner service was now in Ziegfeld hands. She simply came home one day to find the Burkely Crest dining room—whose table seated twenty—smothered in plate. Patty tells the story: "There were soup plates, bread-and-butter plates, dinner plates, dessert plates, salad plates, tureens, platters, cups and saucers, compote dishes, teapots, samovars, and . . . a twelve-branch candelabrum and a mammoth urn sprouting bronze eagle wings."

When Billie came to, she ascertained exactly what all this was and where it had come from. And when she asked Ziegfeld how much it had cost, he hesitated long before admitting to $38,000. Ah!—but the butler can start stacking it right away.

And where would he stack all this? Billie asked. "In Madison Square Garden?" Finally, "For the first time," Billie said, "I understand exactly what the Russian Revolution was about."

Unfortunately, *Louie the 14th* never quite came together. One reason was Romberg, who seems to have been all tuned out after *The Student Prince*. Perhaps Romberg couldn't respond to musical comedy any more; virtually all his seventeen shows after *Louie* were in the grand manner. Besides the dependable Errol, the show's one ace performer was Ethel Shutta, who went into the special summer edition of the 1925 *Follies* while still in *Louie the 14th*. A police escort sped her to the New Amsterdam and back.

That is, back to *Louie the 14th*'s theatre, the Cosmopolitan, on Columbus Circle. That's a full eighteen blocks north of Forty-Second Street, and from its opening, as the Majestic, in 1903, it was a playhouse with a jinx: its location. This was the surburbs to the average theatre-goer, who came to Broadway by subway to Times Square and chose his attraction locally. Ziegfeld and Urban troubled to give the Cosmopolitan a makeover: to no avail. Opening on March 3, 1925, *Louie the 14th* closed after only 79 performances. At least Errol was a touring draw, and Ziegfeld sent the company off in the fall with a good chance of making money after all. But the house jinx extended even out of the house. Even out of *town*. Errol suffered an accident, and the production shut down forever.

Buffs of old Hollywood may have alerted at the name "Cosmopolitan." That was William Randolph Heart's movie company, as we know: Hearst had bought the old Majestic, in 1923, as a showcase for his films. It was he who paid for the refurbishing of the theatre, and surely he who arranged for the police escort for Ethel Shutta's nightly back-and-forth through midtown. Ziegfeld was, by 1925, very big yet not police-escort big. That would have to have been Hearst. And there is that footnote running through the text of Ziegfeld, that he believed success depended on alliances with extremely powerful men, from Erlanger to Hearst.

Again, it was a Chicago point of view. New Yorkers could defy the system—Fiorello La Guardia, for instance. There were no La Guardias in Chicago. Further, men of power were comfortable in Ziegfeld's company, because while they were ruthless plutocrats and he an artist, he didn't speak like an artist. He spoke like them, in fluent Chicago.

There is this, too: Ziegfeld wanted his own theatre. Other producers were assembling lots, throwing new playhouses up. The 1920s saw an astonishing accumulation of new theatre hardware, with a concomitant mushrooming of play production, which led to the unprecedentedly busy—but also dangerously overextended—season of 1926–1927. Of course, like everyone else, Ziegfeld had no inkling that the American theatre industry was overbuilt and overplaying and would suffer a catastrophic implosion even before the Wall Street Crash.

No, all that Ziegfeld knew, in 1925, was that Charles Dillingham had his theatre and Arthur Hammerstein had his theatre. And the Shuberts and Belasco and Henry Miller had their theatres. Ziegfeld was no longer a Syndicate operative. He wanted to continue to use the New Amsterdam, yes—as a supplement to something Broadway had not yet known: a Ziegfeld Theatre, different from others outside and in, as Ziegfeld's art was different from that of other producers. Its content was different and its look was different. The New Amsterdam was so often filled with *Follies* and *Sally* and other Ziegfeldian presentation that the public thought the place was Ziegfeld's. No: Ziegfeld would show them what a genuine Ziegfeld Theatre could be, new and thrilling as Anna's shows were, as the *Follies* was at its inception, as *Sally* was.

And William Randolph Hearst said yes.

CHAPTER FIFTEEN

Any Girl Who Changes or Twists Her Hat Will Be Fired

Hearst was unlike all of the other Ziegfeld backers—the Diamond Jim Bradys, Palm Beach playboys, and bootleggers who spiced his finances from the Anna days to his very last production. Hearst was unseen, ubiquitous, and sociopathic. Whatever he wanted to happen would happen. In Europe, you would have to be Napoleon to get what Hearst got; in America, you need only be a press lord with Ambitions.

It happened that Hearst had decided to develop Manhattan's Sixth Avenue in the mid-Fifties, even though it was still blighted by an elevated railway. Maybe Hearst believed he could take over the railway and demolish it, only to be stopped by the election of the incorruptible La Guardia; who knows? It is certainly true that the Hearsts of the world often look for a front in the arts. Not an arts idealist such as, say, Eugene O'Neill, and not an arts loon such as Robinson Jeffers, crying to the muses in his crazy tower. Rather, a Hearst seeks out an artist with, above all, a popular profile. Such as our own Florenz Ziegfeld Jr.

Hearst had ordered the design and erection of the Warwick Hotel, set to rise in 1927 on the east side of Sixth Avenue between Fifty-Fourth and Fifty-Fifth Streets, and Hearst rather fancied a Ziegfeld Theatre facing it across the road. The Warwick was to serve as the New York caravanserai for Hearst's coterie, especially his Hollywood contacts, and while Ziegfeld was almost entirely innocent of connection to the film industry, he still represented the great world of prestige and influence that

Hearst moved within. There was a symmetry, Hearst thought, in a block of Manhattan real estate representing the combined importance of Ziegfeld and Hearst.

Most interesting to the public was the beyond-the-pale location: these two moguls were in effect pioneering. Today, Sixth Avenue teems, a typical Manhattan gorge running through a world of high-rise power, but in the 1920s it was a nowhere under the El. On January 9, 1925, Ziegfeld announced that ground was to be broken, that Joseph Urban would design the building—remember, he was an architect before he turned to stage art—and that this showplace would open with the latest of the Great Ziegfeld Shows.

What show would that be, precisely? Some incredible Ziegfeld invention? A new kind of musical?

Unlikely, that. Twenties musicals were so generic that they didn't really come in kinds. There were musical comedies as opposed to operettas, of course. And while one attraction might offer the dancing Astaires, another the comical acrobat Fred Stone, and still a third depend on an ensemble of farceurs, as in, say, *No, No, Nanette,* no one thought of these as kinds of musical.

Of course, Ziegfeld could always mount a *Follies.* Not only was this title the Most Famous Thing on Broadway: it bore the Ziegfeld name. Still, was it *special* enough to consecrate the house? Hadn't the *Follies* imitations run revue as a whole into the ground? Yes, Ziegfeld's revue of rococo devilry remained ineffable. But by now the revue annuals that hadn't given up were starting to resemble each other. Designers played musical chairs with the various series, even James Reynolds, whose hip bohemian art was an identification point for the *Greenwich Village Follies.* John Steel—Ziegfeld's Roscoe, without whom one could not imagine the Girls descending the stairs—went over to the *Music Box Revue.* So did Fanny Brice. Ann Pennington shuttled between *Follies* and *Scandals,* and W. C. Fields, after six *Follies,* did a *Scandals* and even a *Vanities* for that tinpot panderer Earl Carroll!

Anyway, hadn't the *Follies* already reached ultimate completion? True, each entry introduced at least one major novelty. In 1920, Ziegfeld featured Art Hickman's Orchestra, and later editions brought in jazz kings Paul Whiteman and George Olsen, leading, respectively, the most famous and the hottest of the big white bands. In 1922, a number called "Lace Land" created a sensation with the use of an extremely tricky coloring process that, in darkness, discovered kaleidoscopic patterns on the girls' white lace costumes.

This 1922 *Follies* also gave birth to a major show-biz trope in a duet for (Edward) Gallagher and (Al) Shean in explorer togs, the former in a solar topee and the latter in a fez. Entitled "Oh, Mr. Gallagher and Mr. Shean," and published as "by themselves about themselves," the song recounted adventures and traded philosophies of life, each verse running up to a match of sassy salutes, such as "Merry Christmas, Mr. Gallagher!/Happy New Year, Mr. Shean!" and, everyone's favorite, "Positively, Mr. Gallagher?/Absolutely, Mr. Shean!" The piece became so well known that it was referenced and imitated by composers from Jerome Kern (in *The Cabaret Girl*, [1922]) to Jerome Moross (in *The Golden Apple*, [1954]).

As it happened, the 1923 *Follies* was a respectable evening, peaking in an authentic reenactment of a talent contest that the very young Fanny Brice had entered, complete with her original number, "When You Know You're Not Forgotten By the Girl You Can't Forget," the everthreatening hook, and catcalls from plants in the audience. As before, Brice won the contest; this time she beat Ann Pennington.

Still, some critics now found revue—all of it—a creaking galley of exhausted concepts. "The most dreary, stupid, pointless, unbeautiful, unfunny show that Broadway has ever seen," Arthur Hornblow called the 1923 *Follies* in *The Theatre*. Surely it wasn't. Yet why had the customary gaggle of big names dwindled into one or two—Will Rogers in 1922, Brice and Pennington in 1923, Rogers and Pennington in 1924, W. C. Fields in 1925, recycling material from the Newark casualty, *The Comic Supplement*? Why was Ziegfeld forever peddling precision kicklines, Van and Schenck in one for set changes, or those "bring on the girls" sequences? One *Follies* song (in 1922) was actually called "Bring On the Girls," as if the audience were in for a novel treat. What, with that staircase again, too?

So we can be certain that the Ziegfeld Theatre will not be opening with a *Follies*. Meanwhile, the 1925–1926 season began, and its first major book shows were *No, No, Nanette, Dearest Enemy,* and *The Vagabond King,* all within a single week. One night after *The Vagabond King* came the show that all New York (and especially Florenz Ziegfeld Jr.) had been waiting for: *Marilyn Miller's Revenge.*

Actually, Dillingham gave it another title: *Sunny*. Still, this was Marilyn's attempt to prove to Ziegfeld that it was her talent, rather than his showmanship, that put her over. It was as well Dillingham's attempt, in effect, to revive *Sally* while changing as little as possible—for starters, just one vowel and the double consonants.

To be fair, *Sunny* is not really a replica of *Sally* in its particulars. Jerome Kern was again the composer, but he was now working with Otto Harbach and Oscar Hammerstein, and while *Sally* was a compositional hodgepodge, *Sunny* is consistently the work of the three authors. Then, too, *Sunny*'s characters are different from *Sally*'s, with a lead comic (the hot-dancing Jack Donahue) very unlike *Sally*'s rubberlegs old-timer, Leon Errol. *Sally,* furthermore, was really a show of the previous generation with a state-of-the-art production; *Sunny* was ultra-twenties with a Jazz Now feeling, as in bringing on Cliff "Ukulele Ike" Edwards to sing his risqué party pieces, giving the orchestra pit to George Olsen's band, or letting Pert Kelton loose to imitate tango dancers and Charlie Chaplin.

However, these are details. The driveline of the event, to borrow the head of the unsigned *New York Times* review, was "Glorifying Marilyn Miller"—and "Glorifying" belonged to Florenz Ziegfeld almost as much as Marilyn Miller did. *Sunny* was *perceived* as Ziegfeldian in style, even if *Sally* raised its curtain on a humdrum locale into which Marilyn got a trick entrance of deceptive modesty. She was all but hidden in rags amid a passel of orphans similarly clad, till the New Amsterdam began to buzz with recognition.

That's Ziegfeld's surprise; Dillingham gave *Sunny*'s first scene a craze of delight. Here's *The Times* again: "The curtain rises upon a circus scene, crowded with men and women spectators, freaks, barkers, snake charmers, and the following scene involves a colorful circus parade, replete to the band." It sounds terrific—and at the height of it all Marilyn appeared, all in white as Queen of the Circus on a real-life horse as the audience let out a roar of welcome.[1]

One wonders what Ziegfeld let out at that moment, for his experience with Mary Eaton proved that there was no alternative enchanting beauty who combined the virtues of Mary Pickford, Pavlova, and Mata Hari, as Marilyn did. Showgirls grow on trees. But one cannot build a show on beauty alone—and let us repeat, for emphasis, that one reason why the name of Ziegfeld meant so much was his love affair with talent. He was a rare American businessman who enjoyed sex more than money; yet he enjoyed talent most of all. His good friends were millionaires. But his best friends were Will Rogers and Eddie Cantor.

Sunny was almost as big a smash as *Sally,* with a long Broadway run and a long tour, hit tunes, and an important memory. This could only have intensified Ziegfeld's need to distinguish himself in the book musical—and to find the unimagined masterpiece with which to open the Ziegfeld Theatre, which would be ready about eighteen months after *Sunny* opened. But first, there was an immediate hurdle to jump: Ziegfeld was blocked by law from producing a *Follies* in 1926.

Or, more precisely, from producing a "Ziegfeld Follies." The phrase was a trademark, and Ziegfeld didn't control it. "His" *Follies,* remember, had begun as a Klaw and Erlanger property. Of course, Ziegfeld developed the *Follies* format till it—and to an extent the very genre of revue—was his invention. So Ziegfeld mixed the contents; the *Syndicate* owned the container. And, as the Syndicate was now extinct, it was all

---

[1]Here's an odd note to sound: in 1934, Jerome Kern and Hammerstein were in London preparing an original musical for Drury Lane, *Three Sisters*. This show, too, employed a horse, and someone told Kern it was the same beast that Binnie Hale had ridden in on for *her* entrance in the London *Sally,* eight years earlier. Amused, Kern, at the piano, broke into Sunny's entrance music . . . and that wonderful horse pricked up its ears, retrieved its muscle memory, and went right into his circus routine as if back onstage at the Hippodrome with Binnie Hale.

over but the lawsuits: concerning theatre realty, artists' contracts, and such niceties as who exactly owned the "Ziegfeld Follies." Not until the attorneys were done could any one producer put one on—not even Ziegfeld himself.

He could, of course, produce a revue, even a *Follies* in some alternate wording—just not *Follies of 1926* or *Ziegfeld Follies of 1926,* because these precise titles were owned by . . . who? Yet to rechristen *his* show seemed awfully retro now that *The Ziegfeld Follies,* quoting Ziegfeld himself, was "a national institution" dedicated to "glorifying the American girl."

So Ziegfeld abandoned the *Follies* for the moment, to produce an alternate variety show in an alternate locale: Palm Beach. Joseph Urban came down to renovate the Palm Beach Supper Club, which Ziegfeld planned to reopen as the Club de Montmartre. The new name recalled the roof gardens where the *Follies* began—the Jardin de Paris and Moulin Rouge—almost as if Ziegfeld were starting from scratch.

Of course, he wasn't—not with the faithful Urban in tow. Further, both Edward Royce and Ned Wayburn directed the new piece (at different times). However, an unfamiliar tech credit was added to Ziegfeld's stock cohort, that of John Harkrider. Just twenty-five at the time, Harkrider became Ziegfeld's main costume designer. Lucile was over; the old-time *Follies* was over. Ziegfeld needed a twenties look when not producing story shows set in the cowboy west or seventeenth-century France. Lucile was fabulous but limited, like the Empress Theodora. Lucile suited the old Ziegfeld, who micromanaged the outfits so intensely that he once sent a telegram to a *Follies* company manager that I quote (in full) as the title of this chapter. That was fine for the Ziegfeld of the 1910s and early 1920s, busy with one *Follies* and sometimes one other title per season. From 1927 on, however, Ziegfeld was busy with two or three story shows a year, with costumes oriented to character rather than wild gimmicks. Harkrider promised the producer a breezy new look, the kind of thing Ruby Keeler or Eleanor Powell might wear.

Banked by the usual pep rally of millionaires, the Palm Beach show resembled the *Midnight Frolic* that used to top off the *Follies* on the New

Amsterdam Roof. Like them, it began late, encouraged dancing to the band after the performance, served supper, and invited clotheshorses to present themselves in the mode.

The entertainment was a nightclub kind of thing, not worthy of the name *Ziegfeld Follies* in any case. And the atmosphere was pure Palm Beach, showy but thin. It was theatre for the rich and powerful in a town whose main attraction, for Ziegfeld, was the gambling den at Edward R. Bradley's beach club. Ask the average leading lady what word she hated, and the answer was "co-star." Ask Billie what word she hated, and the answer was "Bradley's," where Ziegfeld could know to repletion the risk and thrill that had been his in his youth with Anna during their footloose European summers. As father to Patty and husband to the easily exasperated Billie, Ziegfeld could not map about as he once had done; Bradley's Beach Club was his Europe and perpetual ruination now.

Ziegfeld Palm Beach Nights opened in January 1926, with tickets at $200 each. I told you it was theatre for the rich. After the first night, seats went down to $12, still more than double the Broadway top. Yet the cast came cheap. James Barton and Ray Dooley led the comics, and others included Louise Brown (whom Ziegfeld had major plans for and who went absolutely nowhere here, though she worked prominently in England), a close harmony quartet called the Yacht Club Boys (known to aficionados of minor Fox movie musicals in the 1930s), singer Charles King, and dancer Barbara Newberry. To reassure his plutocrat public, Ziegfeld started the show with nothing but a great pailleted silver globe hanging in the air, a diamond as big as the Ritz. Lowered to the floor, the ball broke into top and bottom halves, and out stepped Claire Luce in a spectacular luminous gown to match the globe.

For some reason, Ziegfeld changed the show's title to *Ziegfeld's Palm Beach Girl*, and, by June 24, when it opened in New York at the Globe Theatre, it was entitled *No Foolin'*, after its best-appreciated song, by James Hanley and Gene Buck, introduced by *favorita* Louise Brown. Came then another title change: *Ziegfeld American Revue of 1926*, although switching poster billing during a run can only confuse the public.

The titles kept coming, however, for Klaw, Erlanger, and their attorneys finally closed their Chinese box of legal disputes. So, when this show began its national tour, Ziegfeld officially sanctioned it as *Ziegfeld Follies of 1926*. Still, it was the U.F.O. of the series, the one unlike the others—not least in an astonishing shuffling of talent. The piece that started out in Palm Beach offered a substantially different cast than the one that played New York. High-art dancer Greta Nissen and choreographer Michel Fokine, for instance, were brought in for Broadway, as if Ziegfeld realized that his real public longed for the arty touch that would have irritated the Palm Beachers. Ben Ali Haggin, too, was interpolated into the doings for the last of his teasy tableaux. In the end, the event got PR and eked out a very small profit. In fact, none of Ziegfeld's personal *Follies,* from *1907* through *1931*, failed to pay off, though the later ones, because of Ziegfeld's pound-foolish capitalization, spent rather than made fortunes.

Ziegfeld not only spent but lost a fortune, on his first book musical in, he hoped, Jazz Age style. We note with pleasure Ziegfeld's first commissioning of a score by one of the New Teams of the Twenties: Richard Rodgers and Lorenz Hart. *Yes!* Even if the rest of the writing squad were the usual hacks and kibitzers: Irving Caesar (more typically a lyricist) and David Freedman wrote the book, which was "revised by Anthony Maguire" (Ziegfeld house librettist William Anthony McGuire, in the slightly altered billing he occasionally used at this time). McGuire also staged the show, with choreographer Sammy Lee.

This group and Ziegfeld collaborated on a supremely chaotic production, as the powerless and generally ignored Rodgers and Hart looked on in alarmed wonder. Sometimes a great idea for a musical undergoes faulty execution, but this time the idea itself was at fault. It started when Ziegfeld got Billie's permission to go trotting off to Europe with J. Leonard Replogle, one of his Palm Beach buddies. Billie knew that at least one of them would return bankrupt. In fact, they both returned with raves for a singer they had heard on the boat coming back, and Ziegfeld had plans to build a show around her. She is almost as unknown today as the show itself: Belle Baker in *Betsy*.

Popular in vaudeville, Baker was celebrated for the soulful acting of her vocals at a time when most singers just sang. Baker's contralto was the most emotionalized of the day, with an elaborate portamento that deepened charm songs and made ballads into novels. One wonders why Ziegfeld had never taken notice of Baker before this; she would have been ideal for the Big Lady singer slot that Emma Carus and Nora Bayes occupied in the first *Follies*. He certainly noticed her now: by the time the boat docked, Belle Baker had all but signed to make her Broadway debut in a Ziegfeld show.

So that was the idea for *Betsy*, along with Caesar and Freedman's premise that Baker would play a spinster whose sister and three brothers can't get married till Baker does. Unfortunately, the narrative went little further than that: the brothers fix Baker up with a cute guy who raises pigeons, but he falls for the sister. Baker must face heartache, then decides to forego love for the usual Ziegfeld apotheosis, success in show biz. Everybody else in sight gets engaged. Curtain.

Not counting an early mishap and a couple of revues, Rodgers and Hart had given Broadway three musicals, all smash hits. And they knew something that Caesar and Freedman didn't: musical comedies need lots of plot and plenty of it. Rodgers and Hart weren't even writing from a script but from "little more than a rough outline of the action," as Rodgers recalled. Working off a treatment was in fact customary in the writing of a score, but Herbert Fields, Rodgers and Hart's partner on their three hits, was more collaborative, and readily available. Hart would just as soon go off to have fun in any case, but Rodgers took composition seriously, and he found it frustrating to work in a void. "*Betsy,*" says Rodgers, "turned out to be the worst experience of my career—the worst, that is, until I did another show for Ziegfeld."

That show will be *Simple Simon,* discussed below. Right now, the point is how cavalier Ziegfeld could be about the integrity of composition. Fastidious about the Girls' costumes, the lighting tech, and the PR hooks, Ziegfeld let the unities take care of themselves. Thus, some of his titles ended up more or less consistent in their writing (and one of his titles ended up as *Show Boat* in its writing), while others, like *Betsy*, ended up without even the fluffy substance on which most musicals depended.

Betsy's second-act script and some of its songs have vanished, but the critics can fill us in. In *Judge*, George Jean Nathan called *Betsy* "little save a Keith vaudeville show dolled up for the expensive Broadway trade." George Goldsmith in *The Herald Tribune* noted that "no ingenuity for stage effects could make Miss Baker a musical comedy heroine." "A butchered show," said Sime Silverman in *Variety*. "It is a waste of time to give it any attention."

Interestingly, *Betsy* was one Ziegfeld piece made not of ethnic variety but ethnic homogeneity. This was a tale of New York's Lower East Side, and virtually every character spoke in dialect. Here's the mother of the brood, Mrs. Kitzel, scolding her sons, Louie, Moe, and Joe:

> TRELDA: What are you doing here? Don't answer me! You told me you're going to a party, ah? Keep your mouth! But you didn't told me *what* party and *when* party and *why* party! Shut up! And *who* party! . . . I don't want to make here a scandal, but at home I'll give you already!

For Baker's support, Ziegfeld hired a mixture of second-line regulars (Barbara Newberry; Allen Kearns, eventually to play *Girl Crazy's* hero, was the pigeon master) and nobodies. Ziegfeld normally cast from the highest division, but this was the 1926–1927 season, the biggest thus far in Broadway history, and the hot names had already signed their contracts when *Betsy* was hiring. Ziegfeld did bring in a unique music-and-comedy troupe, Borrah Minnevitch's Harmonica Symphony Orchestra, for specialties in both acts, and veteran Al Shean (of Gallagher and) played a certain Stonewall Moskowitz, a sort of guru of East Side culture.

But then, who could save a work patched of odds and ends? Consider this snippet of a scene in the Kitzel family clothing store, when a customer wants something for a shooting trip out west and is shown a "hunting suit":

CUSTOMER: Why is this a hunting suit?

LOUIE: I been hunting for the pants two years.

It's solid twenties humor—except the line had been used in any number of clothing-store sketches, including one called "Joe's Blue Front" that Eddie Cantor had played in *two* Shubert revues, *The Midnight Rounders* (1920) and *Make It Snappy* (1922), while he was on the outs with Ziegfeld.

Given that Rodgers and Hart knew as much about *Betsy*'s plot and characters as my readers do, they came up with some very pleasing numbers. The Baker spots took in the amusingly syncopated "Sing," a highly endearing up-tune in "If I Were You," and, addressing the deep tug of Baker's *espressivo*, "This Funny World (makes fun of the things that you strive for)." Unfortunately, none of the three was enthusing the public, a humiliating flaw in the tunestack of a singing star. Luckily, the New York premiere unveiled an instant hit for Baker, still popular today. And apparently the only people connected with *Betsy* who didn't know about it were Rodgers and Hart.

This first night occurred on December 28, 1926 at the New Amsterdam, after a single week of tryouts in Washington, D.C. "It should have been kept on the road for months," says Rodgers, recalling everybody fighting and Ziegfeld "charging around the theatre, screaming like a wounded water buffalo." To his wife, Dorothy, Rodgers wrote, "I don't like it at all."

And he downright hated it shortly after the second act began, when the orchestra struck up music unfamiliar to Rodgers, and Baker put forth lyrics Hart had never heard. The call is coming from inside the house: the song was "Blue Skies," by Irving Berlin. Ziegfeld hadn't warned his songwriters that he had commissioned an interpolation (though the song was listed in the program), and the producer added to Rodgers' misery by directing a spotlight to isolate Berlin during one of Baker's encores, so he could rise to acknowledge the public's applause.

It's an incomprehensible story, however often told. First of all, there were other interpolations in *Betsy* that Rodgers knew of, written or cowritten by the busy Irving Caesar. Did Rodgers object to those as well?

And did Rodgers really have no idea that "Blue Skies" was going in? *No one* in the production gave him a heads-up? The first-night house presented Berlin with a warm welcome, but if "Blue Skies" had been a secret, wouldn't folks have been bewildered? Who's the little guy in the spotlight?

Betsy was gone in 39 performances: a debacle. Nonetheless, Ziegfeld was enjoying the completion of his monument. The ceremonial setting of the final stone into and the dedication of the Ziegfeld Theatre took place before a huge crowd on December 9, 1926, amplified for live radio relay and saluted in massive national press coverage.

In some ways, this theatre was the greatest of Ziegfeld's many innovations. He created formats for playmaking, generated a demotic style in show-biz ethnicity, invented the exploitation of scandal in the building of careers, and created a handful of the biggest stars in entertainment. Now, like Richard Wagner devising an opera house of the future at Bayreuth, Ziegfeld revealed the auditorium of the Never Before. It smashed the traditions of the bourgeois theatregoing parlor, with the side boxes for grandees, the flutings, doodads, and antiqued painting that equated theatre with Western power structures.

Instead, the Ziegfeld Theatre's interior was not unlike the inside of an empty eggshell, seating 1,622 and decorated with one endless molecule of art. This was a Joseph Urban mural running from top to bottom, over the ceiling and then down the sides. A prevailing gold and black was stippled with every other color, the whole a gallimaufry of images. "From romances of all time and myths of all ages" was how the theatre's official brochure described it, "to give the liveliness of color and fantasy of pattern to the simple domical envelope of the auditorium."

Now. What work would suit the inauguration of this beautiful monster. As we've said, it couldn't be the *Follies,* or even any other of the kinds of show that Ziegfeld was associated with. And that may be why a legend grew up that Ziegfeld was planning to open his house with *Show Boat,* that *Show Boat* wasn't ready, and that Ziegfeld then stuffed some other thing onto the Ziegfeld's stage. Perhaps this legend simply wants the first attraction in the Ziegfeld Theatre to be historical: but Ziegfeld wanted it to be Ziegfeldian. The theatre itself would make the history; the attraction would serve as an exhibition piece in a complementary way, to let the theatre get the attention.

Besides, *Show Boat* could not possibly have been ready. Its writers, Jerome Kern and Oscar Hammerstein, did not secure the rights for a stage version from the novel's author, Edna Ferber, till less than four months before Ziegfeld's theatre was to open its doors. Counting two months for rehearsals and tryouts, that would leave Kern and Hammerstein about six weeks to write the biggest musical to that date. Shows could be written with surprising speed—even haste—in the 1920s. But *Show Boat* into six weeks does not go. In any case, when the two men and Ferber signed their contract, on November 17, 1926, Ziegfeld had already commissioned and cast the other piece that was to consecrate his playhouse, and was just about to put it into rehearsal.

Most unusually, Ferber did not sell her novel outright. She, Kern, and Hammerstein each held one-third of the musical, so she was eager to learn which producer her partners had in mind. A playwright herself, she knew how crucial his role would be. The men had been noncommittal on the subject, if only because of divided loyalties. Kern wanted Ziegfeld, but Charles Dillingham had produced most of Kern's twenties shows. In fact, *Sunny* (which Kern and Hammerstein had written with Otto Harbach) was still running. Then there was Arthur Hammerstein—Oscar's uncle. Both Dillingham and Uncle Arthur were known for the scope of their productions. Dillingham, we know, had even managed the colossal Hippodrome for a while.

Still, as I say, Kern wanted Ziegfeld, and rather passionately at that. Three and a half weeks after he and Hammerstein made their deal with Ferber, they signed *Show Boat* up with Ziegfeld. Even then, Uncle Arthur, who had somehow understood that he was to be *Show Boat*'s producer, instituted legal proceedings to take the property from Ziegfeld in early 1927. By May, the suit was withdrawn.

We may never know why Kern and Hammerstein chose Ziegfeld. We do know that the idea of adapting Ferber's epic—at once a family saga, a backstager, and a study of the tumultuously evolutionary nature of American culture—was Kern's. And it was Kern who wanted Ziegfeld. We know also that Kern's experiences with Ziegfeld were unhappy, in the fight with Victor Herbert on *Miss 1917* and on *Sally*, the hit he hated. So, again, why Ziegfeld?

Could it have been Ziegfeld's ease in mixing ethnicities? *Show Boat* is partly about race relations and partly about how show biz changed its tones over the two generations leading up to the late 1920s. Arthur Hammerstein was still so old-timer in his race casting that his *Golden Dawn* (1927), a vast operetta set in Africa, gave the black speaking parts to whites in blackface. Perhaps Kern and Hammerstein feared that such thinking would sabotage the presentation.[1]

Then, too, there was Ziegfeld's flair in casting. Yes, he put on spectacles, dazzled the eye, but mainly he was a magnet for talent. Ziegfeld knew theatre; is that what it was? He *surprised* his public, and wasn't *Show Boat* to be the musical made of surprises? The musical with no limits? And this, too: Ziegfeld came from Chicago, where much of *Show Boat*'s second act takes place. So Kern called Hammerstein, told him of Ferber's novel, and what a great musical it would make. That million-dollar title! And what a show for Ziegfeld!

Keep in mind that Ziegfeld was in an almost sorry state at this point, despite the glorious unveiling of his showplace. His book musicals had been flopping, his *Follies* was sagging, yet Kern wanted to take the newest show to this oldest of managers, whose first Broadway production had opened thirty years earlier.

Of course, no one, including Ziegfeld, could have known that he was about to put on six smash hits in a row. But Hammerstein, of a theatrical dynasty, was aware that, in the theatre, you're never down till you're dead.

"Is Ziegfeld enthusiastic?" Hammerstein asked Kern.

With a chuckle, Kern replied, "He doesn't know anything about it yet."

---

[1]Ironically, one of *Show Boat*'s leads *was* a white in blackface—but on a technicality that we'll get to later.

CHAPTER SIXTEEN

Impresario Extraordinaire

That is what one read on Ziegfeld's business card at the time of the opening of the Ziegfeld Theatre, on February 27, 1927: *impresario extraordinaire*. And who could doubt it, as the public gaped at the innovative great open space of the auditorium and the Urban art all about? The Ziegfeld's curtain rose for the first time in its public life on the "romantic musical comedy" *Rio Rita,* a south-of-the-border tale in which a Texas Ranger loves a kind of Irish señorita while pursuing that notorious bandit the Kinkajou.

It's very slightly reminiscent of *Rose-Marie* (1924), with a Rio Grande accent instead of French-Canadian. The baritone hero is even named Jim (as in *Rose-Marie*), and *Rio Rita*'s score uses the augmented harmonies heard in *Rose-Marie* as "Indian" music.

In any case, *Rio Rita* was an odd item for a Ziegfeld show. True, the loose narrative structure allowed for plenty of production numbers and showgirl parades. However, half of the show—the "romantic" part—was *extremely* operetta, and Ziegfeld worked only in musical comedy and revue. Even more oddly, the show's "musical comedy" part comprised a comic duo having scarcely any relationship with the romantic characters. So it's very slightly reminiscent also of *Ariadne auf Naxos,* the opera in which figures of myth are forced to share a stage with figures of spoof. *Rio Rita* is two shows in one, with operetta's Florid Lady and Law

Enforcement Baritone on one side and a shyster, his stooge, and their girl friends on the other. One half expects the two teams to introduce themselves and shake hands during the curtain calls.

Rio Rita's score was the work of the *Kid Boots* writers, Harry Tierney and Joseph McCarthy; the book was by Guy Bolton and Fred Thompson. This was a musical-comedy lineup, without question, and, in truth, the operetta scenes never quite rise to the ecstatic level of, say, late-twenties Sigmund Romberg. Still, *Rio Rita* strikes the indicated poses, and the many divertissements—"Eight Little Gringos" danced by the Gringo Girls, "The Spanish Shawl," "The Charm Dance," "Moonlight Ballet," "The Black and White Ballet"—waltz and tango and march along with brio. And, as so often in twenties musicals, there was a New Dance Sensation, "The Kinkajou." Few of these numbers gave much instruction in the actual performance of the steps, but "The Kinkajou" is virtually a secret message. It does have the distinction of launching its verse (in c minor!) on the dominant ninth chord.

Rio Rita's comedy half has great jokes but not much melody. "Five minutes with me," the shyster tells a comely chorister, "and you're a girl with a past." As the audience giggles, the orchestra breaks into "The Best Little Lover in Town," whose only purpose is to revive a hoary cliché, Comic Prances With Girls. Yet in matching *Follies* veteran Bert Wheeler (the stooge) with Robert Woolsey (the shyster), Ziegfeld created a major comic team of the 1930s, albeit of the second division. Woolsey was as skinny as a thief, with a cigar, glasses, and a pompous delivery. Wheeler was Little Boy Blue. The two were indispensable; RKO retained them, alone of the stage cast, for the 1929 *Rio Rita* film. Certainly, Hollywood felt more comfortable with local folk (Bebe Daniels and John Boles) for the operetta half of the piece. On Broadway, these two were tempestuous Ethelind Terry and stalwart J. Harold Murray, but then who else would sing "If You're in Love, You'll Waltz"? Rita, who speaks fractured English, scorns this ranger who would arrest her brother as the hated Kinkajou. "*Gringo!*" she cry. Yet she save him from bad guy's trap. At length, the real Kinkajou exposed, Rita shows up for the finale already in her wedding gown, as if she were Fran Drescher.

Never before had Ziegfeld been so confident of success. *Rio Rita* was almost—I say *almost,* mind—a *Follies* with a storyline, and the *Follies* had never failed him. The show worked, the theatre worked, Broadway worked. The American stage had been expanding through the 1920s at a reckless rate, despite the rival cinema and radio. As I've said, *Rio Rita*'s 1926–1927 season was the biggest ever: too big. There were too many new theatres, too many new productions, too many star discoveries for theatregoers to accommodate. As a result, the 1927–1928 season saw a painful contraction, in the proportion of flops to hits—one of those self-adjusting capitalist convulsions. Then, of course, the stock-market crash would cut off most of the theatre's cash flow altogether.

In February 1927, however, *Rio Rita* and the Ziegfeld Theatre were what the culture loves most: handsome and lucrative. As first-nighter Brooks Atkinson reported, "Ziegfeld, no less than his patrons, was in a holiday mood last evening. Telegrammed to death with felicitations, he weakly displayed messages from President Coolidge, Mayor Walker and Eddie Cantor as evidence of the democracy of his friendships."

Apparently, Ziegfeld didn't read the one from Will Rogers, addressed to his boss at "Ziegfeld's own theatre on the ragged edge of Park Avenue." It said, in part:

I FEEL THAT THIS IS JUST THE STARTING FOR YOU OF A CHAIN
JUST THINK OF WHAT SHUBERT AND SCHULTE AND LOEW AND
NEDICK AND THE OWL AND CHILDS ALL DID WITH ONE IDEA . . .
I HOPE YOU NEVER HAVE TO PUT IN A MOVIE SCREEN YOUR OLD
HIRED HAND WILL.

Of the theatre itself, Atkinson took appreciative note of Urban's interior mural, "one of the most extravagant and bizarre cycloramas of imaginative designing to be found this side of fairyland." Atkinson referenced Socrates' notion that "Beauty is perfection in usefulness," and gave the new playhouse a high rating thus, for it was "not only splendid but appropriate." For once, an auditorium actually looked like a place of magic. Not a home for Shakespeare, Katharine Cornell, or the Theatre Guild, no. A place of musical comedy: of Ziegfeld.

Rio Rita did tremendous business despite the out-of-the-way location, for the PR established the notion that theatregoers had to collect the experience of, so to speak, seeing things Ziegfeld's way. When *Show Boat* was finally ready, Ziegfeld opened it at his *hôtel particulier* by moving *Rio Rita* down to the Liberty and then the Majestic, allowing the production to tot up 494 performances before setting out on tour. In 1930, a London staging opened a second theatre, the Prince Edward, where *Rio Rita* lasted less than two months.

Ziegfeld wasn't responsible for the London version, and this only reminded one and all how irreplaceable was his Touch. Certainly, Marilyn Miller now thought so; in March 1927, just after *Rita* had opened, Ziegfeld announced that Marilyn was returning to his management. Unfortunately, while feverishly seeking something suitable for the princess of musical comedy amid his typical pileup of projects, Ziegfeld suffered a bout of bronchitis. Theatremaking is stressful even when one is single-minded and deliberate; at Ziegfeld's encompassing pace and survey, theatre is murderous. He needed rest. Not a vacation—Ziegfeld's vacations were gambling and telegrams—but a period of recuperative emptiness. At that, Kern and Hammerstein refused to mount the customary Ziegfeld treadmill in turning out *Show Boat*. The piece was going to be dense, and they would write long. Ziegfeld had to release his first three *Show Boat* hires from their contracts: the aforementioned Elizabeth Hines and Guy Robertson, along with Paul Robeson.

Consider: twenties musicals were not based on novels. Most were originals, meaning that they arranged new combinations of public-domain clichés. Those based on existing sources tended to measure a score to the dimensions of a comedy hit from, say, six or seven seasons before. There was a handful of titles drawn from fiction: *Princess Flavia* (1925), from *The Prisoner of Zenda*; *Hello, Lola!* (1926), from *Seventeen*;

A Connecticut Yankee (1927). But these novels readily accommodated a three-hour slimdown. Edna Ferber's *Show Boat* is epic.

Of course, Hammerstein longed to take the musical to places it had never visited, and Kern—though he preferred above all the old-time charm shows, innocent of jazz—had ambitions, too. And one thing about *Show Boat* above all other things must have fascinated them: it couldn't be done.

Not, that is, under the musical's prevailing guidelines. How do you handle the guy abandoning his wife and daughter? He never returns! How do you write the second heroine, who ends up in a bordello? What about the ugly race stuff? How, even, do you do the boat?

Ironically, Ferber hadn't known about the floating playhouses of the midwest and south and their nineteenth-century programs mixing melodrama and minstrel olio, till a producer brought up the topic at one of those tip-top New York glamour brawls. (The novel is dedicated "To Winthrop Ames Who First Said Show Boat To Me.") Aroused, Ferber called a halt to everything else in her life and journeyed to the Mississippi to see for herself the world of the show boat's unpolished players and naïve audience, "little children listening to a fairy tale." So she writes in the novel, as "they saw, believed, and were happy . . . Virtue was rewarded, evil punished. . . . It was Anodyne. It was Lethe. It was Escape. It was the Theatre."

Further, Hammerstein liked strong women, and so did Ferber. *Show Boat* has two: the phallically aggressive Parthenia Ann Hawks, nagging, snorting, decreeing; and her daughter, Magnolia, the sweetheart who rules by force of charm. At one point, that alternate heroine, Julie Dozier, is exposed as a mulatto and evicted from the all-white show boat company by Mississippi law. Parthy tries to cheat Magnolia out of a proper farewell, but the girl turns on her mother, slaps her face, and runs to Julie: "And when finally they came together, [Julie] gathered the weeping child to her and held her close, so that as you saw them sharply outlined against the sunset the black of the woman's dress and the white of the child's frock were one."

The emotional power of the scene—and its colors symbolically urging racial harmony—typifies the novel's character relationships generally, beyond what musicals could express even in operetta. Kern and

Hammerstein must have known they were in on their own breakaway, a work of career-defining importance. But there were sure things in the material, too, such as Parthy's husband and the head of the show boat troupe, Captain Andy. The henpecked husband always works, especially when he adds tension by occasionally standing up to the spouse from hell. Ferber drowned him in the Mississippi; the musical can't reach its final curtain without him. Why miss a chance for the laugh of the evening when, late in Act Two, Parthy, offstage, lets off her trademark steam-whistle summons of "Annnn-*dy!*" and the captain starts off in response. Why, he is asked, after all these years, does he still jump at her call? What is this woman's magic? What has she got?

Let's play this correctly. Captain Andy stops and turns to gaze at his interrogator with an absolutely immobile and unreadable face. What has she *got?* Three beats. Then:

ANDY: She's got a mean disposition.

As Kern and Hammerstein explored *Show Boat*'s song spots, they realized that while the story and characters lay beyond the musical's normal borders of operation, the score wasn't going to: if the music works, the show will, too.

Thus, one day, Kern showed up at Edna Ferber's apartment to play her "Ol' Man River." We have no record of how Ziegfeld reacted when *he* first heard it, for neither he nor the authors kept a journal nor shared a memoir. But we do hear from Ferber. Keep in mind that "her" topics were the fight for social justice, a distaste for idlers and sellouts, and a passionate unrequited love for George S. Kaufman. There was very little left over for musicals.

Nevertheless, like most New York intellectuals, Ferber was vaguely aware that, in these 1920s, the musical had become a force of some mysterious power in the culture in a way that it wasn't back when Anna Held broke the house record at the Casino.

Remember, too, that Ferber had not signed *Show Boat* away. She owned a third of the musical; she had, as they say, an "interest." So when

Kern performed "Ol' Man River" for her that day, "My hair stood on end, the tears came to my eyes, I breathed like a heroine in a melodrama." Exactly: her show boaters not only play characters in melodramas but live melodramatic lives. That is part of "Ol' Man River"'s power. The score's sole unconventional number, it holds a center of purity and honesty in a world of hoity-toity and whirligig.

At that, some of the conventional numbers are used unconventionally. "Bill" was no innovation when it was written in 1918 for the Princess show *Oh, Lady! Lady!!*. In *Show Boat*, however, slowed from *allegretto* to *andante moderato*—but, really, from wistful to morbid—it became tragedy by oxymoron. In *Oh, Lady! Lady!!*, "Bill" failed to land in at least three out of the four tryout stops; to Kern's frustration, it had to be dropped. In *Show Boat*, the song redefined the very purpose of writing for Broadway: Julie breaks your heart with an up-tune. Beyond this simple use of a song that smiles by a character who can't, we see history preparing the ironies of *Carousel*'s Bench Scene, the title song of *Cabaret*, and "Send in the Clowns." "Ol' Man River" is *Show Boat*'s greatest song. But its use of "Bill" is its most influential event. In a way, Kern and Hammerstein didn't adapt Ferber's novel. They adapted the American musical itself.

But how much input did Ziegfeld have on the mission? Surely it was his suggestion to place the Chicago scenes specifically at the 1893 World's Fair and the Trocadero nightclub, for these turn pages of Ziegfeld's biography: they aren't in the novel. Indeed, *Show Boat*'s second-act opening, "At the Fair," mentions Sandow and brings on that nonexistent celebrity Little Egypt, complete with her hoochy-kooch music. There is another in-joke: the small role of Jim, the Trocadero manager, is in effect Ziegfeld himself, though the time is 1904, when Ziegfeld of course had long departed his hometown. Still, Jim shows a Ziegfeldian flair of showmanship. At one point, he worries about the risk involved in mounting "a two-thousand dollar production!"

That's his idea of the Big Time, though all he's putting on is a variety show. On the other hand, *Show Boat* could be called the ultimate variety show in a literal sense, as an entertainment on serious matters, a dizzy musical comedy with operetta love songs, and a revolutionary work that covers a complex scene change by throwing out a dancer for a specialty spot.

Is *that* why Kern and Hammerstein singled out Ziegfeld as their producer? Because *Show Boat*'s mixture of what has always worked and what hasn't yet been tried was pure Ziegfeld? Even the casting mixed old and new, for Charles Winninger and Edna May Oliver (the Captain Andy and Parthy) were familiar figures destined for stardom while the sweethearts, Howard Marsh and Norma Terris, were journeymen destined for obscurity. (To be fair, Marsh originated the tenor lead in the three longest-running musicals of the 1920s: *The Student Prince, Blossom Time,* and *Show Boat* itself.) The dancey comic couple, Frank and Ellie, were Broadway veterans Sammy White and Eva Puck, while the black couple, Joe and Queenie, were Jules Bledsoe and "Aunt Jemima" (the stage name of blackface artist Tess Gardella), known more for singing than playacting.

Show Boat has no star role, yet it launched a star career for the Julie, Helen Morgan. She had actually begun in a Ziegfeld title, in the chorus of the twenties equivalent of a bus-and-truck tour of *Sally*—not the Marilyn Miller–Leon Errol original but that cutdown version for smaller towns that Ziegfeld licensed and then forgot about. Morgan was a speakeasy singer more than an actress, and—unlike today's contralto Julies—she sang in a shrinking-violet soprano that made her the most vulnerable creature of the day. Remember, Julie is racially oppressed, a loser in work and love, and a generous soul in a selfish world. It's the Lillian Gish part in a stage full of Lillian Lorraines.

No one in *Show Boat* is that bane of twenties musicals, the stereotype, not even the two comics, only slightly derived from characters in the novel. But Julie must be the musical's first rich character—richer, even, than in Ferber. It is not a long role but it is a large one, so astutely observed that her every line seems loaded with subtext. For instance, while a rejected suitor denounces Julie's parentage to the sheriff, the action as originally written offers a core number, "Mis'ry's Comin' Aroun'," sung by the black chorus. Prodded by an unsuspecting Julie, Queenie says, "When I got outa bed dis mornin', Ah knowed somethin' was goin' to happen."

JULIE: Well, what's happened?

QUEENIE: Nothin' . . . *yet.*

Clarifying her bond with this mystical black awareness, Julie "has started rocking and swaying like the others." She even joins in the chorale, but then, suddenly hysterical, cries, "*Stop that rotten song!*" as if confronting nemesis and self at once. Minutes later, the sheriff arrives, and somethin' is goin' to happen.

It's an extraordinary sequence, and it all but broke Kern that the vastly overlong production cut it during the tryout. Revivals restore it, and today "*Stop that rotten song!*" makes Julie the show's exponential character, the one who *almost* understands the forces of race, industrial progress, and entertainment culture that battle for control of American life. Julie is the nonconformist, the libertarian . . . the Edna Ferber, perhaps. She can't control the race thing but she can affect the entertainment thing: she puts Magnolia into show biz and staggers out of the story to drink herself to death.

"Not enough comedy," said Ziegfeld. He hectored Kern to get Hammerstein to liven up the second-act book, if necessary with a collaborator. (Hammerstein had written only one libretto on his own, and all his hits were the work of two or even three librettists.) Some writers have inferred from Ziegfeld's jitters that he never really liked *Show Boat*; is it because they can't connect the glorifier of Girls to a work of art? In fact, Ziegfeld knew from the start that *Show Boat* had tremendous potential. He simply thought it needed more laughs in Act Two. In fact, it did. It *still* does.

Meanwhile, Ziegfeld had decided to produce one last *Follies*, at least for the time being. This one seems to have been a revenge *Follies*, to outdo one Ziegfeld imitator in particular: George White, of the *Scandals*. Because White was known for one thing that Ziegfeld wasn't: an ear for music. Not a single *Follies* to this point had a score by one writing team. The *Scandals* never had anything else. First it was composer George Gershwin (with, admittedly, various lyricists), then it was De Sylva, Brown, and Henderson, whose dynamite tunestack for the 1926 *Scandals* doubled the revue's typical run to 424 performances. Most galling to Ziegfeld was the not-so-secret identity of this 1926 *Scandals*: it was George White's *Follies* in all but name, a shameless use of Ziegfeld's format.

So Ziegfeld decided to do some imitating of his own. In the George White manner, Ziegfeld hired Irving Berlin to write the score for *Ziegfeld Follies of 1927*. Not just much of it, as in 1919: all of it. For the first time in a *Follies,* there were to be no interpolations. Well, hardly ever. Further to unify the work, Ziegfeld virtually gave it to Eddie Cantor, its sole first-division star and collaborator with Berlin in laying out the evening's material. Cantor foresaw a great deal of overwork in that aassignment, but he needed to make nice with the boss in order to finagle a release from their long-term contract. Cantor was versatile enough to be Ziegfeld's most useful star; he always had work for Eddie. And Ziegfeld paid Cantor well. Still, Hollywood's pay rates dwarfed anything on Broadway, and Cantor feared being trapped in the theatre and thus locked out of movie musicals.

Of course, there weren't any as yet. But all show biz had its eye on Warner Bros., just now readying the 1925 play *The Jazz Singer* as the first narrative sound feature. A part-talkie (that is, a silent film enlivened by sound sequences for vocal spots), *The Jazz Singer* would not play to the public till very late in 1927. To Cantor, however, it was news enough that Hollywood was going musical—especially with *The Jazz Singer*: because its protagonist works in blackface.

There were only a few blackface performers prominent enough to be thought casting material at the start of a potentially industry-changing cycle. At that, one of the few, Frank Tinney, had retired two years before after a scandal involving—of course—a *Follies* Girl. That left George Jessel, Al Jolson, and Cantor. Jessel had played *The Jazz Singer* on stage. Jolson was doing the film. What did that portend for Cantor?

So Ziegfeld agreed to drop a year from Cantor's contract if he'd superintend and star in *Ziegfeld Follies of 1927*. The boss even gave Cantor poster billing, the first time any performer was so honored in the *Follies*. After the revue, Cantor and Ziegfeld could finish off their deal with a book show, and Cantor would then be free to film. Cantor jumped at the plan, and he even had the idea for the book show, a musical version of *The Nervous Wreck,* Owen Davis' hit 1923 comedy about a milquetoast among Arizona cowboys.

Cantor really was a nervous wreck at this time, because like so many who had come up from nothing, he saw success as the winning of a lottery, fabulous but ephemeral. He had been driving himself with little rest since he had first punched out at that *Midnight Frolic* in 1916, telling himself that, after all, he had four daughters to support. And his wife, Ida, was pregnant again!

This is pure mania, surely. Plenty of families maintained ample households on far, far less than Cantor made. The comic should have taken lessons in how to enjoy success from Irving Berlin, who had also come up from nothing but knew how to balance productivity with a light touch in living. Berlin had an interesting take on show biz that could be summed up roughly as "After the money is settled, everything else falls into place." Ziegfeld settled Berlin's money for the new *Follies* very handsomely, giving the songwriter a percentage of the gross. This, too, was unheard of, though Berlin's associates began to hear of it constantly. Once, Berlin and Cantor were crossing Times Square when the former suddenly pulled the latter out of the way of a passing taxi.

"For heaven's sake, Eddie, be careful!" Berlin cried. "Think of my royalties!"

Ziegfeld Follies of 1927 opened at the New Amsterdam on August 16. Harold Atteridge (normally a Shubert writer) collaborated with Cantor on the sketches, Sammy Lee and Albertina Rasch shared the choreography, and the star's support included singers Ruth Etting and Franklin Baur, waggish ukulele guy Cliff Edwards, Claire Luce (who rode a live ostrich), and duo pianists Fairchild and Rainger. Building on the 1922 *Follies'* introduction of the "glorifying" slogan, *1927* put forth the Keatsian "He who glorifies beauty glorifies truth."

Ziegfeld spent $289,000, and it showed. For "Shaking the Blues Away," Etting, in white with red trim, led a huge corps of dancing girls in red with white trim; and the first-act finale, "Melody Land," offered an all-girl orchestra, tuba and all. As always blurring the distinction between *Follies* life and real life, Ziegfeld opened the evening with "We Want To Be Glorified," set in his own office as he himself (Andrew Tombes) did some casting and likenesses of Dolores, Fanny Brice, Marilyn Miller, and Ann Pennington appeared. There were further impersonations, now of people in the news, taking in Cantor's Jimmy Walker and, of special interest to Ziegfeld a few pages hence, Charles Lindbergh and Queen Marie of Romania.

A wonderful show: and Cantor's health collapsed. After co-writing and putting it on, he could not carry it as well. Cantor's doctor ordered a vacation, and when Cantor telegraphed the news to Ziegfeld, the star was granted a few days off.

No, a *long* vacation, said the doc. Ziegfeld felt he had a fatherly relationship with young Eddie, but YOU ARE A NAUGHTY EXPENSIVE CHILD TRYING TO RUIN ME, Ziegfeld wired. He brought Cantor up on charges before Equity, a nice irony when one recalls how fiercely Ziegfeld resisted the union when Cantor championed it, in 1919. Cantor offered to submit to an examination by any doctor Ziegfeld approved. Ziegfeld accepted. And that doctor found Cantor in need of, yes, a *long* vacation. *Ziegfeld Follies of 1927* went dark after 167 performances and did not tour: the one *Follies* to flop, albeit on a technicality.

While it was in midrun, Ziegfeld was busy with *Show Boat*'s rehearsals and tryout and the writing and producing of the Marilyn Miller show, which occurred simultaneously. It seems an impossible task for a producer as picky as Ziegfeld—but, again, he was largely letting Kern and Hammerstein steer their craft to port, if you will. Ziegfeld was of course on hand when *Show Boat* started its tryout, at the National in Washington, D.C., on November 15, 1927. Something unusual happened even before the curtain went up: Charles Winninger came out to warn the public that the piece runs long. Right: some four (in some tellings, four and a half) hours long.

Another ballooning Ziegfeld legend needs puncturing here, that this first *Show Boat* audience didn't clap at the end, but simply filed out in silence, like Germans after *The Diary Of Anne Frank*. Ziegfeld's secretary, Goldie Clough, said as much. On the contrary, it took a good ten minutes to clear the house after the final chorus of "Ol' Man River" at a time when ovations were uncommon and standing ones occurred at most two or three times a decade, at New York premieres only. Washington's *Show Boat* was very well clapped, and as it moved through Pittsburgh and Cleveland to Philadelphia, the last leg of the tryout, word spread to The Street that Ziegfeld had finally topped himself.

Wasn't it Kern and Hammerstein who had done the topping? Not in the terms of the day. Producers were perceived as onlie begetters, as if, somehow, they infused writing and staging with their personal creative tonic—as if Ziegfeld had not merely contracted with Kern and Hammerstein to make *Show Boat* but had animated them into being able to make it. Part of this is because, not so long before, producers really did more than sign contracts, but most of it is because, then as now, very few outside the theatre know what a producer really *does*.

For the record, Oscar Hammerstein directed the piece that he and Kern had written, though he gave the credit (literally as "dialogue staged by") to Zeke Colvan, a Ziegfeld regular who often co-directed shows with the choreographer. *Show Boat*'s was Sammy Lee. Victor Baravalle conducted Robert Russell Bennett's orchestrations, and Urban and Harkrider designed.

The name of Ziegfeld, joined with general interest in Edna Ferber's bestseller, empowered the six-week tryout to do radically good business, and a sizable fraction of the show's capitalization had been redeemed by the New York opening—of course at the Ziegfeld—on December 27, 1927. True, the show's weekly operating bill was steep, not least because Ziegfeld insisted that his costumes look fresh and constantly ordered the building of new ones. It seems a monumental trifle in the maintenance of a work playing a 1,622-seat house. But Ziegfeld produced as if every member of the audience were in the center of the fifth row of the orchestra.

The premiere was spiffy. "Potential song hits were as common last night as top hats," *The New York Times* review pointed out. (It was unsigned, the work of a lowly stringer, because Brooks Atkinson had instead attended the opening of Philip Barry's *Paris Bound,* with the intention of catching up with *Show Boat* in his regular Sunday roundup.) And, of course, *Show Boat* was a smash, one of the few classics to be almost instantly reconized as such.

One important historical point never discussed needs airing here: the rather large gap between how deeply a work might treat race relations in its content and how "unrelated" the races might be in the staging itself. By unwritten law, whites and blacks were not to fraternize overmuch in public view—yes, even as late as 1927. Ziegfeld had broken the color bar seventeen years earlier in casting Bert Williams in *Follies of 1910,* and Williams—as we know—at first steered clear of the (white) women in his eight *Follies* appearances but quickly enough integrated himself. Still, this was bold defiance. And note that there was no one comparable—i.e., black—in the *Passing Shows, Scandals,* or *Vanities.* And this: among the ensemble players, whites and blacks were still used as separated groups, observing a clarity of mutual distance.

Some of this inheres in *Show Boat*'s setting, from the post-bellum south up to Chicago and back again, ending in 1927. In the first scene, the black chorus generally tends to the upkeep of the levee and associated tasks, while the white chorus, entering later, is composed of "mincing misses" and "town beaux." The two races occupied the stage at the same time, but they did not mingle, and they didn't, ever, in the rest of the piece. During the performance of *The Parson's Bride,* the blacks were in the balcony,[1] while the whites sat downstairs. In the first-act finale, the black dancers ran onstage for the cakewalk but then ran off, leaving the whites to play out the curtain action. (PARTHY: He's a murderer!

---

[1] Director Hammerstein had to violate the segregation clause in this sequence, setting two hillbillies and Parthy Ann in the balcony with the black spectators. This is a shocking offense against narrative honesty: the imperious Parthy in the balcony? White trash sitting in "nigger heaven"? But the three characters have important business in the scene, and needed to be within the sightlines of every seat in the Ziegfeld Theatre. Placed down in the parterre, they would have been lost to view.

ANDY: I killed a man when I was nineteen. [Parthy faints.] ANDY: Good! Now we can go on with the wedding! WHITE CHORUS: Last A of "Can't Help Lovin' Dat Man.")

Show Boat not only reorganized the American musical: it reorganized how theatregoers regard these shows. Before, musicals were disposable—Broadwayed, toured, terminated. *Show Boat* was Broadwayed and toured but then revived a very short time later. It had to be Broadwayed all over, because everyone wanted to see it again.

This is modern-day thinking: the irreplaceable work. *Carousel, Gypsy, Sweeney Todd*. Art so rich that it can't be collected in one or two viewings. When Ziegfeld started, the American musical was so primitive that many theatregoers' first show had been *The Black Crook*. Ziegfeld lived into the Golden Age—helped create it, in fact—and then produced its emblematic title, *Show Boat*. So Ziegfeld got the notices. Was there no one else like him?

Well . . . not in America. In England, Charles B. Cochran might seem equivalent. "Cocky," five years younger, was, like Ziegfeld, primarily known for the lavish staging of revues and book shows. He often went from rich to bankrupt overnight, famously pillowed with his Girls, and enjoyed a marquee billing with a musical-comedy darling famous for her dancing, Jessie Matthews. Further, the two men got into sport early on, Cochran singling out not a Sandow but a boxing star.

Yet differences between the two define Ziegfeld's art ever more clearly for his innovations. Cochran got into ballet, Eugene O'Neill, Sean O'Casey. Ziegfeld concentrated on the evolution of the musical stage. Cochran had ideas about revue but did not create a revue genre from the ground up, as Ziegfeld did. Lastly, Cochran often imported American or continental titles—a *Music Box Revue, Little Nellie Kelly*, Offenbach, Kern, Porter, Lehár. After the French importations for Anna Held, Ziegfeld was too busy engineering his own projects to take sloppy seconds off another producer—except once. Coincidentally, that producer was Charles B. Cochran, as we'll presently see.

The most important Cochran observation is that his work did not alter the direction of the English musical; what direction it had, Cochran followed. Ziegfeld was incessantly remixing the elements, so that *Sally* was old-fashioned for 1920 while his second Marilyn Miller book show, *Rosalie,* will be startlingly theme-driven for 1928. Cochran adorns the history of the English musical, while Ziegfeld, in America, is defining. Or why are his images still with us? How did Ziegfeld know that Bert Williams + Fanny Brice + Will Rogers + Eddie Cantor + W. C. Fields = American show biz? Because Chris Rock + Barbra Streisand + Tom Hanks + Nathan Lane + Steve Martin = that same show biz a century later. What did Ziegfeld know about us and when did he know it?

CHAPTER SEVENTEEN

Ziegfeld's Broadway

Of all Ziegfeld's hits, *Rosalie* is the one that means nothing today. *Rio Rita* is familiar if only because of the silly title. *The Three Musketeers* got a cast album (in London). *Rosalie* is forgot, though to Ziegfeld it was very nearly the show of the decade. Second of all, he named the heroine after his mother. But *first* of all, it marked the Return of Marilyn Miller. To him.

Whether by accident or design, *Rosalie* is actually about something: the superiority of musical comedy over operetta. Or no: the drive of jazz vs. the languor of the hesitation waltz. Well, more generally: the vitality of democracy as opposed to the pantywaisting senility of monarchies. The hero is Charles Lindbergh, and the villain is Queen Marie of Romania. Most recently, they were subjects of impersonation in *Ziegfeld Follies of 1927*. Here, however, they are more than celebrities: symbols. He is the bold, true blue achiever, and she is everything you ever hated about Europe.

Another of the gossip-column VIPs invented in the 1920s, Queen Marie actually had a lot of content, as a Scots lass of high pedigree who married the king of Romania. Patriotic in her new home, she came to the U.S. to secure a loan, bringing two of her children to texture the quality of her photo ops. The royal tour, in 1926, moved from one press conference to the next as reporters thrilled their notebooks, flash cameras sizzled, and Marie became Celeb of the Year. As Noël Coward put it, anent the first-night cast party for his Broadway flop of the autumn of

1926, *This Was a Man*: "The Queen of Roumania [in the spelling of the day] with son and daughter came . . . so we were all very grand." That was a typical note. A *famous* note comes from Dorothy Parker's little poem "Comment," of exactly the same time, which starts, "Oh, life is a glorious cycle of song" and was to give rise to a national catchphrase in its final line, "And I am Marie of Roumania."

Along the way, the queen made a tour of West Point, and Ziegfeld saw a show in all this—*eventually*. First, Lindbergh and his *Spirit of St. Louis* had to make their headlines, in late May of 1927. Then Ziegfeld saw it: Lindbergh as a West Point cadet with a thing for aviation. That cute little Romanian princess could be aged up into Marilyn's role: she's Lindbergh's sweetheart! Of course, the queen would forbid this casteless romance, and the princess could rendezvous with her love disguised as a West Point cadet!

Marilyn in uniform drag leading the cadets in a martial number sounded like show-stopping material. And because dancing comic Jack Donahue had scored so well with Miller in Dillingham's *Sunny*, Ziegfeld signed Donahue to play Lindbergh's sidekick. Give Donahue a girl friend for the indispensable secondary couple, give Queen Marie a silly king—you know, the dithering Frank Morgan type—and stick in a snobbish Captain of the Guard in Europe who rivals Lindbergh for the princess' hand. The queen will not only favor him but will be manipulative, vindictive, and cruel. Ziegfeld now has his plot, and *Rosalie* is thrown together in a flurry in the fall of 1927.

Because all of Broadway was at its busiest, Ziegfeld found it difficult to secure a first-division team for the songs. Everyone was out of town: Rodgers and Hart with *A Connecticut Yankee*, the Gershwins with *Smarty* (soon to be renamed *Funny Face*), Sigmund Romberg with both *The Love Call* and *My Princess*, Kalmar and Ruby with *The 5 O'Clock Girl*. Even Ziegfeld faithfuls Dave Stamper and Gene Buck had struck out on their own to produce and write *Take the Air*; they, too, were in tryouts. Rudolf Friml was rehearsing *The White Eagle*, Kern and Hammerstein were of course involved in *Show Boat*, and De Sylva, Brown, and Henderson were still with George White.

Who was left? Cole Porter was not Ziegfeld's type and also not yet famous. Irving Berlin had just done the *Follies*; he may have demanded a Ziegfeld Break. Vincent Youmans was free, and he had the musical gifts to encompass *Rosalie*'s musical-comedy America and the operetta Romania, here dubbed "Romanza." Youmans in fact was to work for Ziegfeld, but not yet. The producer had decided that there was only one team to dramatize this *Romeo and Juliet* of Dick Fay of West Point, U.S.A. and Princess Rosalie of Romanza. Only one team could provide one score made half of rhythm and half of rhapsody, and that team was George and Ira Gershwin and Sigmund Romberg and P. G. Wodehouse. George and Ira would substantiate the Americans, Romberg and Wodehouse the Romanzans. The audience would hear the difference in the very sound of the songs.

Now, it was not all that rare for two different composers to collaborate on a show on a half-and-half basis at this time. *Apple Blossoms, Two Little Girls in Blue, Wildflower, Poppy, Rose-Marie, Song of the Flame, Golden Dawn,* and *Rain or Shine* were all co-composed. However, not one of these was planned to field two specifically warring musics.

Even so, Gershwin and Romberg were both, as said, too busy to take on a show to start rehearsals in a few weeks. But Ziegfeld could be persuasive—or cynical—when urging writers to serve as tools of his will. He told the two to rework trunk material. "You'll probably be dropping hit numbers from *Smarty* any minute now," Ziegfeld might have told George. (He was: "How Long Has This Been Going On?" zipped out of *Smarty* right into *Rosalie,* as did "Dance Alone With You," given a new lyric as "Ev'rybody Knows I Love Somebody." Other songs filed in from *Lady, Be Good!, Oh, Kay!, Strike Up the Band,* and an English show, *Primrose.*)

Rosalie's book was written by William Anthony McGuire and Guy Bolton, good-enough hacks when they were good. So virtually all of *Rosalie*'s thematic power lies in the score. None of the Romanzans speaks in operettaese for more than a phrase or so—but there is, at least, a taste of the notion that the American male is a sportsman and the European a courtier.

Thus, the first book scene, set in Romanza and following Romberg's opening chorus of "Here They Are," presents Jack Donahue's girl friend,

Mary (Bobbe Arnst), for some establishing dialogue with the snobby captain of the guard (Halford Young). Because young American women didn't gallivant around Europe unescorted, Mary is with her father. His role is nugatory, but as long as he's there the authors make him a prizefighter. We get it: Americans are physical. The rest of the scene is a typical jokefest edging into the first real number, Mary's "Show Me the Town":

CAPTAIN: Would you like some of our Romanzan vodka? Are you warm enough?

MARY: No one's ever complained yet.

And with a single brass note for her cue, she starts the verse with "Looking for a good time, I've come here to get some action," our first Gershwin of the evening. The battle of the musics is begun.

The royal parents don't figure strongly in the score. The Romanzan queen (Margaret Dale), who wants an American loan just as the real-life Romanian one did, is a non-singing part, and the king (Frank Morgan himself) is mainly around for that Frank Morgan bumbling. At that, hero Dick Fay (Oliver McLennan) has less of a role than Jack Donahue, who danced not only with Bobbe Arnst but with Marilyn. Their success together in *Sunny* led to no less than two dance duets in *Rosalie,* which makes a hash of her romance with the other guy.

At least Romberg gave Fay a spritely anthem for his Stouthearted Men spot, "West Point Bugle." Slipping over from his exotic invocations in Romanza, Romberg concocted a quick march with zesty syncopations in the accompaniment, suggesting a very modern and even jazz-hearted man. Then, in the next number, Gershwin returned, with "Say So," for Fay and Rosalie, a jittery charm song designed to democratize her for marriage with His Majesty the American.

Rosalie's glory is this harmonious civil war of a score, as Romberg trots out a minuet while Gershwin counters with the trusty blue notes of "New York Serenade." And Gershwin wins, because "Yankee Doodle Rhythm" propounds the irresistible modernity of New York, America, and jazz. "Everything else," it squeals, "is passé!"

Here was another reason why Ziegfeld did so little fiddling with *Show Boat*: he was obsessed with perfecting *Rosalie*. It opened on January 10, 1928 at the New Amsterdam, and sold very, very well almost to the end of a ten-month run. This is a smash even before the tour. Yet *Sally* remained the Ziegfeld-Marilyn legend. *Rosalie*'s songs never caught on except with cognoscenti, and the film version, for Eleanor Powell and Nelson Eddy, dropped the entire score for new titles by Cole Porter—his one link with Ziegfeld.

Marilyn was happy, even so. *Rosalie* was her personal triumph, thanks to Ziegfeld, yet she was no more pliant now than before. They were embedded in each other's lives, but lovers in art and business only. A famous tale, possibly apocryphal, finds Ziegfeld shyly knocking on Marilyn's dressing-room door and asking, "Will my Princess Rosalie deign to see me tonight?"

She would have to, sooner or later, because Ziegfeld was producing her next show. He was also putting on another book show even as *Rosalie* opened, moving from Sigmund Romberg to Rudolf Friml for *The Three Musketeers*, with Dennis King as D'Artagnan and Vivienne Segal as Constance. Here was another smash—one wholly in the operetta format in which Ziegfeld had so little interest. Moreover, *The Three Musketeers* has the least imposing score of all the famous twenties operettas. Still, by the time Ziegfeld was finished warning the girls not to twist their hats, talking Friml out of an overture, and advising the lighting techies to up three amps on the follow, iris the reds, and peak the frammis, the piece played like dynamite.

It opened on March 13, 1928, solemnizing a precedent: Ziegfeld had four smash hits running on Broadway at the same time: *Show Boat* at the Ziegfeld, *Rosalie* at the New Amsterdam, *The Three Musketeers* at the Lyric, and *Rio Rita* now at the Majestic. And note that these were four fastidiously produced smash hits (as we expect from Ziegfeld), and four totally different kinds of musical. Perhaps, after all, *that* is why Kern and Hammerstein took *Show Boat* to Ziegfeld: he had a genius for putting on great shows.

Time magazine thought so: it set Ziegfeld on its cover on May 14, 1928. Within *Time*'s invariable red frame, the photograph revealed the subject with the trace of an impish smile, befitting the king of curious entertainments. "Ziggy" was the title of the article, though in fact almost everyone in show biz called him "Mr. Ziegfeld"—and the formality sounds much more like our man.[1] Indeed, *Time* didn't give its covers to a passing story. One had to achieve greatness first, or an official, industry-wide "Mr." or Heavy Numbers. Ziegfeld's, of course, were the Heaviest on Broadway. The article revealed that Marilyn Miller's *Rosalie* salary netted her $5,000 weekly and, through a percentage of the gross, another thousand or so. To be able to afford such talent was impressive in itself, and Ziegfeld ran his own theatre, too—an edifice, *Time* reported, "as imposing as a village bank."

That is: it dwarfs its neighborhood, just as Ziegfeld, by now, dwarfed his colleagues, with the Ziegfeld Touch. But what exactly was this Touch?

Time asked. And Ziggy answered, "Splendor and intelligence."

That response is so empty of precision that we wonder if Ziegfeld simply defies the art of the profile. *Time* tells us next to nothing of the producer and *nothing,* neat, of the man. His art was actually not all that abstract; it simply couldn't be described in the communication of the day because show biz changes its communication so dynamically, so quickly, that few discern the changes till a generation after. As for the man himself, Ziegfeld's father and two brothers were dead by this time, yet we have absolutely no evidence anywhere on how deeply Ziegfeld might have been affected.

But then, Ziegfeld did not define himself in family, in marriage, in bourgeois concerns. He was, first of all, F. Ziegfeld Jr. Presents. So we ask not how he mourned their deaths. We ask what is the next show for Marilyn: now we'll get to know Ziegfeld.

He has commissioned a Gershwin score for an adaptation of Samuel Shipman and John B. Hymer's *East Is West,* a comedy from 1918 about a Chinese waif in love with a white American. Ming Toy is Marilyn's character, and because she only plays title roles, *Ming Toy* is the show.

---

[1] Billie called him "Flo," but after his death, in the third person, she, too, referred to him, by historical invocation, as "Mr. Ziegfeld."

Ziegfeld has also opened up a shop in Hollywood. *The Jazz Singer* has appeared, to general wonder, and the studios are preparing talkies. What would a Ziegfeld movie musical be like? Ziegfeld shows had undergone the silent treatment—Colleen Moore headed *Sally* and Eddie Cantor himself filmed a *Kid Boots* (in a different plot, with Clara Bow). And the novel *Show Boat* is in production at Universal, although, after the introduction of the part-talkie, audiences may be expecting soundtrack participation from the already beloved stage score.

Ziegfeld and Hollywood! The possibilities entice, but for now he entered into just one agreement, with Paramount's Adolph Zukor, to produce a film based on nothing more than the *Follies* slogan "Glorifying the American Girl." There was a plot premise, at least: the rise of a nobody into a Broadway star. This, we know, is Ziegfeld's favorite story, especially when the heroine ends up starring in the *Follies*.

Alas, Paramount turned out to be sluggish in putting the film into production. One reason might have been the very transitional nature of filmmaking in the late 1920s: sound was coming, but in what form, and to what effect? Show biz generally was in flux, because that overextended theatre season of 1927–1928 made start-up money scarce and one's millionaire friends dubious. *Ming Toy* began to seem too expensive even for Ziegfeld, not to mention bizarre. Marilyn Miller as an Asian? It was especially frustrating in that the Gershwins had written a core score in charmingly "Oriental" style. One, "In the Mandarin's Orchid Garden," was more artistic and nuanced than anything yet heard on Broadway—not a bold call like "Ol' Man River" but a wispy lament in art deco, a gingerbread doll baked by Erik Satie. It would have been either cut in Boston or the talk of the season, and whether or not Ziegfeld appreciated it, it does tell us how free writers must have felt after *Show Boat*.

As *Glorifying the American Girl* languished in the Paramount workshops, Ziegfeld returned to the stage and won ego gratification with his fifth consecutive smash. This was *Whoopee*, the Eddie Cantor cowboy piece, which had its premiere on December 4, 1928, at the New Amsterdam.

The Arizona setting gave Ziegfeld a new ethnicity for his mix, because the central romance, like that of the aborted *Ming Toy,* was racially miscegenative: Wanenis (Paul Gregory), an Indian, loves Sally Morgan (Frances Upton), a white girl. Just to make things interesting, she is promised to Sheriff Bob (John Rutherford), a bad guy. Not a law-breaker: a bigot. Nowadays authors tell us whom not to like by making them cigarette smokers. In Ziegfeld's theatre, the dislikable characters don't appreciate Fanny Brice or Bert Williams. This being an Eddie Cantor show, Ziegfeld brings in the Jewish thing, but *Whoopee* really spends a lot of time among the Indians. In the end, Wanenis turns out to be white, adopted in infancy, which *really* irritates Sheriff Bob. But we know the tale is true, for we have it from Black Eagle, one of those inscrutable, taciturn characters who, when he finally says something, proves oracular. "*Indian never lie!*" he thunders. Further, Black Eagle was played by a real-life Indian, Chief Caupolican,[1] filling out his numbers with the vocal tone one normally heard only in operetta.

Cantor's foil, as his nurse and would-be sweetheart, was Ethel Shutta. *Whoopee*'s pop singer was Ruth Etting, the dancer was Tamara Geva, and the pit band was that of Shutta's husband, George Olsen (spelled during the run by Paul Whiteman). Joseph Urban, John Harkrider, and William Anthony McGuire were on hand: the Ziegfeld stock company, one might say. Only the score brought in names new to Ziegfeld, composer Walter Donaldson and lyricist Gus Kahn.

Whoopee was pure star-comic musical comedy, like *Kid Boots* and *Louie the 14th,* traversing a driveline (Cantor and the girl run off together with Sheriff Bob in pursuit) with detours every ten minutes or so for an

---

[1]The chief is one of opera's great footnotes. Everyone knows who broke the color bar at the Metropolitan: Marian Anderson. *Wrong!* Anderson was the Met's first black singer, in 1955, but Janet Collins, a black dancer, beat her to the venerable stage four years before. However, neither of these two was the first nonwhite at the Met. That was red man Chief Caupolican, who sang the title role of Karel Weis' *The Polish Jew,* in 1921. The piece was so unpopular that it lasted but three nights, and Met manager Giulio Gatti-Casazza openly stated that he invited the chief over from his reign as vaudeville's classical baritone only because no one in the Met company would learn the part.

unintegrated set piece. This can be almost anything—Cantor making waffles, Cantor and an older comic arguing over who has the worst surgery scars, Etting turning up in a daisy field to sing "Love Me Or Leave Me." In its minor key, with a plangent drop of an octave in the first line, the tune sounds dire. But this is no "My Man." The number is there to provision Cantor's dressing-room rest break, to beguile the audience, and to lend a title to the eventual Doris Day Ruth Etting bio. *Whoopee* was so stuffed with such guiltless entertainment that it ran forty minutes overtime out of town, yet no one could figure out where to cut.

Of all *Whoopee*'s set pieces, the prize was the showgirl number, in the Indian reservation sequence. On a crag overlooking a mountain pass, Chief Caupolican sang the beautiful yet dirgelike "Song of the Setting Sun," a call to his tribe to see day's end as symbolic of their own passing. In any other producer's show, this would give way to a solemn dance; Ziegfeld puts on a solemn skin number. As the orchestra pounded out the refrain over and over, the Girls paraded down the path, each wrapped in a picturesque blanket which she then opened to display John Harkrider's notion of tepee chic. As the music built in crescendo, so did the skin, the Girls now riding in on horseback wearing virtually nothing but headdresses, each topping larger than the one before. (The horses were led by Indian braves, the Boys almost as cute as the Girls. Ziegfeld was an equal-opportunity panderer.) The last squaw bore a shooting fountain of feathers, with rods to keep the thing from capsizing.

In all, *Whoopee* was probably the best and also the most typical musical comedy of Ziegfeld's later career. The emphasis on fun over romance is very Ziegfeldian, as is the placement of a hot band in the pit. Orchestrations for the orderly mustering of strings, woodwinds, and brass, laid out by a master like Robert Russell Bennett or Hans Spialek, were appropriate for (respectively) *Show Boat* or *The Three Musketeers*. An Eddie Cantor riot of 1928 all but demanded the letting loose of jazz, just as Ziegfeld's art generally aimed at the letting loose of not entirely stable elements of the culture.

This is where the Girls kept coming in, whether or not they were undressed. Consider "Makin' Whoopee," a larky disquisition on marriage and divorce sung just before the heroine jilts Sheriff Bob at the altar. The program credits Cantor "And the Misses Finley, Glad, Ackerman, Smith, Forbes, Dunbar."

What are the Misses doing in the number? Close-harmony backup? Perhaps a dance? Reader, you know Ziegfeld better than that by now: they're Ziegfeld Girls, and not the Marilyn Miller or Ruth Etting kind. They don't sing or dance. They come on and stand there, three to Cantor's left and three to his right. The plot almost motivates their appearance, because they're on their way to the wedding in John Harkrider's exquisite pastels, and Cantor casually invites them to hang out while he carols. That's why the Misses Finley, Glad, Ackerman, Smith, Forbes, Dunbar are in view: to embody the reason why whoopee is made.

With all Broadway for his domain, Ziegfeld actually partnered up with Abe Erlanger and Charles Dillingham in a corporation they called Newam (for the New Amsterdam), as if reviving the Syndicate. He revived as well the *Midnight Frolic*, on December 29, 1928—the first *Frolic* since 1921. The cast list was almost shockingly top, featuring *Show Boat*'s Helen Morgan, *Whoopee*'s Paul Gregory, the Duncan Sisters, Lillian Roth, Paul Whiteman's band, and opening-night-only kibitzer Eddie Cantor. Further, after a month Ziegfeld added in Maurice Chevalier, the most unZiegfeldian of stars, the very opposite of Fanny Brice or Bert Williams or Will Rogers, the opposite even of Anna Held.

However, roof shows seemed horribly corny all of a sudden, no matter who was in them. New York's latest place was the speakeasy, more relevant in a brash and impious time. A Ziegfeld *Midnight Frolic* in the 1928–1929 season felt like something by Ludwig Englander at the Casino Theatre, once the first choice for big shows but now—again, all of a sudden—out of fashion. In fact, it would be demolished a season later: and the 1928 *Midnight Frolic* would be the last.

So roof shows were over; and Hollywood continued to look like Ziegfeld's show-biz ideal, the next permanent novelty. Still frustrated with Paramount's slow development of *Glorifying the American Girl*, Ziegfeld nevertheless made a deal with Universal to let the studio paste onto the finished *Show Boat* film a two-reel prologue offering Helen Morgan, Jules Bledsoe, Tess Gardella, and a chorus in five of the stage numbers, introduced by Ziegfeld himself.

It was a last-minute decision, for Universal had been hoping simply to film a bestselling novel in the usual silent manner and ended up haunted by Ziegfeld, by Kern and Hammerstein, and above all by radio baritones singing "Ol' Man River." Even as Carl Laemmle's outfit wrestled with the new talkie technology to insert sound sequences into the picture, that wonderful Broadway score stood as a reproach: for Laemmle had tried to save money by commissioning his own *Show Boat* music. He even offered *his* "Ol' Man River," Nathaniel Shilkret and Gene Austin's "The Lonesome Road," dreary where "Ol' Man River" is ecstatic. And so, three weeks into January 1929, Ziegfeld and his troupe were hustled onto a New York–area soundstage to put a Broadway imprimatur upon the movie.

It was, at least, a prestigious entry, Universal's Picture of the Year. The cast—Queen of the Lot Laura La Plante, charismatic Broadway hunk Joseph Schildkraut, Alma Rubens, Otis Harlan, and Emily Fitzroy—means nothing today. However, Universal booked a main-stem house, Dillingham's Globe, for *Show Boat*'s premiere, on April 17, 1929.

Ziegfeld's "other" great twenties book show, *Sally,* had also appeared in its talkie version the previous month, starring Marilyn and in two-strip Technicolor. At last, the entire nation could savor Ziegfeld's Queen of Broadway in her *Schicksalsrolle,* the part her destiny had led her to. Faithful in general, the film did fiddle the score, because something had happened since the 1920 stage show: the jazz age. So a bit of the original Kern was, so to say, charlestoned up with "After Business Hours (That Certain Bizness Begins)" and "All I Want to Do, Do, Do Is Dance."

And then *Glorifying the American Girl* went into production, at Paramount's east coast studio in Astoria, Queens. *Show Boat* and *Sally* were adaptations of Ziegfeld shows, but *Glorifying* had been an original Ziegfeld film from the outset. And while the delays exasperated this master of the whirlwind production, at least now it could be a full-fledged talkie. Ziegfeld was sound and light, a frenzy of entertainment, not a bumble of title cards or soundtrack pops as the microphones get plugged in.

So we're grateful for an authentic taste of the style, but we notice that the story takes place in 1927, the year it was supposed to have been made and released in. Why didn't Paramount update it, or at least change the year? In fact, how much of this movie is actually Ziegfeld's?

Except for its lead, Mary Eaton, it doesn't offer a Ziegfeld cast. It's not even a Paramount cast; these actors are B-budget unknowns. Sarah Edwards plays Eaton's treacherous mother, Dan Healy the creepy vaudeville loser who exploits Eaton, Edward Crandall the nice guy Eaton loses, and Olive Shea the girl who gets the guy. We are treated to a strangely self-effacing impersonation of Ziegfeld, and "Pop" Morgan— obviously Ned Wayburn by other means—manages to be realistic and unbelievable at once. He looks like Wayburn, and projects a fascinatingly grizzled lack of interest in anything. But that includes the dance rehearsal we see him running: he stares down at the stage floor, lost in thought. This is Ziegfeld's idea of a director-choreographer? Worse, as written by J. P. McEvoy and the film's director, Millard Webb, *Glorifying the American Girl* makes no attempt to glamorize show biz. On the contrary, it's a cautionary tale.

And that isn't Ziegfeld. He believes in show biz as the redemptive force in American culture, very much as Michael Bennett was to, later on. *A Chorus Line* might be seen as a look at heaven's waiting room, as the Unseeable Authority separates the elect from the damned. Remember the girl who celebrates Being Chosen by raising her arms and touching her wrists together, her head aimed skyward? Ziegfeld knows that girl. But Paramount's "Ziegfeld" ends with a close-up of Mary Eaton glorified yet miserable.

At least we get a taste of the *Follies,* in a finale in more two-strip Technicolor. This enjoys real-life newsreel documentation: the arrival of the first-night magnificos, complete with mellow-toned radio announcer Norman Brokenshire, who says everything twice while calling off the names of Otto Kahn, Ring Lardner, Mayor Walker and his wife, and even the Ziegfelds. Once the camera moves into the auditorium, we see some dancing but, mainly, two Ben Ali Haggin tableaux that prove just how erotically charged Ziegfeld's stage could be.

The star acts, preceded by an absurdly unnatural chorus of frantic whispers from the audience, are less representative. Rudy Vallee, foisted on Ziegfeld by Paramount, is extraneous in every sense, but Helen Morgan and Eddie Cantor offer genuine Ziegfeld style—even if, as already noted, Cantor's tailor shop sketch, "Joe's Blue Front," comes from two Shubert revues.

In all, Ziegfeld's Hollywood experience was a disaster, though it did not stop him from entering into another undertaking of the same kind, now with Samuel Goldwyn, to produce movie musicals starting with *Whoopee*. Why the dictatorial Ziegfeld thought he could produce anything in tandem with the autocratic Goldwyn is one of those mysteries; perhaps the agreement gave Ziegfeld seed money for his next project. This was to be a stage musical to encapsulate the jazz age in a wisenheimer slangfest, as if Walter Winchell's column were to sing and dance. Clearly, the score must be Gershwin and his New York Serenade and the heroine will be Peggy Hopkins Joyce, in her literary form as Anita Loos' Lorelei Lee of *Gentlemen Prefer Blondes*. The stage adaptation, by Loos and her husband, John Emerson, had played Broadway in 1926. Now, three years later, the property was still hot—but when Ziegfeld tried to acquire the rights, he found that Loos had signed away all the possibilities in Lorelei to *Blondes'* producer, Edgar Selwyn.

So Ziegfeld looked around for the nearest thing, and he found it in a bestseller of 1928, *Show Girl*. The good part of that was the book's author, J. P. McEvoy, who had already worked for Ziegfeld. The bad part of that was J. P. McEvoy, because his work gave Ziegfeld two of his bombs, *The Comic Supplement* and *Glorifying the American Girl*.

But McEvoy did have an ear for the vernacular, of English in jazz. He describes his heroine, one Dixie Dugan, as "the hottest little wench that ever shook a scanty at a tired businessman." No, it's not wit. It's the fast, cynical, know-it-all Manhattanese that the first year of the Hollywood talkie—this year, 1929—promulgated as the argot of the minute. And the show that Ziegfeld would make from McEvoy's book would be the musical of the minute. *Show Girl*: was that or was that not the perfect title for a Ziegfeld show?

Note that Dixie Dugan is very unlike Lorelei Lee: a tough little cookie from the Metropolis itself. And while Lorelei is a gold digger, Dixie is looking for the two things besides money: sex and fame. However, what arouses one's interest is less her agenda than her way of expressing it, with mean-streets similes and kennings hardwired into her every utterance. "Flat as egg on a vest." "Genuine imitation pearls." "When he tangoes the floor smokes." Or: suffering a hangover, Dixie says, "Oooh, do I feel," and her sister replies, "And do you look!"

Show Girl's plot is—here we go again—Dixie's rise to Broadway stardom while trying to choose among a quartet of beaux: a stockbroker, a greeting-card salesman, an excitable South American prince, and the tabloid stringer who writes the script of Dixie's show. Peppering the events is a litany of the Higher Names of the day—Aimee Semple McPherson, B. F. Keith, Fanny Ward, Jeanne Eagels, Otto Harbach, Fanny Brice, Wallace Beery, and of course "Ziggy." To keep the pace breathless, McEvoy let fly with a series of telegrams, letters, hotel-stationery notes, detective agency reports, and newspaper items; anything that couldn't be expressed thus McEvoy simply wrote as script scenes, so the novel was already halfway to being a musical as was. A musical about show biz, gossip, and crime—just like America itself.

It was the era of "debunking," and *Show Girl* was the debunking musical, but the piece was thrown together hastily. No doubt Ziegfeld feared that any delay would date this hot dog right out of its bun. At that, Hollywood filmed it so fast, as a part-talkie with Alice White as Dixie, that the movie appeared four months after the book did.

Ziegfeld bade the Gershwins cease work on the now officially "postponed" *Ming Toy* and throw themselves into *Show Girl*. As so often with Ziegfeld, the bookwriters—McEvoy and William Anthony McGuire— had done so little that the Gershwins had to scan their tunestack out of the novel, hoping that they had correctly anticipated the script. Of course, Ziegfeld habitually excited a show into instantaneous being, not out of an aesthetic plan but because he was impatient. But it is worth noting that Ziegfeld's one incontestable classic, *Show Boat,* took Kern and Hammerstein almost a year to write.

In the end, *Show Girl* found a way to juggle Dixie's four boy friends into its plotline, but very little of McEvoy's satirical view of how scandal and crime sell fame came through. *Show Girl* finished as a backstager with a lot of music it didn't need—a digest version of Gershwin's tone poem *An American in Paris* for Harriet Hoctor and the ballerinas and Duke Ellington's band, along with the Gershwins' own numbers and interpolations for the chief comic, Jimmy Durante (with his partners, Eddie Jackson and Lou Clayton). Ruby Keeler, in her first major role, played Dixie opposite: Austin Fairman, Eddie Foy Jr., Joseph Macauley, and Frank McHugh, respectively, going back to their quartet of jobs in the novel. Dixie ended up with the writer, the musical's one act of union with the book, for Ziegfeld seemed intent on laming McEvoy's wild plotting with a succession of onstage scenes. *Show Girl* actually began during a made-up Ziegfeld show called *Magnolias* (an intended reference to *Show Boat*?), went on to spend a great deal of playing time in performing or rehearsing spaces, and climaxed back onstage at a Ziegfeld show: the *Follies,* starring Dixie.

Some writers have suggested that Ziegfeld mounted *Show Girl* because Hollywood had made backstagers trendy from the first full-out musical film, MGM's *The Broadway Melody.* However, Ziegfeld's more likely inspiration was a George White stage show, *Manhattan Mary* (1927), not only a backstager but one in the Ziegfeld manner, about putting on a George White show, even unto presenting a character named George White *played by George White himself*!

Ziegfeld had been topped. And by an ex-*Follies* hoofer, no less! Historians (and MGM's bio-salute, *The Great Ziegfeld* [1936]) cite Charles Dillingham as the official Ziegfeld rival, yet we have seen Dillingham as Ziegfeld's longtime on-and-off partner in various ventures. And when the Ziegfeld or the New Amsterdam was booked, it was Dillingham's Globe that Ziegfeld put his work into.

No, it was George White who was the Other Ziegfeld. This inhered not in lavish décor or in a stream of book musicals, though he did have a couple of hits thus. Where White challenged and irritated Ziegfeld was in the uniqueness of the *Scandals*: alone of the truly long-lived annuals, White's had its own atmosphere, even if White did pinch Ann Pennington from the boss.[1]

At least those George White family retainers De Sylva, Brown, and Henderson failed to get a hot score out of *Manhattan Mary*. No doubt Ziegfeld expected the Gershwins to deflate White with dazzle, but the boys did not come through. Nor could Ziegfeld brag about his new star. Ruby Keeler definitely had a lovable clunky something, but her performing skills per se were on the perfunctory side. Still, whom did that uppity George White try to pass off as *his* new Broadway discovery? He started with Elizabeth Hines in the title role, and—let's be fair—that was Ziegfeld's first choice as *Show Boat*'s Magnolia. But Hines quit *Manhattan Mary* after the first night of the tryout: it turns out that she had married a millionaire during *Mary*'s rehearsals. Strapped for replacement magic during Broadway's hottest season, White had to open with Ona Munson. A *nobody*!

And at least Keeler and the Gershwins gave Ziegfeld something else that *Manhattan Mary* didn't have: a big number. And that brings us to another famous story—in fact, a tiresome cliché of Broadway history. It seems that Ruby Keeler had also recently married a millionaire. Hines' was a banker; Keeler's was Al Jolson. Indeed, Ziegfeld billed his miss as Ruby Keeler Jolson, exciting curiosity. No one else in the cast had any ticket draw, for the four men playing Dixie's beaux were unknown (though Foy was to punch out in time). Clayton, Jackson, and Durante were a nightclub act making a Broadway début. Indeed, the most interesting thing about *Show Girl*'s performers was the chorus, for beside the

---

[1] In a famous tale, a fed-up Ziegfeld offers White $2,000 a week to rejoin the *Follies*, which he had last graced in 1915. White snaps back with an offer of $3,000 if Ziegfeld and Billie Burke step into the *Scandals*. This must be true—it has the ring of Broadway sharpshooters turning a feud into free publicity.

Albertina Rasch Dancers there were thirty-seven song-and-dance girls and seventeen Girl girls, but no chorus men whatsoever.

Now for the tiresome story: during *Show Girl*'s Boston tryout, Keeler is nervous about that big number, "Liza (All the Clouds'll Roll Away)." Keeler can get through a song, but not that one, with its seven sustained notes in each A section. So, as her voice starts to quaver, the faithful and so much more experienced Jolson jumps up from his orchestra seat and sings along, encouraging the nervous Keeler to complete the vocal and then triumph in her dance. Yowzah!

Not to put too fine a point on it, the story is a crock. Though born in Nova Scotia, Keeler was a New York Woman, all spit and vinegar, fearless in the street and on the stage. Years later, she told what happened in that singular Keeler charm, as devoid of nuance as *Dragnet*: "I wasn't nervous. Al just stood up and started singing."

The real story is that Ziegfeld was aware that Keeler couldn't handle the vocal, keeping the number from landing big. So Ziegfeld hired Nick Lucas to join the company in New York while Jolson lit up Boston and the Broadway PR circuits with his stunt. Lucas, one of the smooth-singing "crooners" invented by the radio microphone, would handle the "Liza" vocal before Keeler's dance; unfortunately, that meant giving Lucas also a self-contained performer spot elsewhere in the running time—the last thing the plot-hungry, song-stuffed show needed. Worse, Ziegfeld wanted Jolson to repeat his "improvisation" during the first week in New York: but now Jolson would be encouraging Nick Lucas, which made absolutely no sense at all.

We are not surprised to discover that Lucas left *Show Girl* before the first month was over, but then the work was undergoing a major shake-up all around. Three numbers were dropped. An attempt was made to rationalize the comings and goings of the four beaux. Keeler was replaced by Fred Stone's daughter Dorothy, an established Broadway sweetheart. But more music came in with Stone; what self-respecting young diva would go replacement without adding in her own personal Tambo Dance in the *Magnolias* sequence?

It didn't help. *Show Girl* had too much story yet too little script, too many boy friends for one ingénue, and too much music about nothing. Opening on July 2, 1929, at the Ziegfeld, it was over in 111 performances.

For his next show, quickly to fill the empty theatre but also for failure insurance, Ziegfeld bought another producer's finished hit production to present as his own. In partnership with Arch Selwyn (brother of Edgar), Ziegfeld imported London's biggest hit, Charles B. Cochran's Noël Coward operetta *Bitter Sweet,* in its original designs, choreography, and direction, the last by Coward himself. As the original cast was still playing in London, Ziegfeld hired replicas. Matching Cochran's Peggy Wood was Evelyn Laye, who had been offered the part in the first place but turned it down; she and Cochran were tiffing. It created an interesting history, for Laye—one of the greatest divas of operetta—made only two appearances in New York, and this one, in *Bitter Sweet,* was supposedly one of *her* greatest assumptions, period.

There is a story that Ziegfeld tried to bolster *Bitter Sweet* with showgirl insurance as well; this seems unlikely. Ziegfeld didn't vex operettas with the erotic. He understood that operetta runs on different rules, tilting toward the music where musical comedy tilts toward blasphemy.

Still, we have Coward's word that both Ziegfeld and Selwyn interfered during the Boston stand. Coward says he banned them from the theatre, but one did not ban Ziegfeld from anything, especially his own production. Besides, the show was playing like a hit, not least because of Laye. "She certainly does knock spots off Peggy [Wood]," Coward wrote to his mother. *Bitter Sweet* was coming into town as a made hit; producers like Ziegfeld don't haggle with hits. Taking a night off in New York, Coward attended *Whoopee,* and Eddie Cantor, forewarned—as was the press, of course—stopped the show at one point to direct a spotlight at Coward, introducing him as "the greatest theatrical genius alive today."

Today, we would be startled at such breaking of the fourth-wall contract, but Ziegfeld's shows, as I've said, cultivated that dangerous improvisational quality that the theatre had had even before he took power. The theatre was giving it up in the 1920s: not Ziegfeld. This isn't Shakespeare. This is fun. No rules.

Bitter Sweet opened on November 5, 1929, at the Ziegfeld. Brooks Atkinson's very positive review included the heads NOEL COWARD'S ARTISTIC OPERETTA FROM LONDON IS COMPOSED OF MUSICAL MINIATURES and EVELYN LAYE IS RADIANT. A rave. And yet, until two years before, a Ziegfeld production got Ziegfeld reviews. Discussing *Bitter Sweet,* Atkinson didn't mention Ziegfeld at all (except in a passing reference to the theatre). Nor did he mention Selwyn or Cochran. The review centered on Noël Coward: "the virtuosity of his talent amounts to genius."

As *Bitter Sweet*'s auteur in every sense, Coward certainly deserved all the praise for this most dashing yet most modern of operettas, set in a charlestoning London with a flashback to the Vienna of the drinking song and flirtation by waltz. This is where Coward unveiled his most quoted, touching, and appalling line, about having no more than "a talent to amuse": an operetta with worry, a truly rare work, still revived. And a masterpiece: all Coward's. Two years earlier, they spoke of "Ziegfeld's *Show Boat.*" Finally, they got the byline right.

Yet critics seemed, in the end, not to get Ziegfeld even when he *was* the author of the piece. They knew him in costume, as the Great Glorifier, the showman. But when he showed up in other clothes, they couldn't see him. Did any of them sense the contradiction of the man— that he had democratized show biz while remaining the pet of snobs? Did anyone outside Ziegfeld's circle appreciate his menu of entertainments, whether *The Three Musketeers* or an Eddie Cantor goof-up?

The month in which *Bitter Sweet* opened saw yet another "Ziegfeld" Hollywood success when RKO released its *Rio Rita,* nearly a soundstage filming of Broadway. With its last third in Technicolor, and with silent Bebe Daniels making one of the great transitions into sound in the title role, *Rio Rita* was both expensive and a moneymaker. That's a very Ziegfeldian combination, and the film earned out as RKO's picture of the year.

However, the time is out of synch with celebration, as this is also the month of the Wall Street panic selling known as The Crash. Ziegfeld was of course wiped out: would this inveterate gambler have failed to take part in the national risk fever of buying on margin? Ziegfeld had gambled and gone broke many times before, but he could count on men with more stable finances to help him out. Or he could promote his current show to a duly thronging public.

No more: most others were wiped out, too. And there was no public for *Bitter Sweet*. Ziegfeld suffered a nervous breakdown in miniature; Billie found him sobbing, genuinely unmanned. "I'm through," he told her. Had he ever had occasion to say that before?

Some really were through. Charles Dillingham, Arthur Hammerstein, and Alex Aarons and Vinton Freedley lost their theatres, and the first two were out of business within a year. One cure Ziegfeld could effect immediately: inaugurate that partnership with Samuel Goldwyn by closing *Whoopee* and shipping the cast to Hollywood for a *Whoopee* film. And what about radio? True, what was a listening medium to the man who had reinvented how shows look? Still, many of Ziegfeld's stars went over well on the air—Fanny Brice, Eddie Cantor, Will Rogers. They had a sound, a presence beyond the view of them. Could there be a *Follies of the Air*?

And then Abe Erlanger died, on March 7, 1930. He was not a Ziegfeld intimate, he gave a hard time to everyone who worked for him—that included Ziegfeld—and he was reactionary where Ziegfeld was innovative. Erlanger's death could be seen as liberating, if only in a symbolic sense. Still, the deaths of Sandow, Anna Held, and Bert Williams took away chapters in Ziegfeld's biography; and Erlanger's was in one way the significant chapter. He was the Syndicate, and the Syndicate was The Theatre when Ziegfeld set foot in it, all that way back. It was Erlanger who asked for the *Follies*—no, wait: Erlanger asked for *something,* and Ziegfeld gave him the *Follies.*

Without the *Follies*, Ziegfeld could not have become Ziegfeld. Erlanger did not create Ziegfeld, but he did make it possible for Ziegfeld to create himself. Now Erlanger was dead, and his age was over. In two years, Ziegfeld would be dead, too. But his age was just getting started.

CHAPTER EIGHTEEN

The Passing of Ziegfeld

Ziegfeld died a failure, if only in the material sense. In the last two and a half years of his life, from 1930 into the middle of 1932, Ziegfeld could get almost no idea to work. *Show Girl* was Ziegfeld's newfangled invention; it flopped. *Bitter Sweet* was someone else's London smash; it struggled.

Now Ziegfeld tried putting on someone else's *Broadway* smash—actually a smash series. It was Charles Dillingham who fostered a line of fairytale extravaganzas, a genre dead but for the flair with which Dillingham presented it. His stars were Dave Montgomery and Fred Stone, then, after Montgomery's death, Stone as a solo. And every title was a mint.

So Ziegfeld readied his own fairytale extravaganza: *Simple Simon,* with that giddy toon Ed Wynn. A *Follies* graduate, classes of 1914 and 1915, Wynn was to play a Coney Island "character" who dreams the show into a storybookland of Cinderella, the Prince, Jack and Jill, Bluebeard, and the like. It reeks of the family fare that Dillingham and Stone flourished in, as when in *Stepping Stones* (1923), seventeen-year-old Dorothy Stone made her entrance to the mincing "Everybody Calls Me Little Red Riding Hood" and duetted with her father in cunning Raggedy Ann and Andy getups for "Wonderful Dad."

"Lots of wolf," Ziegfeld told his people: Urban and Harkrider as always, choreographer Seymour Felix, director Zeke Colvan. Ed Wynn himself collaborated on the book with Guy Bolton, and Rodgers and Hart wrote the score.

I warned you they would be back—but why? Especially after the poor working conditions they suffered on *Betsy,* and then the humiliation of "Blue Skies." We know why Hart said yes: he thought all producers equally treacherous, and writing musicals was what he did. It was the philosophy of "Ziegfeld, Schmiegfeld." Rodgers had a different take, because he distinguished among producers. Some he loathed, and some he *really* loathed.

In fact, Rodgers and Hart said yes because they were temporarily jobless. Charles B. Cochran had commissioned them to write the score for his new Jessie Matthews musical. Remember, Cochran was the English Ziegfeld, so to say, but a rational and methodical producer where Ziegfeld was an anarchy of lightning strikes. Cochran was noted, too, for a sophisticated taste in music; Cole Porter and Noël Coward were very Cochran. Rodgers and Hart had worked for him before, and Rodgers liked him.

On top of all this, Jessie Matthews was Cochran's special favorite. This was to be her first book show after years of revue, her first alone-above-the-title starring role, and Cochran had to be planning something prestigious. In fact, he wasn't planning anything yet: Cochran offered to let Rodgers and Hart work up a treatment for the show. This was especially appealing to Rodgers, because he thought the quality of book writing so poor that if you couldn't get Herbert Fields you were better off doing it yourself. Cochran's giving Rodgers and Hart this imposing responsibility tells us that he was very different from Ziegfeld in at least one way: Ziegfeld's conservative side guided him toward an older view of songwriters as mere helpers in the creative process, not originators.

The Cochran show was *Ever Green,* and Rodgers saw it as a breakthrough for not only Jessie Matthews. He and Hart had become trapped in a line of standard-make shows after a brilliantly nonconformist beginning; *Ever Green* might restart them. Consider: Matthews had twice before come to Broadway to repeat a Cochran West End hit. Wouldn't she do so on this one, too?

Then *Ever Green* got postponed. Rodgers was short of cash, and Ziegfeld's commission for *Simple Simon* was the only offer he and Hart had. So they took it.

After all, *Simple Simon* didn't have to be another *Betsy*. For one thing, Ed Wynn was going to be the muscle in the production, the unifier—one thing *Betsy* never had. And Wynn's collaborator on the book, Guy Bolton, was a dependable pro. He could be dreadfully uninspired, but at least he knew what he was doing. Then, too, the elements of spectacle and magic, intrinsic to extravaganza, could keep *Simple Simon* busy with events. No, this one would be very, very different from *Betsy*.

There was one problem, also intrinsic to extravaganza: it completely lacked consistency. It doted on anachronistic jokes, unmotivated pageantry, and, especially, the specialty numbers that Rodgers and Hart's generation wanted to abolish. Ironically, *Simple Simon*'s one lasting song hit was a specialty. Everyone *else* in the fairytale dream was Little Boy Blue, Bo-Peep, Hansel and Gretel, or two men in a horse suit, but suddenly Ruth Etting showed up on a "bicycle piano," driven and played by Wynn, to sing "Ten Cents a Dance." The lament of a taxi-dancer, it begins "I work at the Palace Ballroom" and goes on to a line that aficionados savor, identifying the singer's customers as "pansies and rough guys." How on earth have pansies and rough guys found their way into a dreamland of Cinderella and Jack and Jill?

But then, Ziegfeld's art never lost contact with the world of Anna Held Eyes Songs, of the war of the managers, or of breaking the house record at the Casino, which was being torn down literally during the first weeks of *Simple Simon*'s run. Ziegfeld knew that Rodgers and Hart were hot; everybody said they were. But they were so *earnest* about their work, especially Rodgers. The nifty thing about that Ziegfeld stalwart Irving Berlin was his sense of proportion: success must come first. Somehow or other, the art always followed—but Berlin didn't start with the idea of being artistic. He started with the idea of having a hit.

So, once again, Rodgers and Hart saw Ziegfeld plop an interpolation into their (no, Ziegfeld's) score, though here it was Walter Donaldson's unimportant "Cottage in the Country." In general, the show was a better-than-average Ed Wynn freak piece, an almost vast treasure in its costuming above all. As a Rodgers and Hart show, it was filled with wonderful things, not least in the authors' treatment of Cinderella and the Prince as twenties musical-comedy types without a trace of operetta in word or tone.

But the book was long and, when Wynn wasn't around, dull. The reviews were mixed, from John Mason Brown's "A very grim fairy tale" to Gilbert Gabriel's "A Ziegfeld show up to the hilt." Still, the show lasted 135 performances and toured for six months. It would have made money but for Ziegfeld's habitual unrealistic capitalization.

During *Simple Simon*'s run, Ziegfeld took the train to Hollywood to work with Samuel Goldwyn on the *Whoopee* film. Remember, this was to have inaugurated a partnership in the producing of movie musicals, even though they must have known that neither man functioned as anyone's partner. Indeed, while *Whoopee* was Ziegfeld's show, it was Goldwyn's movie; Ziegfeld could function as Broadway Adviser: meaning that Ziegfeld should do as little advising as possible and be back on Broadway sooner than *that*. Opening in October 1930, the eventual *Whoopee* film, presented entirely in that early Technicolor, was a smash, and at least Goldwyn gave Ziegfeld top producer billing.[1]

Meanwhile, Ziegfeld was indeed back on Broadway, irritated as always at the arrogant ignorance of Hollywood. That was the difference between movies and the stage, as Ziegfeld saw it: the Californians had no respect for talent. They simply paid more for it. One can only surmise that it was these repeated defeats in trying to crack the movie business that kept Billie off the screen at this time, and by Ziegfeld choice.

---

[1] The "F. Ziegfeld Jr." that Ziegfeld had used for the "presents" line on the posters finally eased into both "Ziegfeld Production" and "Florenz Ziegfeld" by the mid-1920s. These gave way to the definitive "Florenz Ziegfeld" in 1930, and so it read—yes, directly atop Goldwyn's own name—on the *Whoopee* window cards.

Hollywood was eating up stage stars to fill their talkies; surely they were going after Billie. One imagines her turning them down out of loyalty to her man.

When in doubt, star Marilyn. Better, add in two of the biggest other Broadway stars, Fred and Adele Astaire, for what we might call marquee shock and awe. Noël Coward provides your concept; he's the wonder boy of the age. And for the music, try the "other" Gershwin, Vincent Youmans. It almost positively can't miss.

This show started as *Tom, Dick and Harry*. It told of three American soldiers who rescue a French orphan waif and take her to New York, where they play godfather as she grows up. She joins the Salvation Army and reforms a snooty brother and sister of the idle rich.

That's the concept: a big empty container for the appropriate mixture of distinctive melody, snazzy dancing, and the usual satiric hooligans in secondary roles. The story itself doesn't matter as long as everything else does—provided the story doesn't get in anything else's way.

But Ziegfeld's *Tom, Dick and Harry* librettist was once again the very erratic William Anthony McGuire, and McGuire created the disaster. Late as always, he started writing without having ascertained what relationship Marilyn's character had with her three guardians, because she might have a romance with one of them, or with Astaire, or maybe . . . But wouldn't the former soldiers be too old for her? She was a kid when they "adopted" her, and ten years have passed. And who was Adele's love interest? Another of the soldiers? One is a hunk, one's a comic, and . . . what's left for the third to be? And is Marilyn in the Salvation Army because it will affect the narrative, or because she'll look cute in the uniform? Can she still go into her Big Ballet? Where, in the Salvation Army meeting hall? Do they do that there? Or should we throw in the ever-handy Society Shindig? Ziegfeld sure loves those.

There was also the problem of the title. This kind of upbeat stars-and-score musical comedy liked snappy ones: *Lady, Be Good!, Oh, Kay!, Heads Up. Tom, Dick and Harry* was snappy, but after *Sally, Sunny,* and *Rosalie,* Marilyn did not relish giving up her eponymous rights. Besides,

MARILYN MILLER FRED AND ADELE ASTAIRE

in

TOM, DICK AND HARRY

would suggest a gender bender. It turned out that someone wanted the soldiers to represent one part each of the victorious allies—one American, one Brit, one Frenchman, and one Italian. So *four* soldiers it would be, each in a different ethnic delivery, and the title was changed to Marilyn's character, Smiles. In a way, the marquee would read

MARILYN MILLER FRED AND ADELE ASTAIRE

in

A RADIANT SHOW

It had great potential. And now Ziegfeld's troubles really began.

McGuire's book broke a cardinal rule of the style: it kept getting in the way. Nor did it ramp up to the numbers properly. Ziegfeld knew how to get a show to *look* right, and he seldom lacked for unique staging coups. Here was a great one for Fred Astaire: in "Say Young Man of Manhattan," he and the chorus men were all in tails. It's all so debonair, but Astaire doesn't like the competition, so he shoots the line down, one by one, with his cane. The stunt so tickled him that he repeated it at RKO in *Top Hat.*

The look of the piece and staging coups, yes. But the age of Ziegfeld trapped him a terminal case of librettoitis. In the previous generation, in his youth, audiences accepted incoherent books; they didn't know any better. In the next generation, after his death, they knew better; so did the book writers. Unfortunately, the 1920s counted few writers who could please a progressively more demanding public. Richard Rodgers, we know, was acutely aware of this. Why wasn't Ziegfeld? His cure for the ailment, William Anthony McGuire, was capable enough when following someone else's lead—Eddie Cantor's on *Kid Boots* and *Whoopee*, Alexandre Dumas' on *The Three Musketeers. Smiles'* wee concept left him without a narrative agenda.

Actually, Ziegfeld had one. He wanted to treat the jazz-age public to a nostalgic recollection of Gustave Kerker's *The Belle of New York* (1898). A flop in New York but a smash in London, the show made a star of Edna May (whom we remember zealously guarding her grandeur on Billie's first hit, *The School Girl*). The score became a favorite on the parlor piano, even as the work itself floated around the hinterland in numerous revisions. Like *Smiles, The Belle of New York* featured a Salvation Army lass reforming various New York types, and Ziegfeld spiced his piece with many an *hommage* to the older one. But he fudged the plot. Even with its specialties and comic "bits," *The Belle of New York* had actually been a more consistent show than *Smiles*.

So a wonderful Vincent Youmans score babbled, as characters broke into song illogically. To cite just one instance, *Smiles'* sole standard-to-be, "Time On My Hands," found Marilyn and the American soldier (Paul Gregory, *Whoopee*'s Wanenis) launching a romance after virtually no preparation in the storyline. Youmans was so difficult that he had to change lyricists for each next project; on *Smiles*, he discovered a Harvard senior, Harold Adamson, and put him to work as soon as he was graduated. Adamson (and Mack Gordon; *Smiles* was littered with lyricists) had supplied Marilyn and Gregory with a kind of all-purpose love song: with time on my hands, there's "you in my arms," and so on. Marilyn refused to sing it, and Ziegfeld had to bring in Ring Lardner to create for her a special lyric to Youmans' music as "What Can I Say?"

No one seems to know why Marilyn rebelled; my guess is that the confident "Time On My Hands" sounded so odd on the chaste Smiles, and so premature for her first-ever romantic moment—at that, with one of her adoptive fathers—that the audience got confused. We do know that this now classic song went over so badly that it was dropped in Boston while Lardner effected his remedy, to be restored in New York. And, sure enough, Lardner's corrective lyric addressed the awkward relationship between this young girl and her protector. "It's just too bad," ran the second A strain, "You are my dad." No wonder these words were never heard again once the show closed.

Smiles should have made history as the outstanding title between

Lady, Be Good! and *Anything Goes.* Instead, it went through that tryout hell that everyone keeps wishing on Hitler. Ziegfeld went wild, because failing with Marilyn Miller and the Astaires in a single show—a *Follies*-like starburst that no book musical had ever had before—would be worse than failure. It would be disgrace.

Ziegfeld spent the Boston time bullying and threatening—not McGuire, the guilty party, but Youmans: because the score wasn't playing, and we know why. Even Marilyn got into the act, because her Boston reviews were unappreciative. An enormously talented but easily aroused figure, she did what many stars do when in trouble: find a scapegoat and have him fired.

Marilyn picked the show's orchestrator and conductor, Paul Lannin, with whom Youmans had co-composed his first Broadway show, *Two Little Girls in Blue* (1921). Youmans had remained close with Lannin, and he interceded on his behalf. With the New York premiere looming and much work to be done, Ziegfeld and Youmans went to law over Lannin. Ziegfeld prevailed, and Frank Tours took over the baton.

Yes, that must be why *Smiles* wasn't working: the conductor. The production opened at the Ziegfeld on November 18, 1930, one of those first nights that every single New Yorker attended, witnessed, or read about in the columns. The reviews were terrible; stung, Ziegfeld fired off a telegram to Percy Hammond of *The Herald Tribune,* though Hammond had been no harder on *Smiles* than anyone else. Ziegfeld accused Hammond of failing to appreciate *Smiles'* elevated moral climate, its wholesome nature, its old-fashioned Edna May charm. "Some people," Ziegfeld stated, "still accept a show without naked women, filth and slime."

All right, cut the mikes. Florenz Ziegfeld Jr. is outraged at not getting credit for producing *clean*? The man who kept vital the musical's link with its shady beginnings as an all-male revelry of cigar smoke and lewd catcalls is angry at being denied the Good Housekeeping Seal of Approval?

One can only presume that Ziegfeld hoped to create a PR controversy. In any case, *Smiles* sold scarcely a ticket after the critics told their tale. The show lasted two months and did not dare a tour, losing its entire investment. And, remember, Ziegfeld's investments were so heavy that we don't hear such numbers again till the most expensive shows of the 1950s—*The King and I, Make a Wish, My Fair Lady,* and *Candide.*

Ziegfeld was so short of cash that he couldn't pay the Astaires. He didn't try to stiff Marilyn: she would have ripped him up in a riot at Broadway and Forty-Fourth Street for all *Variety* to see. The Astaires took the matter to court and eventually accepted a settlement, but in fact Billie was now the Ziegfeld family breadwinner.

And her husband was no longer her manager. Together, they had presented one musical and four straight plays: this was not a Florenz Ziegfeld *cartellone.* Ziegfeld put on musicals—and mainly not cute ones like Billie's *Annie Dear.* Big, wild *Whoopee* stuff. Yes, Billie could sing: Mamie, I've a little canoe. But a Ziegfeld star was a comic or a real singer. Or Fanny Brice. They were crazies from the planet Mars. Billie was a girl a guy might marry.

So Billie had gone freelance—Noël Coward's *The Marquise* (1927), *The Happy Husband* (1928) for Gilbert Miller, *Family Affairs* (1929), which died in a week, and one hit, *The Truth Game* (1930), a Shubert production by the other Noël Coward, Ivor Novello, who played the lead. It was journeyman's work, even if Billie always claimed the Novello as the play that freed her for once and all to play the quirky comedy that, on film, assured her immortality.

Unfortunately, year-round stage acting meant touring; the work drove Billie and Patty apart from Ziegfeld. There was nothing to be done about it: theatre was their daily life and also how they got through interesting times. At least, no matter what town Billie was in, Ziegfeld's telegram would find her: GOODNIGHT DEAR I MISS MY TWO BABIES PERHAPS EVERYTHING WILL TURN OUT SUCCESSFUL AND I WILL SOON BE WITH YOU LOVE EAT AND SLEEP.

The younger of the two babies enjoyed the one professional appearance of her life during Billie's tour in the Novello, in 1931. The show was playing Philadelphia during the Easter school vacation, and an actress playing a maid fell ill. Patty turned out to be, as they put it, a "quick study," and went on with aplomb. Her father came down from New York for the Saturday night, to take her back to school and forbid her ever to do that again. One actress is enough for any family.

After his quartet of four more or less disappointing book shows, Ziegfeld decided to bring back the *Follies*. His stars were all in California making talkies, so this *Follies*, the first since 1927, would in fact also be the first since—incredibly enough—1909 not to boast at least one of the core squad of Bert Williams, Fanny Brice, Eddie Cantor, Will Rogers, W. C. Fields, and Ann Pennington. But at least the *Follies* never failed.

Historians like to point out that by 1931 the big twenties annuals were dinosaurs, edged out of the Darwinian struggle by a lighter, airier new species, the "little revue." Smart and sophisticated, these new shows were more unified than the larger model, forging of their headliners and featured players an ensemble troupe ready for anything from a solo to a production number.

However, these historians are working from the hindsight that knows how scarce the twenties annuals were about to become. In 1931, they were as popular as ever before—and, in any case, Big Revue didn't go out of style for another twenty years or so. The form simply turned into the "theme" revue, with throughline subject matter: newspaper headlines, a world tour, army life, life after the army, a trip around the U.S., a trip around Manhattan, Bette Davis sings.

Two of Ziegfeld's imitators put forth arguably their best entries in 1931. George White, as always using the savviest ear in the business, opened a *Scandals* studded with good music. B. G. De Sylva was in Hollywood, but Ray Henderson and Lew Brown were in top form, and the voices included Ethel Merman's, Rudy Vallee's, opera baritone Everett Marshall's, and—thinner in tone but engaging nonetheless—Ray Bolger's. "Life Is Just a Bowl of Cherries" is the standard, but a spirited tunestack included also a list song in the naughty Cole Porter manner— "(Ladies and Gentlemen) That's Love!"—and "That's Why Darkies Were Born," Marshall's blackface lament in *Pagliacci*-Jolson style. You know, like "Ol' Man River," only grand.

The 1931 *Vanities* was as numbingly derivative as ever, but Earl Carroll still upstaged everyone by presenting it as the opening attraction of a Carroll Theatre to challenge the Ziegfeld: even bigger, more centrally located (on Seventh Avenue at Fiftieth Street), and sinful with luxury. The box-office staff wore tuxedos, and the back of each seat held a light so patrons could follow the acts in the program listing and drive one another crazy switching the little beam on and off. Then, too, this *Vanities* had a terror lizard in the cast—a fake one, of course, but animated enough to need seven men to operate it.

Thus, Ziegfeld was reviving the *Follies* in a busy atmosphere—and while the *Follies* bore the proudest of the trademarks, it was all the same a venerable one by now. George White and Earl Carroll were still in high school when the first *Follies* appeared. And Ruth Etting, Ziegfeld's current favorite girl singer, hadn't even been born then, though she did come into being while it was touring.

Etting was the closest thing to a Ziegfeld star in the 1931 *Follies*, having played three leads for Ziegfeld. Helen Morgan was the other important woman singer, not yet Ziegfeld-fledged beyond *Show Boat* and her one number in *Glorifying the American Girl*. And Gladys Glad was the official Ziegfeld Girl, anointed as "The Follies Girl of 1931." All the other stars were new to Ziegfeld: skinny dancer Hal Le Roy, dialect (his own) comic Jack Pearl, singer Harry Richman, black duo (Ford) Buck and (John W.) Bubbles, soon to be in *Porgy and Bess*, the Collette Sisters for the customary Ziegfeld twins stuff, and exotic *je ne sais quoi* Reri.

It was the Ziegfeld chowder of ethnicities and talents, as always, lacking only the Absolutely Guaranteed Famous that the *Follies*, more than anything else in show biz, represented. Remember, the notion of bunching stars in movies had yet to be invented (in MGM's *Grand Hotel*, one year after this *Follies*). Ziegfeld's inventive PR and his vision in getting genius performers to "collide" their specialties into a unique entertainment created the *Follies'* identity as Event Theatre. Was *that* why Ziegfeld got *Show Boat*? That piece was the Event Musical, just as Sandow was Event Physique and Anna Held's arrival in New York was Event Début. Eddie Cantor, Will Rogers, W. C. Fields, and Fanny Brice playing a sketch was Event Comedy, and the Ziegfeld Girl was Event Sex.

But the *Follies* lineup in 1931 lacked Event. So Ziegfeld had a brainstorm. *This* one will be at once the newest yet the oldest *Follies* possible. It will bring its audience back to the days of Rector's lobster palace while considering the latest problem in show biz: movie actors who can't talk. Such bygone personalities as Lillian Russell, Nora Bayes and Jack Norworth, Hazel Dawn, Sam Bernard, and even the Nell Brinkley Girl from the 1908 *Follies* will be impersonated or invoked. Old songs will be revived, including the *Follies'* own "Shine On, Harvest Moon."

At the same time, in a bow to the ensemble practices of Little Revue, singers Morgan and Richman and dancer Le Roy will extend themselves to play sketch comedy. Also new wave was the Albertina Rasch franchise. Her dancers spent the 1920s pirouetting; now she was ordered to effect the New Dance, made of ballet combined with hoofing, that was to colonize the best musicals in the work of George Balanchine, Agnes de Mille, Jerome Robbins. Note that Ziegfeld got there first, in this *Follies* designed simultaneously to "begin" and close out the series—even if Ziegfeld could not have foreseen this one as Final *Follies*. In fact, others would produce *Follies* entries on Broadway for the next twenty-five years. *Ziegfeld Follies of 1931*, however, was the last one signed by Florenz Ziegfeld himself.

Opening on July 1 at the Ziegfeld—the only *Follies* to play Ziegfeld's house—the work went over well. But the *Follies* was supposed to go over like Niagara Falls as a rule. It was the Depression, it was Hollywood, it was stay-at-home radio. "Show business has changed so," Ziegfeld stated, in a letter to Patty. Who had done more to change it? It was a case of Be careful what you wish for, perhaps.

Then, too, Ziegfeld was so pelted with lawsuits that avoiding process servers became part of his office procedure, with the use of back exits and secretary Goldie creating distractions so the boss could slip away. Florists, writers, actors, designers: Ziegfeld owed everybody. Years before, his attempts to cheat his hires of their fair payment seemed part of the devilry of Broadway, the price of leadership. Now it seemed like desperation.

It is touching to note, then, that throughout these travails Ziegfeld not only wrote his long letters and sent his doting telegrams to Billie and Patty but, using what connections were left him, eased their logistical arrangements. Wherever Billie was touring, Ziegfeld took care of her accommodations as if by magic. There was always a driver to chauffeur her to where—always security, really. It was as if Ziegfeld was obsessed with protecting his wife and daughter from men like him, for Billie and Patty were the only important women in his life who were not Ziegfeld Girls. Though German and Belgian by ancestry, Ziegfeld maintained the Italian view that a man dates whores but is related to saints.

For her part, Billie was settling into her new Fach of the Flighty Woman Who Listens to Anyone Except Somebody Else. During the run of the last *Follies,* she was in California, playing Mary Boland's role in Paul Osborn's *The Vinegar Tree* (1930), a domestic comedy filled with mismatched couples. George Cukor happened to see the show while he was casting his film *A Bill of Divorcement,* and he tapped Billie for the second woman lead (after Katharine Hepburn, in her movie debut). It was a lucky break for Billie, and also for us, as her talkie career preserved classic turns as the Flighty Woman. She hits her apex as a Flighty Sorceress in *The Wizard of Oz,* but of special interest to us is her Millicent Jordan in *Dinner at Eight,* also for Cukor. Here, she gets to play what she in fact had been: the wife of an achiever whose business is a wreck and whose days are numbered. The real Billie knew what her husband was going through; the woman she played in *Dinner at Eight* cannot begin to conceive of it, living as she does on the Planet Me. This is the portrayal of not only a skilled actress but a skilled humanist, and it is fair to say that thirties Hollywood is inconceivable without the contribution of Billie Burke.

Show business has changed so. Ziegfeld's Hollywood associations had failed conclusively, and now he decided to make overtures to radio after all, even as he conceived and discarded countless ideas for the next book show. A radio deal seemed very potential—but then, out of thin air, one of George White's star writers approached Ziegfeld with the perfect show: Bert Lahr, on the lam in Mexico, accidentally ends up as a torero in the bull ring. At the time, this was Lahr's signature shtick: the zany good-for-nothing who accidentally champs out when thrown into the arena—as a boxer in *Hold Everything!* (1928) and an aviator in *Flying High* (1930).

In fact, this new Lahr show was supposed to have been White's *Flying High* follow-up project, with White's new prize contractee Lahr and a score by White's own personal music men, De Sylva, Brown, and Henderson. All right, they were only Brown and Henderson by now. Anyway, on the opening night of the 1931 *Scandals,* Lew Brown and White got into a slugfest. They were quickly separated, and, though it became a town topic, neither of the communicants ever explained the reasons why except to intimates. All that New York knew was that the historical union of George White and the team that had made his music during the *Scandals'* golden age was ended—the team, moreover, that to many epitomized the sound of the 1920s and of George White.

And now here was Lew Brown, with Ray Henderson in tow, offering Ziegfeld the next George White show. To make sure that White got the insult, Ziegfeld engaged *Flying High*'s co-director, Edward Clark Lilley; and its choreographer, Bobby Connolly; and its conductor, Al Goodman; and its costume designer, Charles Le Maire; and its set designer. But then, *he* would have been working for Ziegfeld anyway, because it was the moonlighting Joseph Urban. The only major *Flying High* credit missing was that of B. G. De Sylva, who of course was in Hollywood, but who may have broken with Brown and Henderson because of Brown's battle with White.

Remember when Ziegfeld offered White a star salary to come back and dance in the *Follies?* This was the nearest that Ziegfeld could get to making good on that bid, for now White's art would dance on Ziegfeld's stage. Brown and Henderson wrote the book, with Mark Hellinger. They called the piece *Hot-Cha!* and Ziegfeld filled it with folk new to him— Lupe Velez as Lahr's vis-à-vis, with June Knight and Buddy Rogers for the ballads. Gangsters Waxey Gordon and Dutch Schultz supposedly backed the production; it was the only way Ziegfeld could get his capitalization. Gangsters were the millionaires now.

Hot-Cha! was a risqué piece, even a smutty one. (Its subtitle, supposedly at the insistence of Gordon and Schultz, was *Laid in Mexico*.) This was very unlike Ziegfeld—but his matrix, *Flying High*, had been the hit of its season at 357 performances, and its comedy had been *very* low. Some of the critics expressed reservations at this crass new tone on Broadway, redolent of the excesses of late, degraded burlesque.

But musical comedy in general was turning earthy, partly in support of the enfant terrible rebellion of Herbert Fields, who—shall we say?—refused to write his father's musicals. No, Herbert would write the book to Rodgers and Hart's *Chee-Chee* (1928), about the son of the Chinese Grand Eunuch who rejects the family business because he doesn't want to . . . you know, lose his dick. (Herbert's father, Lew Fields, produced it anyway.)

This is an astonishing leap from the flirtatious innocence of the Anna Held shows. Even in the more outspoken 1920s, Ziegfeld kept his earthiness light. Suddenly, to keep up with the show business that has changed so much, he had to accede to the more blatant pandering of the George White school.

Hot-Cha! was another of those musical comedies that came up thin in both the music and the comedy. However, it was spared tryout hell simply because there was nothing wrong with it: it just wasn't good enough. Worse yet, Ziegfeld spent almost all of that period in his hotel room, with a severe respiratory virus that was finally diagnosed as pneumonia. His show went on to open at the Ziegfeld on March 8, 1932, and finished as the fifth-longest-running musical of that year (in a tie with the Bea Lillie-Bobby Clark revue *Walk a Little Faster*) at 119 performances. So *Hot-Cha!* was less a flop than a casualty of the Depression.

Still, it did lose money. And while Ziegfeld may have rejoiced to have lifted Brown and Henderson from George White, they gave him the most vapid of tunings. To Ziegfeld, it was a *personal* matter: George White was cocky and maniacal, just as Charles Frohman was a guttersnipe dressed in James M. Barrie. You know a man by his style. However, to the public, it was an *artistic* matter. *Hot-Cha!*'s humor was forced and its songs drearily derivative, most offensive in "It's Great To Be Alive!"

This number rounds up the usual nature clichés in an anti-Depression cheer-up ditty, as if "flowers," "trees," and "birdies" made the bankruptcy of a nation bearable. Ziegfeld actually praised this point of view in an interview during the Washington, D.C. leg of the tryout, quoting its palliatives and then saying, of the economy, "It's all in the people's minds to a great extent." Was theatregoing a cure of some kind? *Hot-Cha!*'s program cover presented a line drawing of Lahr and Velez with three of the Girls, Lahr in a torero's cap that looks like a señorita's winter muff with attachments of grapes on either side: fun and beauty. Isn't that the Ziegfeld aesthetic in three words? Eddie Cantor and Dolores. W. C. Fields and Joseph Urban. Or simply Marilyn Miller: and it wasn't working any more.

At least radio said yes. Ziegfeld now put together a weekly show for Chrysler, each a half hour of Ziegfeld-level talent, starting on April 1, 1932. One might have expected the first show to promote *Hot-Cha!*, given Ziegfeld's belief in PR, but all he offered was comic Jack Pearl (from the last *Follies*), a new find in vocalist Jane Froman, and an unknown singer named Art Jarrett, who was to take over for Buddy Rogers in *Hot-Cha!* the following month. Al Goodman conducted, and the boss himself introduced the guests.

Loyal Billie called the Chrysler show "magnificent," and ensuing shows did involve more notable participants, including Fanny Brice and Ruth Etting. EVERYBODYS RAVING ABOUT LAST NIGHTS RADIO PROGRAM, Ziegfeld wired Billie. YOU MUST GET WITH [Will] ROGERS IMMEDIATELY AND LET US KNOW IF YOU AND HE WILL HAVE AN IDEA FOR THE [show on April] EIGHTH ALL MY LOVE.

Ziegfeld's own idea was to fill the air with retrospectives of the theatrical past—of a time when he was master of the arts and George White was facing a destiny as a tango dancer. The plan for Billie and Will Rogers, for instance, was for them to duet on "My Little Canoe," the number that put Billie over way back in 1903 in *The School Girl*.

Then Ziegfeld decided that his next show would be something he had never done before: a revival of one of his own shows. One of his recent ones, in fact: *Show Boat*. Odd as it sounds, this was an innovation, for in those days musicals were virtually never revived, and recent musicals never revived at all. Perhaps because the two-reel prologue of Kern and Hammerstein songs had exhilarated audiences at Universal's *Show Boat* movie more than the movie itself, Ziegfeld realized that this score had not yet been absorbed and collected. Surely, this was great music. Not operetta great, like *Rose-Marie,* nor musical-comedy great, like *No, No, Nanette,* but timeless art great. Permanent.

Casting Dennis King and Paul Robeson as Ravenal and Joe, Ziegfeld otherwise set the original production back on stage with its original cast virtually intact. He reopened it on May 19, 1932, at the new Casino—formerly Earl Carroll's fabulous house, lost like so many others in Depression insolvency. Did these guys never stop honking each other out of the way? Ziegfeld appropriates George White's next show, invades Earl Carroll's theatre . . . and, remember, he took one of Charles Frohman's house virgins for wife.

The second *Show Boat*'s first-nighters reacted as though they had never seen a musical before, so Ziegfeld finally had a hit, even if it was the same one he'd had before. Then, too, he was collapsing under the weight of more lawsuits than can dance on the head of a pin. Ziegfeld even got into some sort of wrangle with Joseph Urban and the stage-hands' union. Still touring *The Vinegar Tree,* Billie was listening to the Chrysler show in California, and something in Ziegfeld's voice warned her that he was in physical distress.

Indeed, he was. In a letter to Eddie Cantor, Ziegfeld wrote, "Doctors demand I take eight weeks' rest—no business." Fat Chance. Ziegfeld never rested; he produced as if his life depended on it. "Would like to do another show with you," he added, "before I pass on."

Here's a hero: Homer Curran, producer of *The Vinegar Tree*'s west coast company. Billie asked him to close the show so she could go east and take care of her husband. And he did! Shooting on *A Bill of Divorcement* had already begun at RKO, but Cukor, too, gave Billie the needed space to go east and take Ziegfeld out of the legal and financial storm that was buffeting him, to nurse him in Los Angeles.

The train trip from New York told Billie that the matter really was serious, as Ziegfeld floated in and out of consciousness. Counting the stations as they neared Los Angeles—Lavic, Haslett, Newberry, Daggett—she took her husband off the train at the next stop, Barstow, in San Bernadino County, to avoid reporters in Los Angeles. Strangely, when Ziegfeld emerged from his troubled sleep, he insisted on seeing Will Rogers. "He will tell us what to do," Ziegfeld explained. But Rogers was in Europe that summer—and, anyway, when did Florenz Ziegfeld Jr. ever need someone telling him what to do?

What was left of Ziegfeld's business had collapsed; back east, the company manager of the *Show Boat* revival could not meet the cast's salaries. For the last time, one of Ziegfeld's millionaire friends stepped in: A. C. Blumenthal, husband of former *Follies* Girl Peggy Fears, guaranteed the weekly nut.

So *Show Boat* sailed on even as its captain's condition worsened. Billie was to start work on *A Bill of Divorcement*, so she had Ziegfeld hospitalized, taking a pied-à-terre nearby to stay with him when not shooting.

And here the story ends. Felled by overwork, or living too well, or dying too often with his beautiful Girls, Ziegfeld went out in the hospital before Billie could get to his bedside. He died of complications of complications, of the stimulation, one might say, of spending his life with the exciting personalities that the entertainment industry made available because Ziegfeld said it had to. Managers weren't usually friends with their attractions, yet from Sandow to Eddie Cantor, Ziegfeld was very close to his headliners. They were confidants, drinking buddies, informal family—as much as possible for the most secretive man alive.

But then, Ziegfeld also lived in worship of talent, a true son of the man—the first Florenz Ziegfeld—who idolized Beethoven and Brahms. Ziegfeld also worshiped power, as a true son of Chicago. And he combined his awe of talent and power in his *Follies,* adding in the popular art of sex, because if show business has changed so it is because Ziegfeld changed it.

In *The Los Angeles Times,* Will Rogers wrote Ziegfeld's obituary in a letter to the editor. That "he picked us from all walks of life" is self-evident, because show biz is caste-blind. Or did Rogers mean less "walks of life" than "different ethnic groups"?

In closing, Rogers said that Ziegfeld left them all with something "that hundreds of us will treasure till our curtain falls, and that was a 'badge,' a badge of which we were proud, and never ashamed of, and wanted the world to read the lettering on it."

The lettering on it. Different eras claim different kinds of heroes. Odysseus might say—as, incorrectly called by the Roman "Ulysses," he does in the recent movie *Troy*—"I lived in the time of Achilles." A French *philosophe* might have said, "I sometimes dined with Voltaire."

The badge that Will Rogers imagined read, in its majestically quiet tumult, "I worked for Ziegfeld."

Florenz Ziegfeld Jr. died on July 22, 1932. No record states with certainty an official cause of death. He was sixty-five years old.

CHAPTER NINETEEN

Ziegfeld's Legacy

Who was Ziegfeld? An unassuming-looking midwesterner with a cultured background, he embodied more than any other Broadway leader the idea that commercial success in American culture is built on an imposing public profile with no personal content whatsoever. Everybody has heard of you, but no one knows who you are.

What everyone knew was the *Follies,* because it was the pinnacle of show biz: what, in America, is bigger? To restate it all: in speed of delivery, democratic ethnic diversity, unrivaled array of star talent, and its strange combination of the oldest show-biz tropes with the latest gizmos and shtick, the *Follies* inspired so much imitation through our entertainment that it never really closed.

It has, however, lost much of its Ziegfeldian glamour. Further, public profiles now leak a great deal of personal content. In Ziegfeld's day, the chief of achievers was William Randolph Hearst, as unknown as a medieval emperor of Japan. Today his like chatter on television talk shows.

The *Follies* itself outlived Ziegfeld, at first in Shubert productions bearing the title (and nominally produced by Billie Burke) in 1934 and 1936. Both featured Fanny Brice, an authentic link. A third Shubert *Follies,* in 1943, offered Milton Berle, Ilona Massey, Arthur Treacher, Jack Cole, and the Bil Baird Marionettes. Would they have been Ziegfeld headliners? They lacked that essential Ziegfeld quality of top and lasting fame potential. Ziegfeld preferred creating stars to hiring them off the rack, but none of 1943's lineup totally punched out except Berle, at that only temporarily and in television, a medium Ziegfeld would have thought limited. Television offers canned stardom, strictly for those who tailor their material to rules of the usual federal white breads.

Oddly, the 1943 edition was the biggest hit of all the *Follies,* running 553 performances. Two *Follies* in the mid-1950s made no history; one even failed to come in. Then the concept of *Follies* gained the status of myth in the Stephen Sondheim–James Goldman–Hal Prince–Michael Bennett musical *Follies* (1971). This is the other Great American Musical, the older one being *Show Boat*; they make a pair because both use show biz as a metaphor for American life. *Show Boat* would have happened without Ziegfeld—but not *Follies.* Without Ziegfeld, modern show biz has no ghosts.

Very unremarked in the Ziegfeld literature is the way he in particular changed the role of the manager, from the nineteenth-century theatre building realtor and tradesman in stock stage ware to the latter-day begetter of art. Reactionary and revolutionary at once, Ziegfeld kept dragging the musical back to the contextual signifiers of its youth—the Girl and the clown—while forcing the musical into newer contexts. He made theatre not only central but irreplaceable, because he was a magnet for all sorts of playacting, from the notoriety of headlines to the immortality of doom. Dying relatively young was a Ziegfeld category: Marilyn Miller at thirty-seven, Anna Held at forty-five, Sandow at fifty-eight, Fanny Brice at fifty-nine. Olive Thomas ingested those poison tablets at twenty-five. Deliberately? Or is Ziegfeld's a magic that befuddles?

The boss himself died at sixty-five, but George White made it to seventy-eight. Charles Dillingham suffered the humiliation of being so Depression-broke that he slipped into the box office of his former theatre, the Globe, and made off with the take. Earl Carroll was killed in a plane crash. Charles Cochran died most horribly, boiled to death in his bath because arthritis made it impossible for him to grasp the hot-water tap and his screams were drowned by the maid's vacuum cleaner.

But the Ziegfelds themselves lived happily. Of the Chicago family, after Ziegfeld's father and brothers had predeceased him, mother Rosalie was not informed of her firstborn's death lest the shock do her harm. She died soon after; Ziegfeld's sister, Louise, survived them all. Billie Burke lived long enough to become a movie star with her own Character, leading to the inculcation of the "Billie Burke type." Sometimes Billie herself played the roles. She returned to the stage in 1941 to tour once more in *The Vinegar Tree,* the work that had cast her in talking pictures, and returned to Broadway in two new works that did not run. She had only just paid off the end of the huge debt her husband had left her with. Interestingly, she glimpsed but never actually met the other three of Ziegfeld's great loves, Anna, Lillian, and Marilyn.

Billie died on May 14, 1970. She was buried beside her husband in the Kensico cemetery in Valhalla, New York. The statue of a woman overlooking the graves represents not Billie but her mother, Blanche. Ziegfeld's stone is a plain rectangle giving his birth and death date, set flat against the earth. Daughter Patty stayed out of show biz except for that one escapade in Philadelphia. She married, raised kids, memoired her parents, and died in April 2008, at the age of ninety-one.

Ziegfeld's other child, the Ziegfeld Theatre, did not fare so well. The offbeat location made it ultimately the least useful house in all Broadway, and after Ziegfeld's death William Randolph Hearst took possession of what was in fact his property. There is revealed another aspect of commercial success in America, the precept that reads "Know a millionaire." Hearst rented the Ziegfeld to MGM as a cinema; Billy Rose bought the place in 1943. The refurbished house reopened with Rose's would-be Ziegfeldian revue *Seven Lively Arts* (1944). Thereafter the theatre got the shows no one else wanted, though *Brigadoon* (1947), *Gentlemen Prefer Blondes* (1949), and *Kismet* (1953) were surprise hits. The Ziegfeld was demolished in 1966. A cinema built to the west of its lot, in the middle of Fifty-Fourth Street, is also called the Ziegfeld; some people think it is the theatre that Ziegfeld built.

But then, he left a number of confusions behind, among them the pronunciation of his name. They were calling him "Ziegfield" in his lifetime, and even in his deathtime, for the rent-a-cleric who delivered the eulogy at the funeral had not been briefed and repeatedly called him "Ziegfield." Repeatedly? "Every two seconds" was Eddie Cantor's count.

Another ambiguity: was he the tyrannical manager or a practitioner of the Broadway Realpolitik, keeping his face clean in a business that is essentially a gigantic pie fight? Was he glorifier or exploiter? An obsessive spendthrift who simply couldn't pay, or a shameless cheater of his creditors?

The exploiter and the cheat do not inspire loyalty. The tyrant has no friends. No one ever said, and proudly, "I worked for Erlanger." Ziegfeld loved women. We call it exploitation now; they called it sex then. Anyway, he was a liberal avant la lettre: open to what was different. He brought people onto his stage whom many in the audience didn't even know existed. Ziegfeld spotlit them, made them basic to glamour. The man got so big in a big culture that he was able to tell Americans what was entertaining and they agreed. He democratized the musical, the theatre, American life, and we enjoy that action yet today.

Did he plan all that? Would he himself have stated it so? How can one be so consistent in one's agenda and not know what one's agenda is? Yet there is this: in Ziegfeld's "other" theatre, the New Amsterdam, Olive Thomas' ghost still walks. Those who have seen her have the odd feeling that she is trying to explain something. She seems to be saying that what happened . . . well, it was just a crazy accident.

Sources and Further Reading

The archivist is in luck, for papers on Ziegfeld, Billie Burke, and Anna Held all reside at the same address, on the third floor of Lincoln Center's Library For the Performing Arts. A fascinating miscellany awaits in unitemized boxes, from tax returns to fragments of scripts. Here, too, one can explore the discrepancies between Anna Held's French memoirs (in typescript) and the published version. For instance, Anna notes that Joe Weber's spoof of *The College Widow* allotted her only ten lines. The English translation, as edited by the spooky Liane Carrera, doubles the figure. Why?

The library is rich in scrapbooks, clippings files, and microfilms of first-night reviews and other matter. The books vary from those kept by relatives or fans to the extensive series put together by Robinson Locke between the 1880s and 1920. Son of the owner of *The Toledo Blade* and eventually editor himself, Locke was stagestruck enough to function as his own theatre critic, under the name Rodney Lee. Much of his theatrical paperwork resides in Ohio, but the scrapbooks proper are one of the treasures held at Lincoln Center.

Other scrapbooks are devoted to a single title on a level beyond exhaustive, such as the gigantic beast treating Ziegfeld's first show, *A Parlor Match*. This one is so dilapidated that one dare not turn too many pages for fear of wrecking it entirely. Its retrospective of Anna Held's début and subsequent national tour demonstrates how extensive Ziegfeld's PR campaigns could be.

Of books on Ziegfeld, the first to appear was less a biography than an anecdote collection, *Ziegfeld: The Great Glorifier* (A. H. King, 1934), by two who knew the subject personally, Eddie Cantor and David Freedman. Appearing two years after Ziegfeld's death, this slim volume dealt more in legend than in hard data, and Marjorie Farnsworth's *The Ziegfeld Follies* (G. P. Putnam's Sons, 1956) considered the Girls rather than the man himself. For example, Imogene Wilson, of the 1923 and 1924 *Follies*, occupies pages 102 through 107 in a typical saga, as she orders *à la carte* from the menu of disaster. Orphaned in infancy, Wilson attracted many an eye, including that of poster artist James Montgomery Flagg and, through him, that of Ziegfeld. Then she fell in love with blackface comic Frank Tinney, who entered into an affair with her. Somehow or other, Farnsworth always finds a quotation with which to punctuate her tales; Tinney's is "Sure I have a wife, a mortgage and an appendix. But I believe a man should keep his troubles to himself." As Farnsworth recounts it, Tinney assaults Wilson; now Ziegfeld's doctor quotes his way in: "This girl looks as though she had been struck by an automobile." Ziegfeld speaks as well: "My policy is to stand behind all my girls when they are in trouble." Indeed, the scandal destroyed Tinney's career; it was the Girls who were supposed to get into scrapes, not the guys. Wilson goes to Europe, to Hollywood, to the dogs. Farnsworth tracks her down to a jail term for stiffing a clothing bill and at last to the Actors' Fund Home on Long Island. Wilson dies young, penniless, and alone, in the approved Ziegfeld Girl manner. Now Farnsworth herself makes remark: "After all her lovers had done to her, death must have seemed almost like a friend."

The Ziegfeld Follies is filled with such lore in a lavish black-and-white production. No other volume documents the *Follies* so well in its visuals, with rectangle after rectangle of full-stage shots, emphasizing the earliest shows.

One set of the Lincoln Center library boxes holds the papers of Robert Baral, a *Variety* reporter who researched Ziegfeld with an eye to writing his biography. That became Baral's unfulfilled dream, but he did publish *Revue: A Nostalgic Reprise of the Great Broadway Period* (Fleet, 1962). Baral offers chapters on the *Scandals,* the *Vanities,* London and Paris shows, and so on, but over a quarter of the book is devoted to the *Follies.* He writes with an air of personal recollection, breathless and disorganized. And note a bizarre statement on page 87 claiming that a producer named George Wintz "obtained the rights to the title of the Ziegfeld Follies" during the wrangles with Klaw and Erlanger. Baral even tells us that Wintz sent out such a show with dancers Ted Shawn and Ruth St. Denis. *What*? I dare you to verify that. In all, Baral is useful, though the lack of an index is irritating in a volume filled with data.

By the time Charles Higham produced *Ziegfeld* (Henry Regnery, 1972), his subject had been dead exactly forty years yet was only then undergoing his first full-scale life's story. It's too easy to correct the scholarship of the founder of the line, but this is a slippery work even so, filled with comments that betray a narrow grasp of old show biz. On page 123, Higham looks in on the battle over whether Vivienne Segal would sing Victor Herbert or Jerome Kern in *Miss 1917* with a concluding "Jerome Kern never forgave her." Yet Segal played the lead in Kern's *Oh, Lady! Lady!!* one year later. More worrisome is Higham's citing of one Marlon Whitney, "possessor of the most flawless physique on Broadway," as Apollo in *Follies of 1909.* In a holdover from nineteenth-century burlesque, Greek gods were played by women in drag, especially in Ziegfeld's shows. The *Follies* Apollo was in fact *Marion* Whitney. Was anyone named Marlon in 1909? Isn't this Higham's slip of the pen in his notes— so why substantiate the nonexistent Marlon with a caption about his physique? No one knew who had a flawless physique in the theatre of that day because men almost never showed skin. Unfortunately, many of Higham's questionable statements have been repeated by later writers.

The Lincoln Center library lists Ziegfeld as not Florenz Jr. but "Ziegfeld, Flo," and so Randolph Carter names him in *The World of Flo Ziegfeld* (Praeger, 1974). Like Farnsworth's book a text with pictures, Carter's includes color, taking in wonderful replicas of Joseph Urban's set designs. We keep hearing how superior Urban was; Carter shows.

Some of his black-and-whites are either irrelevant or incorrectly identified. A shot of Bert Lahr in *Two on the Aisle,* a revue of 1951, is said to be from *Hot-Cha*; the puppetoon prologue to MGM's *Ziegfeld Follies* is, in Carter's view, from *The Great Ziegfeld*; and out of nowhere we get a reproduction of Reginald Marsh's *Pip and Flip.*

The coffee-table volume arrived in 1993, Richard and Paulette Ziegfeld's *The Ziegfeld Touch* (Harry N. Abrams). The dust-jacket design, a hand-tinting of a shot of Bessie McCoy Davis perched on a crescent moon in *Miss 1917,* aptly sums up Ziegfeld's art. Indeed, the volume gives us the most thorough visual reading ever of Ziegfeld's life and work, with color reproductions of some of Urban's mural inside the Ziegfeld Theatre. As their name all but states, the authors are relations, Richard a cousin and Paulette his wife. This leads us to expect a trove of intel particular to the family—not embarrassing revelations, just more anecdotal material than we find in other books. On the contrary, these Ziegfelds seem to be drawing on the same Lincoln Center boxes that everybody else works from. The first two-thirds of the book is a biography, the last third a compendium of data on shows and personnel. Still, there's little new here except the illustrations.

Family members of more telling consanguinity published memoirs. Billie Burke's, written with Cameron Shipp, is *With a Feather on My Nose* (Appleton-Century-Crofts, 1949). Dedicated to daughter Patty and George Cukor, who of course directed Billie's first talkie, *A Bill of Divorcement, Feather* is Billie's, rather than Ziegfeld's, story. But she was closer to him than any but Anna Held, and there are many stories that bring him back alive. Here's one: Billie throws a dinner in Palm Beach for the usual social high-hats, and Ziegfeld, without telling her, cancels her menu and has Dinty Moore's Manhattan eatery fly in fifty pounds of corned beef and cabbage. "Some of the ladies ate so much," Billie recalls, "that they had to be assisted to their cars." That's Ziegfeld the sport; there's also Ziegfeld the connoisseur of beauty. He spares no one. Someone compliments Patty's looks, and Ziegfeld replies, "Inch too large around the hips."

Obviously, it's a very personal book. Filled with black-and-white shots on coated stock, it spans two completely different show-biz eras, from Charles Frohman's elegant fribble plays to the Big Hollywood of *Dinner at Eight, Parnell, Topper,* and *The Wizard of Oz,* to name four of Billie's films. Too many show-biz memoirs lack the backstage details that Billie builds up so effortlessly. She brings herself back alive, too.

The Ziegfelds' Girl: Confessions of An Abnormally Happy Childhood (Little, Brown, 1964) is Patty's view of it all, told with charm and observation. The tale of Ziegfeld and Marilyn Miller in her dressing room after the *Sally* matinée, one of the most basic of Ziegfeld stories, is entirely Patty's. It's astonishing how well she recalls the undertale, so to say, of the man who would be king confronting Joan of Arc as Jezebel. One odd note: the grown Patricia named one child Florenz. Of course, you think. No: a daughter. Note, by the way, that Billie spells her estate as "Burkely Crest," while Patty renders it as "Burkeley Crest." Who's right?

On the city of Chicago before and during Ziegfeld's time, I found particularly useful William Cronon's *Nature's Metropolis: Chicago and the Great West* (W. W. Norton, 1991) and Donald L. Miller's *City of the Century: The Epic of Chicago and the Making of America* (Simon & Schuster, 1996). Cronon emphasizes industrial Chicago and its great trade in wheat, lumber, and livestock. Miller ranges more widely, with something of a novelist's vitality. One line especially arrests the reader: "Over three-quarters of its residents were of foreign parentage in 1893." This is notable partly because 1893 marked Ziegfeld's real entry into show biz, but also because he must have grown up in a milieu as ethnically tasty as the cocktail he himself poured in his *Follies.*

On the Columbian Exposition, see Reid Badger's *The Great American Fair* (N. Hall, 1979) and Stanley Appelbaum's more pictorial *The Chicago World's Fair of 1893* (Dover, 1980). On that pesky question of whether or not Little Egypt is an urban legend, try Donna Carlton's *Looking for Little Egypt* (IDD Books, 1994). The modern volume on the Iroquois disaster is Nat Brandt's *Chicago Death Trap* (Southern Illinois Press, 2003), a very thorough and naturally quite harrowing read, not least because the theatre burned because of thoughtless and stupid human errors. One is especially haunted by the memory of a lone chorus girl playing a fairy and trapped in her flying harness as the sparks turned to flames and then conflagration while no one troubled to let her down so she could escape.

On Ziegfeld's associates, first of all comes Harry B. Smith's autobiography, *First Nights and First Editions* (Little, Brown, 1931). A book collector, obviously, Smith knew many, many first nights; he himself counts "more than three hundred." His is a vanished art whose recollections teem with stars such as Digby Bell, Lulu Glaser, Peter Dailey, Marguerite Sylva; haunts of the archivist's vault. He does at least bring his age back well, albeit in highly mannered style.

Leaving the dark ages behind, we arrive at reliable volumes on Jerome Kern (Oxford University Press, 1980) and Vincent Youmans (*Days To Be Happy, Years To Be Sad*, Oxford, 1982) by Gerald Bordman, and on their regular collaborator Oscar Hammerstein II (*Getting To Know Him*, Random House, 1977) by Hugh Fordin. Bordman's pair troubled to cite virtually every known number by his subjects, with a separate index of the titles, allowing one to look up a song's provenance. Bordman had hoped to call the Youmans book *I Want To Be Happy*, but Irving Caesar demanded too much money for the use of his lyric. The final title seems more appropriate, given that Youmans' career lasted little more than a decade, ending in thirteen years of frustrated retirement before his death.

These by now venerable offerings have been joined by Howard Pollack's almost extravagantly well researched *George Gershwin: His Life and Work* (University of California Press, 2006), a full 706 pages up to the notes and index and packed with revelation. Pollack, too, seeks out all of Gershwin's songs in both text and index. Where Bordman reprinted the final tunestack of each show, Pollack goes further, citing each number in a detailed plot synopsis.

Richard Rodgers' autobiography, *Musical Stages* (Random House, 1975), was ghosted by an unbilled Stanley Green, though Rodgers filled out Green's structural frame with lots of personal commentary. Interestingly, all of the above composers had bad experiences working on Ziegfeld's shows. But then, any producer obsessed with the way the girls wore their hats would have little concentration left for the sound of music. Ziegfeld's shows were, he thought, less written than performed. Pollack reveals how Ziegfeld not only threw *Show Girl* together around the cast and staging effects but then harassed Gershwin for a hit tune after the work had opened. Worse, when Gershwin refused, Ziegfeld stopped his royalty payments. This would lead to the usual legal scuffling—and, as well, the usual hypocritically warm reception if you crossed his path.

That may be why *Show Boat* enjoyed a good production experience. Here was a Ziegfeld show that wasn't a Ziegfeld show, with little room for tampering. This one was *written*. For once, Ziegfeld put on something larger than Ziegfeld—and it has its own book. Miles Kreuger's *Show Boat: The Story of a Classic American Musical* (Oxford, 1977, on the show's fiftieth anniversary) breaks the saga into chapters on the novel, the show, the part-talkie, the 1932 revival, the first talkie, the 1946 revival, and the last talkie. Appendices abound. The rich illustrative material nails down academic ephemera, such as views of real-life show boats, back-to-back reproductions of the sheet music for the original P. G. Wodehouse "Bill" and Hammerstein's slight revision (two measures of the refrain have different music, too), and many of Joseph Urban's set designs. There are few stage shots of the first production, because few have survived. This is why one most often sees the same three or one of their variants: Helen Morgan fainting during the Miscegenation Scene, Captain Andy finishing *The Parson's Bride,* and the Act One finale. At St. Martin's, we strive for the refreshment of novelty; our *Show Boat* shot has appeared in only one previous book. This was the title that was once every stagestruck young gay boy's first important Christmas present, Daniel Blum's *A Pictorial History of the American Theatre* (Crown Publishers, 1950). Six later editions expanded it till it stretched from 1860 to 1980 in some six thousand photographs. *Six thousand*—and the volumes bore such occult power that straights who as much as glanced here and there in them were instantly struck gay, never to return.

Performers. First, Sandow claims a small library of his own titles as well as modern studies, for he is a historical figure in the world of bodybuilding.

He is as well the first star in the show biz of the Beautiful Male Revealed—another aspect of how "today" Ziegfeld really was. How far is Sandow, after all, from the attitudes and techniques that reach a summit in Daniel Craig's James Bond rising from the sea as the camera lovingly drools, in the recent *Casino Royale?* John F. Kasson's *Houdini, Tarzan, and the Perfect Man: The White Male Body and the Challenge of Modernity in America* (Hill and Wang, 2001) bears a nude of Sandow on its cover and devotes a lot of space to him in the context of gender studies. David L. Chapman's *Sandow the Magnificent* (University of Illinois Press, 1994) is the standard biography.

Eve Golden's *Anna Held and the Birth of Ziegfeld's Broadway* (University Press of Kentucky, 2000) revives this most wonderful figure in not only who she was but what she did and how she saw the world. Golden states that Anna's origins, which I think are ambiguous, are unquestionably Polish and Jewish, but, from very early on, Anna would seem to be distinctly French and Catholic. Maybe this occurred by arrangement; *Paris vaut bien une messe.* A cute touch: Golden's chapter titles revive play and song titles of the day. Some are more or less famous—"The Last Rose of Summer," from Friedrich von Flotow's opera *Martha;* or *The Belle of New York,* the Edna May musical that Ziegfeld was so eager to reference for Marilyn Miller in *Smiles,* later the source of a 1952 Fred Astaire–Vera-Ellen movie. Some are long forgot—David Belasco's adaptation of Ouida's *Under Two Flags;* or *It Pays To Advertise,* a Cohan and Harris smash of the 1914–1915 season. It gives one a sense of Golden's period atmosphere. A very recommendable work; you'll fall in love.

Fanny Brice claims, among several biographies, one that does not exist: Norman Katkov's *The Fabulous Fanny: The Story of Fanny Brice* (Alfred A. Knopf, 1953). Brice's daughter, Frances, found Katkov's portrait unsatisfying, and Frances' husband, producer Ray Stark, supposedly spent a fortune having it suppressed. (Stark was later to produce *Funny Girl* on Broadway and on screen.) Nevertheless, copies survive. The curious can find it on eBay, with its raucous dust jacket cover of stagelights at top and bottom shining on a head cutout of the later Brice. Among the more available titles, I prefer Barbara W. Grossman's *Funny*

Woman (Indiana University Press, 1991), scholarly but full of zip. Grossman plays detective on matters never settled before: did Brice ever perform in blackface for coon songs? Yes. Did audiences at *Ziegfeld Follies of 1921* hear in Brice's "My Man" a keening for her incarcerated husband, Nick Arnstein? Brice said no; Grossman says yes. Like Eve Golden, Grossman writes with the confidence of expertise.

Eddie Cantor writes off the top of his head, in *My Life Is In Your Hands,* again with David Freedman (Harper and Brothers, 1928) and then, with Jane Kesner Ardmore, in *Take My Life* (Doubleday, 1957). One does hear Cantor's voice, but these are highly subjective recollections. A single paragraph on pages 119 to 120 of *Take My Life,* on the senior Ziegfeld, Junior's alleged interest in classical music, Victor Herbert, and Sandow, is a trove of misstatements, confusions, and dizzy legends, including placing father Ziegfeld as a colonel in the American Civil War.

There are biographies of Bert Williams by Ann Charters and Eric Ledell Smith. Charters got there first, so she was able to nab the ideal title: *Nobody* (Macmillan, 1970). Smith's is *Bert Williams: A Biography of the Pioneer Black Comedian* (McFarland, 1992). Certainly, Williams was a comedian—but note that his signature tune, like Brice's "My Man," moves beyond comedy into something emotional and universal. "Nobody" was Williams' curse. "Audiences seemed to want nothing else," he complained. A third life story, Camille F. Forbes' *Introducing Bert Williams* (Basic/Civitas, 2008), has recently appeared, but Louis Chude-Sokei's *The Last "Darky": Bert Williams, Black-on-Black Minstrelsy, and the African Diaspora* (Duke University Press, 2005) is clearly more than a bio, looking back to Booker T. Washington and W. E. B. Du Bois and forward to the Harlem Renaissance. This is a study on the race within race, for here's an odd fact: Williams wasn't precisely an African American. He was born in the Bahamas: a Caribbean. The book's cover sports a photo of Williams in one of his most risible *Follies* getups, as a rooster in a top hat; on the rear is the opposite, a photo of him offstage in a conservative three-piece suit. Between these two shots, perhaps, is that "history of a race" that Ethel Waters heard in Irving Berlin's "Suppertime," which she sang in the revue *As Thousands Cheer* as the widow of a lynching victim.

Still, Williams' appearance at the head of the black emergence in the American popular arts was apolitical. The contextual signifiers of 1910, the year Williams cracked the *Follies,* were strictly about talent.

As for the cowboy, there's a glut of Will Rogers books, but the most interesting is *Will Rogers at the Ziegfeld Follies* (University of Oklahoma Press, 1992) because it preserves his worldview in his words. For instance, Will on how the Ziegfeld Girl pays her income tax: "One Girl wanted to charge off Taxi Cab fares to and from the Theatre. I told her she couldn't do that." Why? " 'As far as the Government is concerned, you can come on the Subway.' She said, 'Oh! What is the Subway?' "

The title of Warren G. Harris' *The Other Marilyn* (Arbor House, 1985) reminds us that there was a National Blond Enchantress before Monroe. The book's cover photo, a profile (in color) of his subject, has the daintily rhapsodic look of a pre-Raphaelite, reminding us that Marilyn Miller capped an older heroine type rather than initiated a new one. Out of public view, Marilyn was a wild thing, as was her second husband, Jack Pickford. Yet their image was that of America's Sweethearts. The deconstruction of the Ziegfeld Girl dates not from Ziegfeld's death, in 1932, nor from Marilyn's, in 1936, but from the rise of Ethel Merman, the new heroine type. Marilyn's opposite in all things, Merman sang belt rather than soprano, did not dance, and learned true love ways in the arms of Ernest Borgnine.

Speaking of Ziegfeld Girls: some stood at the center of Ziegfeld's theatre, like Marilyn. Some seized their fame in other venues, like Barbara Stanwyck (who appeared in the 1922 *Follies* one month shy of her fifteenth birthday) or Marion Davies, Miss 1917. But one above all was famous for being nothing more than a Ziegfeld Girl: pretty and opportunistic, a man's plaything who nevertheless tops the men. This was Peggy Hopkins Joyce, done to a T in Constance Rosenblum's *Gold Digger* (Henry Holt and Company, 2000). Joyce was so dumb she was eloquent; her utterances are a guidebook to survival. "Kissing your hand may make you feel very good but a diamond bracelet lasts forever." That is Peggy once removed, as Lorelei Lee, heroine of two novels by Anita Loos from the 1920s, when the Ziegfeld Girl was America's choice Cinderella. But here comes Skeletor with his havoc staff: Linda Mizejewski's *Ziegfeld Girl: Image and Icon in Culture and Cinema* (Duke University Press, 1999) treats the concept to a text defragmentation. Angela J. Latham's *Posing a Threat: Flappers, Chorus Girls, and Other Brazen Performers of the American 1920s* (Wesleyan University Press, 2000) is useful in citing how many instances of civil disobedience (and punishment) it took for women to achieve legal rights of the most basic sort. One thinks of Velma Kelly of *Chicago* threatening to "roll my stockings down." As Latham reveals, Kelly isn't joyriding but baiting arrest.

Jazz Age Beauties: The Lost Collection of Ziegfeld Photographer Alfred Cheney Johnston (Universe, 2006) is less authored than curated, by Robert Hudovernik. This stunning exhibition tours one through the surprisingly various world of Ziegfeld's house camera artist—of the Girls rather than the shows themselves. Johnston gets around: to more generally known creatures and even to daughter Patricia, simple and stunning, a touch of real life amid the splendor and taboo of her daddy. (Patty's shot isn't in the index; she's on page 50.) The book contains a forward by Julie Newmar, the very last Ziegfeld Girl, having led the parade in that *Follies* that closed in Philadelphia in 1956. The cast included Tallulah Bankhead, David Burns, Joan Diener, Carol Haney, Matt Mattox, Mae Barnes, future *West Side Story* kids Larry Kert and Lee Becker, Timothy Gray, Beatrice Arthur, Sheila Smith, and Sheldon Harnick's brother Jay.

Moving from the Girls to the comics, we find that five of the ten profiled stars in Stanley Green's *The Great Clowns of Broadway* (Oxford, 1984) were Ziegfeld contractees, either importantly (such as Fanny Brice) or almost in passing (Bert Lahr, who did only *Hot-Cha!*, Ziegfeld's last new show). There could have been more. Starting with the Golden Age means omitting Bert Williams, who died in 1922, just as the age began. Green also left out Eddie Cantor, on I think specious grounds, calling him "more of an entertainer-comedian than a buffoon." What does that mean? Still, this is an extremely useful book, from the first writer who devoted his career to the American musical. Green quotes heavily from scripts for authentic witness, offers plenty of illustrations, and preserves swatches of W. C. Fields' *Follies* sketches.

Two works retrieve the Broadway of Ziegfeld's youth, Mary C. Henderson's *The City and the Theatre* (Back Stage Books, 2004) and Nicholas van Hoogstraten's *Lost Broadway Theatres* (Princeton Architectural Press, second edition, 1997). Henderson is useful for her comprehensiveness. Her subtitle runs, in part, *A 250-Year Journey From Bowling Green To Times Square,* taking us back to before the erection of the first major playhouse in Broadway history, the Park Theatre, built in 1798 across the street from City Hall. Van Hoogstraten opens an astonishing scrapbook of black-and-whites of theatres inside and out, covering the Casino (built in 1882) to the Mark Hellinger (1930). He thus focuses on early-twentieth-century Broadway, when the houses that Anna Held first played, such as the Herald Square and the Manhattan, were about to close. Henderson's dust jacket collects antique color views of theatre façades; van Hoogstraten's cover photo presents the Vanderbilt in 1918, during the run of *Oh Look!.* One lone woman stands in front of the building, decorated with the big stage shots once thought indispensable in enchanting walk-in browsers and attended by sandwich boards bearing eight-by-tens. *Kid Boots* and *Rio Rita* lyricist Joseph McCarthy collaborated with composer Harry Carroll on this imitation Princess show, about a penniless young man who crashes society. Harry Fox played the lead, and while the piece didn't catch on in New York, it added the Dolly Sisters to the tour and went, as they say, boffo. Fox celebrated by marrying a Dolly, and when you see this photograph, you'll be back on Forty-Eighth Street buying tickets for *Oh Look!.*

The New Amsterdam has its own book, a coffee-table spectacle with a gatefold opening (Hyperion, 1997), subtitled *The Biography of a Broadway Theatre.* With color at her disposal, our old friend Mary C. Henderson treats us to many an unusual shot, including a close-up of Mary Boland on her *Face the Music* elephant. It should demonstrate, conclusively, that the pachyderm was papier-mâché and not real, contrary to a factoid that made the rounds when Encores! revived *Face the Music* in 2007.

On the musical in general, the standard reference books came out one by one at irregular intervals. Cecil Smith's *Musical Comedy in America* (Theatre Arts Books, 1950) was the first, a history by a classical music critic, written apparently off the top of his head. Smith remembered everything in general very well; some of his detail work is incorrect; Glenn Litton expanded the original volume, in 1981. David Ewen's *Complete Book of the American Musical Theatre* (Henry Holt and Company, 1958) came next, in encyclopedia form organized by composer, lyricist, or librettist, each with a bio followed by individual entries on the major works. Again, minor errors abound. Ewen went into revised editions, as did Stanley Green's *The World of Musical Comedy* (Grosset and Dunlap, 1960). Green's book is more richly illustrated, but he organized it around only the best-known writers—Ewen included an appendix to pick up "Some Other Outstanding Musical Productions," from *The Black Crook* and *Adonis* (at which Ziegfeld met Sandow) to *Happy Hunting* and *Oh Captain!*. Most important, Ewen's survey took in nineteenth- and early-twentieth-century works that were no longer performed and were even falling out of memory. Yet we suffer a deficit of epic without them—*The Prince of Pilsen, The Pink Lady, Chin-Chin*. Ewen also gave bio-and-works prominence to such as Ludwig Englander, Louis Hirsch, Karl Hoschna, and Gustav Luders, major composers in the years ramping up to the Golden Age. Green, however—writing only two years later—started his volume with Victor Herbert, George M. Cohan, Rudolf Friml, and Sigmund Romberg, solemnizing a break with the era of princes and pink ladies. This all but terminated the Englanders and Hoschnas as stops on the boulevard of history. (At that, when updating to collect authors of the Sondheim era, Green had to backtrack and add in a chapter on De Sylva, Brown, and Henderson, ignored in the first edition.)

Gerald Bordman's *American Musical Theatre: A Chronicle* (Oxford, 1978) is uniquely all-inclusive: a paragraph or two or even a mini essay on every Broadway musical production, starting in the eighteenth century. This gives the book a wealth of data that one never quite absorbs; rereadings are necessary. This one, too, has enjoyed updatings. Vaguely comparable if only in completeness is Richard C. Norton's three-volume compendium (Oxford, 2002) of program data. Norton preserves each show's cast, tunestack, and production credits, with special attention to the insertion and deletion of numbers during not only the New York run but the subsequent tour. Norton also warns of discrepancies between song titles as listed in the program and as published. His triptych was released as *A Chronology of the American Musical Theater*.

On vaudeville, Douglas Gilbert's *American Vaudeville: Its Life and Times* is the basic text, supplemented by an anthology of fascinating eyewitness articles, Charles Stein's *American Vaudeville As Seen By Its Contemporaries* (Knopf, 1984). As the *Follies* was in effect Ziegfeld's blending of vaudeville and musical comedy—fitting the former's specialties into the latter's unity of staging expertise—this is basic Ziegfeld reading.

What of the influence of burlesque? This vastly misunderstood form is actually a succession of forms, evolving in each generation. During its heyday in the late nineteenth century, it was a book musical spoofing a tale from mythology or literature, cast essentially with pretty young women and a few male comics. Burlesque was naughty, no more. By 1900, burlesque had become vaudeville using, again, women and comics; burlesque was now cheap and dingy. But by 1930, the women were stripping and the men lewd. Burlesque was dirty.

Robert C. Allen's *Horrible Prettiness: Burlesque and American Culture* is the required study. Allen emphasizes the nineteenth century and deals extensively with burlesque's relationship with the rest of the theatre world at a time when bourgeois values were marginalizing the stag stuff. This is of particular relevance to Ziegfeld, because his *Follies* in effect reclaimed the stag stuff for a milieu ruled by bourgeois values and maintaining cultural prestige. Even as burlesque was in devolution, Ziegfeld rehabilitated its primary elements on the New Amsterdam stage. What is *Sally* but a reinstruction of the burlesque heroine and her comic?

The last great practitioners of classic burlesque in its identity as innocent spoof are celebrated in Felix Isman's *Weber and Fields: Their Tribulations, Triumphs, and Their Associates* (Boni and Liveright, 1924). This saga originated as a series in *The Saturday Evening Post,* and it reads somewhat like a novel, with plot twists, a ton of dialogue, and no index. In the spendthrift publishing style of the day, it offers many black-and-white photographs separately tipped in, with endpapers of

only one who sees him so. Harding's worldview is that of the Fran-cophone Brit, reminding us why so many characters in Mike Leigh's Gilbert and Sullivan movie *Topsy-Turvy* constantly break into French. Harding's books include works on Saint-Saëns, Massenet, Gounod, Mau-rice Chevalier, Jacques Tati, Sacha Guitry, and French operetta. Somehow or other he slipped the Duke of Wellington onto his card page as well.

The Shuberts have come off in style, though no volume explores how thoroughly the Messrs. tried to imitate Ziegfeld's revue in a dumbed-down budget all through the 1910s. There is a hint of this in Brooks McNamara's *The Shuberts of Broadway* (Oxford, 1990), a text-and-pictures with fascinating illustrations culled from the Shubert Archives. McNamara is good, too, in gentle reminders of the Messrs.' anonymous philanthropy, often overlooked because of their reputation as Forty-Fourth Street mamelukes. The two biographies are Jerry Stagg's *The Brothers Shubert* (Random House, 1968) and Foster Hirsch's *The Boys From Syracuse: The Shuberts' Theatrical Empire* (Southern Illinois University Press, 1998). Hirsch is the scholar, with many inset quota-tions from eyewitnesses; Stagg is the *scop* with the saga in the mead hall. Typical of their different approaches is their respective treatments of Georgie Price, a Jolson seemalike who was the target of one of the Messrs.' most sadistic legal maulings. Hirsch deals with it briefly, synop-tically. Stagg spins it out to twelve pages of compulsive reading, replete with on-site conversations based on interviews with Price. Lee and J. J. Shubert hated each other so much that they spoke through intermedi-aries, yet they functioned to outsiders as one. Stagg brings this out beau-tifully, quoting Price at the end of his recollections. Marveling at the irony of the world according to J. J., Price "shook his head in complete wonder. 'How could you figure [J. J.]?' He corrected himself: 'Them.' "

The Shuberts, as we know, fought the Syndicate for the turf we call "Broadway" while Ziegfeld joined the Syndicate as a kind of indepen-dent fellow traveler. Of the volumes exploring that turf, Anthony Bianco's *Ghosts of 42nd Street* (William Morrow, 2004) has a chapter on Ziegfeld "and the Cult of the Chorus Girl." The more expansive *Invent-ing Times Square: Commerce and Culture at the Crossroads of the World*

(Russell Sage Foundation, 1991) treats the geography in which Ziegfeld flourished. An anthology edited by William R. Taylor, *Inventing Times Square* includes Peter A. Davis' "The Syndicate/Shubert War," Gregory F. Gilmartin's "Joseph Urban," Taylor's own "Broadway: The Place That Words Built" (on the lingo of the place, from *Variety* to Damon Runyon), and Richard Wrightman Fox on "The Discipline of Amusement," recounting another war for control of the turf, this one between censors and the impresarios of Fun.

Those in search of the sound of Ziegfeld's Broadway have a CD ready-made: Living Era's *The Ziegfeld Follies* offers twenty-three cuts of authentic witness, such as John Steel in "A Pretty Girl Is Like a Melody," Bert Williams in "Nobody," Fanny Brice in "My Man" and "Second Hand Rose," Gallagher and Shean, Eddie Cantor, Ruth Etting, and so on. Marilyn Miller, who never released a commercial 78, is represented by the opening number from her third and last film, *Her Majesty, Love*. A two-sided, twelve-inch Victor medley of *Ziegfeld Follies of 1927* yields seven titles from the score in the care of original-cast members Franklyn Baur, the Brox Sisters, and duo pianists Fairchild and Rainger. And you'll hear Nora Bayes pull off her Levi-Kelly "slip" in "Has Anybody Here Seen Kelly?"—though, to repeat, the number itself is not from a Ziegfeld show. Will Rogers and W. C. Fields get a look-in, too, on this essential disc.

Perhaps mention should be made here of a strange yet relevant item on Sony called *From Avenue A To the Great White Way*. A two-disc set, it first presents songs recorded by performers of the Yiddish musical scene, then jumps to English-language performances by such as Sophie Tucker, Eddie Cantor, Fanny Brice, Willie Howard, Al Jolson, Ted Lewis, and even Irving Berlin (in his own "What Am I Gonna Do?"). The aim is to trace how the vocal inflections and musical ethos of the Yiddish tradition were carried over into Greater American Show Biz, culminating perhaps in Nathan Glantz's rendition of "Yiddisha Charleston." Some may prefer knowing of this CD set's existence in benign neglect to sitting through twenty-five Yiddish-dialect numbers. But at least the second

(English) disc is filled with extremely rare titles, some never heard beyond the 78 era.

Of cast albums of Ziegfeld's shows, there are none, *except.* The Smithsonian's Recordings Division released in 1977 an LP anthology of 78s of *Ziegfeld Follies of 1919.* However, the *Follies* annuals were flooded with music of all kinds—a New Dance Sensation like "The Broadway Glide," a riff on the latest show ("Chu Chin Chow") or science headline ("The Aero-Naughty Girl"). The Smithsonian's nineteen cuts are almost all specialty solos, unrepresentative of the core score. (The *1927* Victor medley, racing through its seven numbers, some without a vocal, is nevertheless more synoptic.) *Sally, Rio Rita,* and *The Three Musketeers* did get cast albums—in London. These have come out on CD or will surely appear in due course.

The outstanding title in the recording of Ziegfeld is *Show Boat,* almost embarrassingly well represented. Eighty years old as I write, the piece is still under construction; each generation remakes it in its choice authoritative format. In the 1940s, it becomes a Rodgers and Hammerstein musical play. In the 1990s, Hal Prince makes it racially sensitive and Important. Meanwhile, the score has grown as the show has, and recordings dispute the tunestack.

The earliest *Show Boat* discs were miscellaneous singles; Helen Morgan recorded "Can't Help Lovin' Dat Man," but so did Zelma O'Neal while she was still introducing "The Varsity Drag" in *Good News!*. Then the Drury Lane cast made an album, though Paul Robeson's "Ol' Man River" was not released, superseded by his alternate take with Paul Whiteman. (His understudy, Norris Smith, filled in on the album.) That left the English set with one side too many, so "Dahomey" was dropped as well. These two cuts came out many years later.

There is genuine excitement in hearing these first *Show Boat* performers, so mannered in their fairyland timbres and cotton-candy phrasing. The two lovers, Edith Day and Howett Worster, seem to arrive from an alternate universe. The original Irene in both New York and London, Day lived on to grace the West End *Sail Away,* in 1962, holding true to the nautical theme. Worster, however, died in such obscurity that reference books provide no concluding year to a life that began in 1888. As for Helen Morgan, this ravishingly bizarre vocalist not only leaves her trademark on Julie but on the English language, slipping *mm*s and *aoa*s into her diction rather constantly.

We got our own *Show Boat* set in 1932, when the revival inspired Brunswick Records' Jack Kapp to make the first American show album. Kapp, who was to pioneer the "original Broadway cast" over at Decca in *This Is the Army,* then *Oklahoma!* and *One Touch of Venus* and *Carmen Jones,* made the 1932 *Show Boat* with Morgan, Robeson, and radio names. Already, we spot textual variants. The London sides present an eleven o'clock song ("Dance Away the Night") unheard in New York, and four lines of the Washington, D.C. casualty "Mis'ry's Comin' Aroun'" appear as a vocal intro to Morgan's "Can't Help Lovin' Dat Man"—as, indeed, they had done on her shorter 1928 single.

Yet another eleven o'clocker, "Nobody Else But Me," bedecks the 1946 cast reading, Columbia's first entry in the then expanding "original cast album" market. Another textual novelty: the first appearance of a verse to "Life On the Wicked Stage." Beginning "Why do stage-struck maidens clamor," it is invariably heard today—but where did it come from? Was it created specifically for this production? We do know that the authors' musical-play updating led them to write a new quatrain to button the number (heard on this disc), because in 1927 the music ended with a wordless dance exit for Ellie and the girls that looked terribly Princess Show for 1946.

This revival, which played the Ziegfeld in its new Billy Rose–refurbished incarnation, was long in the making. In a letter dated June 30, 1942, Kern responds to Hammerstein's casting suggestions with both yesses and noes, though in the end not one of Hammerstein's group was hired. Kern okays Edna May Oliver and Sammy White of the 1927 gang, but Oliver died four months later and Buddy Ebsen got White's role. (White played the tour.) For Captain Andy, Hammerstein wants Bobby Clark, a bizarre yet compelling notion. Clark was more than a little "dirty" for the part, but he was a star comic, and, as for the original Andy, Charles Winninger, Kern regrets "what the vats and distilleries have left of [him], the sodden old dope." The proposed Magnolia, an unknown "nineteen year old peacherino," Kern adamantly rejects, but he is enthusiastic about Hammerstein's Julie: Dinah Shore! The Ravenal is to be Lanny Ross, a radio singer very popular, Kern notes, "with this country's Aunt Hettys." Admitting that Ravenal has always been hardest to cast of the *Show Boat* leads, Kern actually argues that "Ravenal should never have been played by a singer." He continues, "Not only are singers lousy actors congenitally, but the better Ravenal sings, the less we believe in his having to resort to pawning *the* ring and *the* walking-stick. If the audiences weren't intoxicated with our entrancing words and music (a detonation from the Bronx) they would say, why doesn't the son-of-a-bitch get a job as a singer?"

Fascinating, no? The composer wants less voice in *his music*. Dinah Shore's almost-Julie points toward taking this character down from a soprano to a mezzo, one of this revival's lasting alterations, though the Julie was, finally, Carol Bruce. Its ephemeral alteration was "Nobody Else But Me," which turned up at the City Center in 1961 but was not generally offered for performance with the rest of the 1946 script and parts. It does slip onto a contemporary *Show Boat* album on Victor, in which Tommy Dorsey and his Orchestra give eight numbers the mellow background-music treatment, with bandstand vocal refrains by such as Stuart Foster, Peggy Mann, and the Sentimentalists. Hearing these blithely insipid readings disguise the show reminds us, through irony, that this is a truly intense score. At once unique and folkish, it stirs with recollection of Americana, from the "Hearts and Flowers" on Captain Andy's violin to fairground hoochy-kooch, and moving past Princess Theatre style (in "I Might Fall Back On You") through operetta power waltz ("You Are Love") to the colossal "Ol' Man River."

Not till LP days could such a score be surveyed as a whole. Victor's dreary 1956 studio disc under Lehman Engel offered the first recordings of "Till Good Luck Comes My Way," "I Might Fall Back On You," and the second-act opening at the Chicago World's Fair, in conjunction with which the real-life twenty-something Florenz Ziegfeld Jr. made his entry into show biz. Victor's is the opera cast, with Patrice Munsel, Risë

Stevens, and Robert Merrill, a Ravenal who also takes on "Ol' Man River" in B Flat, working one step lower than the written key, as Paul Robeson did. But Merrill takes *all* his music down a step; it's Rigoletto in *The Parson's Bride*.

This is a selective, rather than complete, *Show Boat* discography, and we should skip past Columbia's skimpy yet ponderous 1962 studio version (with another disc premiere, of the first-act finale). Major *Show Boat* revivals are often recorded, and Victor caught the 1966 Lincoln Center staging. As I write, this version is to be "restored" for a concert, at Carnegie Hall in June 2008. It's the musical-theatre equivalent of "guaranteed genuine imitation leatherette," because the 1966 version was ersatz from start to finish, missing a lot of music and going especially lame at the climax, the first important New York mounting with no eleven o'clock spot.

Lincoln Center 1966 was the politically correct *Show Boat*. "Dahomey," the big dance number for the black ensemble in Act Two, was meant to recall the first full-length black musical to play Broadway, *In Dahomey* (1903). Though not popular outside the theatre, the song is integral to *Show Boat*'s retrospective of the nation's arts, invariably performed even as late as 1961, at the aforementioned City Center revival. Suddenly, it's Don't Ask, Don't Tell—so "Dahomey" was cut, and the work's very first lyric, "Niggers all work on the Mississippi," was suppressed. Previously, it had been changed to "Colored folk work," "People all work," and "Here we all work." At Lincoln Center, in a now famous joke, nobody worked on the Mississippi; even the music was deleted.

We might call it the "appeasement *Show Boat*." The casting took in Barbara Cook and Stephen Douglass, David Wayne and Margaret Hamilton, and Constance Towers, and it was the biggest of *Show Boat*s. Oliver Smith's set featured a kind of *Cotton Blossom* module that revolved and opened up as each scene demanded. At least William Warfield took "Ol' Man River" *up* a half-step, to C Sharp Major, for a wonderfully bright reading. Still, the only performer to enjoy a personal success was Towers. Her "Bill" was encored—but of course one cannot stand at the piano expecting the *bis* when one's heart is breaking. So, in his one distinguished bit of the evening, director Lawrence Kasha had Towers slowly exit and then slowly return to claim the silky black handbag she had left on the piano. The audience was still clapping. So: encore.

The 1971 London revival (on EMI) again argues the text, bringing back "Nobody Else But Me" for the Julie, Cleo Laine, to fill in her story between the Miscegenation Scene and her belated reappearance for "Bill." Bizarrely, Laine sings "Can't Help Lovin' Dat Man" in overtly black style; she's *supposed* to sound like a white girl on a tour. And her "Bill" is much too modern for 1904. Still: a great singer in great music. Generally, the recording sounds very theatrical, with a winning cast headed by Lorna Dallas and André Jobin (at last! a tenor Ravenal once more), with our own Kenneth Nelson as Frank.

At some point, a two-disc LP set appeared with the same cast singing more of the score than had been heard on stage. Then TER released a two-disc CD box of the 1946 text using more of those opera singers, including bass-baritone Jason Howard in music designed to suggest the flighty and insubstantial Ravenal. Remember, we just heard Jerome Kern saying, "Ravenal should never have been played by a singer." TER's return to 1946—the last time that Kern and Hammerstein got to edit their piece—might have made a sound historical document if the label hadn't omitted "Nobody Else But Me." After all, this was the authors' last attempt (of five: Washington, D.C. 1927 tryout, New York 1927 premiere, London 1928, Universal film 1936, New York 1946) to conclude this sprawling work with something . . . well, conclusive. The very structure of the piece and the last scene's bringing together of the many parts of epic demand an *event*—if not a full-out production number, then something striking. Hal Prince's 1994 revision for Toronto and New York (on the Quality label) presented a sixth solution, a reprise of "Why Do I Love You?" Yes, this is New York 1927 premiere, but with the addition of the staging's Parthy Ann. It's illiterate to try to qualify the word *unique*, but if there is a Broadway star who is "most unique" it's surely Elaine Stritch, who was given more to do than any Parthy before her. She invaded "Life On the Wicked Stage" to steal its best line and, in fact, got the first statement of "Why Do I Love You?," singing it to her newborn granddaughter.

Prince's production was a revision with extreme prejudice in many ways, but it provisioned *Show Boat*'s best cast album of all, because so much of its music is heard, not least in two fizzy medley-pantomimes that Prince used to fill in holes in his throughlines—a view of a windswept, staggering Julie, a march by World War I soldiers. (Late in the run, economy measures halved the chorus, and, replacing the recruits, a lone Uncle Sam was drawn in on a cart to point his "I want you!" at passersby.) Unfortunately, the ghost of Goddard Lieberson channeled the CD's producer, leading him to record the underscored dialogue without the dialogue, just as on Lieberson's old Columbia albums. Even Captain Andy's coaching of Magnolia in "After the Ball," one of the key moments in Act Two, is missing.

Meanwhile, John McGlinn, who joined the *riesumazione* of the American musical with Bill Tynes' New Amsterdam Theatre Company at Town Hall, conceived the ultimate exhumation: the complete 1927 *Show Boat,* including the underscored dialogue, everything dropped during composition, rehearsals, and tryouts that had survived, and five numbers written for revisions. EMI spent three CDs on it, in 1988, with Frederica von Stade, Jerry Hadley, Teresa Stratas, Bruce Hubbard, David Garrison, and Paige O'Hara. Note that Ravenal was a tenor again, in a generally excellent cast compromised only by the colorless Andy and Parthy of Robert Nichols and Nancy Kulp.

This is not only *Show Boat* 101, but Writing the American Musical 101: the dropped numbers show us Kern and Hammerstein in the workshop, reinstructing their own instincts. For instance, what better way to illuminate Magnolia and Ravenal's growing romance than with "The Creole Love Song," a sprightly bolero with a deep undertone of passion? Yes, better: for Sigmund Romberg. One imagines Kern and Hammerstein playing through the piece at the keyboard and realizing that they were accidently shoehorning a crazy backstager into formulas devoted to niche fantasy and "To the inn we're marching." What these two lovers are feeling isn't exotic or grand. It's basic: "You are love." No zigzagging. To create the first great musical, one must *create.*

Ironically, one of Hammerstein's two sons was determined to keep this recording from being made. Bill Hammerstein was raised in musical theatre, yet he obsessively believed that musical numbers are cut only because they're No Good. In fact, an excellent song can fail to land because of an inadequate staging or performer, or because George Abbott couldn't get complex music or the audience couldn't get complex music. Bill, however, was impervious to contradictory proofs. He not only didn't want anyone staging lost *Show Boat* music: he didn't want anyone even to hear it.

However, the 1927 *Show Boat* was cut back because there were no four-hour musicals. There are four-hour operas; isn't *Show Boat*, of a sort, the first of Broadway's operas? I'm not suggesting that stagehands, orchestra players, and other workers be asked to labor overtime; I'm asking why there can't be a three-CD historical exhibit of this biggest— in every sense—of Broadway's artifacts.

So Bill said no—but, remember, Edna Ferber didn't sell her novel to Ziegfeld. She entered into a partnership with Kern and Hammerstein, retaining one-third control of the musical in the perpetuity of its copyright. To Bill Hammerstein's one-third no, the estates of Kern and Ferber said yes. And, bit by bit, the "lost" *Show Boat* has been reinstating itself; companies now routinely include "Mis'ry's Comin' Aroun'." Perhaps one day the Metropolitan Opera will reinstall the rest of this deliberately expansive work. The Met puts on four-hour musicals as a rule.

Of Hollywood souvenirs of Ziegfeld's shows, I have noted the more faithful renderings in the text itself. We should now consider the key "other" Ziegfeld film because so many collect from it their Ziegfeld intel—indeed, their Ziegfeld myth. This is MGM's *The Great Ziegfeld* (1936), winner of the Oscar for Best Picture and nearly three hours of almost shockingly authentic biography. Missing is the man's inconsistent personality, phlegmatic except when firing off peremptory telegrams or supervising dress rehearsals. Nor is there anything of Ziegfeld's self-destructive gambling addiction or the use of his office to enlarge his circle of sex partners. William Powell catches Ziegfeld's courtly side, and his strict adherence to discipline among his employees. However, of Ziegfeld the creator we get little more than a last-minute suggestion to the crew on the changing of the lighting—the usual Hollywood short-hand for Great Director. The film has none of the wonder that Edna Ferber experienced one day, when Ziegfeld suddenly turned up at a *Show Boat* rehearsal like a god in his temple.

Marilyn Miller is missing, too. MGM wanted her for no more than a cameo and thus could not give her headliner billing—but Miller had worked extremely hard to earn that billing and she wasn't going to give it up. The studio and Marilyn had what we might call Incongruent Agendas, and a nobody named Rosina Lawrence stands in as a sort of Marilyn in a single scene. Shockingly, Ziegfeld stylists Ann Pennington, Gilda Gray, and Leon Errol filmed scenes cut from the release print; the DVD does not restore these, so they may be lost. Will Rogers and Eddie Cantor are faithfully enacted by others; Buddy Doyle's "If You Knew Susie" brings Cantor to life right down to the farewell handkerchief. (Note that he is filmed at a distance and in blackface, giving one the notion that it might actually be Cantor.) Lillian Lorraine's difficult life necessitated an *à clef* "improvement": Virginia Bruce plays her as Audrey Dane. And Frank Morgan Frank-Morgans away as one Jack Billings, whom everyone takes to be Charles Dillingham.

However, Fanny Brice plays herself in one of the greatest single reels of thirties Hollywood (and in a correct restoration of what burlesque was like in 1910). Further, many numbers suggest the true Ziegfeldian opulence; Ziegfeld intimates such as William Anthony McGuire (writing the script) and John Harkrider (designing costumes) substantiated The Legend of Ziegfeld; and Luise Rainer delivered stupendously as Anna Held.

Hers is an all but indescribable performance, mannered and even rococo—but so, it may be, was Held. The film sees Ziegfeld as a man involved with three woman: the mercurial Held, the reckless Audrey Dane, and the sensible Billie Burke, played by Hollywood's most sensible star, Myrna Loy. But this is not a sensible film. It's a Best Picture fantasy on how crazy those theatre people are. So Loy has little to play, and Bruce can covet jewelry and disgrace a *Midnight Frolic* with a tipsy curtain speech. It is Rainer who has The Role, and she, too, won an Oscar: for acting crazy.

Too often, the physics of the Hollywood bio demanded that the subject be denuded of its matter. George M. Cohan never divorced. Lorenz Hart and Cole Porter are straight. Richard Rodgers is nice. Yet *The Great Ziegfeld* is about a suave, sentimental, and superstitious guy who keeps changing the rules of his business, moving from a fairgrounds sideshow to a Broadway so exalted (in part by him) that he dies staggering to a window to gaze, one last time, upon the marquee of the Ziegfeld Theatre, where *Show Boat* is playing. But Ziegfeld died in July 1932, when the *revival* of *Show Boat* was playing *five blocks from the Ziegfeld* at the Casino Theatre. Where is Ziegfeld supposed to be, in a Nedick's?

And yet. Ziegfeld was suave, sentimental, and superstitious. He did keep changing the rules of his business. And he moved from a kind of fairgrounds sideshow to a Broadway that he, among others, exalted. "I worked for Ziegfeld"—remember? *The Great Ziegfeld* gives us a sense of what Will Rogers means by that. Not in the gargantuan end of Part One—the film was a road-show special with an intermission—in which 182 performers move up and down a wedding cake spiraling up to a glorified Virginia Bruce, to the tune of $220,000 for that number alone. It's wonderful, but it's misleading. Ziegfeld didn't produce at the Hippodrome. His theatre wasn't huge: it was beautiful.

No, what Rogers is referring to is that exaltation of what in his day was called "the show business." Ziegfeld didn't glorify only the American girl: he glorified Broadway. He left it different than he met it, and even today he is its only synonym. There's an excitement in the word "Broadway," and it's a Ziegfeldian invention. The ever-touring Mrs. Fiske thought Broadway no more than a stop in her season's itinerary. "New York's just a stand," she said.

No, Mrs. Fiske. Ziegfeld made Broadway the identity of American art.

Index